W9-BVN-435

"SPLENDID . . . THE FINEST COMPREHENSIVE HISTORI-CAL SYNTHESIS YET WRITTEN. Evenhanded in ideology and in its portrayal of leading players, sprightly and often witty in style, and probing and balanced in perspective, *Freedom Bound* offers the ideal point of departure for scholarly inquiry into a generation of black protest and the larger context of American ethical values."　　　　　　　　　　　　　　—*Choice*

"Takes the movement from the mountaintop in Montgomery to the valleys of the Reagan years . . . Puts the actors and actions in the larger national political context, and in the struggle between warring liberal and conservative factions . . . an important addition to civil rights historiography."　　　　　—Julian Bond

"Authoritative and clearly written."　　　　—*The New York Times*

"Excellent . . . Thoughtful, fair, and thorough . . . Distinguished by vivid mini-biographies of everyone in the movement from Martin Luther King to lesser knowns like the fiery Fannie Lou Hamer, and also by dramatic renderings of all the key events from the Brown decision to Watts to the Bakke ruling."　　　　　　　　　　　　　　—*Kirkus Reviews*

"Should soon be accepted as the best one-volume history of the civil rights movement."　　　　　—*American Quarterly*

ROBERT WEISBROT is professor of history at Colby College. He is the author of *Father Divine and the Struggle for Racial Equality.*

Also by Robert Weisbrot

Father Divine and the Struggle for Racial Equality

The Jews of Argentina
from the Inquisition to Perón

Freedom
Bound

MOVE ON OVER
OR
WE'LL MOVE
ON OVER YOU
MOVE ON OVER
OR
WE'LL MOVE
ON OVER YOU

Freedom Bound

A History of America's Civil Rights Movement

Robert Weisbrot

With the research assistance of Dolita Cathcart

A PLUME BOOK

PLUME
Published by the Penguin Group
Penguin Books USA Inc., 375 Hudson Street,
New York, New York 10014, U.S.A.
Penguin Books Ltd, 27 Wrights Lane,
London W8 5TZ, England
Penguin Books Australia Ltd, Ringwood,
Victoria, Australia
Penguin Books Canada Ltd, 2801 John Street,
Markham, Ontario, Canada L3R 1B4
Penguin Books (N.Z.) Ltd, 182–190 Wairau Road,
Auckland 10, New Zealand

Penguin Books Ltd, Registered Offices:
Harmondsworth, Middlesex, England

Published by Plume, an imprint of New American Library, a division of Penguin Books USA
Inc. This is an authorized reprint of a hardcover edition published by W. W. Norton and
Company, Inc.

First Plume Printing, January, 1991
10 9 8 7 6 5 4 3

FRONTISPIECE PHOTOGRAPH: Marchers displaying signs of militancy enter Jackson, Mississippi, June 26,1966. *AP/ Wide World*

MAP ON PAGE xi BY: Ben Gamit

Acknowlegments
    Selection from "Ka 'Ba," in Imamu Amiri Baraka, *Black Magic: Collected Poetry, 1961–
1967.* Copyright © 1969 by LeRoi Jones (Amiri Baraka). Reprinted by permission of Sterling
Lord Literistic, Inc.
    Selection from "Note on Commercial Theatre," in Langston Hughes, *Selected Poems.*
Copyright © 1948 by Alfred A. Knopf, Inc. Reprinted by permission of the publisher.
    Selection from "Of Liberation," in Nikki Giovanni, *Black Feeling—Black Talk—Black
Judgement.* Copyright ©1968, 1970 by Nikki Giovanni. Reprinted by permission of William
Morrow and Co., Inc.

 REGISTERED TRADEMARK—MARCA REGISTRADA

Library of Congress Cataloging-in-Publication Data

Weisbrot, Robert.
Freedom bound : a history of America's civil rights movement
/Robert Weisbrot.
        p.   cm.
    Includes bibliographical references and index.
        1. Afro-Americans—Civil rights.   2. Civil rights movements—
United States—History—20th century.   3. United States—Politics
and government—1945-   4. Liberalism—United States—History—
20th century.   5. Afro-Americans—Economic conditions.
I. Title.
[E185.61.W394   1991]
323.1'196073—dc20   90-46194   CIP

Printed in the United States of America.
Original Book design by Marjorie J. Flock.

For William and Linda Cotter

Contents

Photographs follow pages 100 and 206

Sites of the Civil Rights Movement

Preface

THE ALLIANCE between black and white liberals, which transformed American race relations during the 1960s, was a source of both power and disillusionment to civil rights advocates. Black leaders of the decade's nonviolent protests expressly invoked liberal ideals that centered on greater federal protection of liberty, opportunity, and citizenship rights. Their protest campaigns often seemed designed to spur Presidents Kennedy and Johnson, as well as the Congress, to extend the liberal creed fully to issues of racial justice. This faith in the democratic promise of liberal reform appeared widely vindicated in 1964 and 1965, with the passage of laws banning the caste lines that had long existed in much of the country. Yet the persistence of prejudice, poverty, and ghetto slums, despite these legal changes, exposed deeper barriers to equality that impelled many blacks to question not only the courage and consistency of white liberals but also the core values of liberal belief.

A basic assumption of liberalism in the 1960s was that equal protection of constitutional rights would afford all Americans, regardless of color, an equal chance to amass wealth, influence, and stature. Yet civil rights laws alone could not overcome the effects of past discrimination and lingering prejudice, nor did these laws substantially alter the economic system that had long permitted vast disparities of wealth and privilege, to the disadvantage of most blacks. Leaders such as Martin Luther King, Jr., therefore sought to stretch the liberal vision beyond endorsement of limited welfare programs, to an insistence on freedom from poverty as a basic civil right that required immediate and unreserved national commitment. Unlike the earlier drive for desegregation and voting rights laws, however, this demand for equality of condition failed to sway most liberal reformers, who held that the social order was already basically sound and that merit, rather than race, class, or other circumstances of birth, chiefly determined one's life chances.

The liberal coalition of the 1960s thus wrought, in effect, a self-limiting revolution that abolished formal barriers to equality while leaving intact the basic features of a system in which blacks had played a subordinate, marginal role. For all these limitations, blacks never wholly rejected the liberal alliance, which provided a mainstream vehicle for advancement that no alternative political course could rival. Ghetto-based separatists offered racial pride and solidarity, but no means to transform on a large scale the social and economic conditions of black people. Both black and white socialists failed during the 1960s to win support from the masses they professed to represent, while a range of violent revolutionary groups proved completely outmatched by the government forces they sought to overthrow. The ascendancy of conservative politics at the close of the decade, moreover, highlighted the value of gains achieved through liberal coalition and made clear that the limits of liberal readiness for change represented to a great extent the limits of Americans generally.

This book explores the peak years of the struggle for racial equality in America, with a special focus on the increasingly turbulent relations between black activists and white liberals. My central aim is to relate the civil rights movement to broader currents in American political reform, in the belief that the black quest for justice and the national crusade for a "Great Society" are best understood in relation to each other. I hope, as well, to shed light on the dilemmas and possibilities that have faced advocates of social change and that still shape the course of America's democratic evolution.

Colby College afforded critical support for this project, by granting me a pretenure sabbatical to draft the initial chapters and by helping greatly to defray the costs of research assistance. I am also indebted to Nathan Huggins of Harvard University, who in 1983 generously made available the facilities of the W. E. B. Du Bois Center for Afro-American Studies. Finally, the chance to draw on resources at the University of California at Berkeley, in 1985 and 1987, facilitated the tasks of research and revision. In the course of this study I benefited from the talents of many individuals, whom I am privileged to acknowledge here.

Dolita Cathcart provided invaluable assistance during the first two years of this project. She shared the tasks of examining archives and conducting interviews with civil rights leaders, while offering insights that helped shape and enhance this study, particularly regarding poor blacks in the Northern ghettos. Ms. Cathcart also performed the herculean task of reviewing ten years of issues of the *New York Times,* which afforded me a crucial collection of documents as well as a penetrating and sprightly commentary on them. In all, I could not have asked for a more brilliant or energetic associate.

Steve Forman, my editor throughout six years of work on this book, directed my thoughts toward broad issues in American history, vigilantly patrolled successive manuscript drafts for stylistic lapses, and provided deeply valued support for the project from its inception. Professors John Morton Blum and Howard Zinn, whose own writings on American history have inspired me with their elegance and insight, offered numerous perceptive criticisms and suggestions for revision. William Cotter kindly read the book amid his many tasks as president of Colby College and provided an incisive critique of every section, which I found especially valuable for those passages treating legal subjects. The manuscript is at once shorter and stronger thanks to the editing skills of my friends John Mizner and Tom Mullen. In the final stages of revision my copy editor, Otto Sonntag, reviewed the text with extraordinary thoroughness and an enviable gift for grammatical precision.

Several research assistants measurably aided the completion of this study. Lori Pierce located and ably annotated materials at the State Historical Society of Wisconsin, the Amistad Center in New Orleans, and the Lyndon Baines Johnson Library in Austin, Texas. Marianne Campbell spent a year energetically helping to document the book, and offered astute editorial advice on varied sections. Mary McNear documented two chapters in a summer of tenacious research. I am also grateful to Andrew Grossman, Ahmed Arif, Kim Matthei, Andrew Simons, and Eric Zolov, for carefully checking the manuscript, and to Frances Parker, for sharing her expertise in varied statistical sources.

David J. Garrow generously facilitated the revisions for this new edition. John Hayworth, Rebecca Birrell, and Tom Dorion also assisted by ably rechecking the citations.

Finally, I would like to express a personal word of appreciation to Linda and William Cotter, whose warm friendship has so deeply enriched my stay at Colby College; to my wife, Andrea, for her loving support of my writing, her keen critical eye, and her many innovative suggestions, including the book's title; and to my parents, Louis and Dora Weisbrot, who have assisted my work as patient and probing readers, while providing boundless encouragement on this project, as in all else I have undertaken.

Freedom Bound

Chapter 1

Origins of the Movement

EZELL BLAIR, JR., David Richmond, Joseph McNeil, and Franklin McCain seemed an unlikely band of revolutionaries. At North Carolina A&T College, a black school in Greensboro, these four freshmen moved quickly into anonymity among three thousand other undergraduates in the fall of 1959. They were sharply different individuals: Blair, short and lively, roomed with the studious physics major, McNeil, while the towering, plain-spoken McCain was paired with Richmond, a slender, shy student pondering a future in the ministry. Yet the four youths soon proved kindred spirits. They ate together, studied together, and spent long evenings in their dorms resolving the world's problems, armed only with unlimited idealism and several cans of cold beer. As befitted college bull sessions, their bantering exchanges roamed from eternal philosophical quandaries to the immediate horrors of campus food and the relative charms of local coeds. Inevitably, though, their conversation returned to a single, gnawing question: when would blacks do something about the racial barriers that mocked their ambitions and self-esteem?

Their impatience centered on the failure of recent federal edicts to protect Negroes from continued discrimination. Five years after the Supreme Court had ordered an end to segregated education, over 99 percent of all Southern black children still attended separate schools. Congress in 1957 affirmed the voting rights of adult citizens regardless of race, yet blacks in much of the South still went to the polls at peril to their jobs, or worse. Negroes did register notable gains in the armed forces, where they now served in integrated units. At home, however, the legal segregation of many public places reminded returning black veterans that, out of uniform, they ranked no higher than Citizen, Second Class.

As the four students talked on, night after night, the questioning became more personal, inescapable: at what point would they, the younger generation of black Americans, take their stand against injustice? When their deepening friendship gave them, in McCain's words, "that little bit of incentive and that little bit of courage,"[1] their vague discontent with the state of race relations turned into a specific plan for defiance.

Nurturing this budding rebellion was a white storekeeper and local NAACP member of Syrian descent, Ralph Johns. As a young man Johns had shown a disregard for social convention, crashing the gate at boxing matches in the 1930s. In Greensboro during the mid-1940s his friendships with black customers channeled his flamboyance into a new, deeply felt cause, seen in the message he would chalk on a slate outside his clothing shop: "God hates segregation." In 1949 Johns advised a black student to test Greensboro's Jim Crow laws, leading the astonished youth to blurt out, "Man, what do you want to do? Get me arrested? All I want to do is get my diploma and get out of the South."[2] After ten years of similar scenes with young Negroes, Johns approached Joseph McNeil with the idea of acting against segregation. McNeil pressed him for details.

The plan, endlessly discussed by McNeil and his three friends, was to break the taboo on interracial dining by seeking service at the Woolworth's "white" lunch counter. The sixty-six-seat, L-shaped counter was the single largest money-maker in downtown Greensboro and, as the sole spot in the Woolworth's store where blacks were barred from making purchases, it represented segregation at its most arbitrary and demeaning. Johns offered the four boys a sobering assurance that he would have bond money ready when police officers came to arrest them for disturbing the peace.

What did the students expect their daring gesture would accomplish? No one had any clear idea. When one of the four offered the morale-building thought "We'll stay until we get served," Ezell Blair replied, "Well, you know that might be weeks, that might be months, that might be never."[3] Doubts also surfaced over the punishment they might incur from white authorities and black college officials. But on the last night of the semester Franklin McCain brought the months of earnest, anguished discussion to a sudden resolution. Pounding a dresser, he dared his hesitant friends, "Are you guys chicken or not?"[4] The next morning, February 1, 1960, Blair, Richmond, McNeil, and McCain entered the Woolworth's, determined to give Jim Crow a blow that would not soon be forgotten.

Sundry purchases in different departments established the four students as paying customers at Woolworth's; and then came the test: "Coffee, please." Behind the counter a black dishwasher, who feared for her job and for the boys, gruffly attempted to set them straight. "You're acting stupid, ignorant!" They should know that the counter was for white people. "That's why we can't get anyplace today, because of people like you, rabble-rousers, troublemakers."[5] To the students this lecture belonged to an age of race relations they had resolved to end. They listened patiently but were not about to leave the counter.

A white policeman standing behind the four youths paced the aisle, tapping his club against his palm and, as McCain recalled, "just looking mean and red and a little bit upset and a little bit disgusted."[6] The boys were trembling inside (one of them to the point of emptying his bowels), but the policeman proved too disoriented even to swagger effectively, let alone make arrests. In their quietly determined way the youths had turned the policeman's world upside down, disregarding his presence yet without provoking him severely enough to warrant use of his club or gun. The store manager, too, could think of no better solution than to let the four Negroes sit undisturbed while acting as if they were not there, violating his "white" counter. Gradually it dawned on the students that, for a moment at least, they had stymied the city's white establishment. "By then," McCain remembered, "we had the confidence, my goodness, of a Mack truck."[7]

As Greensboro's white residents streamed through Woolworth's, the seemingly solid South reacted in surprisingly individual ways to the presence of the four students. Some predictably heaped curses on them. Others, inclined toward paternalistic courtesy, pointed out that the youths did not belong at a white counter. But a couple of elderly white ladies patted them on the back and praised their action. One of them added, "Ah, you should have done it ten years ago."[8]

Though the four freshmen were not served that day, they returned to campus to discover that they had become heroes. Their act had elevated them past the status of straight-A students, past even the veneration reserved for A&T's gridiron stars. Ultrafashionable coeds who had been too busy the past semester to notice these freshmen now rushed to announce a sudden clearing of their social schedules. Even A&T's president, Warmouth T. Gibbs, known for his deference to white authorities, reacted with unexpected benevolence when students told him of the sit-in. Although the motives for targeting Woolworth's puzzled him (as he believed that the store had never enjoyed a reputation for fine food), Gibbs declined to call for expulsions, suspensions, or any other disciplinary measures. Soon the four freshmen found that their impact on campus was extending beyond student adulation to include widespread emulation. One boy described the rush to the forbidden lunch counters: "It was like a fever. Everyone wanted to go. We were so happy."[9]

The second day of February 1960 found twenty other A&T students joining their protest; by the fourth day, the first white students joined in from the University of North Carolina Women's College in Greensboro. Then these newly christened "sit-downs" spread to half a dozen towns in the state. The targets now included shopping centers, drugstores, theaters, drive-ins, the whole range of public accommodations. As the sit-ins spread, reporters asked Blair, Richmond, McNeil, and McCain, "How long have you been planning this?" They answered for a generation of young blacks: "All our lives!"[10]

American Dilemma

The barriers that students protested, charging that they denied full humanity to nineteen million Negroes, stood on a national tradition more than three hundred years old. Until 1865 nine of every ten blacks in America lived as slaves, concentrated on Southern plantations. Thereafter racism assumed new forms, ceding blacks limited rights while confining them to the bottom rungs of a caste system based on color and sanctioned by the highest courts. The planning of student protests therefore began in a shared historical experience with all Negroes who were caught in a web of customs and laws designed to maintain the racial status quo.

The ninety-five years spanning the end of slavery and the advent of the student sit-ins marked a twilight period of black American history, in which the promise of equality often shone brightly but never came fully within reach. The cataclysm of civil war, which imposed military rule and political reform on the South, ushered in an era of revolutionary gains in black legal status. Between 1865 and 1869 Congress adopted three amendments to the Constitution that for the first time guaranteed blacks freedom, citizenship, and suffrage. Escorted by Union troops, Southern Negroes only recently in bondage flocked to the voting booths, and hundreds served in federal or state office. Yet this era of Reconstruction, as the forcible reshaping of Southern society became known, proved that old social values could survive military defeat and that "white supremacy" was perhaps the South's most stubbornly resilient feature.

Throughout the post–Civil War years the heart of the old slave system, black dependence on white landowners, continued to beat vigorously. Four million Negroes received little or no land as compensation for their slave labor; rather, they were set free without resources in a region devastated by war. Of necessity most freedmen contracted to work white-owned farms for a minimal livelihood, incurring debts that bound them to the land in virtual serfdom. Negroes were now legally independent persons rather than property to be owned and sold, but in practice they could survive only at the sufferance of white planters, merchants, and creditors.

Improvement in the Negro's civil status during Reconstruction also appeared more impressive on federal law books than in daily life. Southern communities varied widely in respecting the rights of blacks to use public facilities, to testify in court, even to walk the streets unmolested. Armed whites, angered by the imposed changes in racial mores, rioted in cities ranging from New Orleans to Memphis, slaughtering hundreds of blacks with impunity. Guerrilla bands like the robed and hooded cavalry of the Ku Klux Klan meanwhile gained heroic reputations terrorizing and murdering Negroes, whom they despised as symbols of Northern rule. When Southern whites regained full political control over their region, aided by the withdrawal of Union troops in 1877, the limited roots of black advancement were glaringly exposed and systematically pruned.

The decades after Reconstruction witnessed a reversion of Negro status in the South to a level near slavery. Segregation and disenfranchisement of blacks became the chief business of local and state legislators, and lynching gained the approval of entire white communities as a way to enforce the new racial order. Mob murder of black people, with the accompanying mutilations, crowd cheering, and racial taunts, occurred over two thousand times between 1890 and 1910, mainly in the rural "Black Belt" counties stretching from Virginia to Texas. Georgia's popular agrarian leader Tom Watson summed up the predominant Southern white mood at the turn of the century, praising lynch law as "a good sign" that "a sense of justice yet lives among the people."[11]

The successful imposition of Jim Crow, as the South's racial rules were dubbed, depended on Northern acquiescence, which in time ripened into sympathy and encouragement. By the late nineteenth century Northern whites had lost interest in Southern Negro progress as they grappled with the problems of industrial development, abuses by corporate "robber barons," public corruption, and the influx of swarthy European workers who stimulated their own racial fears. Northern editors, scholars, ministers, and politicians increasingly affirmed the wisdom of permitting the South—by which they meant the white South—to handle its "Negro problem."

The Supreme Court, composed mainly of Northern appointees, early placed its imprimatur on Southern laws that codified black inferiority. In 1883 it overturned a congressional act ensuring Negroes access to hotels, restaurants, and theaters. Thirteen years later the Court found Homer Adolph Plessy, a black Louisianan, too sensitive in claiming that a railroad porter had committed an act of discrimination by tossing him from the coach reserved for whites. Plessy had sued on the grounds that a Louisiana statute requiring segregated streetcars violated his right to equal citizenship under the Fourteenth Amendment. Eight members of the Court dismissed his contention, ruling in *Plessy v. Ferguson* that "separate but equal" facilities implied not race discrimination but merely "race distinction." In his solitary dissent John Marshall Harlan branded the ruling "pernicious," though he, too, affirmed a sense of pride in white dominance.

In the quarter century after *Plessy* Southern white racial attitudes hardened into rigid legal patterns. Separate and second-class facilities marked the Negro's lot in public education, health care, and public lodging. Whites used rest rooms designated "Men" or "Women," while blacks followed signs for "Colored." Separate entrances to buildings were standard in Southern towns, though blacks seldom found any entrances at polling booths. Legal ruses, racist registrars, and lynch law kept elections "white folks' business." Even in death, where all presumably were equal, blacks and whites remained separate, because cemeteries were segregated, along with funeral notices in local papers.

Daily humiliation of Negroes was woven into the fabric of Southern life in patterns as variegated as a community's imagination permitted. In 1905 Georgia prohibited Negroes and whites from using the same park facilities; donors of land for playgrounds had to specify which race could use them. Until 1940 Negroes and whites in Atlanta, Georgia, were not able to visit the municipal zoo at the same time. In 1915 Oklahoma authorized separate telephone booths for white and Negro callers. A Mississippi ordinance of 1922 barred members of different races from sharing a taxicab unless the vehicle held more than seven passengers and was traveling from one city to another. New Orleans struck a quaint blow for morality by separating Negro and white prostitutes. Many public libraries permitted black and white to mingle only in the pages of books, while otherwise reserving the buildings exclusively for white use. Separate Bibles for oath taking in courts, separate doors for whites and Negroes, separate elevators and stairways, separate drinking fountains, and separate toilets existed even where not required by law.[12]

Outsiders sometimes noted with surprise that the proliferation of Jim Crow laws coexisted with the most intimate contact between Negroes and whites. The mass of Southern blacks continued to labor on white plantations and in white kitchens. More discreetly, racial barriers often set with the Southern sun, permitting white men to have covert sexual liaisons with Negro women, a practice that since antebellum times had contributed many light-skinned offspring to black families. Such behavior scarcely aided the vocal white drive against racial mixing, but at heart the defense of Jim Crow had less to do with purity than with white power and privilege.

The substance of Southern racial attitudes changed only modestly through the mid-twentieth century. Whites regarded blacks with strong emotions, affection as well as fear, but seldom in a way that allowed them fully human dimensions. For their part blacks who wished to retain self-esteem amid directives to isolate or humble themselves had to retreat into stoic disregard of their surroundings. The white reporter Pat Watters, growing up in Atlanta during the 1950s, observed the strain on Negroes who tried to keep their spirit along with the rules meant to break it:

> While I was in high school I worked on Saturdays and during the summers at a men's clothing store in a cheap section of town, catering to poor whites and Negroes. I can still see the old Negro man who came in one evening and, with big, work-thick fingers, picked through the selection of our Sunday "dress-up" felt hats, and finally, painfully, reaching a decision, took one down and then, with a dignity to the indignity of it, reached slowly into his overalls pocket, pulled out some tissue and carefully lined the band of the hat with it before setting it on his grey head and stood, head cocked, to see in the mirror how it looked on him.

Rare though not at all alone among white Southerners, Watters welcomed the student protests that bid to end "this kind of spectacle, so demeaning to him and to us."[13]

The Southern caste system still flourished on the margins of America's conscience as the country stretched toward the 1960s. Yet it was not quite so impregnable as in the past. Expanding textile, oil, lumber, and chemical industries had drawn 60 percent of the region's population to the urban centers, undermining the traditional plantation culture with its strict distinctions of race and class. The logic of business growth favored a more widely educated labor force, employed by merit rather than color, and a domestic market unhampered by racial division of consumers or disruptive social tensions. To a rising if reticent minority of merchants, manufacturers, and professionals, Jim Crow was becoming an embarrassing, and costly, anachronism.

National currents further unsettled the white South's control over race relations. Until 1910 some 90 percent of all blacks lived in the South, but over the next half century a demographic revolution reduced the proportion to under 60 percent, freeing more Negroes from Jim Crow laws than the Fourteenth Amendment had done. Droughts, floods, and boll weevils devastated Southern agriculture early in the century, priming the flow of Negro tenants and croppers out of the region. War in Europe hastened this rural exodus by cutting off white immigration late in 1914 and creating a demand for Southern Negro factory labor. The resulting desertion of Black Belt plantations stripped some counties so thoroughly that the few Negro barbers, undertakers, and merchants also departed, for lack of patronage. Some migrants became domestics and unskilled workers in Southern cities. But most followed the lure of booming industries, higher wages, and relative freedom in the urban North.

Resettlement in impersonal, slum-ridden black ghettos entailed wrenching adjustments, yet it also released black energies from the thrall of white rural overlords. By the 1930s northward migration had added several hundred thousand ghetto dwellers to the voting rolls, clustered in key Northern industrial states. These newly enfranchised citizens drew overtures from candidates of both major parties and helped blacks escape the political isolation that had kept them a largely powerless minority.

The ascendancy of liberal reform politics in the 1930s afforded blacks a particularly crucial vehicle for advancing their rights. Impelled by the need to reduce widespread hardship and discontent during the Great Depression, liberal leaders advocated more vigorous federal safeguards for all citizens regardless of background. There emerged a vast welfare apparatus, designed and controlled by officials in Washington, D.C., which advanced the ideal of aiding "forgotten Americans." Though this development sprang mainly from economic rather than from racial concerns, it coincided with black aims of participating more fully in the benefits of American society.

The substantial inclusion of blacks in federal assistance programs, though marred by frequent instances of discrimination, helped cement the ties between Negroes and liberals. In 1936 blacks voted in record numbers for the Democratic President Franklin Roosevelt, responding to his job and relief measures at a time when work even as a salesclerk could garner front-page coverage in Harlem journals. The rapid entry of blacks into the Democratic camp formed a growing counterweight to the party's white Southern wing, with its insistent cry of "Segregation forever."

The rise of industrial unions in the mid-1930s added to the political leverage of blacks. Unlike the established craft unions that blatantly excluded blacks, emerging unions in steel, automobile, and other mass-production fields enlisted Negroes as equal members rather than risk having companies hire them cheaply as strikebreakers. Walter Reuther of the United Auto Workers and John L. Lewis of the United Mine Workers spoke out against the caste system that divided labor in the South and impeded union organizing. As black employees increasingly joined strikes and factory "sit-downs," helping to win heftier pay envelopes for all union members, white coworkers warmed to the cause of racial tolerance as being sound philosophy and still better economics.

The fusion of Negro and labor interests, though incomplete, advanced a loose Democratic coalition of blacks and numerous other rising social groups. In the preceding decade Republican administrations had almost exclusively championed corporate interests while showing little concern for either the poor or the ethnic minorities. The onset of the Great Depression, discrediting both business leadership and the idea of single-interest government, encouraged Negroes as well as Catholics, Jews, Irish-, Italian-, and Slavic-Americans, unions, the Farm Bureau, women's organizations, social workers, and intellectuals to assert their claims on President Roosevelt's "New Deal" policies. Blacks were by no means the strongest of these lobbying forces, but their respectful treatment by the President and Northern congressmen signaled a sharp turn away from the politics of white supremacy.

Critics of racism gained a more respectful hearing in this tolerant political climate. The German-trained anthropologist Franz Boaz had long since debunked "scientific" claims of black inferiority based on cranial capacity, jaw protrusion, and mortality rates. During the 1930s scholars increasingly built on his findings, which emphasized environmental rather than genetic influences on human behavior and treated the term "race" as a product of myth and ignorance. Otto Klineberg's work *Negro Intelligence* (1935) exposed flaws in widely cited Army tests purporting to show that blacks and Jews were mentally inferior to other Americans. Current popular literature also highlighted the influence of environment, including works by the black novelist Richard Wright, whose tragic heroes raged against a society that would not recognize their humanity. These cultural winds by no means swept away the nation's deeply ingrained racial sentiment, but they corroded it to the point where blacks, too, widely appeared entitled to at least some rights and opportunities.

Negroes assisted these developments with escalating protests against discrimination, anchored by the foremost civil rights group, the National Association for the Advancement of Colored People (NAACP). During the 1930s the "N–Double A–CP" launched a concerted attack on school segregation that slowly stripped the judicial fences around Jim Crow. The association's source of legal inspiration, known to insiders as the Margold Bible, built on a single proverb by the attorney Nathan Margold: that the reform climate of the New Deal favored appeals to equal opportunity but not demands for integration. The NAACP therefore challenged the 1896 *Plessy* decision by indirection, claiming that inferior facilities mocked the claim of "separate but equal." In this way it desegregated graduate and law schools in Maryland, Missouri, and other states unable to persuade federal courts of an equal commitment to black and white students.

The President and Congress also received relentless tutoring from black leaders on the need for stronger commitment to human rights. Lobbyists armed with graphic pamphlets helped the NAACP expose a surge of racially motivated, unpunished, and uninvestigated lynchings in Southern states. Federal antilynching bills twice passed the House of Representatives in the 1930s, though they failed to surmount the obstructive oratory of Southern senators and the timorous silence of President Roosevelt. The stalemate on civil rights legislation nonetheless accompanied a growing openness in national politics about the long-forbidden subject of federal responsibility for racial justice.

During the early 1940s civil rights activism rose amid a military buildup that increased white employment but left blacks angrily stirring over exclusion from defense plants. As late as May 1941 the president of the North American Aviation Company explained that despite the firm's "complete sympathy with the Negro, it is against company policy to employ them as aircraft workers or mechanics . . . regardless of their training." He pledged "some jobs as janitors for Negroes."[14] That summer the Negro union leader A. Philip Randolph, founder of the Brotherhood of Sleeping Car Porters, warned President Roosevelt that over fifty thousand black men would rally at the capital against Jim Crow in the armed forces and war-production industries. Randolph's prediction was more a desperate gambit than an informed estimate, given the paucity of Negro activism outside the Northern ghettos. But in a time of approaching war Roosevelt chose not to test this rippling of black political muscle. He created an advisory committee to promote fair employment in munitions factories, in exchange for Randolph's agreement to call off the march. A limited step, it was also the first presidential order for civil rights since Reconstruction—and the first intended chiefly to quiet an emerging Negro mass movement.

American entry into the Second World War in December 1941 intensified black gains—and discontents. Two million Negroes secured jobs in munitions factories, yet they worked mainly in the least-skilled, lowest-paid positions. Half a million black soldiers served in the European and Pacific theaters, nearly all of them in segregated units under white command, just like their fathers a quarter century earlier in the First World War. Such treatment spurred a frustrated black leadership to fuse patriotism and protest, urging a "Double Victory" over the enemies of democracy at home and around the globe.

With federal leaders intent on avoiding any intervention in the social order that could weaken the war effort, race relations on the home front drifted between surface harmony and open violence. Campaigns for national unity often withered on contact with race issues, as in the sign that urged bus riders in Charleston, South Carolina, to "pull together" for victory by obeying the laws seating whites from front to back, and Negroes from back to front.[15] Farther north, patriotism again deferred to racial custom when German prisoners of war dined at a lunch counter in Salina, Kansas, while their black captors received only a rebuke, "You boys know we don't serve colored here."[16] In Detroit, where black migration compounded the competition for scarce housing, white violence led to a full-scale race riot in 1943 that claimed thirty-four lives. By 1945, as Americans celebrated first V-E Day, to mark victory in Europe, then V-J Day, with the surrender of Japan, black leaders grimly prepared to revive the languishing war for democracy at home.

The social atmosphere in postwar America proved unexpectedly tonic for civil rights leaders. Growing numbers of religious, civic, labor, and intellectual spokesmen addressed the issue of segregation, not just as a "Negro problem" or a sectional one, but as a challenge to national values. The call for tolerance rang louder with the emergence of second- and third-generation Americans, Catholic and Jewish, who participated more assertively in the country's economy, politics, and culture in the years after World War II. Will Maslow of the American Jewish Congress summed up the attitude of varied ethnic organizations: "You can't fight discrimination against one minority group without fighting it against others."[17]

Social scientists reflected and reinforced the popular mood by combining critiques of racial theories with bolder prescriptions for a national assault on Jim Crow. Only a society already gripped by anxiety over segregation could have raised to popular heights the 1,483-page tome *An American Dilemma,* in which the Swedish sociologist Gunnar Myrdal charted the gulf between the nation's democratic ideals and the reality of discrimination. Published to immediate acclaim in 1944, Myrdal's volume moved beyond its own detailed indictment of prejudice to sound a widely shared hope: "The main trend in [the country's] history is the gradual realization of the American Creed."[18]

Foreign policy considerations indirectly contributed to the nation's growing tolerance toward Negroes. Four years of war against Hitler's Germany helped awaken Americans to the dangers of racial ideology. Although racist policies at home were less extreme than Nazi atrocities in the name of Aryan supremacy, they seemed to many Americans uncomfortably similar in spirit.

Blacks also found a strange but potent ally in the anti-Communist fervor that gripped the country after 1945. Although this mood lent itself to political conformity, it nonetheless made the hue of one's ideology rather than that of one's skin the overriding test of a worthy American. Similarly the obsession with "godless Communist tyranny," despite right-wing overtones, encouraged a celebration of American society for its guarantee of freedom for every citizen. Competition with the Soviet Union for the favor of emerging nonwhite nations further enhanced the cause of black rights, as racism became a damaging embarrassment for a people claiming for itself the virtues of a democratic society. The preoccupations of the Cold War thus spurred Americans to achieve at home the ideal of liberty on which they based their assertions of moral superiority abroad.

A prolonged postwar economic boom sustained these egalitarian forces. Gloomy predictions of a slide back into depression following World War II gave way to astonished relief, then to an easy confidence about the limitless capacity of American capitalism. Mass production and advances in technology delivered a cornucopia of refrigerators, washers, vaccuum cleaners, "miracle drugs," the first widely sold televisions, and other staples of the good life for a majority of American families. Blacks shared this bounty, more than doubling their median income in the period from 1940 to 1960. The northward migration of nearly three million blacks brought gains in professional, white-collar, skilled, and semiskilled occupations. Yet whereas in the hard times of the 1930s whites competed with Negroes for even the lowest-paid jobs, in the postwar years employment and salaries spiraled upward through the late 1940s and 1950s, easing fears that black gains would threaten white affluence and security.

As barriers lowered for all minorities, Negroes shared in some of the symbolic "firsts" that promised fuller acceptance. The UN diplomat Ralph

Bunche won the Nobel Peace Prize in 1950 for arranging a Middle East armistice, though he later declined an appointment as undersecretary of state rather than subject his children to Washington's Jim Crow laws. Baseball's Brooklyn Dodgers allowed the first black into the major leagues when the team installed the former track and football star Jackie Robinson at second base. In 1947 Robinson silently withstood abuse by spectators, players, restaurant owners, and hotel managers while going on to win rookie-of-the-year honors. By season's end the league's sole dark-skinned hero was exchanging shouts, insults, and arguments with umpires and opponents on a nonracial basis, to the delight of fans in every ballpark. With less publicity, black actors, writers, singers, union organizers, lawyers, and soldiers joined Robinson in chipping away at traditional enclaves of segregation.

Registration of over two million blacks by the late 1940s drove one of the deepest wedges into the racial status quo. President Harry Truman, who as a Missouri politician had always welcomed black support as heartily as white, appointed a committee in 1946 to investigate violations of Negro rights. Known as the Noah's Ark commission, because it boasted pairs of businessmen, labor leaders, Southerners, Negroes, educators, women, Catholics, and Jews, this prestigious task force urged comprehensive federal action to end segregation. In 1948 Truman acceded to a strong civil rights plank that liberal delegates had inserted in the Democratic national platform. He then weathered defections by a minority of Southern whites to win a second term, aided by 70 percent of the Northern Negro vote. Two years later he began desegregation of the armed forces to heighten military efficiency for the Korean War and to quiet restive black leaders. These gains were scratches on the social order, but together they signaled the growing importance of Negroes in the complex ethnic mosaic of Democratic politics.

By the late forties Negro breakthroughs in many fields encouraged the NAACP's special counsel, Thurgood Marshall, to abandon the Margold Bible for a newer legal testament: all-out opposition to *Plessy.* Marshall argued that segregation was inherently unconstitutional, for it stigmatized an entire race and thereby denied it "equal protection of the laws" as guaranteed by the Fourteenth Amendment. The Supreme Court, badly fractured along personal and ideological lines, continued for several years to rule for the NAACP without directly addressing whether segregation could ever be justified. Then in 1954 a new chief justice, with a fair skill at law but a surpassing talent for compromise, persuaded his judicial brethren to issue a single, unwavering statement on the contradiction between segregation and citizenship. In four cases known collectively as *Brown v. Board of Education,* Earl Warren wrote for a unanimous court that "the doctrine of 'separate but equal' has no place" in the nation's public schools. Jim Crow, having leaned comfortably on a legal precedent for fifty-eight years, abruptly found itself at odds with the law of the land.

By threatening white supremacy so forthrightly, the *Brown* case intensified Southern resistance to civil rights progress. Although some officials pledged to implement the law, headlines and thumping electoral victories went to those who vowed to defend segregation. District attorneys sought injunctions to prohibit NAACP branches from operating, and in Alabama they were entirely successful by 1957. The Ku Klux Klan, the White Citizens Council, and other fringe vehicles of racial hate experienced overnight revivals after the Court decision. The Supreme Court took stock of this frenzied reaction by issuing a dovish addendum to *Brown* in 1955 that acknowledged the difficulty of changing educational systems and asked only that states act "with all deliberate speed." A phrase of deliberate ambiguity, it encouraged attempts to evade school desegregation indefinitely.

The conservative tenor of national politics further inhibited progress in race relations following *Brown.* After experiencing years of rapid reform and rising presidential power, Americans were reluctant to extend federal authority for any purpose, let alone to upset established racial patterns. As President, Dwight D. Eisenhower reflected this attitude by refusing to lend his immense prestige to the *Brown* ruling. Avoiding public comment, he privately criticized the Court decision as rash and impractical. His own decision to appoint Earl Warren as chief justice Eisenhower called "the biggest damfool mistake" he ever made.[19] Heartened by the President's policy of neutrality, officials in the Deep South kept Negroes from attending "white" schools for over three years.

Little Rock, Arkansas, became the site of a test case of federal commitment to civil rights when a federal court ordered public schools there to begin desegregation in September 1957. Governor Orval Faubus dispatched a unit of the National Guard to Central High School on opening day to prevent Negro students from entering. His action antagonized but also paralyzed white moderates, while encouraging mobs to form outside the schools as a grass-roots veto of the *Brown* mandate. The President, whose earlier inaction had contributed to this anarchic scene, now painfully moved to uphold the integrity of federal law.

A summit meeting between Eisenhower and Faubus relieved the tension only briefly, for the governor still refused to withdraw the National Guard. If Faubus intended merely to get an early start on his reelection campaign by playing to racial fears, he succeeded handily. If, however, he hoped to outbluff the former Allied supreme commander in World War II by barking commands at state reserve units, the governor was out of his depth. On September 24, 1957, Eisenhower federalized the National Guard and ordered part of the crack 101st Airborne Division to Little Rock. By 5:00 A.M. paratroopers had ringed the school, bayonets fixed. Several hours later nine black children arrived in an Army station wagon and filed past their armed escort en route to their first experience with integrated education.

The need to secure a public school with infantrymen confirmed to Eisenhower, and to much of the nation, that local race relations were best left alone. With the President maintaining his nonaligned stance on *Brown,* Negro students bore the brunt of Little Rock's experiment in school desegregation. They went dutifully to classes, prepared their homework assignments, ignored insults and threats, coped with slaps and beatings, steeled themselves against constant danger to themselves and their families. "Nothing has changed," Carlotta Walls, sixteen, commented on her determination to remain in school the morning after a bomb containing three sticks of dynamite tore a three-foot hole through her brick house. With those quiet words to a reporter, Walls rode off to Central High School, where she and four other black students daily studied beside dozens of hostile white classmates.[20]

The clash at Little Rock sobered many blacks and whites who hoped that a purely legalistic approach might quickly and neatly dismantle Jim Crow patterns. Still, the *Brown* case exerted an impact on race relations far beyond the scant immediate changes in Southern schools. It provided a yardstick of color-blind justice against which Americans could measure their progress toward the ideal of equal opportunity. It also conferred a symbol of legitimacy on black activists, who prepared bolder assaults on segregation in the South.

An Awakening Movement

Before *Brown* Southern Negroes had periodically defied Jim Crow, though with limited continuity and effect. James Farmer, Jr., son of a black divinity scholar in Holly Springs, Texas (Klansmen were heard to call him "Doctor"), began organizing a Negro resistance movement in 1942. Inspired by India's nonviolent protests against British rule, Farmer drew on his contacts in Christian pacifist circles to cofound the Congress of Racial Equality, or CORE, as a vehicle for nonviolent Negro revolution. Yet his vision held little interest for blacks at a time when two million were winning jobs in defense plants and several hundred thousand others were fighting fascism in Europe, albeit in segregated regiments. Nor did the white South appear ripe for conversion by CORE's nonviolent crusaders. "Are you Gandhi?" James Farmer, Sr., asked his son. "The British threw him in jail. The 'Bamians and Mississippians would shoot him. Dead." Young Farmer replied that CORE radicals would be ready to give their lives, when the time came.[21] But reality jostled even the most determined CORE idealists: they based their headquarters in Chicago, where mortality rates for integrationists compared favorably with those in Alabama and sister states.

In 1947 CORE sent an interracial team of bus riders through the Upper South to desegregate interstate travel. This "Journey of Reconciliation" quickly ended, however, when unreconciled border-state sheriffs arrested most of the riders. Some, like the black socialist Bayard Rustin, finished their trip in police custody and later spent weeks in hard-labor camps, to the vast indifference of the nation. The setback left CORE a small, Northern-based group staffed mainly by whites, vainly seeking an occasion to trigger a Negro mass movement.

Sporadic local protests also sent a message of growing Negro assertiveness, but few, black or white, received it. In November 1953 forty-eight black soldiers in Columbia, South Carolina, were arrested and fined more than

$1,500 because one sat next to a white girl on a bus. That same year a Negro boycott of buses in Baton Rouge, Louisiana, lasted a week before officials permitted blacks and whites to occupy some seats on a first-come, first-served basis. These and other campaigns, generally brief and unavailing, failed to produce either a guiding philosophy or a spokesman to forge a social movement. Within months of the second *Brown* decision, however, a racial confrontation in the heart of the South suddenly provided Negroes with both.

In the years leading to the *Brown* verdict Montgomery, Alabama, had witnessed recurrent though isolated acts of resistance by Negroes seeking to stir a lethargic community against segregation. On one such occasion a black rider whose feet were tired and whose patience with Jim Crow was exhausted sat in the section of a bus reserved for whites and refused the driver's command to move back. When ordered off the bus, the rider stood in the aisle and asked how many other blacks would also leave the bus. Not a single person responded. A few days afterward the rider, the Reverend Vernon Johns of the prestigious Dexter Baptist Church, chided a woman who had declined to join his protest. She spoke for her fellow passengers in replying, "You ought to knowed better."[22]

Several years later, with the *Brown* ruling a warm memory, a white driver scolded Rosa Parks, a former NAACP secretary and another habitual violator of Jim Crow seating patterns on Montgomery buses. The driver had ejected her from a bus twelve years earlier; this time he called for police backup. On December 1, 1955, the forty-two-year old seamstress was arrested and imprisoned, charged with disorderly conduct for refusing to yield her seat to a white man. But in the aftermath of this incident people in black Montgomery were not saying that Mrs. Parks should have known better. They were too busy organizing against the bus company, the city government, and the Jim Crow system.

Jo Ann Robinson, a college English teacher and head of the black Women's Political Council in Montgomery, reacted to the arrest by mimeographing protest leaflets until four in the morning. "The next time it may be you, or your daughter, or mother," she wrote, and urged blacks to stay off the buses in a daylong gesture of solidarity with Rosa Parks.[23] By the afternoon of December 2 she and two student volunteers had delivered fifty thousand of these appeals to schools, businesses, barbershops, beer halls, and factories. The nearly unanimous sentiment for a bus boycott delighted some black leaders and pulled along others who had grown accustomed to placating white authority.

Helping to push away decades of inertia was a tough union organizer, E. D. Nixon, who pressed Negro spokesmen about a possible boycott of the buses. "Brother Nixon," said Martin Luther King, Jr., new pastor of the Dexter Baptist Church, "let me think about it awhile, and call me back." When Nixon called him again, some sixteen persons later, King had resolved to move ahead. "I'm glad you agreed," Nixon said, "because I already set the meeting up to meet at your church."[24]

Racial deference was so ingrained that some ministers at the Dexter Baptist Church meeting suggested publicizing the boycott with unsigned leaflets in order to conceal their role in the protest. E. D. Nixon sat there "boiling over, so mad [he] didn't know what to do," then impulsively jumped up and, forgetting they were in the balcony of the church, yelled, "What the hell you people talkin' 'bout?" Were they grown men or cowards? he demanded to know.[25] Cut by Nixon's challenge, King shouted back that he was no coward. Within the week a bus boycott was under way, guided by the newly formed Montgomery Improvement Association (MIA), with King as its president.

Martin Luther King, Jr., carried with uncommon erudition the heritage of Negro folk religion. Born in 1929 to a Baptist minister's family in Atlanta, he was reciting stretches of biblical verse at five, and wielding a vocabulary that seemed several sizes too big for such a small child. He moved through an adolescence of spiritual doubt, inwardly disdaining Negro religion as otherworldly and overly emotional. But college contact with educated, "modernist" black clergy led him to enter divinity school in the faith that an activist church could save more than souls.

At Crozer Theological Seminary in Pennsylvania and then at Boston University, King explored ways to relate spiritual values to social needs. His erudition spanned the writings of ancient Greece, the French Enlightenment, and German Idealism, but he displayed greater interest in homespun American philosophies of justice. Since college he had drawn inspiration from Henry David Thoreau's 1849 essay, "Civil Disobedience," which defended nonviolent resistance to oppression. Thoreau denied that obedience to the civil law was a citizen's highest responsibility and insisted, "Under a government which imprisons any unjustly, the true place for a just man is also a prison."[26]

Foremost among the American religious thinkers who impressed King was Walter Rauschenbusch. This early-twentieth-century minister stretched the idea of "social Christianity" to radical lengths by exalting Jesus as a revolutionary and by defining salvation as the fulfillment of America's democratic promise. In *Christianity and the Social Crisis* (1907), a book King especially lauded, Rauschenbusch distilled his earthbound religious focus: "The championship of social justice is almost the only way left open to a Christian nowadays to gain the crown of martyrdom."[27]

No one captured King's admiration so fully as Mohandas Gandhi, the ascetic whose nonviolent resistance to British rule accelerated India's movement toward independence. Gandhi advocated confronting authorities with a readiness to suffer rather than inflict harm, in order to expose injustice and impel those in power to end it. Before reading Gandhi, King had sadly concluded "that the ethics of Jesus were only effective in individual relationship. . . . When racial groups and nations were in conflict a more realistic approach seemed necessary." But Gandhi's message imbued him with hope that one could "lift the love ethic of Jesus" to make it "a powerful and effective social force."[28]

The rigorous discipline of nonviolence offered King a path toward mastery of his own volatile nature as well as a tool for combating injustice. Although King had always enjoyed charm and popularity, from his earliest years his life was freighted with intense, often agonizing emotions. As a child he twice leaped from an upstairs window to mourn a close relative. That fragile sensitivity coexisted with proud self-restraint, which emerged in his response to frequent corporal punishment. "He was the most peculiar child whenever you whipped him," King, Sr., related. "He'd stand there, and the tears would run down and he'd never cry."[29] Yet this child was not so long-suffering toward other male relatives. Once he stopped his younger brother from teasing their sister by knocking him cold with a telephone receiver.[30]

The "violent swings in mood"[31] that a high school acquaintance observed in King remained a vital part of his character, forever testing and strengthening his commitment to a higher nonviolent ideal. Like Gandhi, like so many Christian saints, King grappled with an extra measure of inner turbulence to refine a message of faith and understanding. In so doing, he expressed with unique conviction the need of an entire community to turn its grievances into an irresistible moral force.

King liked to say that Rosa Parks, the prime mover in black Montgomery's nonviolent revolt, had been tracked down by the zeitgeist—the spirit of the times. The zeitgeist took a little longer to lay hold of King himself, absorbed as he was with establishing a new ministry and a young family. By the standards of Southern Negro society, which relied on churches to organize communal life and which accorded special eminence to educated pastors, King was an obvious choice for civil rights leadership. Yet in 1954 he declined to run for president of his city's NAACP branch, preferring to spend more time with his family, his congregation, and his doctoral study of the theologian Paul Tillich. A year later he was virtually drafted to direct the boycott, in part because failure seemed likely and, as an acquaintance recalled, no senior black leader "was exactly bucking for the position."[32] Once chosen, though, King revealed some very definite ideas about conducting a protest.

King exhorted Negroes to sacrifice, to go to jail if necessary, not to defeat whites but to free all Montgomery from injustice. With the aid of visiting Northern pacifists, including Glenn Smiley from the Fellowship of Reconciliation and Bayard Rustin of the War Resisters' League, the young minister also deepened his grasp of Gandhian tenets. Gradually he accepted absolute nonviolence as the spiritual bedrock on which to build any movement for justice. After discussions with his wife he rescinded an application for a gun permit and dismissed the volunteers guarding his home, despite dozens of death threats against him and his family. When a bomb narrowly missed killing his wife and children, in January 1956, King upheld his faith in nonviolence by dispersing a vengeful mob that had gathered outside the remains of his dynamited front porch. Hurrying home after the blast, he arrived in time to hear a Negro taunt a policeman, "Now you got your .38 and I got mine; so let's battle it out." As a pale mayor and his entourage stood nearby, fearing an imminent race riot, King told the armed and angry throng that there was a higher way:

"We must love our white brothers no matter what they do to us. We must make them know that we love them."[33] To the astonished relief of white on-lookers, King's Negro listeners quietly returned to their homes.

If the nuances of King's Gandhian preaching eluded many protesters, virtually all blacks in Montgomery grasped his emphasis on unified resistance to segregation. Students at Alabama State College walked or thumbed rides rather than board the city's buses. Some workers rode in cabs or private cars, a few reached their jobs by way of mule, and still others arrived in horse-drawn buggies. Even after efficient car pools formed, many blacks thought the exercise of the spirit worth the walk. One elderly woman waved a car on, explaining, "I'm not walking for myself, I'm walking for my children and my grandchildren."[34]

Astonished whites refused to accept that blacks could defy Jim Crow in such numbers of their own free will. Surely, they reasoned, "goon squads" of black ruffians were keeping blacks off the buses. Police on motorcycles were assigned by city commissioners to trail every bus and keep on the lookout for harassment of potential riders. That first day a college student helping an elderly woman across the street was seized for "intimidating passengers." But the fact was that no one—from the "goon squads" of the city's imagination to officials trying to break the boycott—was intimidating Montgomery's aroused black citizens.

The boycott lasted nearly a year before the city of Montgomery obtained a county court order to end the black car pools, in effect breaking the boycott as well. The local court was still in session, though, when news came of a Supreme Court decision earlier in the day that voided Montgomery's law to segregate buses. NAACP counsels, working in concert with the boycott leadership, were immediately responsible for that verdict, though Montgomery's overjoyed black residents tended to see larger forces at work. "God Almighty," a Negro in the courtroom shouted, "has spoken from Washington, D.C."[35]

Late in December 1956, blacks boarded the buses in Montgomery as unprovocatively as possible, in accordance with the strictures of boycott leaders. Several whites took seats beside Negroes, and there was little violence. The desegregation of Montgomery's buses may have left the city's caste lines largely intact, but the boycott had a transforming effect on traditional attitudes of Southern Negroes. Once the Ku Klux Klan had only to appear in the Negro quarter for residents to scurry home, bolt their doors, draw the shades, and turn off the lights. "Fearing death, they played dead," King explained.[36] After the boycott settlement Klansmen renewed their nocturnal hauntings but found that the old white magic no longer produced the desired display of fear and trembling. When forty carloads of hooded Klansmen moved past Negro homes in Montgomery, they found porch lights gleaming and doors open. After a few blocks the apoplectic merchants of fear realized there were no takers and vanished down a side street.

Whereas earlier protests, like the one in Baton Rouge, had attracted only local attention, news of the campaign reached Negroes far beyond Montgomery. The outcome showed that a black community could strongly challenge racism even in a city proud to be called "the cradle of the Confederacy." It also brought national fame to Dr. King, whose pilgrimage toward nonviolence attracted a gathering caravan of civil rights forces seeking inspiration and direction.

The prospect of further Negro stirrings in the South helped a coalition of liberal, labor, religious, and minority groups press Congress to enact the first Civil Rights Act since Reconstruction. Signed by a mildly supportive President Eisenhower in September 1957, the act created a commission to monitor civil rights violations and authorized the Justice Department to guard black voting rights through litigation against discriminatory registrars. Even advocates of the bill conceded it was a modest triumph, for Southern senators had energetically trimmed away any provisions threatening immediate concrete change. The NAACP's director, Roy Wilkins, grimaced at this "crumb from Congress" but stood by the measure as a potentially important precedent.[37] At the same time black leaders understood that without their heightened initiative, progress toward racial equality would continue to hobble along "with all deliberate speed."

In the years following the emergence of Martin Luther King, Jr., Negroes organized for change with growing confidence and urgency. Early in 1957 Bayard Rustin and other volunteers helped Dr. King form a network of activist black clergymen, the Southern Christian Leadership Conference. CORE continued to be chiefly a Northern group, low in members and funds, but it began mapping plans for Gandhian action in the Deep South. NAACP youth councils proliferated and often outstripped the national office in zeal. Between 1957 and January 1960, Southern towns experienced sixteen sit-ins, short-lived but often widely supported campaigns. One, begun in Durham, North Carolina, late in 1959, offered a vivid model to students in nearby Greensboro.[38]

This activism unfolded in relative obscurity against the gray background of conservative national politics. But as Eisenhower's second term waned, the social complacency that had marked his tenure in office yielded to a clamor for bold leadership in all areas of American life. The new mood mixed a range of elements—fear of advancing Soviet technology, rising concern over hard-core poverty, and the restless idealism of the postwar baby-boom generation that was just coming of age. No group felt these currents more keenly than young blacks in the South. Raised on the promise of *Brown* and the Montgomery campaign, they awaited only a spark to set them against the barricades of segregation, as they heralded their country's reawakening reform spirit.

Chapter 2

The Sit-ins

Catching the Mood

BLACK STUDENTS throughout the country strained for new details of the Greensboro protests, as if listening to word about their own future in America. Word of the event hit sixteen-year-old Cleveland Sellers, a high school honors student in South Carolina, "like a shot of adrenalin" and infused him with "a burning desire to get involved."[1] Seventeen-year-old Ruby Doris Smith ran home from Spelman College, in Atlanta, to catch television coverage of the sit-in, and began thinking that perhaps this could happen in her city, too. A brooding twenty-six-year-old high school teacher in New York, Robert Moses, stared at a newspaper picture of the Greensboro youths and felt immediate kinship. He found on their faces a certain look—"sullen, angry, determined"—that was light-years away from the "defensive, cringing" expression that had marked the Southern Negro. Within months of the first sit-in, Sellers was leading protests in his native town of Denmark, Smith had joined a campaign in Atlanta, and Moses was heading South to devote his full time to the student movement. They were among hundreds, then thousands, of black youths from different backgrounds who challenged the color line, each knowing, as Bob Moses did, that the actions of these four freshmen "had something to do with [his] own life."[2]

The rising tide of protest needed less than a week to spill over state borders into Hampton, Virginia, and Rock Hill, South Carolina. One week more and whites in Chattanooga and Nashville were coping with extensive sit-in campaigns. Over in Little Rock, Arkansas, black students marked a boycott of segregated stores by sporting badges on their jacket lapels that read, "I am wearing 1959 clothes with 1960 dignity."[3] By the end of February the protests had penetrated the Deep South, including the cradle of nonviolent direct action, Montgomery.

Even at Alabama's Tuskegee Institute, a black school dependent on state funds and long unmatched in its avoidance of controversy, students were forsaking farm science for current events. They heeded strict college directives not to engage in sit-ins, but on February 27, 1960, three hundred students marched into downtown Tuskegee to protest the expulsion of nine student activists from nearby Alabama State University.[4] By this gesture of solidarity, students at this most conservative of black campuses affirmed that they, too, felt the spirit of Greensboro.

In the North, sympathy boycotts against Woolworth's and other chain stores whose Southern branches excluded blacks from lunch counters gave the sit-in campaigns added financial muscle. Significant white participation in the boycotts and picketing ensured that corporate management would feel the financial effects of continued discrimination. Among the picketers at Woolworth's stores in New York City was a native Alabaman and former Miss America, Yolande Betzbeze Fox, who demurely explained, "I'm a Southern girl, but I'm a thinking girl."[5]

The contagion of antiracist protest extended even to employees at these chain stores. One CORE worker found that managers sometimes congratulated him for picketing, and at one Woolworth's store a Bible concessionaire came out to greet him: "You're losing me business like crazy—but don't stop. I'd even join you if I didn't have my concession here." Returning to his store he added, "I guess people have been reading my product lately."[6]

The proliferating protests brought to the fore new leaders to inspire the student movement. As young blacks began to seek guiding principles as well as precedents for action, they paid particular notice to the distinctive sit-in campaign unfolding in Nashville. Unlike the freshmen whose act of naïve courage first sparked the sit-ins, the Nashville activists were somewhat older students or graduates who had held their first workshop in nonviolent resistance nearly a year before the protest in Greensboro. As inclined to grapple with Gandhian texts as with white authority, they emerged as models for a movement that, at barely two weeks of age, was fast growing in numbers and vigor yet remained very much in search of its moral bearings.

Among the Nashville activists whose lives exemplified the Christian roots of student activism, John Robert Lewis was perhaps the most single-minded. Short, humorous but intense, Lewis was one of ten children born to sharecroppers in rural Alabama. Fired by the evangelical piety of the Black Belt, he began the Lord's work early, preaching at age four to the family chickens and then duly baptizing them. (He agonized long afterward over having sent one luckless fowl to an early afterlife during a too zealous immersion ritual.) Classmates in high school dubbed him "Preacher" for his Sunday sermons at nearby churches. As a teenager he listened to radio sermons by Martin Luther King, Jr., in the days before the Montgomery boycott and revered him as "a Moses, using organized religion and the emotionalism within the Negro church as an instrument, as a vehicle, toward freedom."[7] By the time Lewis won a scholarship to Nashville's American Baptist Theological Seminary, in 1957, at age seventeen, he was already thinking about the possibilities for religious-based protest against Jim Crow.

In addition to reform-minded seminarians like Lewis and his friends Bernard Lafayette and James Bevel, others came to the Nashville student group from Fisk University, less immersed in formal religious training but just as intent on applying moral principles to black protest. Marion Barry, originally from Mississippi, was studying for a graduate degree in chemistry when the sit-ins erupted. He found his informal study of Gandhi more compelling and joined the protests at the risk of his scholarship. Fisk also brought to prominence a petite, articulate, and iron-willed student named Diane Nash. A Chicago native and a Catholic, she found the sit-ins an example of "applied religion," fostering "appreciation of the dignity of man."[8]

Linking the seminarians and the Fisk students was the unofficial but undisputed leader of the Nashville group, a Northern-born black minister named James Lawson. At thirty-one considerably older than his disciples, Lawson had also undergone a longer spiritual odyssey than most. He chose prison in the early fifties as a conscientious objector during the Korean War. Paroled to the Methodist Board of Missions, he spent three years as a missionary in India but seemed less interested in spreading the news of Jesus than in absorbing the word of Gandhi. He returned to the United States with a deep interest in using the Mahatma's methods to promote social change. The Fellowship of Reconciliation, a pacifist group that had provided most of CORE's early leaders, sent Lawson to Nashville in March 1958 to lead a workshop in nonviolence for black activists. A year later, as a divinity student at Nashville's Vanderbilt University, Lawson drew a small but morally charged following to his regular training sessions in nonviolent protest.[9] They came from the black colleges, young men and women including Lewis, Bevel, Lafayette, Barry, and Nash; absorbed by the Christian ideal of a "Beloved Community," they pledged to accept any risk to bring it about.

The Beloved Community took an unsteady step forward in the fall of 1959, when the Nashville student group staged test sit-ins at segregated city restaurants and lunch counters. Staying just long enough to draw refusals of service, they failed either to change management policy or to draw others into the protest. Lawson's band had outrun the zeitgeist by a few months. With the Greensboro sit-ins of February 1960, though, the Nashville group acquired a prophetic luster. Soon Lawson was directing hundreds of student volunteers in disciplined protests against segregation in downtown stores.

Students listened approvingly as Lawson called for sacrifice to advance justice, and early in the sit-in campaign they saw him set an example. The chancellor of Vanderbilt, after vainly warning Lawson to stay away from the sit-in movement, expelled him from the university. Eleven white teachers turned in their faculty robes and resigned in protest. So did the dean, shortly after bailing Lawson out of jail and personally escorting him back to campus.[10] The divinity school never readmitted its wayward student, but Lawson showed little concern. Like many other young blacks he had found his calling.

In March 1960 an equally formidable though very different center of student influence staked its claim to leadership of the protests as the sit-in movement reached the Queen City of the South, Atlanta. Here, in the South's largest, richest city, lived the region's most powerful and prestigious black community. Here, too, one found the most unabashedly ambitious body of students in all of black academe. They gathered at Atlanta University, a sprawling six-campus answer to Ivy League elitism centered on exclusive Morehouse College, known as the black Harvard, and its sister school, Spelman College. The university's student leaders displayed little of the philosophical erudition that marked the Nashville circle. Indeed, Atlanta's student activists preferred to flaunt their reputation as a freewheeling lot, given to constant improvisation and untroubled by the fine points of Gandhian tenets. Yet they, too, commanded the respectful attention of other students, and only partly because of their enviable position in black society. Their joyous élan symbolized another, vital side of the student movement, suited to a generation fired by unbounded confidence in its abilities and its future in American society.

Tremors from Greensboro unsettled Atlanta University almost immediately, thanks to one uncommonly determined student. Several days after the first sit-in, a lithe Morehouse senior named Lonnie King strode into the university's student hangout, Yates and Milton's drugstore, brandishing a newspaper and looking for allies to take up the new protest. At first glance the powerful King did not appear in need of much assistance. Older than most students because of a stint in the Navy, known as a star football running back, King had enough organizing drive to muster a small student army. Yet he realized that his rough-hewn background as a child of the slums and an ex-boxer (and brawler) might limit his appeal to a student body priding itself on elegance and refinement. He therefore cast about Yates and Milton's for a student with a gift for words and the right touch of suave sophistication, just as dapper Julian Bond sat down to mingle with the toast of black student high society.

In Bond, a fleeting acquaintance since the days of freshman registration, King seemed to have found his complete opposite. Bond was light skinned, the son of an eminent scholar and college dean, a prep school grad, and a former intern at *Time:* in all, a product of privilege, and obviously intent on enjoying college life to the fullest. On campus Bond was known for his fragile good looks, an enthusiasm for jazz, and a literary verve that led Langston Hughes, aged laureate of the ghetto, to include two of Bond's poems in his anthology *New Negro Poets U.S.A.* One of Bond's unpublished college meditations, though, better suggested his approach to life at the time:

> Look at that gal shake that thing,
> We cannot all be Martin Luther King.[11]

Lonnie King nonetheless resolved to add sit-ins to Bond's absorbing extracurricular schedule. King held out his copy of the *Atlanta Daily World,* its banner headline blazing, "GREENSBORO STUDENT SIT-IN, THIRD DAY." "Have you seen that?" King asked. Bond was irritated by King's effort to draw him into the subject but maintained his ever cool aura, which had led classmates to call him the Morehouse Bogey. "Yeah, you know," said Bond, "I read the papers." To Bond's growing discomfort, King persisted:

"What do you think about it?"

"Well, it's all right, pretty good stuff."

"Don't you think it ought to happen here?"

"It probably will."

"Let's make it happen." Bond thought to himself, "What do you mean, *let's?*" but as he later recalled, "You know, Lonnie's a very persuasive guy."[12] They agreed to take separate sides of the drugstore and call students to a noon meeting about organizing new sit-ins. Lonnie King had found his ally, and Atlanta University had just found its protest leadership.

Before Bond and King faced their first white businessman, however, they became mired in the sympathetic counsel of Atlanta University's chief officer, Rufus E. Clement. On Clement's advice they spent several weeks preparing "An Appeal for Human Rights," which called on merchants to desegregate lunch counters. This step, Clement explained to Bond and King, would help the students establish their moral position; he omitted that it might also help preserve his administrative position by averting a clash that could embarrass the university. Clement facilitated student efforts to publish the appeal as an ad in the city dailies, while disavowing any responsibility for its contents. White merchants predictably ignored the appeal. They ignored, too, the scattered sit-ins by maverick students impatient with attempts to conduct a protest movement in the pages of the *Atlanta Constitution.* By mid-March a chagrined Bond and King concurred that it was time students took their appeals, in unison, directly to the city lunch counters.[13]

Two hundred Atlanta students simultaneously marched on ten different eating places on March 15, 1960, at precisely 11:00 A.M., in a display of organizational wizardry that did much to compensate for earlier delays. The focus was on public sites, including bus and train stations, the state capitol, the Federal Building, and other government-owned property. Julian Bond led about a dozen students to City Hall, intent on using the municipal cafeteria. A big sign in front greeted them with the words "PUBLIC IS WELCOME," and so they entered, the young men wearing neckties, the young women dressed as if for a church social. Then the inevitable clash took place.

A heavyset woman manager sternly told the students, "Well, we can't serve you here." "That's not true," the students replied; "you've got a sign outside saying the public is welcome and we're the public and we want to eat."[14] By this time the manager had had more than her fill of logic. She called the lieutenant governor, who had police cart the students off in a paddy wagon and deposit them at the jail called Big Rock.

Tangling with the law was no small step for any black in the Deep South. For relatively sheltered students from Atlanta University, arraignment was especially jarring—indeed, before the Greensboro protests it would have been unthinkable. The defendants drew little comfort from Bond's repeated assurance that they would be in jail for at most fifteen minutes. Nor did it ease their anxiety that their senior defense attorney had been—in his prime—a pioneer for black rights. A. T. Walden, Esq., indeed brought to the hearing a venerable legal reputation, but he was now in his dotage, and, as students gaped in dismay, he literally fell asleep on his feet. The students' inexperience with these proceedings also took its toll. When the judge asked, "Well, how do you plead?" Julian Bond whispered to the junior defense attorney in turn, "How do I plead?" His counsel answered, "Innocent, you fool." As matters went, it made little difference, for the students were indicted on nine counts. These included violation of an antitrespass law (recently signed by the governor for just this purpose), conspiracy in restraint of trade, and violation of a law enacted in the 1870s to deter assemblies by the Ku Klux Klan. In all there seemed to be "enough charges," as Bond reckoned it then, to put him away "for ninety-nine years." The students once more found themselves in Big Rock, impatient, afraid, and, as time passed, none too happy with their leader, Julian Bond.[15]

As happened so often in the young movement, jail proved a crucial testing ground for student commitment. It particularly taxed Julian Bond, who, innocent of prison life, legal niceties, and encounters with police, faced the task of maintaining student morale while musing on the prospect of an indefinite jail term. Impatient students entreated him, "Bond, we've been here about six hours. You said we were getting out in about an hour." "Don't worry about it, fellas," he replied with unblinking nonchalance; "we'll be out in a minute." Much later that night all were bailed out by parents, and inner doubt turned to expansive pride for these unlikely ex-prisoners. In high spirits they poured into the black-owned restaurant and motel called Paschal's; then, as Bond related, they descended on Spelman College where they "could be heroes, you know, among the women."[16] For most of these heroes it was their first and last time in jail. That, however, was enough to crystallize a belief that jail could be a badge of honor for the most proper black Atlantans. It confirmed, too, the exciting notion that shaking society must be the first order of business for students no longer content to attend the best segregated college in the country.

A Movement on Trial: The Rise of White Extremism

The rush of sit-in campaigns through the South exposed the racist underside of public life. Instead of redressing black grievances, communities more often simply jettisoned the old facade of civility that had helped conceal them. As Southern moderates hesitated to assert their influence, extreme racists threatened the safety of student protesters and the survival of their movement.

Alarms from the state capitols sounded a tone of hostility toward demonstrators that paralyzed the moderates among local merchants and politicians. Governor Ernest F. Hollings of South Carolina depressed the level of public discourse on the sit-ins with a warning to blacks who "think they can violate any law, especially if they have a Bible in their hands." He added portentously,

"Our law enforcement officers have their Bibles, too,"[17] leaving unstated that when in doubt these officers would very likely reach first for their billies. Farther south the warnings grew cruder. Governor Earl Long explained to his fellow Louisianans that the protests were the work of "some radical outfit" whose members "should return to their native Africa."[18] Governor John Patterson of Alabama meanwhile alternated calls for crackdowns on outside agitators with orders for police to investigate a black state college that had experienced student unrest.[19]

Not every governor hastened to strip the sit-ins of all respectability. A conspicuous exception was Leroy Collins of Florida, who on March 20, 1960, appointed a biracial commission to promote racial harmony and later appealed to city officials throughout the state to do the same. Collins also decried the inconsistency of excluding blacks from certain areas in stores that welcomed their patronage in all other departments.[20] Yet his words were significant not for starting a trend but for braving one. Collins hailed from a state which, though located in the Deep South, in its social mores seemed suspiciously near the Mason-Dixon line. More often the posturing of state leaders helped legitimize the forces of vigilante law.

As student protest continued, the veneer of racial harmony in Southern cities cracked, then fell away to reveal a core of racial antagonism. The city of Huntsville, Alabama, epitomized this widespread reversion evident even in communities boasting of progress in race relations. When Huntsville experienced its first sit-in, in 1962, many white residents reacted with genuine puzzlement. Race relations in the northern Alabama city were certainly not typical for the state. Huntsville's strong economy generated a civic pride that tended to mitigate overt racial conflict. It was among the fastest-growing cities in the South, thanks to the Redstone missile base that drew foreign and Northern personnel who imparted to the area a cosmopolitan tone. Public transportation, the city library, bus and airport terminals, and the municipal golf course had all been desegregated "without incident or fanfare,"[21] as the interracial Ministers' Association noted in offering to mediate between students and white leaders. But the sit-ins against the still segregated lunch counters alerted Huntsville residents that, like many other self-declared models of good race relations, they had been enjoying a period of silence, not harmony. When blacks started expressing their grievances more openly, the mood in Huntsville turned bitter, and civilities succumbed to the surge of vindictiveness that was sweeping the entire state.

Young CORE workers found that the Woolworth lunch counter in Huntsville served mainly harassment, which was mild compared with the fare at a nearby Walgreen's, where protesting students were arrested.[22] At the county jail, fingerprinting and the taking of mug shots let each student know that Huntsville's police viewed them as common criminals. The students were then incarcerated. One of the prisoners, Mary Jo Hamlett, recorded the women's experience:

Ten of us girls were placed in a cell. There was one bunk—for the cleaning woman who works there. We slept on the floor. Supper was over when we got there; there was no food until breakfast time: 5:30 a.m. We girls found the biscuits, gravy and stewed peaches not too appetizing so we didn't eat. The boys "dug in" as only boys can.

Breaking the gloom was a whispered word of praise "from—of all people—a policeman."[23]

The officer's view was a lonely one among Huntsville's police force. Dozens of students were arrested on frail pretexts. Police hauled in one student who accidentally brushed arms with an officer; the charge was assault and battery. Still, the early confrontations with managers and police had been free of violence, and the city's leading journal pleaded, "Let's keep our baseball bats in the dugout where they belong." Such minimal prudence could "defeat the purpose of those who seek to provoke us into rash and foolish acts."[24]

But as the police began to look the other way, Huntsville's citizenry became emboldened to act on its growing hostility toward blacks. Beatings went unpunished by police. So did an attack in which whites inflicted burns on three white CORE members with oil of mustard, an ingredient used in the manufacture of mustard gas during World War I. Nor were the town's influential people inclined to resolve the worsening conflict, according to a CORE spokesman: "The mayor says the merchants have not shown any desire to change policy, so he is powerless. The merchants await word of the sacred will of the community through its elected representatives, so they're powerless."[25]

The deterioration of Huntsville's race relations, coupled with the climate of violence sanctioned by public officials, typified the fate of Southern communities in which black students challenged Jim Crow. In Nashville, whites pushed lighted cigarettes against the backs of girls sitting at a lunch counter. The KKK pistol-whipped a sixteen-year-old in Jacksonville, Florida, while a black man who was unconnected with the demonstrations but went through a police roadblock was shot to death by a white service station attendant. In Biloxi, Mississippi, a white mob shot and wounded ten blacks at a public beach.[26]

Even where police afforded a bare minimum of protection, residents surrounded student protesters to pour out the community's scorn. As Candie Anderson discovered at McClellan's department store in Nashville, the greatest contempt was reserved for young people like her—whites who were seen as betraying their own race:

There was a rope around the stools, showing that the counter was closed. We climbed over the rope. A policeman stood there and said quite clearly, "Do not sit down," and we sat down. . . . I became suddenly aware of the crowd of people standing behind us. . . . Young kids threw french fried potatoes at us, and gum, and cigarette butts. I looked down the counter at Barbara Crosby in a straight pink skirt and nice white blouse, and at Stephen in a dark suit, with a calculus book. . . . The policemen simply lined up behind us and peeled us two by two off the stools. . . . The crowd in the store . . . shouted out approval. They said about Barbara and me . . . Oh, white . . . WHITE, WHITE, WHITE! Three paddy wagons were blinking at us from the street.

Once more we had to walk through those crowds. Someone spit right in front of me. . . . The TV cameras took lots of pictures and we drove off to the Nashville city jail.[27]

Individual students reeled from the beatings, mass arrests, and vilification—but the movement as a whole drew strength from such adversity. If many students had begun the movement in the spirit of a lark, the ordeal of white counteraction forged a more mature, purposeful commitment. For students who had endured vigilante violence and one-sided justice, the originally airy concepts of nonviolence and brotherly community became more than mere rhetoric.

The protesters compensated for their renunciation of physical force by enriching their store of spiritual weapons, including song. Old Negro spirituals alluding to freedom lent the power of black cultural tradition to the sit-in campaigns. These songs had once expressed an abiding faith in other worldly deliverance, but they also contained an implicit yearning for freedom on earth. That second level of meaning now emerged in the proud chanting of spirituals like "Walking for Freedom":

> I want to be ready,
> I want to be ready,
> I want to be ready
> Walking for freedom
> Just like John.[28]

Students also offered their own compositions, which captured the modern setting as well as the timeless spirit of their venture. Three women serving forty-nine days in a Florida jail for sitting in at a Woolworth's lunch counter created the popular song "Fight On," which blended the tone of the spiritual with a bit of Americana:

> Gone to the jail, without paying our bail
> Justice will come right over the trail. . . .
> We're fighting, we're fighting, for a better land we know.
> For the Constitution tells us so
> Fight on, fight on.[29]

Of the many songs, one stood out for its haunting melody and simple faith in God and man. Black slaves had sung it as a spiritual called "I'll Be All Right," and it had boosted the morale of striking black tobacco workers in the Carolinas during the 1940s. In the late 1950s Pete Seeger strummed the tune for Guy Carawan of Tennessee's Highlander Folk School, a place that welcomed labor organizers, civil rights workers, and good music with equal gusto. Carawan experimented with the formal arrangement to restore a more free-spirited, Baptist flavor. He joined the Nashville sit-ins in 1960 and tried out his song at group rallies, where it served as a powerful bond for protesting students seeking a spiritual testament.[30] In this way "We Shall Overcome" returned to its provenance as a melody rooted in black folk tradition to become the anthem of a movement for racial justice.

While singing of better days to come, students also took more mundane precautions against the days of white rage already upon them. In Nashville, where harassment and assaults beset students from the fourth day of protests, a list of do's and don'ts of sit-in behavior aimed to minimize all unnecessary provocation: "Do show yourself friendly on the counter at all times. Do sit straight and always face the counter. Don't strike back, or curse back if attacked. Don't laugh out. Don't hold conversations. Don't block entrances."[31]

Classes often reinforced these lessons with realistic protest games in which student volunteers improvised varied roles at "white lunch counters" formed from a few tables and chairs. In a typically grueling encounter, the sixteen-year-old high school student James Wooten of Jackson, Mississippi, asked politely for a cup of coffee, and the "waitress," a young black woman, insulted him in her best white manner. Then a "white agitator," the black CORE veteran George Raymond, dutifully rushed young Wooten and slammed him to the floor. He beat Wooten on the shoulders and kicked at his face. The director of this exercise, the CORE leader Dave Dennis, frowned at Wooten's feeble defense. "No, no," he scolded the prostrate protester. "You got too many places open, you could get a judo chop on the back of your neck. Curl up, pull your knees up, crouch up. Let's try it again." By the third beating, Wooten had learned his lesson well: he rolled smoothly to the ground and pulled himself into a tight ball with his hands clasped protectively behind him. "That was good," Dennis said, and moved on to test new volunteers. Later, Dennis questioned students on the purpose of this nonviolent conduct. One youth responded that they wanted to defeat the sin, not the sinner. Another explained, "We're trying to play on his conscience," reflecting the students' faith that with enough spiritual force they would set white racists on the path to understanding and, in time, the Beloved Community.[32]

Buoyed by their songs, their training, and their common cause, students expanded their protests in both size and sophistication to meet the mounting harassment. In Atlanta, where arrests numbered in the hundreds, fifteen hundred picketers encircled the entire downtown area in May 1960. Leaders planned every logistical detail, coordinating a regular shuttle system between a small black church and the downtown area. They also took extra precautions, Julian Bond recalled, such as "special football coats for the girls, with big hoods, because there were a lot of thugs downtown throwing spitballs and stuff at them." Bond added, "We had special laminated signs that wouldn't wash off in the rain." Indeed, the stepped-up harassment seemed only to increase student commitment—and braggadocio. As Bond put it succinctly, "We were hell."[33]

Some student groups went further still, welcoming jail as an act of civil disobedience against an unjust system. The CORE leader Thomas Gaither reflected on the pressures weighing on students who accepted this strategy: "Making a decision to go to jail for the first time was not easy. In some cases, it meant leaving a girlfriend; in others, antagonizing parents who had little understanding of nonviolent action and much fear for their children's safety."

Nearly a year to the day after the first sit-in in Greensboro, Gaither led ten student demonstrators in the first widely noted "jail-in." After a night's detention in the Rock Hill jail, Gaither and his group heard the judge pass sentence for their role in requesting service at two dime-store lunch counters: thirty days' hard labor on a road gang or one-hundred-dollar fines. One defendant paid the fine, but the others shocked the judge by choosing jail without bail. "The only thing they had to beat us over the head with was a threat of sending us to jail," Gaither explained. "So we disarmed them by using the only weapon we had left. . . . It upset them considerably."[34]

Here and there black youths broke nonviolent ranks under the continued fury of white assaults, and cases of black vandalism and attacks on whites were not unknown. The overwhelming number of blacks, however, maintained discipline amid the gravest provocation. This was especially true among the CORE field-workers, whose reports to their national office gloried in their pacifism at any cost. Typical was the recounting of an attempt to use lunch counter facilities in a McComb, Mississippi, bus depot:

The station operator told the Negroes seated at the counter to get out. A [white man] grabbed a cup of coffee and struck one of us, George Raymond, sharply at the base of the skull with the cup, spilling coffee over him. . . . A white tough jumped at me and beat me with his fists, yelling over and over, 'I'll kill him, I'll kill him!' About a dozen whites pummelled our group. They pushed us around and over counters and tables and kicked us through the door.

The author of this report, Jerome Smith, was seized by the mob, tossed repeatedly in the air, and kicked each time he landed on the pavement. His sole, matter-of-fact reference to his behavior and that of his fellow CORE workers during this ordeal was the terse observation "We remained nonviolent."[35]

Other students, though seldom so thoroughly grounded in the rigorous Gandhian techniques of CORE workers, also impressed observers as models of restraint beside their white tormentors. James J. Kilpatrick, the ardently segregationist editor of the influential *Richmond News Leader,* expressed the chagrin of many white Southerners at this inversion of racial stereotypes:

Here were the colored students, in coats, white shirts, ties, and one of them was reading Goethe and one was taking notes from a biology text. And here, on the sidewalk outside, was a gang of white boys come to heckle, a ragtail rabble, slack-jawed, black-jacketed, grinning fit to kill, and some of them, God save the mark, were waving the proud and honored flag of the Southern States in the last war fought by gentlemen. Eheu! It gives one pause.[36]

Nonviolent restraint came the more easily to students who were too innocent for hate and too young for fear. "We didn't really get angry at that age. It was just fun," a veteran of the Nashville sit-ins recalled years later. She had been twenty-three years old and eight months pregnant when a white woman recognized her as a protester and kicked her repeatedly while she sat on the street corner waiting for a ride back to Fisk College. She had been too weak to strike back. Later she said, "But I wouldn't have hit her back if I could—not then. I would now." What had changed since those early movement days? "I don't have the guts I had then."[37]

Perhaps the resolve of students shone brightest when they relaxed their Gandhian principles and resorted to nonviolent American stubbornness. Students had clustered in Rich's department store, the main target of Atlanta's sit-in campaigns. As white patrons and young demonstrators looked on, the manager walked up behind delicate-looking Lana Taylor from Spelman College and grabbed her by the shoulders, cursing her and ordering her out of the store. But as her white lunch counter neighbor, Jane Stembridge, related this "most honest" expression of the sit-in spirit, "Lana was not going." It was a moment to mark the character of a movement:

I do not know whether she should have collapsed in nonviolent manner. She probably did not know. She put her hands under the counter and held. He was rough and strong. She just held and I looked down at that moment at her hands . . . brown, strained . . . every muscle holding. . . . All of a sudden he let go and left. I thought he knew he could not move that girl—ever. . . .[38]

Coming Together: Students and the Black Community

While staging sit-ins against white merchants, students waged a less heralded but equally vital campaign along generational rather than racial lines. Their brash conduct surprised and alarmed many older blacks, who viewed the protests as futile and, worse, dangerously provocative. For their part, students proudly saw themselves as breaching the timidity of the black establishment. The ingredients existed for a conflict that could defeat the movement from within by isolating the student protesters from the rest of the black community. The more perceptive sit-in leaders consequently pursued a taxing dual objective: to maintain their independence while winning the older generation to their cause. It was often a bitter task but not one they could forgo, because only by tapping the resources of the entire black community could students hope to overcome the growing resistance they faced.

Students were clearly challenging parental restrictions as well as white taboos. Until the Greensboro demonstrations Southern Negro youths lived in a world of contradictory values: they were encouraged to get ahead while observing the color line that confined them at every turn. The first sit-in swept away those contradictions in a wave of defiance against the cautioning of their elders. "It's not hard to interpret what our parents mean by a better world," explained an organizer in Georgia's student movement, Cordell Reagon. "You know, go to school, son, and get a good education. And what do you do with this? You get a degree, you move out into some little community housing project, you get married, five kids and two cars, and you don't care what's happening. . . ." For Reagon and for thousands of student peers who came of age in the early sixties, it was time to turn their concerns outward: "So I think when we talk about growing up in a better world, a new world, we mean changing the world to a different place."[39]

Much of the handwringing over student protests in fact stemmed not from anything so abstract as ideological differences but from parental panic over the fate of wayward children. Mothers and fathers who learned that their children planned to lead them to a better life by defying the law and going to jail seldom debated the fine points of civil rights tactics or tenets. "Get out of the movement," John Lewis remembered his mother imploring him. "She didn't [even] say 'movement.' Probably said, 'Get out of that mess, before you get hurt.' " Lewis wrote to his parents that he was acting in accord with his convictions and Christian conscience, adding, "My soul will not be satisfied until freedom, justice, and fair play become a reality for all people." His parents remained appalled.[40]

At another level students faced a more deep-rooted conflict of institutional interests with the black establishment. Local Negro elites—usually older men of wealth, education, or professional standing—held authority in their communities at least partly on the sufferance of white leaders. The sources of dependency ranged widely: black lawyers could expect to try their cases before white judges; black journalists needed white officials to favor their requests for visas and security clearances; black teachers and principals in state-supported schools relied on whites for their jobs. The regular flow of minor political appointments and other favors reinforced this informal system of vassalage, which induced Negro elites to accommodate the white "city fathers" in government.[41]

The sit-ins spurred some local black leaders to discard the old accommodationist etiquette and to side openly with the students. Prominent among these activists were younger ministers and others who shared the students' impatience and enjoyed financial independence from whites. More often, though, the responses of community leaders were painfully ambivalent. Older, settled blacks might have felt the pull of student calls for freedom, but this was not quite enough to make them forget that the bold new world promised by these youngsters might have no room for old patronage networks. In the short run, certainly, their movement threatened to cloud the atmosphere of tranquillity in which white and black establishment figures could do business. The black establishment varied in profile from city to city but generally included many civil rights leaders who had come to view piecemeal, ad hoc gains as the inevitable limit of their labors. Above all, in the indignant view of campus activists, this old guard included college presidents, who tended to see the sit-ins as calamitous for black education and, more immediately, for black educators.

While the occasional college president acted like North Carolina A&T's Warmouth Gibbs, who nodded benignly at the student revolution, or like Atlanta University's Rufus Clement, who sought to temper it, many others tried to undo the revolution altogether. They appraised the students not simply as impulsive idealists but as unwitting saboteurs who were unleashing the enmity of trustees, regents, and state legislators on whom their schools depended. These administrators frequently implemented the plans of state officials to intimidate students. Southern University at Baton Rouge, the largest Negro institution in the nation, suspended eighteen sit-in leaders and forced the entire student body of five thousand to reapply to the college so that it could screen out agitators. Felton Grandison Clark, president of the university, spoke for many Negro administrators in casting his repressive policies as a form of high statesmanship: "Like Lincoln, who sought to preserve the Union, my dominant concern is to save Southern University."[42]

When black college presidents shrank from displaying the necessary Lincolnesque qualities, governors prompted them from the wings. Some preferred the quietly ominous approach taken by Governor Luther Hodges of North Carolina, who wrote to black college heads, enlisting them as allies in curbing demonstrations against segregated lunch counters.[43] Others inclined toward the more open bullying practiced by Alabama's governor, John Patterson, who ordered the expulsion of nine student protesters from a black state college. The school administration complied at once.[44]

The response by other sectors of the black establishment tended to be less severe but equally discouraging. Fissures between the generations ran deepest in Atlanta, where the most prominent Negro elite contended with the most influential student body. Publicly the city's black leaders supported the sit-ins; privately they arranged a summit meeting intended to show students the folly of their ways. The conference revealed two groups sharply at odds—even before the first words had been uttered, as a journalist recorded: "While the students wore slacks and sport shirts, their elders were dressed like New York bankers. Their faces were somber and the atmosphere was somewhat like that of an emergency meeting of the General Motors board of directors." The presiding elder was a pleasant-faced, light-skinned man "who spoke and looked like President Eisenhower." Like his imposing colleagues—an Episcopalian minister, a banker, a realtor, and a lawyer—he spoke on the theme that wisdom dictated caution and, apparently, deference to one's elders. "So you see, kids," the messages droned on, "we've been in this a long time. We want the same things you do, but we know by now they can't be gotten overnight. It's our experience that you have to work slowly to get lasting results. We'd hate to see your movement backfire and spoil the things we've worked so hard for. You need guidance, and we hope you'll have the vision to accept it." The students responded with a disconcerting lack of vision but ample independence. "We are continuing the movement as best we know how," one replied. "We hope you will join us."[45]

This scene was enacted with minor variations in black communities across the South. Established civil rights leaders, usually representing the NAACP, might have bridged the gap between young and old. Yet in the early weeks of the sit-in campaigns many NAACP officials greeted young protesters with head-shaking paternalism, irreparably damaging the organization's credibility with student groups. Cleveland Sellers recalled visiting NAACP leaders in Denmark, South Carolina, as one of the first steps toward organizing a sit-in campaign, only to hear a line repeated at many similar student sessions with NAACP figures: "If you'll just be patient. . . ." Sellers detected more than sage caution in this plea. He also recognized a "familiar glint" in the eyes of this official, one he had seen in the eyes of blacks all his life: "It was fear. They were afraid to work with us. It was as simple as that."[46] Negroes in the town went ahead with their sit-in campaign, thanks to the teenager Sellers and others not much older. The NAACP watched skeptically, and passively.

The students' wariness toward established organizations fueled their desire for a new, youth-oriented network to link their protest campaigns. On April 16, 1960, student representatives from Southern black campuses converged on Raleigh, North Carolina, for a three-day convention to share their experiences and coordinate plans. Behind this initiative for youth solidarity was fifty-five-year-old Ella Baker, who, though executive director for the SCLC, was increasingly at odds with its "establishment" role. In her early years Baker had dreamed of becoming a medical missionary, and though financial realities diverted her from medical study into social work the missionary zeal remained. She worked in New York during the Depression as a community organizer and in the forties as a field secretary for the NAACP. Her contacts in radical circles included Bayard Rustin, who recruited her in 1957 to organize the Atlanta headquarters of King's Southern Christian Leadership Conference. Baker soon soured on King's leadership, however, viewing it as too cautious and self-centered. To encourage the development of institutions rooted in group strength rather than in personal charisma she wrote to student activists, lauding their efforts and inviting them to meet at her alma mater, Shaw University, "to help chart future goals for effective action."[47] The response astonished her: over three hundred students attended, most of them coming from fifty-eight black colleges in twelve states. In keeping with growing liberal support for the sit-ins, nineteen of the delegates came from white Northern colleges. It was a buoyant and boisterous gathering, and it marked a jump in the evolution of the sit-in campaigns into a cohesive protest movement.

The convention gave eloquent expression to student ideals in a declaration of purpose drafted by Nashville's James Lawson. This founding charter of the student movement defined the protests in spiritual rather than in political terms. It exalted nonviolence as not only a tactic for change but also a "philosophical or religious ideal" at the center of the movement's faith. Nonviolence marked the path to "a social order of justice permeated by love," and integration represented "the crucial first step toward such a society."[48]

Integration, the black students decided, would begin in the ranks of the student movement itself, a significant resolution given the rising numbers of Northern white activists as organizers, as fundraisers, and, to a lesser extent, as demonstrators. A workshop on the techniques of nonviolence issued a statement that students conducting sit-ins should fill every other seat in a lunch counter, to "allow the white public to demonstrate their willingness to eat or demonstrate with Negroes." Another session, treating whites and the student movement, invited all forms of white support, explaining, "This movement should not be considered one for Negroes but one for people who consider this a movement against injustice. This would include members of all races."[49]

Students were more divided over an item not on the official agenda but hanging over the conference from the start: should students affiliate with the established civil rights groups? Each of the three major organizations had sent "observers" who doubled as recruiters bidding for student support. Students dismissed the overtures of the NAACP, gave somewhat more thought to joining CORE, the first group to endorse the sit-ins, and—inspired by Dr. King's philosophy of nonviolence—inclined most seriously toward the SCLC. Yet after hours of heated debate students rejected alliance with any established groups. Instead they formed a new organization, later called the Temporary Student Nonviolent Coordinating Committee.

Once more Ella Baker played a major role in pressing students to assert their independence. She warned students that others would try to manipulate them for their own ends and that students "had the right to direct their own affairs and even make their own mistakes," words that resonated with the mood of the delegates. "She was much older in terms of age," John Lewis remembered, "but I think in terms of ideas and philosophy and commitment she was one of the youngest persons in the movement."[50]

Tension between the generations also surfaced in the student response to two of the major speakers at the conference, Martin Luther King, Jr., and James Lawson. King's reputation preceded him; more, it contributed to the meeting's large attendance and extensive press coverage. His address to the students, moreover, anticipated much of their subsequent activity, as he called for a nationwide campaign of selective buying, establishment of a permanent organization, and waves of volunteers who would accept jail terms rather than pay fines, in order to dramatize the moral issue. Yet his talk, while well received, lacked the impact of Lawson's. Lawson was barely younger than King and had assisted him as the SCLC's program director in the late fifties; yet because of his leadership in the sit-ins students saw him as one of their own. The Nashville leader said little that differed with King's address, but he did more to crystallize the impatience of his listeners with the failings of the older generation. "All of Africa will be free," he thundered, "before the American Negro attains first-class citizenship. Most of us will be grandparents before we can live normal lives." He lambasted the NAACP for its timidity, and termed the student protests "a judgment upon middle-class conventional, half-way efforts to deal with radical social evil." Students rose and cheered "the young people's Martin Luther King."[51]

To symbolize its independent status the Temporary Student Nonviolent Coordinating Committee convened in May 1960 and elected a chairman, Marion Barry. The choice had much to do with the hidden workings of student politics: the post had to go to someone in the Nashville circle, which had come to represent the students' Gandhian path; yet it could not favor the religious element too greatly by falling to a minister. Then, too, the powerful Atlanta group had to be placated through what appealed to all concerned as an equitable compromise: all future meetings of the committee would be held in Atlanta. The Nashville circle would chart the path to the Beloved Community, and Atlanta University would be its capital. Beyond the minor intrigues of student politics, the selection of Marion Barry, a twenty-two-year-old native of Mississippi, spoke a broader message to both well-meaning Northern whites and black adults attending the conference. This generation of blacks, the student delegates had resolved, was going to remain the master of its own movement.

Even as students were warding off the advice and warnings of their elders, it was becoming clear that they could not press their movement alone. They needed the NAACP's legal and financial assistance in challenging segregation statutes and police repression of demonstrators. They needed the prestige that civil rights leaders like the NAACP chairman Roy Wilkins and Martin Luther King, Jr., could lend the movement on a national level. Perhaps most important, they required united black support for their boycotts in order to convince recalcitrant store managers that segregation meant bad business. Therefore, with as little fanfare as possible (and no discernible humility), students increasingly accepted the aid of black adults, who themselves acknowledged that the students, in their forward, at times obstinate way, were fighting their battle, too.

The bridging of generations came the more easily because of an underlying unity of beliefs. Student protesters may have spoken of a new day dawning, but their millennial vision drew heavily from mainstream American values familiar to their elders. Although they scorned the hypocrisy that denied them the rights white citizens enjoyed, the students made confessions of faith notably devoid of radical nuances. "All I want," said the student leader Charles Jones of Charlotte, North Carolina, "is to come in and place my order and be served and leave a tip if I feel like it." Less than a year earlier Jones had attended the Seventh World Youth Festival in Vienna, where he loyally insisted to foreign delegations that the racial situation in his country was not so bleak as they claimed. Similarly Diane Nash, the Fisk beauty queen whom Tennessee authorities branded a dangerous subversive, described the student movement as part of the struggle against communism. She added that if blacks received equal educational opportunities, "maybe some day a Negro will invent one of our missiles."[52]

This conservatism lay beneath even the boldest rhetoric in the student movement. At the Raleigh convention in April 1960, students cheered James Lawson's portrait of a militant new generation but immediately afterward revealed that they were as much the products of their society as they were its prophets. Ella Baker followed King and Lawson with an address urging students to broaden their social vision. The protests, she said, must be over "more than a hamburger" at a lunch counter; they must extend to a range of problems afflicting blacks. Looking back, Julian Bond observed that her speech "was probably the best of the three," but at the time it left students indifferent and bemused. "We were just not ready," Bond explained. " . . . To our mind, lunch counter segregation was the greatest evil facing black people in the country and if we could eliminate it, we would be like gods."[53]

Had lower-class blacks played a greater role in these protests, they might have redirected them against basic economic ills such as slum housing, malnutrition, inadequate health care, and the scarcity of jobs at decent wages. But the young activists in 1960 came overwhelmingly from the most privileged, confident stratum of black society: the two hundred thousand college students poised to join the nation's broad middle class. Most of these youths had already attained greater formal education and brighter job prospects than their working-class parents. Negro students who came from wealthier families and attended prestigious private colleges like Morehouse were even more likely to protest against segregation.[54] Their sit-in campaigns drew support from every segment of the black community, for all shared the basic goal of achieving equality before the law. Beyond this, student aims bore the conservative stamp of a group that seldom paused to question the social order in which they were so rapidly ascending.

In July the SNCC chairman Marion Barry sent a message to the 1960 Democratic National Convention that amplified the theme of student loyalty to the country's fundamental political and economic institutions. Responding to charges by former President Harry Truman that the student protests were Communist inspired, Barry deplored Truman's willingness to credit communism with being humane and opposed to tyranny. On the contrary, Barry tutored the ex-President in Cold War doctrine: "Communism seeks power, ignores people and thrives on social conflict. We seek a community in which man can realize the full meaning of the self, which demands open relationship with others."[55]

If students invoked revolutionary leaders, they ignored Marx and Lenin in favor of more widely accepted models. "How can we forget the America envisioned by Washington, Lincoln and Jefferson?" asked CORE's Thomas Gaither, soon to endure weeks of abuse in Louisiana jails for his part in the sit-ins. In the same vein Marion Barry's tradition-laden message to the Democrats traced the impulse for equality to "the truth of the American Declaration of Independence and the Constitution." Intent less on altering than on entering American society, he declared that the American Negro, having for 350 years been sent to the back door, now wanted "to walk into the sun through the front door."[56]

These were the hopes of the older generation as well as of black youth. And as the first shock of student protests abated, black adults began confessing to each other that their children were doing a pretty good job of taking the community where it should have been going all along. "Students have been exposed all their lives to the teachings of the great American scriptures of democracy, freedom, and equality," Fisk University's president, Stephen Wright, declared between efforts to check campus activism, "and no literate person should be surprised that they reflect these teachings in their conduct."[57]

On a more personal level, Julian Bond's mother cried over her son's arrest but then confided to a friend that the students were simply acting the way their parents had always spoken:

> You know how it is with some white people who tell their children that they want them to be tolerant of Negroes and to like Negroes and when the child comes home married to a Negro they're just amazed? They say, "Well, we didn't mean *that!*" And, we'd always told our chidren that we believed in democracy and that there shouldn't be any discrimination, but we didn't have any idea they were going to take it so literally, the way they did![58]

As students continued to expand their protests and articulate their high purpose, the anguished ambivalence among black adults gradually turned to active support of the sit-in campaigns. Typically students made their first successful overtures to those not directly connected to the movement by enlisting the sympathy of black consumers in boycotts of segregated stores. This happened in Atlanta, where students realized that their protests hinged on applying financial pressure to Rich's department store. While students lacked the buying power to force desegregation of lunch counters upon Rich's management, black adults were at first reluctant even to try. "A Rich's charge plate in the black community was like running water," Lonnie King explained. Every black family had a card and viewed it as "a necessity, easy credit, pretty good terms." Students embarked on a massive publicity campaign, delivering pamphlets in churches Sunday morning, working the streets, and saying to blacks that students were "the ones taking the chances" by joining sit-ins and picket lines: "All we're asking you to do is just don't buy, just stay at home." Soon Rich's began to feel the pressure as virtually all black adults throughout Atlanta heeded the student slogan "Close out your charge account with segregation, open up your account with freedom."[59]

The established civil rights groups also began to devote more time and resources to the student cause. CORE worked with many student groups, including the Greensboro youths, almost from the first report of the sit-ins. The Reverend King of the SCLC was at first hesitant in his support, concerned this time not to ruffle senior Negro leaders, including the Reverend King, Sr., in his native Atlanta. But the moral pull of the student protests soon won out, and by early March 1960 King was contributing his unmatched stature and eloquence to the protest campaigns. NAACP leaders meanwhile conducted a painful reappraisal of their fifty-year-old organization in an effort to preserve its pioneering civil rights role during a time of rising mass action.

Since its founding in 1910 by militant blacks, including the scholar W. E. B. Du Bois, and a cluster of white liberals, the NAACP had anchored the movement for racial equality. In much of the white South it had a reputation on a par with the Communist party as a radical threat to the social order. Yet its predominantly middle-class, professional leadership had fought its most protracted struggles in court chambers and congressional anterooms. By 1960 many young blacks whose protests skirted the border of legal propriety viewed the NAACP's reliance on lobbyists and lawyers as obsolete. NAACP spokesmen countered that their organization's hard-won legal victories had made the student sit-ins possible. But these same spokesmen had assimilated more of the younger generation's doubts than they could openly admit or privately resolve.

Three months after the sit-ins began, Roy Wilkins's aide John Morsell shared a gloomy message with the NAACP's inner circle. The sit-ins had uncovered, he wrote, "alarming weaknesses in the areas of alertness, initiative and imagination and . . . disclosed many of our members and units to be ridden by inertia and the struggle for community prestige." Yes, such symptoms were familiar to his colleagues, Morsell went on, "but the extent of the problem seems to have been greater than any of us anticipated." Drawing on his years as a sociologist, he began a calm Weberian analysis of bureaucratization and its ills, "a thoroughly understandable situation . . . being just one more illustration of a fairly common phenomenon." Then the personal stakes brought the NAACP administrator Morsell back to a central, nonacademic point. Ending this stagnation, he said, "is a matter of life and death to us."[60]

Morsell's challenge evoked more agony than enlightenment. The NAACP legal counsel Robert L. Carter saw merit in some sit-ins—for example, at polling places—but warned that too great an emphasis on this tactic "would tie us to something that some other organization has taken and run away with."[61] The program director, James Farmer, formerly of CORE, urged the national office to "maintain the posture of knowing precisely where we are going," while speeding up efforts "to find out where we really want to go." He advised against revealing the national leadership's full confusion, which would merely "increase the demoralization of our rank and file."[62]

The NAACP never fully embraced the student protests, nor did it erase the public relations damage wrought by its glaring doubts. Yet in concrete terms this organization—whose 388,000 members made it by far the nation's largest civil rights group—provided invaluable aid for student protests. Sparked by some bolder local branches and supported by a chastened national office, the NAACP helped fund many campaigns, organized Northern sympathy boycotts, and donated legal aid to student defendants and prisoners.

Mistrust between students and the older civil rights leadership never wholly subsided. Even NAACP leaders who endorsed student actions derided the Gandhian jail-in tactics as impractical. "If someone offers to get you out, man, get out," the architect of the *Brown* victory, Thurgood Marshall, told Nashville students in April 1960, to the enduring indignation of young blacks.[63] Yet despite mutual misgivings students were becoming one part—the critical shock troops—of a movement that increasingly drew in other vital elements of the black community.

Impact of the Protests

The spring of 1960 witnessed the first concessions from local merchants, for whom the virtues of tolerance often became clear after a period of economic coercion. A widely noted breakthrough came in Nashville, though it took the specter of rising disorder as well as falling profits to bring merchants to the bargaining table. In late April an explosion demolished the home of a seventy-two-year-old black attorney for the students and knocked out 147 windows of a medical school across the street. Instead of cowing Nashville's Negro community, the bombing brought two thousand angry marchers to the steps of City Hall.

Mayor Ben West, who had previously shown a rare talent for being out of town during periods of racial crisis, this time made no effort to avoid the demonstrators. Rather, he pondered the twin dangers of growing lawlessness and the prospective loss of black electoral support, and vowed to help end the conflict. The mayor hastily formed a biracial committee, which obliged him by recommending a plan to desegregate downtown stores in stages. Store owners, by this point less in need of private suasion than of public sanction to end discrimination, embraced the plan. On May 10 four theaters and six lunch counters opened their doors to blacks. When neither violence nor retaliatory white boycotts developed, other stores followed suit. The Reverend James Bevel marveled at the way white folks adjusted to the new pattern, so soon after the racist violence in April. Perhaps, he speculated, "The Devil has got to come out of these people."[64]

The devil found more permanent lodging farther south, in Birmingham, Alabama, Orangeburg, South Carolina, and other communities that brutalized protesters into quiescence. Mobs in these cities preserved segregation for several years more with the use of chains, knives, and attack dogs. Frequently they drew confidence if not courage from the racist statements of state and local officials. In Montgomery, Alabama, a city fast regressing from its brief era of racial peace in the late fifties, white vigilantes roamed the streets and beat Negroes with impunity. A majority of the police force reportedly belonged to the Ku Klux Klan, while the city's chief law enforcement officer was a popular speaker at rallies of the White Citizens' Council. By the summer of 1960 repeated violence, several hundred arrests, and the united opposition of white spokesmen had ended Montgomery's sit-in campaigns.[65]

Yet as far south as Texas changes occurred wherever businessmen and politicians forcefully asserted their preference for thriving commerce and racial peace. Galveston and Houston were among the first Southern cities to desegregate lunch counters, without incurring violence. The sit-ins reached Dallas only in 1961, but white leaders adjusted with astonishing rapidity and goodwill, desegregating forty stores and major hotels with minimal resistance. Observers found many reasons for this model transition: sustained black unity, a history of close ties between black and white leaders, a substantial black political and economic presence in the city, low-key treatment in the black and the white press. The fact that blacks formed less than 15 percent of the city's population may also have eased fears about changes in race relations. Most important, though, Dallas featured a cohesive business community that quickly reckoned and rejected the costs of protracted conflict. It promptly met student demands and went right on enjoying boom times, presaging other settlements wherever merchants recognized that racial progress and business profits were inseparable.[66]

In Atlanta protest gains were as uneven as the road to consensus between students and the Negro establishment. The sit-in campaign was from its inception undermined by constant factionalism, a process culminating in March 1961 when black elders engineered a compromise without the students' knowledge. They obtained a pledge from Atlanta store owners to serve Negroes at lunch counters, but beginning only in September, to coincide with the start of court-ordered school desegregation. Negro leaders, on the other hand, agreed to halt all protests immediately to avoid further exacerbating racial tensions. Students charged betrayal. At a mass meeting on March 10 to discuss the settlement, they assailed both the compact and its sponsors. The Reverend Martin Luther King, Sr., known as Daddy King, responded for the old guard. Insisting on deference from the younger generation, he reminded them that he had been a leader in Atlanta for thirty years. "That's what's wrong," a young man shouted back. Many black adults at the meeting also angrily rejected the settlement. "We didn't realize how much we had sold the black community on supporting us until that night," Julian Bond remembered. "Oh, man, there were about two thousand people down there, and they were ready to lynch some people."[67]

Even in Atlanta, though, the unifying force of black protest overcame the bitterness between its older and younger factions. Both sides responded to the impassioned oratory of Martin Luther King, Jr., a man standing uneasily between the students and the community leaders, but who on that day preached enough faith into young and old to move a mountain of accumulated mistrust. Urging both sides to resist the "cancerous disease of disunity," he praised the contributions of Atlanta's black elder statesmen—and now, he said, it was time for the younger blacks to make their contribution. He implored the community to respect the agreement fashioned by his father and others. When King finished, people wept in shame for having humbled their leaders and—Bond and Lonnie King included—accepted the settlement.[68] They accepted, too, the implicit compromise Dr. King outlined for community leadership, which spared the pride of one generation while ceding the helm of the protest movement to the next.

If the Atlanta experience showed that students and community leaders could look past even the sharpest divisions, it also underscored that consensus was by no means identical to harmony. In September 1961, when Atlanta lunch counters began receiving blacks, celebration gave way to renewed tensions as adults insisted on sending "mixed groups" of older and younger blacks. Julian Bond noted that women "came dressed in furs and all their finery to be the first black person to eat at Rich's," elbowing the students aside. His assessment: "Sad, sad, sad."[69] To Bond and fellow students it seemed blatant hypocrisy for the black establishment to jockey for a measure of glory that it had scarcely earned. For their elders, though, a lifetime of patient endurance of racism, moving by slow, painful turns to reach this day of social equality, fully justified their presence at the lunch counters.

Elsewhere in the Deep South, student protests achieved few tangible gains in their first year. Yet it was evident that in many communities Negro activism was driving deep wedges into white public opinion. In Savannah, Georgia, the mayor withstood demands for desegregation only by suspending his own biracial committee, which had affronted him with unanimous recommendations for compromise. Nor did Savannah's businessmen, who lost one million dollars during the first month of boycotts, always wait for their city's politicians in adjusting to black activism. One white grocer placed an ad in a Negro journal repudiating his brother's racist campaign for a seat in Congress, after "unauthorized" black picketers appeared outside his store. The sit-ins brought no quick resolution to the ambivalence besetting this former "tourist paradise," but it was already becoming clear, as one protest leader declared, "Come what may, Savannah will never be the same."[70]

In all, by the summer of 1960, over thirty Southern cities, including twelve in Florida, set up some kind of community organization to conciliate local Negroes. Most settlements occurred in border-state communities, many of them emulating the precedent of phased desegregation implemented in Nashville. Amid the succession of policy changes announced by local merchants blacks took special satisfaction from the news, on July 25, that Kress and Woolworth's lunch counters would henceforth serve Negroes in Greensboro, North Carolina.

By fall the outlines of an enduring student movement were clearly visible. To the dismay of white merchants, many of the sit-in campaigns that had ebbed during the summer vacation revived in September with added vigor. The following month Atlanta University hosted a convention at which 140 delegates from the Student Nonviolent Coordinating Committee formally discarded the word "temporary" from their organization's title. Soon the acronym SNCC (pronounced Snick) became synonymous with daring civil rights workers at a time when authority figures seemed to exist mainly to test youthful courage.

Students at the October 1960 conference also elected a chairman to replace Marion Barry, who had resumed his studies at Fisk. His successor, Charles McDew, was a leader of the violence-ravaged protests in Orangeburg. While a college student in South Carolina, McDew had converted to Judaism after finding that the only white religious leader to permit him in his congregation was the town rabbi. When the sit-ins erupted, McDew explained his involvement by quoting the ancient rabbi Hillel, in words that might have served as SNCC's rejoinder to all counsels of patience and forbearance:

> If I am not for myself, then who is for me?
> If I am for myself alone, then what am I?
> If not now, when?

As SNCC chairman, McDew interspersed his talmudic inquiries with some outspoken declarations to those who hoped the sit-ins would subside after the lunch counter victories. On the contrary, McDew said, in summing up the growing militant tendencies of the students, there would be no end to protests until "every vestige of racial segregation and discrimination [was] erased from the face of the earth."[71]

The Atlanta convention revealed the student movement as still torn between its fiery cries for change and its lingering desire for respectability. Students displayed their conservative side in withdrawing an invitation to the black socialist Bayard Rustin. The reversal followed a threat by the liberal Packinghouse Union, which cosponsored the conference along with Northern students and the SCLC, to rescind its grant if Rustin was allowed to address the conference. To most SNCC students, who had little interest in civil liberties and less in socialism, the sacrifice of their keynote speaker seemed a small matter.[72]

Alongside this expedient conservatism students nonetheless edged tentatively toward the left at this convention. Among the more than eighty observers welcomed by SNCC were representatives of such left-of-center groups as the Young People's Socialist League, Students for a Democratic Society, the Southern Conference Educational Fund, and the Highlander Folk School. James Lawson, once again the most popular speaker among the students, added some Marxist flourishes to his basic address on the need to fight racism. Now Lawson depicted the student protests as the start of a "nonviolent revolution" to destroy "segregation, slavery, serfdom, paternalism," and "industrialization which preserves cheap labor and racial discrimination."[73] Although few students yet harbored such discontents with the capitalist system, they were rapidly coming to agree with Ella Baker that their appetite for revolution could no longer be satiated by equal access to hamburgers.

By the end of 1960 the student campaigns had swept through every Southern and border state, plus Nevada, Illinois, and Ohio. Some seventy thousand blacks and white supporters participated in sit-ins, picketing, marches, and rallies, with thousands more offering financial and moral support. In addition to lunch counters the demonstrations also focused on parks, swimming pools, theaters, restaurants, churches, interstate transportation, libraries, museums, art galleries, laundromats, beaches, and courtrooms. Students further demanded an end to employment discrimination and began voter registration projects as part of a growing interest in grass-roots political organizing. No longer just a series of limited campaigns, the student protests had evolved into a long-term movement for social change. Young blacks looked to ever greater nonviolent triumphs, determined that no part of American life would long remain beyond their supremely confident reach.

In their first year the student sit-ins achieved only a shallow breach in the South's deeply fortified caste system, but they jolted whites and blacks from their long complacency. In the South whites still comforted each other with denunciations of "outside agitators"; but the sight of familiar black faces on picket lines and in "white" sections of stores undercut their words. Moreover, on the national level the persistent resolve and dignity of young demonstrators gradually impressed on Americans the depth of black discontent and the moral force of black demands.

The sit-ins elicited respectful consideration from President Eisenhower at a press conference on March 16, 1960. Although his vague syntax warded off journalists who asked if he endorsed the protests, the President allowed that he was "deeply sympathetic with the efforts of any group to enjoy the rights . . . guaranteed by the Constitution."[74] Privately Eisenhower had long expressed doubts about the wisdom of trying to force the pace of integration, opining that those who sought to do so were "just plain nuts."[75] But his public prudence reflected the favorable opinion that many Americans held of these protests.

Black protest similarly lifted the nation's religious leadership to a belated if not great awakening on the race issue. America's premier evangelist, Billy Graham, declared in April 1960 that race relations posed "the most burning issue of modern times." His ode to tolerance dwelled less on eternal truths than on looming national security concerns. Together with "economic strain" and "moral decadence," race tensions would weaken the nation to the point where communism would gain "the ultimate victory." Then, too, the cold war among organized religions could go against Christianity if "fine Christian political leader[s]" of rising African countries continued to be humiliated on visits to the United States by prejudiced whites. "Seventy per cent of the world's population is colored," Graham also pointed out, and "growing in power, strength and numbers. If we do not end our racial discrimination . . . a hundred years from now the white race may well be extinct."[76]

If Graham's preaching reflected the society's deepening concern with race prejudice, the limits of his conversion said much about the bounds of the national conscience in 1960. While Graham thought it "absolutely ridiculous to refuse food or a night's lodging to a man on the basis of skin color," he believed that "some extreme Negro leaders" were going "too far and too fast." After all, he explained, "the Bible also recognizes that each individual has the right to choose his own friendships and social relationships. I am convinced that forced integration will never work. You cannot make two races love each other and accept each other at the point of bayonets." Yet after wresting the issue of race relations from the political to the religious realm, Graham censured clergymen of both races who made the "race issue" their gospel, when they should have been concerned with saving souls.[77] In all, the tenor of Graham's epistle on racism was that discrimination was foolish, yet more a venial than a mortal sin.

Still, American society slowly began to take the measure of black unrest, as seen in press coverage of the sit-ins. Newspapers had at first ignored the campaigns or treated them as isolated curiosities. Media interest heightened somewhat when established civil rights figures headed by Martin Luther King, Jr., gave the protests new respectability. The tenacity of the students, their growing numbers, and their ability to win concessions also drew media attention. By the end of 1960 the UPI counted the sit-ins among the year's ten most significant events, though the protests were ranked only eighth, just behind the execution of the convicted murderer Caryl Chessman and just ahead of Hurricane Donna.[78] Sandwiched between these two violent events, the nonviolent student protests seemed one more, somewhat enigmatic source of turbulence in a year of upheavals. White Americans only dimly grasped that the sit-ins had created the most potent of storms—that a revolutionary movement was under way and a crisis in American race relations already at hand.

Chapter 3

Mass Protest in the Kennedy Years

The Presidential Campaign of 1960

BLACK political activism in the election year 1960 led presidential aspirants of both major parties to declare a growing—and in some cases newfound—fervor for civil rights. In turn their campaign pledges encouraged blacks to believe that the next occupant of the White House would be far more attuned than Eisenhower to the strains of "We Shall Overcome." John F. Kennedy in particular sparked the imagination of Afro-Americans with his calls to a "New Frontier" of bold reform, a vision that meshed well with hopes for stronger executive leadership on civil rights. In the course of his successful bid for the presidency Kennedy reached out energetically to black Americans, winning not only their votes but also their confidence that a new era of racial justice was as imminent as the November election.

As a contender for the Democratic nomination, the forty-three-year-old Kennedy aimed to establish himself as the party's most vigorous liberal candidate. But while Kennedy was widely known as a war hero, a Pulitzer Prize–winning author, and a staunch anti-Communist, few regarded him as a leader of any social cause. He therefore vied during the spring primaries with a figure of more imposing liberal credentials, Senator Hubert Humphrey of Minnesota, in asserting a commitment to civil rights among other domestic reforms. Later, when Humphrey withdrew following primary drubbings in Wisconsin and West Virginia, Kennedy echoed his former rival's pledge never to sacrifice civil rights for the sake of political expediency. He added, in an interview printed in a black newspaper, that "if anyone expects the Democratic administration to betray that same cause they can look elsewhere for a party."[1]

The sensitive subject of the sit-ins, which were occurring even as candidates canvassed delegate support, gave Kennedy his fullest opportunity to stand apart from the caution of government leaders. Whereas President Eisenhower had distanced himself from the protests, Kennedy praised them as signaling that the American spirit was "coming alive again." The goals of the sit-ins merited both individual and government support, Kennedy declared, adding, "It is in the American tradition to stand up for one's rights—even if the new way is to sit down."[2]

At the Democratic convention in July, Kennedy's strategy of emphasizing his Northern liberal ties contributed to a first-ballot victory, aided by nearly unanimous support among black delegates. It resulted, too, in a party platform that called for wide-ranging civil rights reforms to be implemented by "strong, active, persuasive and inventive" presidential leadership, words tailor-made for both Kennedy's progressive image and more specific NAACP designs. The new nominee moved quickly to mend his Southern fences by selecting as a running mate his chief convention rival, Senate Majority Leader Lyndon Johnson. The maneuver brought shrill objections from liberals, union leaders, and especially Negroes, but it soon became evident that the Texas senator was eager to transcend his conservative regional base. Ever alert to recognize a national trend on the march, Johnson assured blacks who criticized his nomination that a Democratic administration would "do more in the field of civil rights than has been accomplished in the last century."[3]

Republicans, too, stirred to the sounds of a more assertive black constituency. Their presidential nominee, Vice-President Richard Nixon, was widely respected by Negroes as a progressive influence on race matters within the Eisenhower administration. Moreover, Nixon agreed to a strong civil rights plank in the Republican platform as a way of unifying the party's liberal eastern wing behind his nomination. At the outset of the campaign, therefore, Nixon looked to win a substantial portion of the Negro vote, despite his ties to an administration that was rapidly becoming anathema to civil rights groups.

Once the presidential campaign got under way, however, Kennedy displayed greater energy and clarity of purpose in pursuing the black vote. In part this reflected a generally superior campaign organization and an excellent staff of committed advocates for black rights, including his brother-in-law Sargent Shriver, a prominent black Democrat, Louis Martin, and Harris Wofford, a Southern white activist who studied Gandhian thought in India, earned his law degree at a black university in Washington, D.C., and served for three years as an attorney for the U.S. Commission on civil rights. In drawing on these aides Kennedy recognized that blacks were essential to the Democratic coalition and that strong support for civil rights was a key aspect of his call for a revitalized society. As he had said in accepting the nomination, "The New Deal and the Fair Deal were bold measures for their generations," but new reforms were needed in these rapidly changing times, including support for the "peaceful revolution" that was "demanding an end to racial discrimination in all parts of our community life."[4]

In contrast, Richard Nixon's interest in civil rights and the black vote seemed frail next to his hunger for Southern white support. The result was a tortuous campaign in which his denunciations of the "radical" Democratic platform sounded much louder than his general praise for progress in race relations. His lone Negro staff member found himself isolated from the candidate and from key campaign decisions. He was therefore unable to prevent embarrassments such as Nixon's denial that race would be a factor in Cabinet appointments, just after his running mate boasted that the Nixon Cabinet would feature at least one black member.

Nixon's staff minimized his identification with civil rights, to the point of countering a claim by Georgia's Democratic governor, Ernest Vandiver, that Nixon was a member of the NAACP. To many Southern whites this organization was a symbol of subversion, and the Nixon camp squirmed away from this seeming skeleton in the candidate's closet. The Vice-President had merely been made an honorary NAACP member by a California chapter, his assistant press secretary explained. "He has not contributed any money or effort to the operation of the NAACP. He is not now an active member and never has been,"[5] the aide insisted, much as other Americans of the day indignantly denied past or present association with the Communist party.

Nixon's emerging coalition also gave pause to black leaders. "I felt a bit frightened by the forces lining up behind Nixon and by the way some among his followers were manipulating the religious issue," Roy Wilkins of the NAACP stated. Against those conservative forces, with their share of anti-Negro and anti-Catholic elements, "Kennedy and Lyndon Johnson looked like shining liberals."[6]

During the televised debates in mid-October, race relations barely emerged as an issue, as the candidates preferred to trade salvos over who could better repel the Communist challenge. It said much about the thrust of national concerns that Nixon's vow to protect the micro-islands of Quemoy and Matsu near Taiwan generated more controversy among the candidates and the press than any question on civil rights. Yet within this circumscribed political atmosphere Kennedy outperformed Nixon in advocating federal measures to achieve racial equality. He also vividly detailed the problems of ghetto dwellers in education, health, and employment, impressing civil rights leaders with his rare ability to convey in personal terms the costs of prejudice to blacks and to the nation.

Later in the month both candidates faced their greatest test of commitment to the civil rights movement. Martin Luther King, Jr., was arrested at a demonstration in Atlanta on October 19 and sentenced to four months of hard labor on the most gossamer of legal technicalities, related to an earlier probation for a minor traffic violation. King's frantic wife, Coretta, feared that he might never emerge from the rural prison where he was being held incommunicado. Nixon considered expressing sympathy for King's plight but was silenced by the priority of winning Southern white support. Kennedy's more single-minded interest in the black vote, and the party loyalty of Georgia's white Democratic officials, allowed him to pursue a more active course.[7]

Atlanta's Democratic mayor, William Hartsfield, who cared more about preserving racial peace than about defending white lunch counters, quietly suggested to Kennedy's staff that the candidate contact King's wife as a gesture of his concern. No one was sure of the political repercussions, but on the moral urging of Harris Wofford and Sargent Shriver, Kennedy called Coretta King on October 26 to assure her of his support. As it happened, Hartsfield had left little to chance or the candidate's discretion: he told a group of Negro reporters that Kennedy had been pressing him to help free King, a fiction that preceded even the call to Mrs. King.[8]

Acting independently of his older brother, campaign manager Robert Kennedy telephoned Oscar Mitchell, the judge whose sentencing of King had created this political predicament. The initiative for his call, too, came from a white Georgian who considered himself a Democrat first and a segregationist second. Governor Ernest Vandiver had discreetly suggested that a timely word to Mitchell from the Kennedy camp might pry King loose from the penitentiary. In any case "Bobby" needed little encouragement; he had been barely able to restrain his anger toward the judge, who had not only violated King's civil rights but also heedlessly endangered his brother's presidential campaign. The day after Kennedy's call, acting under what he later conceded was tremendous pressure, Judge Mitchell rethought the legal nuances of the case and had King released.[9]

At first the impact of Kennedy's actions on the white South seemed so uncertain that he avoided public statements about his intervention. In private Kennedy seemed most interested in the effect of his call on King, Sr., a Baptist minister, who had originally opposed him because Kennedy was a Catholic. Daddy King, as black Atlantans called him, changed his mind on learning that the candidate had wiped "the tears from my daughter[-in-law]'s eyes." "Imagine Martin Luther King having a bigot for a father!" Kennedy needled Harris Wofford. Then he added, with a grinning reference to the moral imperfections of Joseph Kennedy, Sr., "Well, we all have fathers, don't we?"[10]

The story of King's release never gained wide attention in the white South, to the relief of the Kennedy camp, but in the black community the contrast between Kennedy's intervention and Nixon's passivity made a strong impression. The Democratic party spread the good news in black districts, and a pamphlet that contrasted "A Candidate with a Heart, Senator Kennedy" with " 'No Comment' Nixon" became a staple of Democratic campaign literature. Martin Luther King, Jr., himself remained officially neutral throughout the campaign, preferring to be "the conscience of both [parties,] not the servant or master of either."[11] "But after learning of Kennedy's aid, King showered the Democratic candidate with plaudits that to the politically untutored ear could scarcely be distinguished from an outright endorsement.

On election day Kennedy won the smallest of pluralities over Nixon, scarcely 100,000 votes out of some 69 million cast. Any of numerous groups could claim to have decided his victory—Irish, Italians, Poles, Catholics, Jews, and, as some pundits whispered, the heavy graveyard turnout in parts of Texas and Cook County, Illinois. Yet the black vote was also undeniably crucial. Some 70 percent of all black ballots went to Kennedy, providing the margin of success in such key industrial states as Pennsylvania and Michigan. In the South, Negro support exceeded Kennedy's margin of victory in Texas and South Carolina. Afro-Americans were thus doubly pleased by Kennedy's triumph—as a candidate pledged to vigorous leadership to achieve racial justice and as a politician indebted to blacks for their decisive loyalty. When John Kennedy captured the presidency, many in the civil rights movement believed that they had done so as well.

Kennedy in Office:
The Politics of Expectation

John F. Kennedy's vision of a New Frontier had stirred great hopes for change during the campaign. The new President elaborated that vision in his inaugural address, which was memorable not only for its eloquence but also for compressing into a few thousand words a formidable list of the administration's goals. Although the speech stressed foreign rather than domestic affairs, black Americans drew hope from its central theme of defending "human rights, to which this nation has always been committed, and to which we are committed today at home and around the world." The President concluded with an exhortation that people everywhere "ask what together we can do for the freedom of man." Civil rights leaders rejoiced as they prepared to ask this question with growing assertiveness in the years ahead.

The advent of the New Frontier infused Washington with more vitality than at any other time since the inauguration of Franklin Roosevelt in 1933, when every reform plan seemed to merit a hearing, if not an agency. Like Roosevelt at the outset of the New Deal, Kennedy recruited large numbers of young, exceptionally talented aides and put them to work on ambitious new programs. The White House spurred efforts in space exploration, designed the Alliance for Progress to aid economic growth in Latin America, and created the Peace Corps to tap student idealism for service in developing lands. On the domestic front Kennedy weighed plans for a tax cut to stimulate the economy and proposed legislation to raise the minimum wage, expand federal aid to education, and subsidize health care for the aged. As part of this broad-based effort to "get the country moving again," Kennedy looked favorably on measures to promote racial equality. Initiatives in this area could be discerned almost from the outset of his term of office.

The most visible change in federal policy was an immediate and dramatic rise in the appointment of blacks to government posts. Previously blacks had been almost wholly excluded from crucial areas of federal service. Of 950 attorneys in the Justice Department in 1960, 10 were black (though all of the department's 56 messengers were black). The more than 3,600 foreign service officers included only 15 blacks, and other departments showed a similar, discriminatory pattern. In each of the upper ranks of the federal civil service, there was only one black employee. To eliminate this apparent discrimination the new President created by executive order the Committee on Equal Employment Opportunity, chaired by Vice-President Johnson and affecting more than 20 million workers. Kennedy instructed the committee "that federal money should not be spent in any way which encourages discrimination,"[12] a sharp signal not only to government administrators but also to corporations dependent on federal contracts. Lockheed Aircraft was among the major companies that "voluntarily" began recruiting Negroes, especially in Southern branches that once hired only whites. The President also persistently pressured department and agency heads to present specific progress reports on the hiring and promotion of Negroes. As the impact of these directives began to tell, it became a joke around Washington, as Roy Wilkins related, "that Kennedy was so hot on the Department heads . . . that everyone was scrambling around trying to find himself a Negro in order to keep the President off his neck."[13]

In all, Kennedy appointed some forty blacks to high federal positions. Robert Weaver, chairman of the board of the NAACP, was chosen to head the Housing and Home Finance Agency, which Kennedy hoped to upgrade to Cabinet status. Frank D. Reeves was named a special assistant to the President, and the campaign veteran Louis Martin became deputy chairman of the Democratic National Committee. In September 1961 the President nominated the NAACP's legendary lawyer Thurgood Marshall for a judgeship on the Second Circuit Court of Appeals in New York, the most prestigious of the eleven federal appellate courts then existing beneath the U.S. Supreme Court. It was Marshall who had anchored the NAACP case in *Brown v. Board of Education,* a fact the Southerners on the Senate Judiciary Committee perversely honored by delaying his confirmation for nearly a year. In the end Marshall's nomination won Senate approval, and Kennedy received praise from black leaders for his staunch support of the man widely admired in the black community as "Mr. Civil Rights."

Afro-Americans were also welcomed in White House social circles, a marked departure from Republican practice. Society editors of the *Washington Post* could not recall Eisenhower ever entertaining Negro guests except for foreign dignitaries and possibly the distinguished UN official Ralph Bunche.[14] On rare occasions White House receptions had also included E. Frederic Morrow, a black assistant on Eisenhower's staff and himself something of a foreign dignitary as the administration's token Negro.[15] By contrast the Kennedys regularly invited blacks to social gatherings at the White House and at "Hickory Hill," Robert Kennedy's Virginia home. The spirit of social equality even led high federal officials to break ties with prestigious but racially exclusive clubs in Washington. Foremost was the Metropolitan Club, an august institution barred to Negroes and Jews. Attorney General Robert Kennedy quit the club in September 1961 after trying in vain for six months to get its board of governors to admit Negroes. The President's application for membership in the exclusive Cosmos Club was withdrawn after the rejection of Carl Rowan, the black deputy assistant secretary of state for public affairs. Such gestures were largely symbolic, but they were warmly valued by civil rights leaders who believed that recognition of racial equality should begin at home—especially when that home was the White House.

The President's efforts to combat discrimination centered on the Justice Department, under his brother Robert. Bobby, as the thirty-five-year-old attorney general was called with widely varying degrees of affection, had assumed his Cabinet post amid cries of nepotism and indignant criticism that he had never tried a case in court. Yet the indispensable coordinator of his brother's presidential campaign quickly proved a gifted attorney general and a trusted adviser in nearly every area of government. His appointment was a boon to the civil rights movement, for he turned the Justice Department into a versatile force in the battle against racism.

The department's Civil Rights Division had plodded along to little effect since its creation in 1957. It was painfully understaffed, underbudgeted, and led with the same lack of élan that had characterized the Eisenhower administration's general approach to civil rights. Under Robert Kennedy the division changed quickly. He assembled a staff of extraordinarily able deputies, headed by a soft-spoken but brilliant Washington lawyer named Burke Marshall. Robert Kennedy encouraged his aides to move frequently from their Washington offices into the field, which could be anywhere race troubles were simmering. John Doar, first assistant in the Civil Rights Division, recalled of his chief in the Justice Department, "He was always wanting to move, get something done, accomplish something, and when I first went up to see him—probably April 1961—he was for filing seventy-five cases by Thanksgiving."[16]

Southern resistance to school desegregation first tested the Justice Department's commitment to civil rights. In 1960 New Orleans officials had pleaded with President Eisenhower to endorse a school desegregation plan that was under attack by local extremists and state leaders. Eisenhower refused to take sides, and the Justice Department followed his retreat by disclaiming responsibility. Mob action filled the vacuum of authority, closing two of the New Orleans schools before the desegregation plan could begin in the fall term. Early in 1961 the new attorney general fired off a very different message of administration intent. To Louisiana officials, who had voted to cut off the salaries of teachers in integrated schools, Robert Kennedy warned that he would ask the federal court to hold them in contempt and put the state superintendent in jail. He pressed them to ensure the smooth, desegregated operation of all the affected schools in New Orleans. When Burke Marshall started court proceedings, the state yielded.[17]

The Justice Department also encouraged moderation by sending its chief Southern aides to reason with community spokesmen in cities like Dallas, Atlanta, and Memphis. "I'd go in, my Southern accent dripping sorghum and molasses," John Seigenthaler, an aide from Tennessee, recalled. Then Burke Marshall would explain the law to them.[18] The President expedited these efforts by issuing the first White House endorsement of school desegregation. Kennedy praised the principals, teachers, students, and parents "on the front lines of the problem." Their adherence to the Constitution was "contributing to the education of all Americans."[19]

In May 1961 Robert Kennedy carried the gospel of integrated education into the heart of the South. He spoke at the University of Georgia, which had recently obeyed a federal court order to readmit two black students, Charlayne

Hunter and Hamilton Holmes, who had been suspended after whites rioted in response to their presence. Kennedy lauded the school's respect for law and hailed as "freedom fighters" the two black youths who had weathered threats in returning to campus. Terming race discrimination a national rather than a sectional problem, he called for acceptance of the *Brown* ruling as a matter of right, of law, and of America's international image. This mixture of candor and respect for Southern sensibilities drew a long ovation and the gratitude of white moderates. "Never before, in all its travail of by-gone years," marveled the *Atlanta Constitution,* "has the South heard so honest and understandable a speech"[20] from a high federal official. Such messages could not in themselves end white extremism, but they strengthened the elements of Southern white society that wanted to spare the region further turmoil and bloodshed in yet another "lost cause."

The intimidation of Negroes seeking the ballot was a second major concern of the Civil Rights Division. It investigated possible violations of voting rights in nearly sixty counties and filed unprecedented lawsuits in such problem areas as rural Mississippi. The division's attorneys soon found, however, that the skein of discrimination was so tightly woven into the whole fabric of race relations that it could not be broken by litigation alone. In Fayette and Haywood counties in Tennessee, resistance to Negro voting approached a state of war and tested the Justice Department's resolve to outflank such obstruction by all means short of military force.

Blacks in these two rural counties began registering in significant numbers for the first time in early 1960, when whites retaliated with a boycott against eligible Negro voters and their families. One black woman reported her experience as a newly registered citizen of Fayette: "One night when my baby got sick, I went to get some medicine. . . . The druggist told me he couldn't sell me anything. The grocer I've traded with for years won't sell me a loaf of bread and I can't buy clothes anywhere in the county." A black Baptist minister who had led the registration campaign in Fayette was denied a crop loan. The local gas company confiscated his storage tanks, so he could no longer drive his tractor. As added punishment his wife and other black employees were discharged from their cafeteria jobs in the local white school. For a Negro grocery store owner in the town of Brownsville, registering to vote became equivalent to liquidating his business. He was forced to drive fifty miles daily to Jackson, Mississippi, or Memphis in order to buy wholesale merchandise that the nearby white merchants denied him. Tobacco firms removed their cigarette vending machines from his store, and other companies stopped delivering bread and other goods on the grounds that they would otherwise lose business with local white merchants.

When blacks were able, on rare occasion, to persuade companies to deliver goods, police stopped the trucks on the road and turned them back. Many Negroes were summarily evicted from the lands they farmed; they erected a "tent city" in desperation but still could not obtain adequate food. Frantic petitions were sent to the federal government toward the close of the Eisenhower administration, but the President ignored them. Black families were by this point kept alive largely through parcels from relatives outside the counties. But the economic siege was tightening, and it threatened mass starvation.[21]

When Robert Kennedy became attorney general, he reacted in near disbelief to news that a brutal war of attrition was in progress against thousands of Americans. He speeded litigation that the Justice Department had begun in December 1960 against eighty-two Tennessee merchants and bankers for conspiracy to deprive blacks of their voting rights. While these cases were pending, Kennedy enlisted the aid of the Departments of Agriculture, HEW, Commerce, and Labor to provide food for victims of the boycott. Bureaucratic inertia blocked these efforts at every turn, but the Kennedys persisted down to the last obstacle, as Harris Wofford has related: "The Agriculture Department, with its network of white Southern extension agents and its dependence on congressional appropriations, preferred to get a presidential order rather than act on its own. So we arranged for the President to write to the department, and before long surplus food was being provided directly to some 14,000 people in those two counties."[22] This account overlooked one last convulsion by the machinery of government, which delivered food that excessive storage had partly spoiled. Yet despite this checkered outcome the episode confirmed the new administration's commitment to protecting blacks through unconventional initiatives.

For all these signs of bold innovation in civil rights policy, in important respects the New Frontier stopped at old political borders. Kennedy had promised during the campaign to submit major civil rights legislation to Congress, but even before his inauguration he concluded that he could not afford to alienate Southern congressmen whose key committee chairs would enable them to shepherd his liberal legislative program either to passage or to oblivion. The Democrats' 1960 loss of twenty-one seats in the House and two in the Senate gave Kennedy additional cause for delay, for this meant that in the best of circumstances it would be a struggle to pass any of his reform measures. Even Harris Wofford conceded in an early memorandum that "on most controversial social and economic issues, the Republican-conservative Southern Democratic coalition could probably muster a majority in the House, and successfully invoke a filibuster in the Senate." There existed virtually no chance of passing civil rights legislation, and any attempt to do so would "endanger all the rest of the administration's program, including measures of great importance to most blacks [such as the plan to raise the minimum wage]. It would demonstrate the President's weakness at a time when he needed to build strength."[23] Kennedy therefore deferred plans to submit a civil rights bill, giving priority instead to a range of social welfare reforms.

The President sought to placate Negro leaders by assuring them that a strategy of "minimum legislation, maximum executive action" on civil rights offered the best hope for concrete results. Yet here, too, Kennedy hesitated for fear of Southern conservative reaction in Congress. He delayed so long on his campaign pledge to end housing discrimination "with the stroke of a pen" that an "Ink for Jack" campaign deluged the White House with bottles of ink and hundreds of pens. He could not find one that felt politically right for nearly two years, then issued an order so embarrassingly limited in scope that he deliberately timed its announcement for maximum obscurity.

This deference to conservative Southern congressmen bordered on servility in the area of judicial appointments, several of which went to advocates of white supremacy. The Kennedys listened dutifully when the arch-segregationist James Eastland of Mississippi, chairman of the powerful Senate Judiciary Committee, alerted them to the availability of a close friend and influential attorney for a post on the federal bench. Civil rights leaders groaned that the appointment would be a disaster for the rights of nearly one million Negro Mississippians. The President, however, found it politically imperative to believe better of Eastland's crony, who was soon nominated and confirmed for a judgeship on Mississippi's Fifth District Court. From that strategic vantage point, Judge William Harold Cox went on to become a tenacious obstructor of black rights.[24] He also became a symbol to civil rights leaders of the Kennedy administration's seemingly unbounded flexibility in adjusting black interests for the sake of a broader liberal program.

The New Frontier was further constricted in its approach to civil rights by a preoccupation with Cold War tensions. During the first two years of his presidency, Kennedy spoke, acted, and risked political capital for one overriding goal: an America strong enough to deter Communist expansion around the globe. This all-absorbing outlook meant that domestic reform—particularly on controversial issues like civil rights—would be relegated to a comparatively minor level of federal activity. For the nation as for the President, the challenge to democracy was symbolized far more by the Red hammer and sickle than by a white hood and burning cross.

A final impediment to federal action was Kennedy's own, limited empathy with Negro outrage. The new President considered civil rights an admirable goal, but one that should not occasion undue passion or federal provocation. This detachment surfaced during Kennedy's first week in office, after complaints by African diplomats that Southern restaurants en route to Washington were refusing them food and water. "Can't you tell them not to do it?" Kennedy complained to his chief of protocol, Angier Biddle Duke. When Duke began to describe his progress in persuading some restaurant managers to accept Negro patrons, Kennedy cut him off: "That's not what I'm calling about. Can't you tell these African ambassadors not to drive on Route 40? It's a hell of a road. . . . Tell these ambassadors I wouldn't think of driving from New York to Washington. Tell them to fly!" Afterward Duke asked Harris Wofford, "Are you sure the President is fully behind our efforts?"[25]

Kennedy's early civil rights record far excelled that of his predecessor in the White House, but it fell short of the growing hopes for decisive executive action that Kennedy himself had done so much to encourage. To civil rights leaders who had trusted a single government figure to transcend all the congressional and electoral pressures weighing against their cause, the resulting disillusionment offered a sharp reminder of political realities. Most of these leaders remained optimistic about Kennedy's sincerity and the opportunities for continued advances toward equality. But they increasingly believed, as Kennedy himself had often said during the 1960 campaign, that he could do better. They resolved, too, that with growing pressure from civil rights activists, he would.

Freedom Rides

In the spring of 1961 CORE's executive director, James Farmer, outlined plans for a series of interracial "freedom rides" on public buses throughout the Deep South. Their stated mission was to test compliance with court orders to desegregate interstate transportation terminals. An underlying objective was to spur the federal government to protect Negro rights more vigorously by precipitating acts of racial violence in the heartland of Jim Crow.

Farmer came to this campaign a respected veteran of protest activity. Reflecting the basic similarity of values among civil rights leaders, CORE had just plucked its founding father back from the NAACP, where he was serving as program director. CORE was then seeking a charismatic figure who could attract broader public interest and donations. Its first choice, inevitably, was Martin Luther King, Jr., who declined in order to remain president of the Southern Christian Leadership Conference.[26] But Farmer in some ways cut an even more striking figure. A man of robust physique and hearty laughter, he spoke with the precise diction and deeply resonant tones of a Shakespearean actor—one who might have been equally convincing as a tragic Othello or as an ironic Falstaff. Farmer's commitment to Gandhian protest tactics went back further than King's, and his organization's Journey of Reconciliation presaged much of the nonviolent direct action in the early sixties, including the freedom rides. Though committed to nonviolence, Farmer also believed in the tonic value of confrontation in advancing civil rights. He explained the premise behind the freedom rides: "We put on pressure and create a crisis [for federal leaders] and then they react."[27]

CORE secured warm support from the SCLC and numerous NAACP branches, which pledged housing, food, and—perhaps most valued by the CORE riders—prayer. Only an occasional flash of territoriality checked the enthusiasm of local leaders for CORE's proposed trip through their towns and into the national media. Mississippi's NAACP field secretary Medgar Evers, remembering earlier raids on his membership by CORE, SNCC, and the SCLC, spurned a request to obtain lodging for the riders and help them address student rallies. "As much as we would like to be of help," Evers wrote five weeks after CORE contacted his office, "we feel that CORE's coming into Jackson at this time . . . will not have the effect intended and possibly hamper some of the efforts already in progress." He suggested that CORE direct its efforts to cities "currently outside the NAACP area of concern" and noted, in the manner of a sheriff waving on undesirables, "It would perhaps be better for you to bypass Mississippi and proceed to your destination."[28]

Yet even the NAACP's Roy Wilkins, who preferred discreet lobbying to what seemed quixotic provocation, set aside both tactical doubts and organizational rivalry to urge support for the CORE volunteers. Disdainful of the seemingly endless caution of New Frontiersmen, Wilkins could not help admiring Farmer's "desperately brave, reckless strategy, one that made those touch-football games played by the Kennedys look like macho patty-cake."[29] Perhaps, too, Wilkins thought back to the day late in 1960 when Farmer almost apologetically tendered his resignation in order to rejoin CORE. Aware that his departing program director had written many action-oriented memos, all of which had succumbed to bureaucratic snarls, Wilkins gazed out his office window, smiling wistfully. Then he turned to Farmer with a prediction of dynamic times for CORE: "You're going to be riding a mustang pony—while I'm riding a dinosaur."[30]

Seven black and six white volunteers left Washington in early May 1961 on two buses bound for Alabama and then Mississippi. All were veterans of social movements, most of the blacks having participated in sit-ins and the whites coming from a background of socialist or pacifist activism. Yet they knew that the risks of this trip were of an order beyond anything they had experienced. John Lewis summed up the prevalent attitude of his fellow passengers in stating that he would "give up all if necessary for the Freedom Ride" because human dignity was "the most important thing in [his] life."[31] He came close to doing just that at the Greyhound terminal in Rock Hill, South Carolina, when he tried to enter the white rest room. He explained his constitutional rights to "several young white hoodlums [with] leather jackets, ducktail haircuts, standing there smoking," who blocked his way. "He tried to walk past," James Farmer related, "and they clubbed him, beat him, and knocked him down."[32] Several more isolated incidents of violence or harassment occurred as the bus wound its way south. Then it entered Alabama, and the riders braced for greater danger.

The group also absorbed the unexpected loss of its Gandhian leader when James Farmer left in a swirl of sorrow, relief, guilt, and duty to attend his father's funeral. James Farmer, Sr., had battled a terminal illness throughout the time of the freedom ride, until the moment a copy of his son's itinerary showed him about to enter Alabama. Mrs. Farmer had no doubt that her husband had willed the timing of his death in an effort to save his son's life.[33]

On May 14 the lead bus moved into the town of Anniston, whose residents lined the streets in readiness for the riders. To a CORE field secretary on the bus, Genevieve Hughes, it seemed that everyone in the town had turned out to make them feel unwelcome:

> As we reached the terminal, the bus circled around the building and pulled up in what looked to be an alley. There was some space to the left of the bus, but none to the right. The mob was out—about 30–50 shabby looking men. They walked by the side of the bus carrying sticks and metal bars.[34]

In the absence of police protection for the riders, local anger flared into violence. Vigilantes slit two tires on the bus and tossed rocks at the windows. The bus left Anniston soon afterward, with forty cars following closely, but when the two slashed tires went flat the bus stopped again and the pursuers resumed their work of smashing the bus windows. Then, screaming obscenities and brandishing pipes and chains, they tried to storm the bus. A Southern white man who had boarded the bus in Atlanta, Eli Cowling, moved to the door, a pistol in hand, and held back the mob for more than fifteen minutes.[35] Everyone on both sides assumed that Cowling was an ordinary passenger, despite his extraordinary heroics. But this state highway patrolman had come on orders of Alabama's governor, John Patterson, who did his best to inflame public rage against the freedom riders but did not relish the negative publicity certain to attend the mass killing of travelers in his state. Still, Patterson had Cowling travel in plainclothes—lest white Alabamans hold their governor responsible for frustrating local justice.[36] As it happened, the riders remained under the jurisdiction of mob law a while longer.

Passengers clung to a precarious safety within the bus until, as Genevieve Hughes witnessed:

[A man] thrust a bundle, seemingly of rags through the window opposite me, at the same time lighting it. There was a noise, sparks flew and a dense cloud of smoke immediately filled the bus. I thought it was only a smoke bomb and climbed over the back of the seat. The smoke became denser and denser, becoming completely black. I crouched and figured I was going to be asphixiated.[37]

Then she and other passengers saw flames shooting from the bus and realized that it had been an incendiary bomb. The riders dashed outside, some scrambling through the holes where bus windows had once been. Whites charged the dazed passengers but had scarcely begun to beat them when a gunshot fired in the air changed them from a mob into a cowed assembly. Eli Cowling put a stop to the beatings by warning that he would kill the next person who hit anyone. Shaken riders regrouped across the street, while the people on whose lawn they were standing came out to extend a different Southern welcome. "It's a shame," they said, and invited them inside. Meanwhile state troopers could be seen conversing just as warmly with the mob leaders.[38]

The second busload of passengers was also assaulted at Anniston later that day but reached the Birmingham terminal on schedule. They emerged to find a waiting gang of thirty heavyset young men armed with baseball bats, lead pipes, and bicycle chains. They beat the riders to the point where an FBI informant on the scene reported that he "couldn't see their faces through the blood."[39] One rider required fifty-three stitches for injuries to the head. Throughout the assault no police were in sight. Afterward reporters swarmed around Public Safety Commissioner Theophilus Eugene ("Bull") Connor for an explanation. It was Mother's Day, Connor piously reminded them; no officers were available.[40]

A fuller explanation for the unchecked violence emerged from FBI notes and went considerably beyond Connor's theory of filial piety. The FBI informant Gary Rowe (so zealous to maintain his cover that he helped lead the mob) had alerted his superiors earlier in the week that Connor had promised the Ku Klux Klan fifteen minutes to attack the riders, whom he wanted beaten until "it looked like a bulldog got a hold of them." FBI Director J. Edgar Hoover was in theory bound to report this to his superior in the Justice Department, Robert Kennedy. But the FBI, though nominally an agency of the executive branch, was in fact more an independent fiefdom of its director. Hoover never informed Robert Kennedy of the conspiracy in Birmingham, whether out of opposition to the riders or sheer pique at an attorney general he considered meddlesome. Because Hoover had, in his way, rendered justice blind, Robert Kennedy took only one precaution on behalf of the riders entering Birmingham. He alerted the local police to possible violence at the terminal, unaware that Connor had not only anticipated but arranged that possibility.[41]

The President appealed for law and order following the outbreak of mob violence, and sent Robert Kennedy's aide John Seigenthaler to Alabama to negotiate with officials for the safety of the riders. Seigenthaler led the battered riders from the terminal and flew with them to New Orleans. But John Kennedy was angered by the news that new freedom riders were being readied. He was then immersed in diplomatic crises, including an imminent summit meeting with Premier Khrushchev of the Soviet Union, and did not want to be distracted by a campaign that seemed bent on sparking a crisis within the country. "Tell [the riders] to call it off," the President commanded his civil rights aide Harris Wofford, who had contacts with Negro leaders. "Stop them!"[42] But it was one executive order that no one could implement.

Initiative for the rides passed to scores of student volunteers after CORE halted its own campaign because of mounting violence. With James Farmer's reluctant approval Diane Nash and John Lewis organized a new group of eight black and two white riders, who headed for Birmingham in full knowledge of the brutalities that had just taken place. When they arrived on May 17, police were there to meet them, a situation that turned out to be a marginal improvement over the earlier disaster. They refused to let the passengers leave the bus, despite demands by local black ministers who came to escort the riders from the terminal. John Lewis recalled that some of the riders finally "stood up and tried to get out, and the cops got on the bus and just started knocking people down and sticking people with billy clubs and things." Afterward, Connor and the mayor had the riders placed in "protective custody" and the next morning forcibly escorted them to the Tennessee border, where they were put out on the highway.[43]

The stranded riders were in a position not wholly unlike that of fugitive slaves. They were in territory where hostile mobs could suddenly materialize, where police were more a threat than a safeguard, and where the isolation of back roads meant that no one might learn what became of them. As in antebellum days, too, they counted on cabin dwellers who reluctantly risked their own security to give them shelter. John Lewis described one black family's response to their plight:

The old man and his wife, they were really frightened. They didn't know what to do and at the same time they wanted to be helpful. So we got in, and the man went to different stores—about three or four stores—buying food from different places to keep the people in the community from being suspicious. He said, "If anyone asks, say you're my cousins from Nashville, who came down to visit me, my sister's children."[44]

At the family's home Lewis and his companions ate their first meal in more than three days. Then they called their contacts in Nashville and got a car—to take them back to Birmingham.

Unable to dissuade the riders, the Kennedys focused on smoothing their journey. Greyhound employees by this point refused to take the freedom riders anywhere, their resistance stemming in part from the prospect of having their buses targeted for obliteration. "I only have one life to give and I'm not going to give it to CORE or the NAACP," one driver exclaimed. An irritated Robert Kennedy called the company superintendent in Birmingham on May 19 with a message for "Mr. Greyhound." Kennedy warned that the government was going to be "very upset" unless transportation was quickly provided for the freedom riders, as they were entitled to by law. He clarified the point with a typically blunt flourish. "Somebody," he advised, "better get in the damn bus and get it going and get these people on their way." The next morning the riders were able to board a bus for Montgomery.[45]

The bus depot in Alabama's capital city was strangely quiet as the freedom riders arrived. Lewis, once more in the vanguard of protest, found it "a ghost town. . . . It was an eerie feeling. Complete silence. There were no cabs around that you could see. You couldn't see any other buses."[46] Nor any police. The town had been alerted to the group's travel plans. When the riders got out of their bus, whites suddenly rushed at them from the surrounding buildings. Lewis had his briefcase ripped from his grasp and torn to shreds, then was struck in the head with a wooden soda crate. He lay in the street with a concussion, bleeding from a head wound. When he regained consciousness, a man was standing over him to serve a state court injunction forbidding integrated travel in Alabama. White freedom riders fared no better, including one whose spinal cord was damaged by repeated kicks. Reporters on the scene were treated like allies of the riders. The mob seized the camera of an NBC employee and smashed it into his head, knocking him out. Still no police entered the area, though the station was five minutes from the bus terminal.

Amid the chaos John Doar phoned a desperate eyewitness report to Robert Kennedy. "It's terrible," he said as he detailed the attacks. ". . . People are yelling 'Get 'em, get 'em.' "[47] Another high-ranking aide on the scene, John Seigenthaler, attempted to act as a surrogate for Montgomery's absent authorities. As two young women were assaulted, Seigenthaler stepped out of his car, said, "I'm a federal man," and tried to escort them from the area. He was clubbed from behind and left bleeding on the pavement for nearly half an hour.[48] Seigenthaler's heroism and his fate together said much about the conundrum of federal officials in handling the freedom rides. They instinctively sympathized with the demonstrators and sought to protect them, yet shrank from using force to achieve these ends for fear of overextending their political and legal mandate. In May 1961 the Kennedy administration seemed more prepared to suffer with these reformers than to save them.

Violence again threatened later that evening when Martin Luther King appeared at a church rally in Montgomery. Fearing a repetition of the horror at the bus terminal, Robert Kennedy hurriedly improvised a force of five hundred federal marshals from widely scattered locales and departments, including the Tax and Alcohol Divisions and the Border Patrol. Most of the marshals held sedentary patronage positions, lacked experience in law enforcement, and, as white Southerners, were reluctant to guard black demonstrators. The attorney general and his aides shared doubts, only partly in jest, about whose side the marshals would take.[49]

On May 20 twelve hundred of Montgomery's blacks meanwhile packed into Ralph Abernathy's Baptist church to show support for the freedom riders, as an angry mob of whites gathered outside. James Farmer, having just returned from his father's funeral in Texas, was then moving toward the crowd on his way to the church. His life may have been saved by his local escort, the Reverend Fred Shuttlesworth, a short, thin man who so astonished the whites by commanding, "Out of the way!" that they parted to let them by.[50] An outburst followed in which the mob torched a car and tossed tear gas bombs through the church's stained-glass windows. There were shouts to burn down the church, but then the marshals began to arrive. They carried no firearms, in accord with the Kennedys' insistence on restraint; but these rawest of recruits kept marauders away from the church until the Alabama Guard took over. This probably saved the lives of the twelve hundred people trapped inside.[51]

The Kennedys now publicly pressed civil rights leaders for a "cooling off" period, fearing that further rides might bring still worse violence. Privately Bobby Kennedy exploded to Harris Wofford at the demonstrators' utter disregard of the President's need for national unity at a time of anxious preparation for the Vienna summit meeting with Khrushchev. But black leaders were adamant. James Farmer observed that blacks "have been cooling off for 350 years. If we cool off any more, we will be in a deep freeze."[52] Martin Luther King lamented that the President and the attorney general "don't understand the social revolution going on in the world, and therefore they don't understand what we're doing."[53]

The disparity of outlooks between the administration and the movement was brought home most vividly when a reporter at the Montgomery terminal darted over to Ralph Abernathy to ask how he could justify embarrassing the President as he was about to depart for Vienna. Abernathy looked evenly at the reporter through the space where a rock had shattered his car window, then said slowly, "Man, we've been embarrassed all our lives."[54]

As riders prepared to leave Montgomery for Mississippi, the leaders of the civil rights movement once more hurried after their followers. Martin Luther King, Jr., came to the Montgomery bus depot to see off the volunteers, but he declined to join them on the grounds that he could not violate his probation. SNCC youths argued indignantly, "Look, I'm on probation too." "So am I." "Me, too." "Me, too, and I'm going."[55] King exhorted the youths but remained in Montgomery. James Farmer also encouraged the volunteers, helping load their luggage and waving them on. But when the CORE worker Doris Castle of New Orleans asked, "Jim, you're going with us, aren't you?" her burly porter hedged. The prospects for a safe journey to Jackson were extremely bleak, and Farmer looked for a polite way to avoid martyrdom. "Doris, I've been away from the office now for three weeks, . . . " but Doris persisted: "Jim, *please.*" This plea was too much for Farmer, though like everyone else he "was scared to death at this point." He issued an exasperated order to a CORE staffer nearby: "Get my luggage out of the car and put it on the goddamn bus. I'm going." After all, he later remarked, "How was I going to face her afterwards if something happened, and I had finked out . . . ?"[56]

The Kennedys also viewed the rides as a terrible danger, though political rather than physical. Unable to stop the rides and unwilling either to send troops or to let the riders face possible death through mob assault, the Kennedys turned to Senator Eastland of Mississippi to keep the peace. In a private conference with the attorney general, Eastland guaranteed the safety of the riders as they traveled through Mississippi to Jackson. In return he received assurances that the federal government would not contest the arrest of freedom riders on charges of traveling "for the avowed purpose of inflaming public opinion." The senator proved as good as his word. This and succeeding rides into Mississippi averted violence, but some three hundred passengers were arrested for their "inflammatory" traveling.[57] Kennedy's bargain was hardly the ringing presidential endorsement of the freedom rides that CORE had set out to extract, but it spared the riders' lives and the President's stature en route to dealing with Chairman Khrushchev.

Harassment of freedom riders now shifted from attacks in the sunlight and the glare of news cameras to abuse within the confines of Jackson's prisons. A visitor to the county jail found fourteen women freedom riders in a thirteen-by-fifteen-foot cell and sleeping on a damp concrete floor. Mary Hamilton, a young black woman from California, reported, "Our blankets all smelled of urine. The sheets were soiled . . . and the mattresses were very dirty." Male prisoners sang freedom songs, which provoked guards to beat them and transfer some to the county prison farm, where they performed hard labor in one-hundred-degree weather. Interrogations of the male prisoners were also taxing. One rider recalled, "Outside we could hear the questions, and the thumps and whacks, and sometimes a quick groan or a cry." The Reverend C. T. Vivian of Chattanooga refused to respond "Yes, sir," to his interrogator and left the room with blood flowing from his head.[58]

City and county jails soon exhausted their ability to crowd freedom riders within their walls. In mid-June 1961 the Mississippi state penitentiary at Parchman began accepting male riders in its maximum-security wing. Later a hunger strike by women riders, who insisted on equal treatment, won them a transfer to the dreaded Parchman institution. The routine there lacked frills: no books, papers, cigarettes, exercise periods, time outdoors, or any other diversion. Food was prepared in the most unappetizing manner, then carefully oversalted; James Farmer lost thirty pounds without even intending to go on a hunger strike. Prisoners who sang freedom songs were, as usual, singled out for discipline, this time with wrist breakers suspending them from the walls. Guards also cracked down on singing by taking away mattresses, forcing prisoners to sleep for nights at a time in their underwear on the steel bed frames, "with fans going full blast to freeze them at night." When the mattresses were returned, guards shut the fans and windows, "causing the heat to be unbearable, making it difficult to breathe." Some prisoners stopped singing, but others could not be cowed. One young Negro told guards who threatened to remove his bed, "Come and get my mattress. I will keep my soul." James Farmer recalled, "Jail was not a new experience for many freedom riders; but the riders were a new experience for the jailers."[59]

Jackson authorities tested the financial reserves of the freedom riders more successfully than their spiritual endurance. By setting high bail and pacing trials slowly, they cost CORE several hundred thousand dollars and forced the organization into severe debt. Farmer contacted Roy Wilkins, who offered one thousand dollars from the constricted NAACP coffers, just enough for CORE to put down a deposit on some chartered buses. But without funds for court expenses the freedom rides seemed headed for defeat, not through intimidation but through insolvency. The momentum of the campaign, however, swept NAACP leaders into CORE's camp. James Farmer, freed from the Mississippi state penitentiary after thirty-nine days, spotted Thurgood Marshall at a cocktail party and renewed his long acquaintance with him.

After hearing of CORE's financial straits, Marshall, then director of the autonomous NAACP Legal Defense and Education Fund, told Farmer about a special bail bond account of a quarter million dollars: "It's not doing nothin'. It's just sitting there, salted away, drawing interest. You might as well use it as long as it lasts." Farmer hugged him.[60]

President Kennedy returned from Vienna in June 1961 to find the freedom rides still going on, and bidding fair to go on without end. In late September, prodded by Robert Kennedy, the Interstate Commerce Commission tightened its regulations against segregation in terminal facilities. Faced with the possibility of Justice Department litigation for defying these new rules, most Southern communities declined to contest the issue further. By November the attorney general was happily bestowing tributes for restraint: "Despite strong personal feelings and even antagonisms, these communities—to their great credit and the credit of the Nation—have peacefully accepted the regulations and respected the law."[61]

The Justice Department meanwhile exerted strong private pressure wherever bus terminals still featured signs for separate white and black waiting rooms, rest rooms, and dining areas. Robert Kennedy's emissaries often received cooperation from local officials and prominent national politicians who preferred quiet change to a federal lawsuit. In Mississippi, Senator John Stennis and Governor James Coleman worked with Burke Marshall to negotiate the removal of Jim Crow signs from bus stations in Meridian, Vicksburg, Natchez, and Laurel. The Kennedy administration left these victories carefully uncelebrated, heeding Marshall, who cautioned, "Neither the negotiations nor the removal of these signs have received any public notice, and I am under commitment not to draw public attention to them." A few towns, such as Jackson and McComb, continued to hold out despite growing political isolation, and in such cases Robert Kennedy obtained injunctions to overcome resistance. By late 1962 CORE announced that segregation in interstate travel had virtually ended.[62]

The larger goal of CORE and its allies—to impel President Kennedy toward stronger civil rights action—proved more elusive. Out of humanity and concern to minimize social disorder the President had, with Bobby's innovative aid, found ways to save the riders while preserving his political standing even in the South. But he remained dubious about the recurrent use of federal force to maintain order in the region. His reservations were in part narrowly political: his plurality of 49.7 percent of the vote had scarcely yielded a mandate for change, let alone to renew memories of Reconstruction. Beyond that, he doubted the legal and practical merits of such a course. As his chief of the Civil Rights Division, Burke Marshall, repeatedly insisted to anyone within earshot,

We do not have a national police force. . . . There is no substitute under the federal system for the failure of local law enforcement responsibility. There is simply a vacuum, which can be filled only rarely, with extraordinary difficulty, at monumental expense, and in a totally unsatisfactory fashion.[63]

This, rather than the urgency of sweeping federal intervention in the Deep South, was the main lesson the Kennedys drew from the ordeal of the freedom rides.

The Albany Movement

In late 1961, once more hoping to stir the White House, Martin Luther King's Southern Christian Leadership Conference assumed direction of a protest campaign in the town of Albany, in southwest Georgia. Like much of the rural Deep South, Albany had resisted reform even as sit-ins and freedom rides spread across the region. But for Albany's Negro citizens, at least, times were changing. They marched in force in October 1961, after the arrest of five SNCC workers, and formed a coalition of community groups known as the Albany movement. Its goals encompassed the desegregation of terminal facilities—the unfinished business of the freedom rides—and the opening of biracial talks with town leaders. The initial response of white officials was to ignore black demands and arrest hundreds of demonstrators, as well as nine "outside" riders. The protest appeared stalemated when in mid-December King arrived to fire up a church rally, then on impulse stayed to lead a march and was arrested. In one stroke the troubled Albany movement was transformed into a symbol of the wider struggle with Jim Crow. Yet even King soon conceded privately that it had been an ill-considered promotion, for events in Albany increasingly threatened to discredit his leadership and the course of the whole protest movement.

From the outset the Albany movement contended with bitter internal divisions. Local SNCC workers believed that NAACP leaders were impeding their bolder organizing efforts. Competition for the loyalty of young blacks was particularly destructive. Bernice Reagon, secretary of her NAACP youth chapter in Albany, was shocked to hear visiting senior officials tell "how SNCC would lead us wrong." Under heavy pressure she and other youth chapter members voted against affiliating with SNCC, but the episode struck her as so pointlessly divisive that she never went to another NAACP meeting.[64] Roy Wilkins recalled the NAACP's view of these tensions: "We paid some of the expenses of the Albany movement, only to be insulted for being on the wrong side of the generation gap."[65] King's arrival succeeded in uniting these and other community groups only in hostility to his own, the SCLC.

No one disputed that King could inspire the mass of Negroes to mobilize, which is why he had been implored to visit in the first place. And his arrival in a community instantly ensured that its protests received wide news coverage. To journalists he was the American Gandhi, who at any moment might galvanize the nation or, also like the controversial Mahatma, face assassination. But the focus of journalists, white officials, and even local Negroes on the Reverend King undermined all except the most secure egos among Albany's black leaders. They particularly disliked the high-handed way in which his aides Wyatt Walker and Ralph Abernathy directed or disregarded them.[66] This struck community figures as a kind of paternalism scarcely more tolerable than what the loosely stitched Albany movement had set out to eliminate.

SNCC leaders also wondered what would happen to the Negro community if its eminent visiting minister should strike a weak agreement for the sake of a symbolic SCLC victory. King made a special effort to conciliate SNCC youths in a private meeting, in which he praised them for pushing him further than he might otherwise go. He left them respecting his sincerity and unexpected humility, but still wary that their long organizing efforts might be compromised by King's caution and his interest in national publicity.[67]

Certainly no one in the movement was prepared for the phenomenon that was the Albany police chief, Laurie Pritchett, "a round-faced, impish-looking man with pink skin and light red hair,"[68] and a cunning unknown to the likes of Birmingham's Bull Connor. Pritchett ostentatiously restrained his officers from using firearms or fire hoses and discouraged the brandishing of a single billy club in arresting demonstrators. The chief went so far as to join protesters in prayer before having them locked up. This veneer of civility obscured frequent violations of black rights in Albany. Dirty cells, periodic beatings of prisoners, an occasional caning or kicking of some unfortunate protester, and hundreds of unconstitutional arrests remained staples of Albany's approach to law and order. But by keeping the most blatant violations off camera and just beyond the reporter's vision, Pritchett stymied the movement's efforts to capture national sympathy. "We . . . met 'nonviolence' with 'nonviolence,' "[69] Pritchett boasted, and at least on the level of public relations it was a fair statement and a devastating tactic.

In July 1962 King tried to dramatize the mistreatment of Negroes in Albany by going to jail rather than paying a $178 fine for an "illegal" protest in December. But he and his fellow prisoner Ralph Abernathy were soon freed on secret orders by Mayor Asa Kelley, just as scores of volunteers were pouring into Albany to insist on King's release. Clashing rumors attributed the payment of the fines to a mysterious benefactor working for a conservative Negro faction, for the town, even for the Justice Department (whose aides had made calls to officials in Georgia). All stood to profit from the reduction in tensions that resulted from King's virtual expulsion from prison. Abernathy alluded to the ulterior motives behind the settlement of the fines when he observed, "I've been thrown out of lots of places in my day but never before have I been thrown out of jail."[70] King was arrested again in August for holding a prayer meeting on the steps of Albany's City Hall, but this time town officials simplified their task by suspending his sentence. Like Pritchett, they wanted the black protesters mastered, not martyred.

The Albany movement reached its nadir shortly after King's release, when an act of brutality against a woman bringing food to black prisoners set off rioting against police in Albany's Negro quarter. Pritchett directed the attention of reporters to "them nonviolent rocks," while a dismayed Reverend King called for a day of penance and a moratorium on protests.[71] This merely accentuated the resentments of SNCC leaders, many of whom considered King too fixated on nonviolence and, worse, intent on gaining control of their campaign. The Albany movement was fast breaking apart.

In August the movement received a spark of encouragement from the President, who until then had been strictly a silent observer of the struggle. As civil rights volunteers and larger numbers of Klansmen entered Albany and tensions escalated, Kennedy urged publicly that both sides meet to ensure the constitutional rights of all. It was "wholly inexplicable" to Kennedy that while delegates of the United States and the Soviet Union were meeting to discuss differences, Albany's government could not "do the same for American citizens."[72]

But when tensions in the city eased, Kennedy declined to speak further on the situation and shied altogether from a more forceful assertion of executive power. He considered his legal options limited and hoped, too, that federal restraint might enhance the chances of the Democratic gubernatorial candidate Carl Sanders, a moderate by the standards of Georgia politics. Local Negroes concluded that the administration's interest in minimizing disorder aligned it more closely with the repressive local government than with civil rights demonstrators. One Negro woman in Albany said she learned then that "even the government is a white man."[73]

By late 1962 the Albany movement existed in little more than name. It had failed to win substantial concessions on the desegregation of public facilities or even to get the mayor and his council to bargain in good faith. King visited Albany sporadically but was already focusing on other projects, while the black community's once great enthusiasm for demonstrations seemed largely drained by a year of sacrifice and setbacks. One activist ruefully summed up the campaign: "We were naïve enough to think we could fill up the jails. Pritchett was hep to the fact that we couldn't. We ran out of people before he ran out of jails." Pritchett himself was still more succinct. "Albany," he beamed, "is as segregated as ever."[74]

For civil rights leaders who proclaimed a belief in the inevitable triumph of their cause, the Albany campaign posed a severe test of faith. King, whose prestige had taken a battering from the debacle, claimed that the experience, while disappointing, still showed that blacks could sustain a citywide protest against segregation in the Deep South. And like all pioneering efforts the Albany movement provided lessons for future campaigns; thus its mistakes also had value.[75] Still, the nearly total defeat of the Albany movement after the gains registered by the sit-ins and freedom rides raised a morale-shaking doubt. In the absence of blatant white violence not even mass protest, it seemed, could guarantee national commitment to the struggle against Jim Crow.

James Meredith and "Ole Miss"

The civil rights movement was still caught in Laurie Pritchett's web of nonviolent repression when a black Air Force veteran named James Meredith defied a governor's blustering and the threat of mob murder in order to register at the all-white University of Mississippi at Oxford. The twenty-eight-year-old Meredith had applied to transfer from a black college the day John Kennedy gave his inaugural address. Meredith was inspired by the new President's eloquence on the issue of human rights and like many young Americans sought to give that vision practical expression. The university at first spurned Meredith's application, but a federal court ruled that this able student could not be denied admission on grounds of race. It soon became apparent, however, that Meredith would register at risk of his life.

The Justice Department took an interest in Meredith's situation when his first attempt to register, on September 20, 1962, was stopped by Mississippi's governor, Ross Barnett, who personally blocked the applicant's path to the admissions office. When Meredith conveyed to the government his intent to try again, Robert Kennedy called Barnett to gain assurances that Meredith would be protected. The governor, however, seemed more concerned to ensure his own political survival. He spoke of state traditions, popular wishes, and forces beyond his control (which he had done his best to set in motion with angry speeches). The attorney general reminded Barnett that Mississippi was a state bound to observe the Constitution, a legal judgment that the governor disputed. "Are you getting out of the Union?" Kennedy asked. "It looks like . . . we don't belong to it," Barnett retorted,[76] as if the Civil War were still continuing. In a way, it was.

Robert Kennedy then dispatched five hundred federal marshals to Ole Miss, as the campus was known, to help Meredith survive the nonacademic rigors of his new college. After Meredith entered his dorm without incident, on September 30, an angry crowd of students and outsiders gathered to shout epithets at Meredith, blacks, and the President. "2-4-1-3, we hate Kennedy" was a refrain heard throughout the evening. Barnett fueled the mob's anger with a radio broadcast that was ostensibly a plea for peace but contained such incongruous phrases as "My heart still says 'Never' " and a reference to the "oppressive power of the United States."[77] The President broadcast a more wholehearted request for order, but even before he began whites were hurling rocks as well as chants at the federal marshals. The marshals fired tear gas at the crowd, but it did not disperse. Instead thousands of outside militants poured onto the campus, many with lethal weapons, and laid siege to the government forces.

The outnumbered marshals were hit with bottles, bricks, buckshot, acid, and flaming gas. Still, they heeded the Justice Department's orders not to use rifles and relied on tear gas and clubs to defend themselves. They resisted the growing mob late into the night, by which time their supplies of tear gas were nearly exhausted and 160 marshals lay wounded, 28 having fallen from gunfire. (Casualties also included a French newsman and a local jukebox repairman, who were killed by stray bullets.) Before sunrise President Kennedy reluctantly ordered the first of 5,000 Army troops onto the campus. They, too, refrained from using rifles but managed through superior numbers to quell the riot. Their presence enabled moderate faculty members to wrest control of the university from the governor, and the soldiers were soon evacuated. Meredith himself remained at the school, surrounded by a federal guard, enduring threats, ostracism, and harassment of his family. He graduated the following August.

The events at Ole Miss did much to reshape President Kennedy's thinking about race, politics, and his role in civil rights reform. He looked, first, with greater skepticism at the notion that moral suasion alone could effect major changes in race relations in the Deep South. His new attitude came partly from his brother, who had endured several conversations with a governor breathing segregationist fire and who had directed efforts to repel the campus mob. The attorney general exclaimed during this time that he understood better now how Hitler had taken over in Germany. "Everyone in Mississippi is accepting what that fellow [Barnett] is doing," he said.[78] The President also found that bolder action on race issues would not necessarily destroy his political base in the South. Although leaders in Mississippi and neighboring Alabama harked back to dark images of Reconstruction, in other Southern states the reaction to the President's use of troops was milder. Many officials recognized that Kennedy had responded patiently to Barnett's provocations and ordered Army units only as a last resort in the face of unrelieved mob violence. Finally, Meredith's ordeal impressed on Kennedy that the widely held view of Reconstruction as simply the tragic imposition of Northern tyranny on a helpless South may have been wide of the mark.[79] Perhaps, Kennedy later remarked to the historian Arthur Schlesinger, Jr., as racial violence continued to worsen, federal intervention had been necessary to protect human rights in that era.[80] The parallel with his own time, a century later, was unmistakable. In attempting to deny a lone black American an education, Ole Miss instead afforded one for the President of the United States on the need for more vigorous civil rights leadership.

Birmingham

"We've got to have a crisis to bargain with," Wyatt Walker noted, expressing the cynicism of a scarred civil rights leadership.[81] King agreed that unless racial tensions reached a more visibly dangerous pitch, the President's goodwill might never translate into bold deeds. "He vacillated," King wrote of Kennedy in October 1962, "trying to sense the direction his leadership could travel while retaining and building support for his administration."[82] It would take a confrontation on a scale greater than the freedom rides, greater than at Albany or Ole Miss, to force the Chief Executive's hand. To create one, the SCLC planned a campaign against segregation in Birmingham, site of the first mass beatings of freedom riders, the most fitting place to expose the horrors of Jim Crow to a morally sluggish nation.

Birmingham had backed into the sixties as a bastion of bigotry. Despite its booming steel industry, Negroes there were confined to menial jobs. They were excluded from "white" water fountains and fitting rooms. Segregated lunch counters reflected the city's determination to act as if the sit-ins had never taken place. Birmingham's police reinforced these patterns not only by routinely terrorizing Negroes but also by punishing whites deemed friendly to black rights. Public Safety Commissioner Connor twice had the manager of the city's bus terminal facilities arrested for flagrantly complying with federal orders to desegregate. No sacrifice for racial separation seemed too great for this metropolis, which closed all city parks rather than obey the secretary of the interior's order to integrate them. The same logic led municipal officials to bar performances of the Metropolitan Opera—which played only to integrated audiences—to prevent the occasional middle-class black from patronizing *Madama Butterfly* along with his social betters. In all ways, then, SCLC leaders were challenging a city justly known as the most segregated in the country.

Vivid memories of the Albany movement—undermined by a nebulous protest strategy and internal disunity—helped shape plans for the Birmingham campaign. King and the local SCLC affiliate Fred Shuttlesworth carefully selected boycott targets among downtown department stores, giving the protests a clear focus and economic leverage. Extensive fund-raising by King and the activist-entertainer Harry Belafonte added several hundred thousand dollars to SCLC reserves for bail money in case of mass arrests. To avert local black resentment of the national SCLC leadership, 250 residents were recruited to teach the techniques of nonviolence in Birmingham's Negro churches. King further placated local Negro leaders by postponing "B-Day" until after the mayoral runoff election in April 1963, in order to aid the less stridently segregationist candidate. With his victory SCLC workers began pouring into the city, which tensed with the expectation of racial disturbances. Under King's direction those disturbances exceeded even the fevered imaginings of Commissioner Connor.

As they moved through downtown Birmingham on Wednesday, April 3, the participants in the first sit-ins and marches found Connor unexpectedly civil. He directed the arrest of picketers but ordered his officers to avoid violence. Connor permitted himself only the indulgence of briefly showing off his attack dogs to the marching Negroes on Sunday afternoon, revealing as well the anger under his fragile persona of restraint. To King and his lieutenants it seemed merely a matter of time before Connor reverted to character.

Eight days into the campaign King was served a state court injunction against further demonstrations. At Albany he had obeyed a similar order from a federal court: he felt he could not blatantly defy the very forces of national law he was seeking as allies. But the state court ruling was a "pseudo" law, King said, designed to perpetrate "raw tyranny under the guise of maintaining law and order." At a press conference King announced his willingness to go to jail, while a nearby policeman recorded his every remark on a pad. He need only have taken down one line. "Here in Birmingham," King told the reporters pressing around him, "we have reached the point of no return."[83]

King was imprisoned and held in solitary confinement for three days—admirers noted that the minister's ordeal lasted from Good Friday to Resurrection Sunday—when the Kennedys intervened to secure him better treatment. But King showed that physical confinement could not silence his appeals to the wider society. When eight Southern ministers and rabbis deplored the protests and praised the Birmingham police for upholding the law, King seized the moment for a polemic to amplify the urgent moral issues at stake. He wrote on scraps of paper with a pen smuggled into his cell by a Negro trusty. Like many political tracts forged in the darkness of prison, King's letter displayed a rare grasp of the value of freedom. In response to claims that the protests were illegal he pointed to a higher moral law rooted in divine justice and opposed to the degrading statutes of segregation. To charges that the protests were ill timed he replied that "freedom is never given voluntarily by the oppressor; it must be demanded by the oppressed." In the past, King observed, "wait" had always meant "never" for Afro-Americans. The letter also swept aside the charge that the protests created ill will between the races. King emphatically denied this, for the entire nonviolent direct-action movement sought only to reveal an existing evil in order to eliminate it:

I had hoped that the white moderate would understand that the present tension in the South is a necessary phase of the transition from an obnoxious negative peace, in which the Negro passively accepted his unjust plight, to a substantive and positive peace, in which all men will respect the dignity and worth of human personality. Actually, we who engage in nonviolent direct action are not the creators of tension. We merely bring to the surface the hidden tension that is already alive. We bring it out in the open, where it can be seen and dealt with. Like a boil that can never be cured so long as it is covered up but must be opened with all its ugliness to the natural medicines of air and light, injustice must be exposed, with all the tension its exposure creates, to the light of human conscience and the air of national opinion before it can be cured.[84]

"Letter from Birmingham Jail," drafted on April 16, was soon circulated in churches as a pamphlet printed by the American Friends Service Committee. It was excerpted in journals like *Christian Century* and in national newspapers. In Washington, too, it was a topic of discussion, with the President among those impressed by its forceful pleas for justice. The letter came at a time when demonstrations already held wide attention but had to struggle against the public reflex to side with the forces of "law and order." King's epistle did much to overcome that moral inertia by vividly depicting the protesters rather than their tormentors as defenders of the Constitution and the human spirit.

On April 20, 1963, King was freed on bail, but he emerged to find the demonstrations waning. "We needed more troops," Wyatt Walker recalled. "We had scraped the bottom of the barrel of adults who would go [to jail]."[85] James Bevel, who had joined the SCLC in 1961 fresh from the Nashville sit-ins, suggested recruiting high school students, and King agreed: "We needed this dramatic new dimension."[86] Soon teenagers were crowding into the churches' nonviolent workshops. So were uninvited younger siblings, who begged to march with the rest. Black parents recoiled at the prospect of exposing their young children to the worst that Connor's uniformed vigilantes could offer. But the SCLC leader decided that no one was too young to sacrifice for freedom in a land where blacks of any age faced legal suppression. The children would march. King hoped in this way to "subpoena the conscience of the nation to the judgment seat of morality."[87] To Gandhian resisters, too, it appeared that the ends could justify ruthless means: King would risk the children's bodies in order to save the country's soul.

On May 2 the children filled the streets with a joy that was untouched by the danger. Bull Connor ordered his hapless subordinates to lock them all up, but this was not so easy. The children playfully set ruses to distract police, with decoys heading one way while larger groups of picketers marched on the downtown stores. The youngsters could also be startlingly serious. An eight-year-old girl was walking with her mother when a policeman stopped her. "What do you want?" he demanded. Looking at the towering figure, she answered without hesitation, "F'eedom." Over nine hundred children went to jail on May 2 for that goal, and the only hesitation visible was on the faces of policemen. One troubled captain confided to a fellow officer, "Evans, ten or fifteen years from now, we will look back on this and we will say, 'How stupid can you be?'"[88]

Bull Connor was not among the doubting. "If you'd ask half of them what freedom means, they couldn't tell you," he scoffed.[89] On May 3 police barricaded the Sixteenth Street Baptist Church, where a thousand Negroes had assembled. When many tried to leave the church, police struck. Using fire hoses at a pressure set to take off tree bark, they blasted adults and children, the jet streams ripping their clothes and leaving them bloodied on the ground. Police swung nightsticks into skulls indiscriminately, and attack dogs set loose among the panicked crowd sank their fangs into three fleeing children. Only twenty Negroes reached City Hall.

Over the next four days King's army lost its discipline and its pacifism to the sustained brutalities of the police. Hymns of love were drowned out by a hail of bottles and bricks as young adult males among the city's poorest blacks retaliated for the ongoing attacks by whites. They formed only a small portion of the demonstrators, but their message reached white Birmingham with unmistakable clarity: the age of the submissive Negro was gone forever. Connor's police predictably became more wanton in their actions. When Fred Shuttlesworth went into the Negro quarter to try to calm the rioters, he was lifted off the ground by a jet stream from a fire hose and hurled against a wall of the Sixteenth Street church. He was taken away unconscious in an ambulance. Connor lamented that he had missed the scene and added, "I wish they'd carried him away in a hearse."[90]

By this point Connor's gleeful vindictiveness no longer comforted many Birmingham whites, who began to fear all-out race war. Businessmen also watched in alarm as sales and profits dropped in the face of the boycotts and the turmoil that discouraged anyone from patronizing the downtown stores. Northern industrialists, encouraged by presidential emissaries, tightened the pressure on local Birmingham executives to reach a settlement.[91] These accumulating worries finally overcame the city's merchants just after they had adjourned a meeting with the mediator Burke Marshall on May 7. They had told him that compromise was out of the question, then stepped outside to view the stark alternative: "There were Negroes on the sidewalks, in the streets, standing, sitting in the aisles of downtown stores. There were square blocks of Negroes, a veritable sea of black faces. . . . Downtown Birmingham echoed to the strains of the freedom songs."[92] Three days later the merchants reached a pact with the SCLC. In exchange for an immediate halt to the protests they would meet all demands for desegregation and the hiring of Negroes during the next three months.

Like most compromises bridging bitter conflicts, this one drew expressions of outrage from both sides. Negro critics charged that King had bartered away their protest weapon for mere promises. Hard-line whites like Governor George Wallace of Alabama disavowed any settlement, and state troopers reinforced Wallace's viewpoint by roaming the Negro quarter with sawed-off shotguns. Bull Connor urged a white boycott of stores that agreed to desegregate. To some this did not go far enough. Two dynamite explosions destroyed the home of King's brother, a Birmingham minister, and blew out part of the Gaston Motel, where King and his aides were thought to be staying. Enraged Negroes threw rocks at police, and state troopers eagerly began beating blacks at random. While King preached in the streets against violence, the agreement he had negotiated verged on collapse. But if the informal settlement could not end Birmingham's racial tensions, the protests had set broader forces in motion that now dragged this metropolis, despite itself, into a new era of race relations.

Television coverage of the clubbings and hosings in Birmingham stirred indignation among Americans who had long been complacent about racist mistreatment of Negroes. One evening the national news featured film of five Birmingham policemen pinning a black woman to the ground, with one officer's knee at her throat. A photograph carried on the front pages of newspapers around the world showed a huge, snarling police dog lunging at a black woman. For the first time the media brought a graphic knowledge of racist violence into every American home.

Amid this public revulsion to events in Birmingham, which Oregon's senator Wayne Morse grumbled would disgrace even the Union of South Africa,[93] the President warned that he would not permit extremists to undermine the recent agreement. On May 12 he ordered three thousand Army troops to draw near the city and prepared to nationalize the Alabama Guard. The bombings quickly ceased, and the way was cleared for a formal ratification of the pact. Local merchants removed racial designations from fountains and rest rooms, desegregated their lunch counters, and hired Negroes for positions once reserved for whites. The new mayor, Albert Boutwell, also heeded the signs of change and repealed the city's segregation laws. Under prodding from black leaders he eventually opened the library, city golf courses, public buildings, and finally the schools to both races. In the nation's most segregated city, a symbol of white resistance and Klan power, Negroes had won a victory, in the Reverend Shuttlesworth's words, for "human supremacy."[94]

The impact of the Birmingham campaign continued to be felt in the White House, for the protest came while broader political trends were converging to promote a bolder civil rights policy. In foreign affairs the ebbing of Cold War tensions after the President's firm handling of the Cuban missile crisis in October 1962 enabled Kennedy to focus on domestic reform more fully than he had in the first years of his administration. At the same time, Kennedy's hard-won experience with Congress had at last convinced him that deferring civil rights legislation could do little to placate conservatives, who in any case opposed his other reform measures such as aid to education and health care for the elderly. So although a crucial tax bill was pending in 1963, Kennedy felt less incentive than earlier in his presidency to sacrifice civil rights in the hope of saving other liberal proposals.

The Birmingham protests also led John and Robert Kennedy to realize that the growth of black activism and white support had given civil rights an urgency unknown even during the freedom rides. Barely twelve hundred volunteers had made those dangerous trips in May 1961 and succeeding months; but in 1963 the Birmingham campaign and the other protests it helped spark over the next seven months engaged over a hundred thousand people and led to nearly fifteen thousand arrests.[95] The Kennedys now found their administration tested in two critical ways. First, could it redress the injustices so glaringly exposed by black protest? Second, could it even preserve national peace amid the growing polarization over the Negro revolution? In facing these questions, the Kennedys in effect also confronted the crisis of a liberal reform tradition challenged to break its long accommodation with the nation's racist heritage.

Toward a "Second Reconstruction"

America's racial crisis reached the Kennedys not only in the spectacle of massive demonstrations and worsening violence in the South but even more directly in meetings with protesters. One session, hosted by the attorney general on May 24, 1963, was notable for the rare candor—and bitterness—with which Negroes addressed the nation's political leadership. On Robert Kennedy's initiative the noted writer James Baldwin had convened a group of Negroes "other blacks listened to" for an exchange of ideas on advancing the cause of racial equality. The gathering included the playwright Lorraine Hansberry, the entertainers Lena Horne and Harry Belafonte, the psychologist Kenneth Clark, and others from varied backgrounds but—Robert Kennedy was emphatic on this point—no conventional politicians like Roy Wilkins or even Martin Luther King. The attorney general stressed that he wanted to learn what Negroes were really thinking. Still, he anticipated a congenial strategy session among fellow liberal reformers.

Instead a young freedom rider named Jerome Smith, survivor of a mob beating, began the meeting by announcing that having to be in the same room with the attorney general nauseated him. Smith meant to convey the degradation of having to plead for his rights, but the phrasing said much about the angry intensity of the Negro visitors, who rallied around Smith when Kennedy disputed him. Smith further shocked the ultrapatriotic attorney general by saying that he saw no obligation to fight for his country while blacks were treated like second-class citizens. As the meeting wore on, Kennedy tried vainly to focus on specific tactical nuances, gradually becoming more silent, tense, and coiled in resentment as blacks lambasted the administration and the country. Afterward one of the participants privately thanked Robert Kennedy for the administration's efforts on behalf of Negro rights. Asked why he had not said this at the meeting, the man explained, "They would conclude I had gone over to the other side."[96] To Kennedy, who had viewed civil rights activists and the federal government as partners in a difficult struggle, the fact that a Negro leader he respected had alluded to white liberals as "the other side" was perhaps even more disheartening than any specific criticism during the meeting.

Blacks leaving the meeting agreed that it had been a catastrophe, for which they blamed the shortcomings of white society generally. Baldwin thought that Robert Kennedy had shown himself, like all whites, unable to understand the Negro's sense of urgency. More charitable toward Kennedy but not toward his liberal values, Kenneth Clark commented that the attorney general's patience during that searing emotional experience showed that he was "among the best the white power structure has to offer. There were no villains in that room—only the past of our society."[97]

Kennedy was little more complimentary toward his guests in appraising the conference. Unwinding from the nonmeeting of minds, he released his frustration to Arthur Schlesinger, Jr.:

> They didn't know anything. They don't know what the laws are—they don't know what the facts are—they don't know what we've been doing or what we're trying to do. You couldn't talk to them as you can to Roy Wilkins or Martin Luther King. . . . It was all emotion, hysteria. They stood up and orated. They cursed. Some of them wept and walked out of the room.[98]

On the face of it the meeting signaled an unbridgeable divide between the pragmatic reform politics of the nation's leaders and the more desperate, urgent sensibility that fired the black protests. Yet in fact the meeting contributed to the forces that were fast pressing the White House and the civil rights movement into a closer, if contentious, alliance. Much like King's conviction that direct action exposed tensions in order to achieve deeper unity, the painful three-hour confrontation of views uncovered barriers that white liberals could not easily acknowledge, and hastened the attorney general's education on civil rights as much as any crisis in the Deep South. A few days after enduring the prolonged verbal battering, a reflective Robert Kennedy offered a thought that belied reports of a stagnant and dying liberalism. Perhaps, the nation's second-most-powerful person mused to an aide, if he were in Jerome Smith's position, he would not want to fight for his country either.[99]

Robert Kennedy's quiet remarks had a way of sending powerful reverberations through the White House. During this time John Kennedy was sounding out aides about addressing the nation on behalf of civil rights, then requesting Congress to enact major legislation. Close aides such as Theodore Sorensen, himself a veteran liberal activist, warned that Kennedy would merely wreck his presidency. Lyndon Johnson thought that further groundwork was needed with Congress before a legislative proposal on civil rights could be made.[100] Luther Hodges, Kennedy's secretary of commerce and a moderate from North Carolina, told the President that many Southerners already resented him for apparently encouraging Negroes to break the law. Further action for civil rights might cost Kennedy reelection in 1964. Alone among Cabinet officers and other aides, Robert Kennedy urged his brother to go ahead. His words resonated with the President's own impulse to act and overcame all pleas for caution. "There comes a time," the President told Hodges, "when a man has to take a stand and history will record that he has to meet these tough situations and ultimately make a decision."[101] It remained only to find a suitable occasion to address the nation, and once more the state of Alabama answered the call.

Alabama was the only state that had not allowed even token desegregation of its public-funded university. It appeared this would change on June 11, 1963, when two Negro students planned to register at the campus in Tuscaloosa. But Alabama's governor, George Wallace, vowed to bar the way. Earlier, at his inauguration, Wallace had sneered at civil rights advocates, "I draw the line in the dust . . . and I say, Segregation now! Segregation tomorrow! Segregation forever!"[102] Now, determined to make his mark in Southern politics, if only a nihilistic X, he stood in front of the college admissions office until federal marshals accompanying the two students ordered him to stand aside. The governor appeased his constituents with this public ritual, but the image he projected on national television was in its way as offensive as that of Connor's dogs. To Americans trying to forget the horrors of Birmingham, the sight of a governor seeking physically to prevent students from entering a school was at once tragic and ludicrous. To John Kennedy it was the moment to warn the Wallaces and Connors of the land that their day was over.

That same evening the President addressed the nation on television in order to confront "a moral issue" that was "as old as the Scriptures and . . . as clear as the American Constitution." The turmoil arising from racial discrimination could not be "met by repressive police action," he said, but only by the efforts of Congress, state and local governments, and private citizens to see that "all Americans are to be afforded equal rights and equal opportunities. . . ." With unsparing candor Kennedy admonished his countrymen that they could no longer tell blacks to "be content with the counsels of patience and delay," nor could they tell each other that the country had "no class or caste system, no ghettos, no master race except with respect to Negroes." The President added that he would soon request Congress "to make a commitment it has not fully made in this century to the proposition that race has no place in American life or law."[103]

Kennedy's address signaled a turning in the history of the civil rights movement. To one historian "It marked the beginning of what can truly be called the Second Reconstruction, a coherent effort by all three branches of the government to secure blacks their full rights."[104] It marked as well the political coming of age for Afro-Americans, whose nonviolent but confrontational politics had pressed Kennedy to act.

Like Lincoln, who signed the Emancipation Proclamation after repeated temporizing and under great pressure, Kennedy issued his epochal appeal for justice at the point where his sense of crisis at last outweighed his persistent caution. Kennedy admitted freely that he had acted in response to mass pressure, and critics have elaborated that even on June 11, 1963, he was still shaping his civil rights policy out of political calculation. There is much justification for this view, though for Kennedy such calculation was impelled by more than mere cynicism. It included in generous measure a concern to promote human dignity, an ability to gauge the tides of history as well as smaller fluctuations in Gallup surveys, and an openness to new insight based on growing experience. Like most leaders of democracies he concluded too readily at times that the path to greatness was not necessarily a straight line. But in the area of civil rights his path took him in less than three years to the center of a movement bearing the nation's highest ideals and enmeshed in its deepest controversy.

Civil rights leaders were unanimous in their praise for Kennedy's speech. King called it "the most earnest, human and profound appeal for understanding and justice that any President has uttered since the first days of the Republic."[105] Yet it was not enough to still the fires of racial hatred. A few hours after the President's address word came that Mississippi's NAACP leader Medgar Evers had been murdered by shotgun blasts in the back as he walked toward his home. When the slain civil rights worker's effects were returned to his wife, she found among them a five-dollar bill whose picture of Lincoln was stained with blood.[106]

The murder of Evers, followed by angry demonstrations in Jackson, Mississippi, and numerous other cities, convinced Kennedy that new efforts were needed to unite the country behind his call for racial equality. On June 19 he requested from Congress a broad law to bolster voting rights, ban segregation in public facilities, authorize the attorney general to initiate suits against segregated schools, and strengthen federal authority to deny funds for programs that discriminated. In the weeks that followed, the President made personal appeals to separate groups of delegates representing educators, lawyers, business executives, governors, mayors, Negroes, Southern whites, clergymen, labor spokesmen, Republicans, and Democrats. With Kennedy's approval, the Democratic party official Louis Martin formed a citizens lobby for the civil rights bill, while the attorney general and Burke Marshall aided the President in meetings with congressional leaders. The outlook for defeating a filibuster in the Senate remained uncertain, and Kennedy's standing in the South continued to drop. But there could be no turning back. The President had fully committed the authority of his office—and his political future—to continued civil rights progress.

The March on Washington

As the legislative process lumbered on, civil rights advocates searched for a way to build political momentum. In July 1963 A. Philip Randolph, the architect of the March on Washington movement in 1941, once more headed plans for a massive rally in the nation's capital. This time the main purpose of the demonstration was to demand strong federal protection of black rights. Unlike the exclusively black march planned (but never carried out) twenty-two years before, this campaign welcomed the participation of whites as helpful to the enactment of civil rights legislation. In its ambitious aims and avowedly interracial character the new March on Washington movement climaxed the evolution of black protest in the early sixties: from the first, piecemeal actions by Negroes in Southern cities, the civil rights crusade had become a truly national coalition directly pressing Congress and the President for reform.

Black spokesmen had alternately brandished and withdrawn the threat of a massive protest in the capital for over two decades. Each time, the fear of harming Negro interests through too strident or too weak a protest led march leaders to abandon their original plans. Randolph had called the 1941 march partly to prevent more radical elements, including the Communist party, from exploiting anger in the ghettos. Having done so, he could more readily defer the rally in return for limited concessions, rather than risk a turnout that did not match expectations. Blacks in the march committee's youth division bitterly denounced this about-face, but Randolph dismissed them as romantics who did not know when to compromise.[107] His words set a pattern for the continuing March on Washington movement, which was marked by few forward strides and a series of abrupt strategic retreats. Randolph's movement provoked bitter ridicule in the ghettos. Harlem rioters in 1943 destroyed the march committee headquarters on 125th Street, then scrawled an epitaph for the movement on one of the walls: "Randolph, why don't you march?"[108]

Randolph's advancing years and the declining strength of his union, the Brotherhood of Sleeping Car Porters, militated against his hopes of leading a mass march. But with the rise of Martin Luther King in the mid-1950s Randolph once more set forth plans for a national protest, aiming now to fuse King's personal stature with the NAACP's organizational strength. In March 1957 Randolph asked King and Roy Wilkins to join him in sponsoring a rally at the Lincoln Memorial. Once more he trimmed his original militant designs in order to broaden his support; at King's urging he rechristened the march a "Prayer Pilgrimage," to avoid any hint of coercion. Randolph also took symbolic cues from Roy Wilkins, who suggested scheduling the march for May 17, the third anniversary of the NAACP's victory in the *Brown* case. The first fruits of Randolph's long labors for a march on Washington made for a poor political harvest. While 25,000 predominantly Negro marchers rallied in the capital, President Eisenhower ignored the event and so did the public. Still, Randolph had established a precedent, which he reinforced with youth marches in the two following years. By 1963, with the Negro revolution bidding to catch up to Randolph's decades-old vision, the seventy-three-year-old leader planned one more rally, determined this time to exact keen attention from the President and the American people.

The coordination of Randolph's idea fell to his chief aide, Bayard Rustin, the most skillful organizer in the civil rights movement.[109] Tall, with flaring gray hair, high cheekbones, and thin features reflecting part-Indian ancestry, his aristocratic diction shaped by long stays in England, the fifty-one-year-old Rustin cut a profile in elegance. From an early age he mingled easily with whites, as one of very few blacks growing up in West Chester, a suburb of Philadelphia. As a young man in the 1930s Rustin, who sang in all-white clubs with such Negro celebrities as Josh White and "Leadbelly," clearly saw the social divide separating the races. But he came to work closely with whites as his admiration for Communist activism against segregation, lynching, and economic exploitation of blacks drew him into the party's orbit. These ties lasted until 1941, when Communist functionaries explained that the German invasion of Russia required dropping all protests against American racism in order to focus all of the party's energy on the "people's war." A disillusioned Rustin instead renounced the party, still believing in the need for interracial alliances but thereafter considerably more critical in pursuing them.

From 1941 Rustin's résumé approximated an outline history of the Negro nonviolent direct-action movement. A volunteer in Randolph's youth division for the March on Washington, he joined in protesting its cancellation. Yet he shared Randolph's emphasis on economic goals that could bridge racial lines, including federal measures to end poverty, and he continued to aid Randolph's efforts to draw labor into the fight against Jim Crow. Raised as a Quaker, Rustin also became a favorite disciple of the grand agitator among American pacifists, A. J. Muste of the Fellowship of Reconciliation (FOR). Rustin shuttled between this organization and its offshoot, CORE, working with James Farmer on varied protests and winning respect for his outward serenity during several beatings. In 1955, convinced that Negro churches held a key to mass action, he went to Montgomery on behalf of Muste to share his experience in organizing boycotts. There Rustin, the urbane activist, dazzled Dr. King with discourses on Gandhian philosophy, which he had studied with disciples of the late Mahatma while spending a year in India. It was Rustin who persuaded King to found a regional network of black ministers and who had principal responsibility for organizing it. It was Rustin again who helped revive the March on Washington movement in the late fifties, organizing all three rallies. By then he had become a trusted adviser to the black labor movement through Randolph, to the black church leadership through Dr. King, to the Northern-based Gandhian movement through FOR and CORE. A fountain of deeply held beliefs, he nonetheless worked effectively with people of different backgrounds, affiliations, and ideologies. An intellectual with a talent for polemic, he was also a technician of change, attentive to every organizational and logistical need. He was perhaps the only visionary in the movement who could be more exacting about the location of latrines along a march route than about the doctrinal positions of the marchers. Small wonder, then, that Rustin was the activist of choice for implementing any vision of Negro protest.

For all this, Rustin remained a remarkably unheralded figure in the movement, not for any lack of personal flamboyance but because other Negro leaders drew back from the controversy that hounded his political and personal life. Whereas most black spokesmen strongly endorsed free enterprise or, like King, at least rejected communism, Rustin had been a member of the Communist party. Even his apostasy in 1941 moved him only as far right as democratic socialism (where he joined his mentor Randolph), and in a time of Cold War conformity Rustin's precise location on the spectrum of leftist thought made little difference. Rustin carried a still heavier political weight: he had gone to jail as a conscientious objector during World War II, and he continued to oppose serving in the armed forces of a society he viewed as racist. It was one thing for the Reverend King to link Negro protest to Christian love and nonviolence; the minister still avoided criticism of American foreign policy and in his memoir of the Montgomery boycott he noted his early doubts about pacifism in world affairs. Rustin's notion of nonviolence, in contrast, seemed more expansive than the civil rights movement could withstand.

Someone of Rustin's talents might have surmounted these political handicaps, but one final, personal matter frightened movement leaders too greatly. Rustin had never hidden the fact that he was a homosexual, and on one occasion he had been arrested on a "morals" charge. Even had Rustin not been black and formerly Red, the social mores of the day would have made him a certain target for defamation by those seeking to discredit the civil rights cause. That concern had led Dr. King, who did not worry unduly about the left-wing views of some aides, to refrain from offering Rustin the directorship of the SCLC. Thus, Rustin remained in the background of the events he guided, as unofficial adviser or "assistant director." He was a pioneer working in the shadows.

In 1963 the flowering of a national Negro protest movement, filled with charismatic leaders but lacking overall direction, enabled Rustin and Randolph to reassert their influence. Now was the time, they believed, for blacks to stage a protest in the capital, supported by white labor and other groups, demanding federal action. Their idea caught hold of the civil rights leadership, whose underlying unity of purpose had never been more evident. Randolph, Martin Luther King of the SCLC, James Farmer of CORE, Roy Wilkins of the NAACP, John Lewis of SNCC, Whitney Young of the Urban League, and others involved in planning the rally exhibited widely divergent ideas about what its character should be. Yet they repeatedly compromised their differences in the interest of promoting common nonviolent action to spur reform.

Randolph and Rustin were the first to alter their vision of the march in order to secure a broad spectrum of supporters. As early as December 1962 they had conceived the march as a labor movement vehicle to press for a federal jobs program. After months of groundwork Randolph appealed to Negro trade unionists in language reminiscent of his organizing speeches in the twenties and thirties. "Let the black laboring masses speak! Negro workers, ARISE and MARCH," he exhorted.[110] The masses, as represented by black union leaders, scarcely responded. In the spring of 1963 it became evident where they were heading, as protests against segregation—but not against the economic system—spread from Birmingham to Jackson. Randolph and Rustin accordingly shifted their focus from a jobs bill to passage of civil rights legislation, and from union spokesmen to black middle-class leaders like King, Wilkins, and Farmer. This required the two veteran socialists to suspend their Marxist view of civil rights protest as a somewhat immature subsidiary of the movement for economic justice. In exchange for this elastic ideological approach they won the support of Dr. King and, with it, the chance to mobilize massive black support for their rally.

Other civil rights leaders followed King's lead. CORE and SNCC spokesmen doubted that a march would exert enough pressure to serve any useful purpose, but when King committed himself to Randolph they joined as well. Similarly Wilkins and Young, on the other side of the civil rights continuum, signed on despite their concern over a confrontation with federal authorities. King, for his part, took pains to reassure the skeptical Wilkins. There would be no sit-in at the Capitol, he promised the NAACP leaders, who feared this would provoke a disastrous backlash.[111] The site of the rally was shifted, too, from the Capitol to the Lincoln Memorial, further attenuating any connotations of protest. As religious, labor, and other groups stepped forward to help sponsor or otherwise aid the march, Randolph's antigovernment protest became transmuted, in the words of the journalist Milton Viorst, from a matter of politics into "a moral witness against evil."[112]

Whitney Young, Jr., of the Urban League, known as the movement's "chairman of the board" for his mediating skills, guided the march organizers past their one trying conflict. The question of who should lead the march threatened to end in deadlock, though not for reasons of ego conflicts or group rivalry. Everyone agreed that Bayard Rustin was uniquely qualified to direct the march, but Roy Wilkins regretfully maintained that Rustin was also uniquely tainted. At a leadership conference in late June 1963 Wilkins cautioned that Rustin "had too many scars—all the talk about his sex life, his political life, and his being a draft dodger." How many liabilities could the march be expected to bear?[113] Anticipating the point, Randolph answered as Young had counseled in a private caucus: Randolph would lead the march himself, but he insisted on the right to name his own deputy director. King, Farmer, and other march organizers assented to Randolph's wishes, again as Young had encouraged them in separate meetings. Faced with this show of loyalty to Rustin and his venerable protector, Wilkins withdrew his opposition but offered a skeptical afterword: "O.K., Phil, I've warned you, but if you want him, you take him, and it's *your* responsibility." Rustin remembered that as the meeting adjourned, Young patted him on the back and said with a laugh, "I'm telling you, black boy, you'd better behave yourself."[114] With harmony preserved, Rustin once more prepared to orchestrate the civil rights movement from a position of calculated obscurity.

The march leaders attempted to enlarge their common ground with federal officials at a White House Conference on June 22, 1963. President Kennedy urged his guests to give their highest priority to enacting his newly proposed civil rights bill and warned that further demonstrations might trigger a conservative backlash. "We want success in Congress," he said, "not just a big show at the Capitol." James Farmer and A. Philip Randolph explained that the march would afford an essential, nonviolent outlet for rising anger among the black masses. Martin Luther King, Jr., added that he had never engaged in any campaign that did not seem "ill-timed." They impressed on Kennedy the inevitability of a march and spurred him to endorse its aims, while he in turn further discouraged them from considering any protest against his administration. This informal détente echoed Kennedy's concluding words to his guests: they might disagree at times over tactics, but they should always preserve "confidence in the good faith of each other."[115]

That faith was stretched by another, more private conference the same day, during which President Kennedy pressed Martin Luther King, Jr., to dismiss an aide whom the FBI had called a Communist agent. The accused man, a white attorney named Stanley Levison, had been involved in varied liberal and leftist causes, but King viewed him as an innocent victim of FBI Director J. Edgar Hoover's belief that all black protests were Communist inspired. President Kennedy recognized, however, that even an unproved hint of Communist infiltration could severely stigmatize the civil rights movement, damage prospects for his bill, and tarnish his administration. As they strolled through the Rose Garden, the President alerted King that the FBI had him "under very close surveillance," and he warned the minister not to let personal loyalty cloud his judgment and jeopardize their common cause. King had to answer to a larger coalition, Kennedy emphasized: "If they [the opponents of civil rights] shoot *you* down, they'll shoot *us* down too—so we're asking you to be careful."[116]

Under the administration's intense pressure (and on the strong urging of Levison himself) King reluctantly agreed to break with his aide and friend. In return the President told a press conference on July 17 that there was "no evidence" to support rumors of Communist influence in the civil rights movement. Robert Kennedy meanwhile wrote senators a similar categorical denial of charges specifically involving King.[117] These statements left the administration vulnerable to a punishing scandal if evidence ever surfaced for any of Hoover's allegations. That the Kennedys nonetheless chose to shield the movement from the FBI director's glare, just weeks before the most ambitious of all demonstrations, attested to the growing convergence of interests between black protest leaders and white liberals in government.

As the march date approached, even the rhetoric planned for the event was monitored and in one instance muzzled for the sake of liberal consensus. John Lewis, the young SNCC leader who had suffered numerous assaults during protest marches and was now covered by a protective layer of political cynicism, planned a speech that made his colleagues tremble. He intended to castigate the Kennedys as hypocrites, the civil rights bill as worse than useless, and American society as despicably racist. His speech promised a "march through the heart of Dixie, the way Sherman did," to "burn Jim Crow to the ground—nonviolently."[118] Other organizers simply refused to let Lewis wreak havoc with their painstaking efforts to forge a broad political consensus. Wilkins, shrewd veteran of many legislative battles, later wrote that it was not so much Lewis's fiery rhetoric that disturbed him but that "Lewis was denouncing the legislative process at a demonstration called in large part to back the Civil Rights Bill—that seemed like a double cross."[119] Randolph, the white-haired sage of the movement, revered by all parties, spoke to Lewis for the others. "We've come this far," he implored. "For the sake of unity, change it."[120] Lewis reluctantly agreed, and the March on Washington went forward with ranks closed for the sake of moving a nation.

The spectrum of Negro unity was not unbroken; it faded before a ghetto-based group called the Nation of Islam, which preferred racial solidarity to integration. Yet their spokesman, Malcolm X, the foremost black critic of an interracial coalition, wavered before the strength of Negro support for the march. Malcolm arrived in Washington in August 1963, ostensibly to mock the event at close range but perhaps also to partake of it from the edges. "This is nothing but a circus, it's nothing but a picnic," he said, by way of dismissing the upcoming rally at a press conference on the eve of the march. Bayard Rustin just then emerged from a strategy meeting and spotted Malcolm feeding his hyperbole to headline-hungry reporters. The march's deputy director strode toward Malcolm and amiably asked his arch-critic whether he would care to repeat his words to Negro marchers the next morning. Recognizing as well as Rustin the direction of Negro sentiment, Malcolm jovially declined. Later that evening Rustin encountered him again and issued the same, genial challenge. Malcolm, a man widely feared by civil rights leaders as devastating in debate, merely smiled, perhaps in the certainty that his day too would come.[121]

On August 28, 1963, under a nearly cloudless sky, more than a quarter of a million people gathered near the Lincoln Memorial to rally for "jobs and freedom."[122] Fifty thousand whites mingled in the crowd and among the prominent speakers. From every area of American life leaders came to donate their talents or simply their stature to the cause: Walter Reuther, maverick labor leader and a Kennedy ally; clergymen of every faith; film stars Sidney Poitier, Charlton Heston, and Marlon Brando; radical folksinger Joan Baez and gospel legend Mahalia Jackson; teachers, students, professionals. It was the largest political assembly in American history. And although many Washington residents anticipated the event in terror—according to Louis Martin the Army had prepared for the rally "as if it were World War II"[123]—the immense crowd was nonviolent and in a largely festive mood.

The sweltering afternoon featured a profusion of speakers, each allotted fifteen minutes, though more than a few found that their accumulated wisdom could not be contained in that brief span. The dominant memory of the rally, however, was the closing address by Martin Luther King, Jr. King began with a formal if powerful recitation of the trials of Afro-Americans struggling for freedom in a society shackled by discrimination. He was gathering up his notes, preparing to sit down, when Mahalia Jackson called out from behind him, "Tell them about your dream, Martin! Tell them about the dream!"[124] King obliged, drawing on imagery from earlier speeches, encouragement from the assembled marchers, and sheer inspiration. To shouts of "Tell it, doctor!" and "Amen!" the minister put aside his text and concluded in a flourish of democratic exaltation and religious exultation:

I have a dream that one day this nation will rise up and live out the true meaning of its creed: "We hold these truths to be self-evident—that all men are created equal." I have a dream that one day on the red hills of Georgia the sons of former slaves and the sons of former slaveowners will be able to sit down together at the table of brotherhood. I have a dream that one day even the state of Mississippi, a desert state sweltering with the heat of injustice and oppression, will be transformed into an oasis of freedom and justice. I have a dream that my four little children will one day live in a nation where they will not be judged by the color of their skin but by the content of their character.

I have a dream today. . . .

When we let freedom ring, when we let it ring from every village and every hamlet, from every state and every city, we will be able to speed up that day when all of God's children, black men and white men, Jews and Gentiles, Protestants and Catholics, will be able to join hands and sing in the words of the old Negro spiritual, "Free at last! Free at last! Thank God almighty, we are free at last!"[125]

Weary with emotion, King stepped down from the podium and into the embrace of his friend Ralph Abernathy, who exclaimed that the Holy Spirit had surely taken hold of King as he spoke. And in the faces of a quarter million black and white listeners, now suddenly released in shouts of praise and elation, King could glimpse his ideal of interracial brotherhood come to thundering, joyful life. James Baldwin, who had often written in withering counterpoint to King's politics of faith, was among the cheering throng. Later he confessed the power and rapture of the minister's vision: "That day, for a moment, it almost seemed that we stood on a height, and could see our inheritance; perhaps we could make the kingdom real, perhaps the beloved community would not forever remain that dream one dreamed in agony."[126]

The vision seemed closer still because of the march's impact on the President. Up until the march date he had been ambivalent about the rally. He had endorsed its objectives at a press conference in July, calling it "a peaceful assembly calling for the redress of grievances . . . in the great tradition."[127] But Kennedy remained wary of possible violence that could discredit the movement; and he declined to speak at the march for fear that if he could not fully meet its demands it might turn into a protest against his administration. Afterward, though, a relieved President publicly lauded "the deep fervor and the quiet dignity that characterizes the thousands who have gathered in the Nation's Capital from across the country to demonstrate their faith and confidence in our democratic form of government."[128] He also invited ten of the main organizers, including John Lewis, to a reception in the White House, offering them warm encouragement and hot coffee. By such symbolic acts he blurred yet again the lines between the movement and the White House.

Negro pride in engineering the greatest peacetime assembly in American history was tempered by worry that even this might not be enough. After the march Bayard Rustin met Malcolm X a third time and saw the Muslim minister's earlier affability give way, not to his usual sly mockery but to foreboding. "You know," Malcolm confided to Rustin across their long political divide, "this dream of King's is going to be a nightmare before it's over." His manner struck Rustin as uncommonly grim, as if he sensed that there would be a hard period ahead. Rustin answered, "You're probably right."[129]

Crucial challenges still faced the movement. The March on Washington had powerfully confirmed the serious and responsible intent of civil rights supporters; but even liberal congressmen like Senator Hubert Humphrey of Minnesota doubted that the rally had changed many votes in Congress. Meanwhile Southern congressmen were punitively tying up even routine appropriations bills while vowing an endless filibuster against the pending civil rights legislation. More ominous was a surge of extremist violence. The following September a bomb exploded in Birmingham's famous Sixteenth Street Baptist Church, killing four black girls. No city official cared—or dared—to attend the funeral service for the victims.

The President spoke out strongly against the unreasoning acts of violence, but increasingly he found himself a target of hatred because of his support for civil rights. In mid-fall a poll showed that four and a half million white Southerners had become disaffected with Kennedy's leadership, a figure that far exceeded the number of new black voters he could hope to gain in 1964.[130] The widespread loathing of Kennedy among those Southerners was captured by the complaint of a North Carolina housewife: "He's stirred up all the colored people to get their vote. It's terrible; he encouraged them to break state laws."[131] The Republican right-wing senator Barry Goldwater, a likely presidential nominee in 1964, was the chief beneficiary of this reactionary ground swell. Throughout the South signs sprang up, "Kennedy for King—Goldwater for President," in a bitter play on Kennedy's support for the SCLC minister.[132]

Kennedy was nonetheless determined to ride out the South's spasms of fury and to encourage white moderates in their efforts to draw the region away from racial extremism. The nation's rapid economic upsurge, particularly evident in the South, provided a basis for optimism. In September 1963 the pollster Louis Harris encouraged Kennedy, "You can well go into the South throughout 1964 not to lay down the gauntlet on civil rights, but rather to describe and encourage the new industrial and educational explosion in the region."[133] The President foreshadowed this strategy with a trip in October to Arkansas, where he appealed to the pride of a region too long "distorted by headlines and headline-seekers." The President also referred to the dams and reservoirs in the region, many funded with federal aid, that "symbolize the new South, for they mean navigation for your commerce, protection for your cities, opportunity for your people." The *Arkansas Gazette* concluded from the warm reception for the speech that the Republicans might be "counting prematurely in adding up all those electoral votes for 1964 from a Solid Republican South."[134]

By late fall signs of progress increasingly broke through the pall of racist violence and invective. Nearly 40 percent of all Southern and border-state communities of over ten thousand people had desegregated at least some public facilities. In Congress, Kennedy's search for a reform consensus took a major step forward on October 29 when the House Judiciary Committee favorably reported by a comfortable margin a bipartisan civil rights measure. The wide-ranging bill included provisions that prohibited discrimination in public facilities or employment and strengthened guarantees of black voting rights. Some of the bill's language had been trimmed to win over moderates whose votes would be crucial for House passage; still, it remained the most sweeping civil rights measure since Reconstruction.

At his last press conference before a campaign stop in the Deep South stronghold of Dallas, Kennedy looked past immediate barriers to a future of bold reforms. Before Congress adjourned, the President predicted, it would pass his civil rights bill together with measures on education, mental health, and taxes. "However dark it looks now," he said, "I think that 'westward, look, the land is bright,' " and he added, "By next summer it may be."[135] Civil rights leaders concurred that the future had never looked brighter, as Kennedy moved in the twilight of his presidency to stake his deepest claim to leadership "for the freedom of man." It seemed then to many blacks and whites who marched for the dream of freedom that the New Frontier was, after all, filled with endless possibility.

Chapter 4

The Great Society

"Let Us Continue"

MARTIN LUTHER KING, JR., and his family sat by their television set on November 22, 1963, "hoping and praying that John Kennedy would not die." Coretta King remembered their vigil:

We felt that President Kennedy had been a friend of the Cause and that with him as President we could continue to move forward. We watched and prayed for him. Then it was announced that the President was dead. Martin had been very quiet during this period. Finally he said, "This is what is going to happen to me also."

As they watched the funeral, their six-year-old son Marty tried to grasp the nature of their loss. "Daddy, President Kennedy was your best friend, wasn't he, Daddy?" Coretta agreed: "In a way, he was."[1]

Black Americans sharing the national trauma over Kennedy's murder felt a special apprehension. He had made their struggle his own; but now its promise flickered with the passing of its most powerful advocate. In parts of the Deep South news of the President's death met with boisterous approval because of his support for civil rights. Cheers and applause in some public schools greeted announcements of the shooting. Without Kennedy to oppose the rising tide of racial hatred, would Congress dare pass intact the civil rights measures he had proposed?

A fog of doubt settled on Kennedy's successor, Lyndon Johnson—shrewd son of the South and longtime obstructor of civil rights legislation, a born-again civil rights convert of suspect motives and fervor. Skeptics found little in Johnson's record to nourish optimism. Though in the thirties he had stood out as a federal administrator in Texas by treating Negroes and whites equally, Johnson early moved his career upward with an adroit turn to the right, voting against six civil rights bills in Congress. Even when he shepherded to passage the Civil Rights Act of 1957, critics noted that he had compromised away the few strong provisions for enforcement. Johnson later excused his uninspiring civil rights record by reasoning, "One heroic stand and I'd be back home, defeated, unable to do any good for anyone, much less the blacks and the underprivileged."[2] But Johnson's view that he had struck a subtle blow for Negro rights by ensuring his own political survival held little appeal in civil rights circles. In 1960 he was the one candidate for the Democratic nomination unacceptable to most blacks, and his presence on the ticket strained their loyalties to the party of Franklin Roosevelt. As Vice-President, Johnson softened this criticism by effectively chairing Kennedy's subcabinet on equal employment and strongly advocating the President's civil rights bill. Still, in the gloom of November 1963, blacks worried that the torch of racial justice had passed to someone less eager to carry it proudly forward than to dampen the fire in some back-room caucus.

Johnson's critics reckoned without his ability to change with the fast-moving events of the era. Keenly aware that black protest had altered the nation's political agenda, he also grasped that Kennedy's presidency—and his martyrdom—had made civil rights an issue no successor could safely defuse. Black protest had also affected Johnson personally, as he came to recognize that he and his fellow Southerners had deluded themselves into believing that the black people around them were "happy and satisfied."[3] The presidency, with its moral authority and an equal moral burden, seemed to liberate Johnson from the easy fatalism that he could do little to change race relations. "In that house of decision," Johnson found, ". . . a man becomes his commitments."[4] In the first, difficult days of his presidency, Lyndon Johnson's commitments made him the nation's foremost champion of civil rights reform.

On November 27, having scarcely settled into the Oval Office, the new President addressed an assembly of congressmen and Supreme Court judges to tell them, along with a grieving nation, that Kennedy's legacy still lived and that Lyndon Johnson was unquestionably in charge of it. "Let us continue," Johnson said, sounding the theme of his young administration, promising that "the ideas and the ideals which [Kennedy] so nobly represented must and will be translated into effective action."[5]

Johnson's new zeal for civil rights remolded his approach to the legislative process itself. While Kennedy was President, Johnson had shared the administration's view that the civil rights bill might have to be pared considerably as it approached its final form. In particular the provisions guaranteeing equal access to public accommodations and equal employment opportunity appeared headed for radical surgery in the familiar committee operations headed by Southern senators. As President, however, Johnson resolved against any compromise that could weaken the civil rights bill. "I had seen this 'moderating' process at work for many years," Johnson later wrote in his memoirs, modestly omitting that he had been the Senate's most unstinting moderator. ". . . I had seen it happen in 1960 [with passage of a weakened voting rights bill]. I did not want to see it happen again."[6]

Johnson's insistence on a bill untainted by compromise appeared to depart from his long reliance on consensus politics but not from a still more deep-seated resolve to master new political realities. Johnson privately recognized that his poor standing with many civil rights supporters demanded an all-or-nothing strategy on the pending legislation. "I knew," he later confided, "that if I didn't get out in front on this issue, they [the liberals] would get me. They'd throw up my background against me, they'd use it to prove that I was incapable of bringing unity to the land I loved so much. . . . I couldn't let that happen. I had to produce a civil rights bill that was even stronger than the one they'd have gotten if Kennedy had lived." "Without this," he added in a blunt postscript on the political stakes, "I'd be dead before I could even begin."[7]

Two days after he asked Congress for rapid action on civil rights, Johnson summoned Roy Wilkins for a private strategy summit. The meeting afforded Wilkins a dose of "the Johnson treatment," a potent brew of flattery, cajolery, sound reason, and sheer physical presence. As Wilkins sat down, a very somber President brought his chair to within a few inches of his visitor's knees. Wilkins "felt those mesmerizing eyes of Texas" on him as Johnson—dominating the conversation—discussed the future of the civil rights bill. He explained that he would insist on enacting a strong bill, which would require every possible Senate vote to defeat the inevitable Southern filibuster. Therefore he needed Wilkins and other civil rights leaders to lobby relentlessly for the bill. "When are you going to get down here and start civil-righting?" he demanded.[8] The President encouraged Wilkins to tell Senate Minority Leader Everett Dirksen and the entire Republican party that black leaders would support the presidential candidate most committed to equality and would go "with a senatorial man who does the same thing."[9] Toward the end of their talk the President leaned forward, poked his finger at the civil rights leader, and said quietly, "I want that bill *passed.*"[10]

Wilkins left that meeting "struck by the enormous difference between Kennedy and Johnson." Kennedy had been sound on matters of principle, Wilkins concluded, but "for all his talk about the art of the possible, he didn't really know what was possible and what wasn't in Congress." By contrast Johnson understood the Congress better than virtually anyone else alive and therefore was much more willing and able to take the measure of the Southern bloc. Johnson "knew exactly what was possible," and he was going to press for the last vote to get it.[11]

Through the early months of 1964 the President took his message of no compromise on civil rights to press conferences, Cabinet meetings, Congress, and other sites no matter how unlikely, including the New York World's Fair. He also held a difficult private talk with his former mentor and patron in the Senate, Richard Russell of Georgia, who had directed successful filibusters against numerous other civil rights measures. In a conversation marked by mutual respect and regret rather than anger, Johnson expressed his hope for a future in which Southerners would no longer stand against the rest of the nation. The two also sounded a common message: there would be no retreat in the battle over the civil rights bill. It would either pass with all provisions intact, or die in yet another Southern filibuster. Johnson later wrote that the situation led him to consider some sound advice by a fellow Texan: "John Nance Garner, a great legislative tactician, as well as a good poker player, once told me that there comes a time in every leader's career when he has to put in all his stack. I decided to shove in all my stack on this vital measure."[12]

Johnson then instructed the lobbyists Clarence Mitchell of the NAACP and Joseph Rauh of Americans for Democratic Action,

You tell [Senate Majority Leader] Mike Mansfield to put that bill on the floor, and tell everybody that it's going to stay there until it passes. I don't care if it stays for four, six, or eight months. You can tell Mike Mansfield, and you can tell anybody else, that the President of the United States doesn't care if that bill is there forever. We are not going to have the Senate do anything else until that bill is passed. And it is *going* to pass.[13]

Mansfield took this Johnson-size hint on congressional strategy. The majority leader managed to bypass the Senate Judiciary Committee of Mississippi's senator Eastland, who had once pledged to "protect and maintain white supremacy throughout eternity."[14] Mansfield placed the civil rights bill directly on the Senate calendar, and Southerners hastened to the deadly earnest business of consuming the Senate's time. At first Senator Richard Russell of Georgia brought a refined touch to the filibustering, as the historian Eric Goldman noted, "by entangling the Senate in a dizzying debate over whether a motion to debate the bill was debatable." In March 1964 these convoluted minuets gave way to a total war of delay that spared no subject of human knowledge, or ignorance:

Senator Russell had a band of eighteen Southern senators whom he deployed in three platoons of six each, a fresh platoon each day. They talked on and on—about the "amalgamation and mongrelization of the races," the source of the grits that people in Minnesota eat, the living habits of Hungarian immigrants, sometimes about the bill itself, calling it, to use the phrase of Senator Russell Long, "a mixed breed of unconstitutionality and the NAACP."[15]

While the Senate spun its webs of arcane oratory, the House of Representatives moved forward on the civil rights bill at a far more rapid clip. In late January a bipartisan committee defeated over one hundred crippling amendments, accepted thirty-four relatively trivial ones, and sent the bill to the floor. It was a formidable measure that strengthened voting rights, banned discrimination in public facilities and in employment, empowered the attorney general to begin suits against school segregation, and authorized the withholding of federal funds from noncomplying schools. Southern Democrats continued to rain weakening amendments on the House floor but secured only one substantial change. This amendment was considered so radical, however, as to imperil passage of the entire bill.

"Judge" Howard Smith of Virginia facetiously offered a "perfecting" amendment that would bar employment discrimination against all women as well as Negroes. He commiserated with women, who, outnumbering men by two million, already were at a disadvantage in seeking spouses. At least, he implied, they should get jobs with equal pay. To many liberal defenders of the civil rights bill this amendment was as preposterous as the lighthearted Virginia gallantry accompanying it. Seventy-five-year-old Emanuel Celler of

Brooklyn, floor manager for the bill, shouted his indignation: "I rise in opposition to the amendment!" "Oh, no!" Smith replied with mock gravity, enjoying the turnaround in liberal sensibilities. Celler went on to censure Smith for upsetting the traditional roles of the sexes and overlooking their "biological differences," while spectators snickered throughout.[16] Judge Smith had succeeded in wreaking havoc with traditional partisan lines by raising the ante for compulsory tolerance past the point many liberals could abide.

The feminist vanguard in Congress divided over the amendment. The Michigan Democrat Martha W. Griffths observed that without the protection of this amendment the civil rights bill would leave white women "at the bottom of the list in hiring," after white men and Negro men and women. She added, "It would be incredible to me that white men would be willing to place white women at such a disadvantage." But another white congresswoman was willing, or at least resigned, to take that risk. Edith Green of Oregon, who had fought for years to guarantee women equal pay for equal work, admitted she might now be called "an Uncle Tom, or maybe an Aunt Jane," but she refused to let one provision jeopardize the whole civil rights bill.[17] Despite her plea, enough liberal representatives—including five of six women—joined with opponents of the civil rights bill to pass the amendment, 168 to 133. But Southern Democrats rejoiced only briefly, for the issue quickly receded for most congressmen into the realm of a minor curiosity. A midwestern Republican who opposed the bill thought that the wily Judge Smith had "outsmarted himself. At this point there was no way you could sink the bill."[18]

Through it all Lyndon Johnson remained in the background, but even at a distance his profile was unmistakable. When the House passed the bill on February 10, by an emphatic 290-to-130 vote, Clarence Mitchell and Joseph Rauh celebrated by trading high-spirited tales of their lobbying feats, until the House corridor pay phone rang. It was Lyndon Johnson, offering terse congratulations: "All right, you fellows. Get over to the Senate. Get busy. We've won in the House, but there is a big job across the way."[19]

Passage of the bill now rested on the ability of civil rights forces to end debate in the Senate. Here the work of a fifteen-year-old federation, the Leadership Conference on Civil Rights, enabled over a hundred lobbying groups to coordinate as precisely as Senator Russell's disciplined delaying band. The rapid growth of this federation during the fifties and early sixties testified to a developing national consensus on civil rights issues. Its founder, Arnold Aronson, an official in the Jewish community, worked closely with leaders in the NAACP, Americans for Democratic Action, the AFL-CIO, the National Council of Churches, and a rapidly expanding list of other groups. Aronson's organization served as a clearinghouse for civil rights supporters to suggest lobbying strategies and ratify a common course. The Leadership Conference could act effectively because beneath the diverse characters of member groups lay a unifying outlook. Their guiding premise was that Negroes deserved full protection of the law and that no political, economic, or moral ground could justify their continued exclusion from society.

An unusual lobbying strategy soon emerged from the Leadership Conference. It was to rely on the churches not only to keep the moral issue in view but also to sway lawmakers in central, southwestern, and far western states where labor unions and blacks wielded little political clout. Clergymen responded with unprecedented enthusiasm for a purely political issue. They met regularly with congressmen and pressed community leaders to do so as well. The issue became for many a test of religious sincerity, eclipsing the routine of church life and drawing many out of a cloistered existence. "This was the first time," marveled James Hamilton of the National Council of Churches, "that I ever recalled seeing Catholic nuns away from the convents for more than a few days."[20] On April 19 the church pressure increased when trios of Protestant, Catholic, and Jewish seminarians staged a prayer vigil at the Lincoln Memorial. It continued around the clock throughout the Senate debate. The seemingly ubiquitous presence of clergymen in and around the Senate building nonplussed Southern legislators; it was difficult enough for them to ward off Lyndon Johnson and the rising force of public opinion without finding themselves unexpectedly ranged against the Almighty.

The administration directed many of its own prayers to the one man who could obtain the votes necessary for cloture, a measure to limit each senator's speaking time on a bill to one hour. Senate Minority Leader Everett Dirksen was a complex partisan whose theatricality, shrewdness, cynicism, and patriotism all were refracted through a powerful ego of unpredictable bent. Dirksen had previously opposed all civil rights legislation. Yet, like Johnson, he recognized that black activism and social turmoil were changing the political picture rapidly. Johnson and his aides appealed to Dirksen's desire to move on the side of history. They also sought to enlist his ego in their cause by encouraging him to stamp the legislative process with several minor amendments. Senator Hubert Humphrey, floor manager for the bill, recalled, "I courted Dirksen almost as persistently as I did [my wife] Muriel."[21] On June 10 Senator Humphrey's persistence once more paid off. Dirksen declared in the Senate chamber that America was changing and growing and that "on the civil rights issue we must rise with the occasion."[22] He then announced his support for cloture. Several days later, with every senator present, the cloture motion passed by 71 to 29, four more affirmative votes than the needed two-thirds. With that the real legislative battle ended. Three weeks later Congress easily passed the Civil Rights Act of 1964, every major provision intact, as Johnson had predicted and demanded.

Feelings remained raw on both sides of the long congressional struggle. A week after President Johnson signed the bill into law on July 2, 1964, South Carolina's senator Strom Thurmond boycotted a subcommittee meeting to implement a section of the act. The Texas liberal Ralph Yarborough tired of these delaying maneuvers and yanked Thurmond by the arm in an attempt to drag his uncooperative colleague inside the committee room. Soon both men were removing their jackets for more strenuous debate. Spotting Yarborough thirty pounds, Thurmond twice managed to pin his distinguished opponent before other legislators could step in to arrange a compromise settlement.[23] Not since 1856, when a melee followed the caning of a Northern senator who insulted a Southern colleague, had congressmen grappled over the issues in quite this way.

It was the magisterial Richard Russell, however, rather than Yarborough or Thurmond, who set the tone for Southern reaction to the act. In a statement carrying the finality and dignity of Robert E. Lee's call for the South to accept the verdict of history, Russell wrote to his constituents, "It is the law of the Senate and we must abide by it." He urged Georgians "to refrain from violence in dealing with this act."[24]

Russell's statesmanlike reaction came the more easily because he understood how strong national sentiment was in favor of this legislation. Roy Wilkins recalled that Senator Russell said a bit gloomily after his legislative defeat that every time he looked up he seemed to be faced with someone from the AFL-CIO, the women's groups, fraternal or civic organizations, or a minister.[25] Also, by permitting a lengthy floor fight, the administration had enabled Southerners to realize that their senators had been defeated fairly. That, Russell told Clarence Mitchell just after the deciding vote, would help make the civil rights law enforceable.[26] Russell left unspoken one final, crucial factor in the acceptance of this law—the President's decision to use the full powers of his office to achieve a powerful, and popular, measure. While Senator Dirksen rightly termed the bill "an idea whose time has come,"[27] Lyndon Johnson's masterful support had surely hastened its safe arrival.

Freedom Summer

During the 1964 drive to enact civil rights legislation, SNCC youths remained in the vanguard of black activism with a project more suited to their temperament and experience: political organizing of Negroes in rural Mississippi. The project risked unprecedented racial violence in a state whose history was pockmarked with the casual shootings of black people. It exposed, too, a subtler but still serious peril to the civil rights movement, as it thrust beyond the bounds of Johnson's political consensus.

Mississippi had always etched its racial lines with a vigor unmatched throughout the Deep South. As a late-booming slave state it had discarded even the trappings of white paternalism in order to regiment Negroes into efficient labor gangs. Although the status of blacks briefly rose during Reconstruction, a period of unrestrained white terrorism soon restored the old ways. In 1890 white lawmakers completed the eradication of black citizenship, rewriting Mississippi's constitution with the express purpose of disenfranchising Negroes. With this act they blazed a path back into the antebellum past that other Southern states eagerly followed.

Through the mid-twentieth century the civil rights movement scarcely challenged Mississippi's caste system, which concentrated wealth and power among a few white families. Oligarchs like Senator James Eastland still controlled vast cotton tracts on which black 'croppers labored "from kin to kain't," or sunrise to sunset, for perhaps fifty cents a day. While Negroes in other Southern states stirred with news of *Brown* and the successful bus boycott in Montgomery, race relations in Mississippi continued much as if the War Between the States had ended at Bull Run rather than Appomattox.

There were always isolated Negroes who were prepared to pay the high cost of first-class citizenship in Mississippi. In 1954 a young man named Medgar Evers became field secretary of the state NAACP, despite his wife's imploring lectures on the importance of staying alive and raising a family. As a college student Evers had taken as a role model Jomo Kenyatta, who became Kenya's first president after helping end white control. (Medgar's oldest son was christened Darrell Kenyatta, and the "Darrell" was hastily slipped onto the birth certificate by Mrs. Evers, who knew that a Negro would find Mississippi lively enough without his bearing the name of Africa's foremost revolutionary.) But Evers turned from thoughts of violent rebellion as he realized, "Not even the southern bigot has much ground to stand on when he tries to rabble rouse about our winning court decisions. But give him a little Negro violence to point to, and he will have a good selling point for stirring up race hatred."[28]

Evers also carried, like many Southern Negroes, an attachment to his native region that oppression seemed only to sharpen. Mississippi, he said proudly, was not just his place of birth: "The state is beautiful, it is home." And as race relations improved, the land could offer a good life to all its inhabitants:

> You know, it may sound funny, but I love the South. I don't choose to live anywhere else. There's land here, where a man can raise cattle, and I'm going to do that some day. There are lakes where a man can sink a hook and fight the bass. There is room here for my children to play, and grow, and become good citizens—if the white man will let them.[29]

In that hope Evers and a handful of other blacks brought the civil rights movement to Mississippi's insular world.

The South's most conservative state also proved to be its most violent. A surge of racial assaults following the *Brown* decision culminated in the lynching, in August 1955, of fourteen-year-old Emmett Till, a Chicago-born youth who was visiting relatives in the Delta. For whistling at a white woman in a grocery store, Till was beaten, shot to death, mutilated, and thrown in the Tallahatchie River. Two indictments quickly followed, but the intensive national media coverage of the Till murder trial stirred local whites to forge a defiant solidarity with the accused. Both defendants were acquitted despite clear evidence of their guilt, after a defense attorney exhorted the twelve white, male jurors, "I am sure that every last Anglo-Saxon one of you has the courage to free these men. . . ."[30]

For black Mississippians who sought to exercise their political rights, the peril from white violence increased many fold. In 1955, while national attention focused on the Emmett Till case, a Negro who tried to register to vote in Brookhaven, Mississippi, was shot on the courthouse steps. That same year economic intimidation against four hundred Negro registrants in Belzoni led all but three to withdraw their names. The Reverend George Lee kept his signature on the voting lists and soon afterward was gunned down at point-blank range. Asked about the pellets found in the late Reverend Lee's mouth, the local sheriff guessed, "Maybe they're fillings from his teeth."[31] Lee's fellow organizer Gus Courts ignored death threats, a tripling of rent on his grocery store, and denial of credit by white merchants, in order to keep his name on the voting rolls. Then he, too, fell from a shotgun blast, barely survived, and left the state. A final holdout, the Reverend Lee's widow, still refused to withdraw her name, but according to one of Mississippi's three black civil rights lawyers she "wouldn't take that long march through the valley of death to the polling place."[32]

Medgar Evers himself became, at thirty-five, the youngest person on a nine-man death list circulated by white extremists.[33] He continued to recruit NAACP members by day while spending extra waking hours at night curled beside a rifle. But though Negroes admired Evers as an inspirational figure, few were as steeled for the dangers of white retaliation. After years of organizing, Evers reported "an apparent decline in the activities of many of our branches." "Violence and police brutality," he said, "still have the upper hand in Mississippi, inasmuch as many of the victims are afraid to speak out because of threats upon their lives or fear of economic reprisals. . . ."[34]

SNCC workers ventured into this unpromising situation in 1961 at the initiative of a shy former high school teacher named Bob Moses. In quieter times this graduate student at Harvard University had spent his days reading Camus and pondering philosophical paradoxes. But with the rise of black protest, Moses had become SNCC's own greatest paradox, a soft-spoken, modest man, whose pursuit of ideals rather than influence led other SNCC staffers to seek his leadership. Moses was never known to tackle a merely difficult task when a more daunting one was available. As a first-year volunteer he pointed out to fellow SNCC members that most civil rights groups based their Southern headquarters in relatively cosmopolitan Atlanta and competed for recruits in urban areas. SNCC could therefore help the movement more by working with rural blacks in places where the NAACP, CORE, and the SCLC had not established themselves. In an organization where daring to the point of recklessness was widely viewed as a sign of grace, the idea won approval, and with a small staff, Moses went into the wilderness of McComb, Mississippi.

Self-styled the Camelia City because of its profusion of delicate roselike blossoms, McComb was also the most violent city in Mississippi. Shortly after Moses arrived, a state legislator, E. H. Hurst, shot a black man to death in broad daylight for disobeying a warning not to register to vote. A coroner's jury acquitted Hurst, ruling his act justifiable homicide. One Negro who witnessed the murder did not get off as easily. When an FBI agent tipped off local police that Louis Allen was ready to testify against Hurst, Allen was beaten and placed under surveillance. Three days before he planned to leave McComb, Allen was found shot to death.[35]

In late 1961, as SNCC operations in Mississippi withered under continued violent harassment, the Kennedy administration offered all civil rights groups unexpected aid. Robert Kennedy implied that if they turned their efforts to voter registration he would help by securing funds from liberal philanthropies like the Taconic Foundation and by giving the project tax-exempt status. Some SNCC workers objected that behind this show of federal friendship lay an effort to manipulate the movement, diverting it from direct action to quieter tasks that would raise vote totals for the Democrats in 1964. But SNCC was desperate for financial assistance, wider recognition, and help with its foundering work in Mississippi. The administration's offer also coincided with calls by the SCLC and SNCC for massive Negro registration. By April 1962 SNCC and other civil rights groups formally launched the Voter Education Project, whose founding charter cited John Kennedy's inaugural address on the need to defend liberty at any cost.

The bulk of project funds poured into Mississippi, where SNCC, CORE, and the NAACP formed an uneasy common front. The Council of Federated Organizations, or COFO, allotted funds and enough titles to mollify all member organizations. Bob Moses became project director; Dave Dennis of CORE became the assistant project director; and the state NAACP president Aaron Henry, who reluctantly withdrew his objections to a joint project, became COFO's president. SNCC provided most of the staff workers, in an effort to exploit its new line to the White House. But a dreary sense of reality set in early. Despite their high expectations of the federal government, SNCC and CORE workers received no protection against local whites, only regrets from Attorney General Kennedy that sustained intervention in the South was simply not feasible.[36]

The Voter Registration Project would register over half a million Southern Negroes by 1964. Yet these gains occurred largely in urban areas and in states where Negroes could already vote with relatively little fear of death. The project showed scant gains in Mississippi, where in two years it added fewer than 4,000 names to the voting rolls and left some 394,000 black adults unregistered. Police frequently arrested SNCC workers and vied with private citizens in administering beatings. Sometimes angry whites went further. In February 1963 Moses and two other organizers were riding a dark road in Greenwood, Mississippi, when thirteen .45-caliber bullets tore through the car, shattering the left window and wounding the driver in the neck. Moses was unharmed if not unscarred by the attempted murder, but the incident reminded SNCC workers yet again that in Mississippi they were outlaws, enjoying no security save that afforded by their own caution.

Still, the work of community organization continued, with SNCC youths pouring into the state in 1963, in defiance of further shootings. They were joined by eighty students from Stanford and Yale, mostly white, organized by

the liberal activist Allard Lowenstein. These volunteers also carried the blessings of Bob Moses, who hoped that the presence of affluent young whites would
focus an intimidating national spotlight on local sheriffs. By October 1963 their
efforts resulted in a rare show of political assertiveness by Mississippi's blacks.
In dozens of cities and towns some eighty thousand Negroes voted for slates of
"Freedom party" delegates in alternate elections to the state Democratic primaries. The votes were never tallied by the party's Jim Crow electoral boards;
but they showed that Mississippi's blacks did care about the ballot, despite
carefully nurtured myths to the contrary. The outpouring of black voters also
led Bob Moses to wonder what a much larger organizing effort in Mississippi
could achieve.

Moses planned a "freedom summer" project for 1964, in which hundreds
of student volunteers would move into every black neighborhood in Mississippi to encourage registration and support for candidates of the "Freedom
party." Black activists already in Mississippi initially balked at the prospect of
white volunteers joining them. Some argued that the presence of an interracial
team would simply antagonize authorities and impede efforts to gain the confidence of local blacks. There was another, widely shared fear among black
activists—that educated white students would so thoroughly assume leadership roles as to undermine their own self-confidence. Resentments still festered
over Lowenstein's skilled but abrasive direction of the registration effort in
1963. But Bob Moses refused to be part of an all-black project. Integration, he
explained, was at the heart of the Beloved Community ideal, which had impelled him and others to nonviolent sacrifice. His counsel helped ensure that
the freedom summer would continue SNCC's interracial traditions.[37]

Not knowing who among the Mississippi workers might be a plant by the
FBI or the press, Moses did not explain another, more calculated motive in his
decision to welcome white volunteers. Privately he and the CORE veteran
Dave Dennis had decided that only if whites shared the risks of violence would
civil rights workers gain federal protection and a national hearing. Dennis later
acknowledged, "We made sure that we had the children . . . of some very
powerful people in this country over there, including Jerry Brown," son of the
governor of California. He reasoned that if volunteers were going to be murdered, the "death of a white college student would bring on more attention to
what was going on than for a black college student getting it. That's cold, but
that was also in another sense speaking the language of this country."[38] By the
spring of 1964 Moses and Dennis were directing invitations to hundreds of
predominantly white colleges to help the cause of freedom in Mississippi.

Applications deluged the COFO offices. Of the nine hundred volunteers
accepted in this freedom army the great majority were white. Typically they
were Ivy League students affluent enough to forgo a summer's employment
and pay their way to Mississippi, idealistic enough to forgo a sheltered suburban life in order to work for social change. They often cited concern with a
broad range of issues, including poverty and the country's growing involvement in Vietnam, but they believed that volunteer work in Mississippi afforded

the best practical channel for their reform commitments. The spirit of service that had led thousands of young people to enter the Peace Corps infused their ranks.[39]

Just how great a contribution a white Northerner could make to a Southern black movement was problematic, and volunteers accepted their limitations with self-conscious diffidence. "The movement is really one of chastened idealism," explained Barney Frank, a doctoral candidate in political science at Harvard. "We're not really making a one hundred percent commitment to what is a very tough fight that lasts the year around."[40] A tall, intense senior at the University of Michigan, Sam Walker, touched on the image of liberals as more inclined toward token gestures than deep commitment to change—an image that sobered the students while it impelled them to volunteer:

> As to why we're going down, if anyone gave a simple answer, I'd be suspicious. Part of it is the American dream, you know, and part is shame. I feel a very real sense of guilt. But I hope I'm not going down there to get my little red badge of liberalism, to be able to go back home and tell everyone how I spent two days in the Jackson jail.[41]

At least, one student wryly observed, the volunteers could serve as "cannon fodder" to swell the ranks of the civil rights movement.[42]

The freedom summer project revived the youthful idealism that had propelled the sit-in campaigns, but like the sit-ins it highlighted tensions within the movement. Established civil rights groups believed that SNCC's focus on Mississippi was folly. The NAACP had branches in the state but few were active. The SCLC placed the bulk of its resources in Alabama and Georgia, very deliberately treating Mississippi as beyond imminent redemption. King's trusted aide Andy Young once told SNCC members that Mississippi was simply too brutal for them to make any headway there. "We tried to warn SNCC," Young recalled, but for these exuberant youths a warning was not easily distinguishable from an invitation.[43]

More serious than these family quarrels among black activists were the fault lines in the liberal coalition that the freedom summer project also uncovered. The young volunteers may have seen themselves as acting out the highest impulses of American reform, but to the father of the Great Society they were wayward, disruptive children who had to be disciplined. President Johnson feared that the Mississippi project could lead to violence and in turn threaten party unity at the Democratic convention in August. To quash the project in its planning stages the administration signalled prospective donors to reconsider promises of aid to SNCC.[44] That did not prevent wealthy whites from participating, but it severely curtailed black participation. Johnson further warned the planners that he could not provide protection for the volunteers. The price of disobedience was thus set high: the volunteers would enter Mississippi at peril to their lives.

Mississippi mobilized for the arrival of civil rights workers as if threatened by a foreign army. Governor Paul Johnson won legislative approval of an increase in the number of state highway patrolmen from 275 to 475. In Jackson the police force grew from 200 to 390 officers. Mayor Allen Thompson bought 250 shotguns and had them loaded with buckshot and mounted on squad cars and motorcycles. The mayor also readied his "Thompson tank," a six-ton armored vehicle complete with 12-gauge steel walls, bulletproof windows, and a submachine gun mounted on the turret. As a final precaution, the state enacted a "bill to restrain movements of individuals under certain circumstances," a euphemism for declaring martial law.[45]

Although danger deterred few students, it had quite a different effect on parents, as Stokely Carmichael and Cleveland Sellers learned while recruiting black youths for the summer project. They were chatting on a porch with Carol Martin and Doris Wilkerson, recent volunteers, when two middle-aged women sternly ordered the girls home—and out of the Mississippi project. "We're not going with you, Mother," Carol Martin said. Carmichael tried to mediate the ensuing vehement argument but reconsidered when warned away by one of the women. The mothers finally hailed a passing police car and told the officer that the girls were runaways. When the policeman learned that the girls were eighteen and could not be legally detained, the mothers called after their daughters, "If you don't come home with us tonight, don't come home at all. If you go to Mississippi with *these* people, you can consider yourself homeless!" The daughters cried throughout the night, but a week later they set out for Oxford, Ohio, to join the other volunteers in training for the rigors of this freedom summer.[46]

Students at orientation camp heard a series of speakers tell them that where they were going they would have no rights worth mentioning. R. Jess Brown, one of four lawyers in the state of Mississippi who would accept civil rights workers as clients, pointed to his young audience and gave them his best legal counsel: "If you're riding down somewhere and a cop stops you and starts to put you under arrest even though you haven't committed any crime—go on to jail." He added with a smile, "Mississippi is not the place to start conducting Constitutional law classes for policemen, many of whom don't have a fifth-grade education." The students broke out laughing, though it seemed to another black attorney there, Len Holt, "the kind one blurts out when the real reaction is to cry." Another orientation leader talked about the likelihood of violence: "There's not even a sharp line between living and dying; it is just a thin fuzz." Jim Forman put it most simply: "I may be killed and you may be killed." Len Holt appraised the orientation as reasonably successful: when the students arrived in Oxford, they "were merely scared," but by the time they packed their belongings for the trip to Mississippi "they were terrified."[47]

Perhaps the single greatest shock at Oxford came from a federal spokesman, John Doar, who had hoped simply to list the achievements of Presidents Kennedy and Johnson in race relations. But when Doar briefly warned that the FBI could serve only as an investigative agency, a spectacled black man in overalls screamed, "What are you going to do to enable us to see the fall?" "Nothing," Doar replied, and elaborated logically, "There is no federal police force. The responsibility for protection is that of the local police. We can only investigate." Students shouted in protest at this seeming abdication of concern for their lives. In the privacy of their rooms, many cried.[48]

On June 21, as carloads of volunteers arrived in Mississippi, they learned that a Negro church in the town of Philadelphia had just been set on fire, one more attempt to break the morale of local blacks before the summer project could take root. Two workers from COFO's Meridian office, Michael Schwerner and James Chaney, joined by the summer volunteer Andrew Goodman, immediately set out for Philadelphia. They traveled through thirty-five miles of swamp, scrub pine, and scraggly cotton land, bristling with indignant white onlookers, to reassure Negroes that COFO would aid them regardless of harassment.

The stocky, goateed Michael Schwerner came to this unenviable mission as one of few white volunteers familiar with the terrain and the terror. Six months earlier the twenty-four-year-old social worker had left a settlement house on Manhattan's Lower East Side to organize Meridian Negroes on behalf of CORE. All concerned received him coolly. Negroes were predictably wary and whites threatening. Meridian's only rabbi offered a private sermon that afforded little spiritual comfort. Whites in Mississippi were already labeling Schwerner "that goddamned bearded atheist communist Jew," the rabbi berated him. He went on to point Schwerner back north, explaining that the youth's impetuous actions were "not helping Negroes but hurting Jews."[49] Schwerner stayed. With his wife, Rita, he helped blacks build a community house that served as a pilot project for CORE's work in southwest Mississippi. The Meridian native James Chaney, at nineteen a high school dropout working as a plasterer's apprentice, joined Schwerner early on, despite limited family enthusiasm:

"Mama, I believe I done found an organization that I can be in and do something for myself and somebody else, too."
"Ain't you afraid of this?"
"Naw, mama, that's what's the matter now—everybody's scared."[50]

Now Chaney accompanied Schwerner to Philadelphia in order to quiet those fears in others. Twenty-year-old Andrew Goodman came from a background more typical of the volunteers, as a Queens College anthropology major from New York who had never before set foot in Mississippi. But as a worker assigned to Schwerner's task force at Oxford, Goodman demonstrated his maturity and courage to his colleagues. He was a welcome passenger on a lonely ride no one could be sure of completing.

Schwerner gave a coworker in Meridian his standard good-bye: "There's an immutable rule here: no-one is to remain in Neshoba [County] after four P.M. If for any reason we aren't back by four P.M., you should alert [the COFO office in] Jackson and begin checking every city jail, county jail, sheriff's office, police station and hospital between Meridian and Neshoba. O.K.?"[51] By 4:00 P.M. on June 21, volunteers were beginning their inquiries, to no avail. By the next morning veterans like Cleveland Sellers had assumed the worst: Schwerner, Chaney, and Goodman had become the first martyrs of the freedom summer.[52]

Fear and gloom pervaded the camps of volunteers waiting for word of the three missing workers. A young woman wrote to her parents that the news had an air of unreality about it: "They were in Oxford only a few days before—they couldn't already be in such danger." But suddenly the reality hit with the chilling image "that it could be you. And then there's this weird feeling of guilt because it wasn't you. . . ."[53]

The significance became even clearer when Lyndon Johnson once again signaled his annoyance at the summer project and his refusal to support it. The President sent a personal emissary to Mississippi in the wake of the Philadelphia disappearances, the former CIA director Allen Dulles, but his tone appalled Bob Moses, Dave Dennis, and the other heads of COFO. Dulles tersely informed them that he was about to meet with the governor and added, "We want this mess cleaned up." Aaron Henry of the NAACP stood up and said, "What do you mean?" Dulles explained that civil rights demonstrations were causing friction and that the administration would not allow this to continue even if it had to send troops. This may have been Johnson's oblique way of cautioning Mississippi authorities, who were likely to have bugged or infiltrated the civil rights meetings. If so, it did little to soothe COFO's leaders, who reacted in astonishment. Henry replied that Dulles was "talkin' to the wrong people," but Dulles seemed more interested in keeping Mississippi out of the news than in keeping civil rights workers out of harm.[54]

Weighed down by a sense of constant danger and abandonment by the federal government, the volunteers threw themselves into the work of canvassing local Negroes. This, too, had its pitfalls. Many blacks responded to their white visitors politely, deferentially, but with no intention of defying the local authorities by registering to vote. For volunteers who had expected an enthusiastic rush of sharecroppers to the nearest white-run registration office, the results were frustrating and at times embittering. Yet many realized, in the words of one volunteer writing home, that reluctance to register reflected "a highly rational emotion, the economic fear of losing your job, the physical fear of being shot at. Domestic servants know that they will be fired if they register to vote; so will factory workers, so will Negroes who live on plantations. In Mississippi, registration is no private affair. . . ."[55]

The presence of so many white volunteers compounded the difficulties in reaching local blacks. Negro sharecroppers who had known a lifetime of nearly absolute dependence on white landlords and servility toward white authorities typically looked upon the white volunteers with bemusement, suspicion, and more than a little fear. One white student from Harvard who had participated in the Albany movement and other campaigns thought that the "problem" of whiteness was not insurmountable, as some believed, but it was deep-rooted and could be crippling if not faced honestly and quickly. He cited the case of a "white college girl down in Terrell County for SNCC, with long hair, silver

Mrs. Rosa Parks, of
Montgomery, Alabama.
Flip Schulke

Sit-in at the Greensboro Woolworth's lunch counter, on the second day, February 2, 1960.
From left: Joseph McNeil, Franklin McCain (two of the original protesters), Billy Smith,
Clarence Henderson. *Greensboro News & Record Library*

Burning bus in Anniston, Alabama, during the first freedom ride, May 15, 1961. *AP/Wide World*

From left to right: the Reverend Martin Luther King, Jr., Dr. W. G. Anderson, leader of the Albany movement, and the Albany sheriff Laurie Pritchett, December 16, 1961. Pritchett tells the two ministers that they are under arrest for leading a protest march after they could not produce a permit to parade. *The Bettmann Archive*

Roy Wilkins (*left*) with James Meredith, 1962. *AP/Wide World*

Bull Connor, police commissioner of Birmingham, Alabama, addresses a White Citizens' Council meeting, 1963. *AP/Wide World*

Martin Luther King, Jr., jailed during the protests in Birmingham, Alabama, April 1963. *Flip Schulke/Rev. Wyatt T. Walker*

Governor George Wallace of Alabama reviews National Guard troops, 1963. *AP/Wide World*

Birmingham, Alabama,
May 3, 1963.
AP/Wide World

Hosing of demonstrators, Birmingham, Alabama, May 6, 1963. *Charles Moore/Black Star*

Robert F. Kennedy addressing civil rights demonstrators in Washington, D.C., 1963.
Capital Images

Bayard Rustin. *Leadership Conference on Civil Rights*

A. Philip Randolph, flanked by SNCC's John Lewis *(left)* and Norman Hill (Leadership Conference on Civil Rights). *Leadership Conference on Civil Rights*

The March on Washington, August 28, 1963. *AP/Wide World*

Martin Luther King, Jr., at the March on Washington. *AP/Wide World*

President Kennedy meets the leaders of the March on Washington. *From left:* Whitney Young, National Urban League; Dr. Martin Luther King, Southern Christian Leadership Conference; John Lewis, SNCC *(rear);* Rabbi Joachim Prinz, American Jewish Congress; Dr. Eugene C. Blake, National Council of Churches; A. Philip Randolph, AFL-CIO vice-president; Kennedy; Walter Reuther, United Auto Workers; Vice-President Lyndon Johnson *(rear);* and Roy Wilkins, NAACP. *AP/Wide World*

earrings, and sandals, bouncing confidently along a Georgia road to a share-cropper's shack, exhorting the awed and worried Negro who opened the door to register, and insisting that he call her by her first name."[56] Such conduct did less to promote reform than culture shock, and seemed to many blacks only marginally preferable to the predictable racism of local whites.

The volunteers persisted. Despite the reserve of local blacks and harass-ment by whites, the young workers began to see changes. Negroes came to registration classes and to adult literacy programs. There they learned to fill out the proper forms and to analyze the Mississippi constitution, a voting requirement whose unequal application had long served to disenfranchise blacks. The group sessions imbued participants with a hitherto unseen resolve to assert their right to the ballot. In McComb, which featured the state's highest incidence of racial violence, a volunteer observed the black commu-nity's determination:

The voter registration classes are slightly tense, but what is more present is hope, positiveness. The people dress up carefully. They shake each other's hands, await ea-gerly the return of those who have gone down to the courthouse already. Two func-tional illiterates have come, and so many others have so much trouble filling out the form. But they're going down. . . .[57]

The heart of the new political activism did not depend on registrars at all. On July 21, 1964, local Negroes chaired precinct meetings of an independent organization, the Mississippi Freedom Democratic party, intended as an alter-native to the Jim Crow Democratic gatherings. COFO staff assisted on procedural matters but generally found that homegrown community spokes-men abounded in numbers and initiative. Volunteers remarked in amazement and some pride at the way previously apolitical people needed all of ten min-utes before setting to issues of taxes, fairness, and rights with the confidence of longtime activists. The same vigor marked the Freedom party's county con-ventions later in July and its state convention beginning August 6 in Jackson. Sixty-eight delegates, including four whites, were picked to attend the Demo-cratic National Convention, less than two weeks away, and to persuade the national party to bring democracy to Mississippi politics.

Despite these ties to the liberal Democratic coalition, the young people who ran the summer project were concerned mainly with fostering indigenous social movements regardless of partisan lines. For many volunteers the most important work did not involve voter registration or political organizing but rather the creation of "freedom schools" for the children of local Negroes. These schools provided remedial academic instruction and classes on Afro-American history, race relations, and other subjects no Mississippi public school would dare permit black children to hear about, let alone speak about. In the largely free-form classes of the freedom schools the children spoke up often, with an eagerness and confidence that augured a new, very different generation of Mississippi blacks in the making.

Working with minimal funds and equipment—standard conditions for a SNCC operation—the freedom schools expanded to forty-one sites by the end of the summer and taught well over twenty-five hundred children. Among the classes most frequently requested by the students were foreign languages, arithmetic, art, drama, typing, and journalism—none of which were available on a regular basis to blacks in Mississippi's public schools. The opportunity to learn after years of enforced ignorance resulted in a flourishing of student initiative: in Holly Springs a student-produced play, "Seeds of Freedom," about Medgar Evers; in Clarksdale a "freedom press," typed and edited by the students; in Hattiesburg, the center of the Freedom School movement, a student-written declaration of independence petitioning for racial equality in Mississippi.[58]

The quality of the freedom school teachers ranged widely. Some volunteers unwittingly proved that the rhetoric of liberation made a poor substitute for classroom skills. Yet at their best, in the hands of naturally gifted instructors, the freedom schools became models of classroom creativity. One volunteer observed Stokely Carmichael lead a class in which a lesson on proper speech radiated to issues of social conformity and acceptance. After writing four sentences on the left side of the board in local black dialect ("I wants to reddish to vote") and their counterparts in standard English on the right side, Carmichael elicited student views on language and life:

STOKELY: If most people speak on the left, why are they [teachers] trying to change these people?

GLADYS: If you don't talk right, society rejects you. It embarrasses other people if you don't talk right.

HANK: But Mississippi society, ours, isn't embarrassed by it.

SHIRLEY: But the middle class wouldn't class us with them. . . .

STOKELY: Will society reject you if you don't speak like on the right side of the board? Gladys said society would reject you.

GLADYS: You might as well face it, man! What we gotta do is go out and become middle class. If you can't speak good English, you don't have a car, a job, or anything.

STOKELY: If society rejects you because you don't speak good English, should you learn to speak good English?

CLASS: No!

ALMA: I'm tired of doing what society say. Let society say "reddish" for awhile. People ought just to accept each other.

ZELMA: I think we should be speaking just like we always have.

ALMA: If I change for society, I wouldn't be free anyway. . . . If the majority speaks on the left, then a minority must rule society? Why do we have to change to be accepted by the minority group? . . .

STOKELY: Let's think about two questions for next time: What is society? Who makes the rules for society?[59]

These freedom school challenges to "standard" American values reflected a growing responsiveness by civil rights activists toward poor blacks, who had steadily swelled the movement for racial equality since 1960. SNCC in particular recognized that calls for racial integration could not fully satisfy the needs of lower-class blacks; it sought instead to help them assert their own identity and interests. In that cause tutors like Stokely Carmichael conducted their classes as models of participatory democracy—in which leaders questioned, the mass of people guided, and any idea for change was viewed as a realistic possibility.

Although the summer project stretched the reform vision of these young volunteers, it also exposed them to the tenacity of racial prejudice even in their own ranks. Southern Negro activists seethed with feelings of envy and insecurity as white Ivy Leaguers slipped into key leadership roles in the movement. For their part the white volunteers tended at times to romanticize—and patronize—Mississippi's blacks. The black novelist Alice Walker later drew on her memories of civil rights workers in portraying a white volunteer named Lynne who could not help thinking of "primitive" Southern Negroes as "art" or resist the temptation to slowly comb her long hair near black female workers.[60] The summer project volunteers included many "Lynnes," who had journeyed South to fight racism without having conquered, or fully examined, their own parochial values.

Those values included gender as well as race prejudice. Some female volunteers, both white and black, wondered aloud why male workers always assigned them to housekeeping and coffee-making chores in a movement for human dignity and liberation. Notions of male supremacy were nonetheless so ingrained in the civil rights movement, as in the wider society, that only a small minority of women dared protest and nearly all the men reacted with amusement and incredulity. Stokely Carmichael, one of SNCC's most uncompromising advocates of racial equality, conveyed the patronizing attitude of male workers with his usual flair for derision. "The only position for women in SNCC is prone," he declared in late 1964, with an insider's reference to the summer's many sexual liaisons.[61]

Sexual tensions across the color line further strained relations among the volunteers. Many black men pursued white female volunteers—often the first friendly white women they had ever known—as the forbidden fruit, the final barrier to status in white society. White women frequently responded in kind, seeing black men as the exotic, primitive sexual force of American myth, at once alarming and inviting. COFO's leaders stressed the pitfalls of attraction that drew on racial stereotypes, and warned recruits against all interracial romance, which they believed could tarnish the project as a serious political venture. But their strictures had little influence over human nature. The Beloved Community began to acquire unintended shades of meaning, as volunteers intent on treating all men like brothers showed less resolve in viewing all women as sisters.

Although interracial courtship sometimes led to love, for the movement as a whole it unleashed crippling acrimony. If white women rejected black suitors, they risked the dread label "racist"; and if they entered relationships with black men, they risked the anger of black women scorned.[62] While some black female volunteers also shared in the summer's interracial romances, the sexual exploits of black men with white women formed a more conspicuous and compulsive phenomenon. Unlike white feminists, who sought recognition as being more than decorative sex objects, black women complained that Negro men viewed them as able coworkers fit for the rigors of the field but lacking the soft refinement of white middle-class girls. The black psychiatrist Alvin Poussaint found that "so much energy was expended by both black males and females in discussing white girls that on many days little project work was accomplished."[63] These discussions illuminated, but scarcely resolved, the problems of trying to build a new society with values rigidly conditioned by the old.

As suspicions tore at the movement from within, outside threats placed the operation of freedom schools and voter registration projects in a state of unrelieved terror. White Mississippians viewed the young organizers seriously enough to harass them daily with arrests, obscene and threatening phone calls, and Klan surveillance. In Drew, police jailed volunteers for distributing voter registration material; in Hattiesburg workers were beaten; a freedom house in McComb was bombed. The constant sense of mortal danger was described in a letter by a volunteer who had witnessed many violent incidents and been beaten in broad daylight: "I wake up in the morning sighing with relief that I was not bombed, because I know that 'they' know where I live. And I think, well, I got through that night, now I have to get through this day, and it goes on and on." While this volunteer wrote his letter, an anonymous phone caller threatened to bomb the office.[64]

President Johnson meanwhile pressed an FBI manhunt for Schwerner, Chaney, and Goodman, amid a growing public outcry. Four hundred sailors dredged nearby waters, a move that quickly recovered corpses of several blacks who had been shot. In early August the search ended at an earthen dam in Philadelphia, where seamen uncovered the bodies of Schwerner, Chaney, and Goodman. Autopsies showed that Schwerner and Goodman had been shot through the head once each with a .38-caliber bullet. Chaney, the lone black, had been shot three times and beaten savagely. A doctor examining Chaney's body at his mother's request stated that in twenty-five years' experience as a pathologist, he had "never witnessed bones so severely shattered."[65] Evidence soon pointed to Philadelphia's deputy sheriff Cecil Price, who had arranged for the three civil rights workers to be "released" from jail just long enough for several whites to waylay and murder them.

Newsmen located Rita Schwerner in CORE's Washington office and asked about her feelings. She offered a brief word on the nation's loss: "Three good men were killed—three good men who could have done a great deal for their country." The newsmen pressed her to state whether some good might yet come from the triple murder. Her reply captured the hopes and growing doubts of all the volunteers: "That is up to the people of the United States."[66]

"It was the longest nightmare I have ever had: three months," Cleveland Sellers said, in summarizing his experience in Mississippi during June, July, and August 1964.[67] In all, he and his coworkers suffered one thousand arrests, thirty-five shooting incidents, thirty bombings of homes, churches, and other buildings, and eighty beatings. In addition to Schwerner, Chaney, and Goodman, at least three other civil rights workers died violently. Several more survived snipers who barely missed them with rifle fire in the dark. By summer's end most of the project workers headed back north, reflecting on the cost of their efforts or, in some cases, trying to forget their collective nightmare.

Some three hundred of the volunteers, more than a third, remained in Mississippi. For these veterans there were few illusions about transforming race relations in Mississippi. The demoralizing effects of local harassment and internal bickering were everywhere apparent. By fall 1964, COFO project centers presented a picture of collective burnout:

Staff and volunteer discipline has broken down so far that the state headquarters has had several race riots, white workers are often subject to severe racial abuse and even violence from Negro workers, staff and volunteers have assaulted the fellow workers, cashed checks (for their own personal use), clothes and supplies have been stolen totaling several thousands of dollars. Negro workers are frequently played-up-to and looked-down-on by white workers, juvenile delinquency sometimes appears to have taken over certain offices. . . . many workers drive cars as fast as they can, figuring COFO will pay their fines and get them a lawyer no matter what they do. Former SNCC staff going to Tougaloo steal and act rowdy in the Jackson office. . . .[68]

A semblance of the movement survived. The freedom schools lingered for another year, and a second, more decentralized freedom project brought white and black volunteers to Mississippi in June 1965. Yet long before the project finally disbanded that September, it had become clear to dispirited COFO workers that Mississippi's traditions of white supremacy were amply fortified against a summer's Northern breeze.

The Movement and the Party

The atmosphere of extremism that had poisoned race relations in Mississippi spread widely in 1964 as the far Right fed on white fears of rising Negro status. In St. Augustine, Florida, where Martin Luther King, Jr., led demonstrations in June and July, white vigilantes with police support terrorized merchants who served Negroes. One businessman who owned forest lands near the city placated St. Augustine's right-wing element for fear that his property could be incinerated by "anybody with a book of matches." A merchant who had dared to seat blacks in his restaurant paid that same night when every window of his restaurant, car, and home was smashed. After this incident the man once again affirmed the sanctity of segregated dining patterns. He explained the facts of life in St. Augustine to a reporter: "People are scared. They are banded together. You need to survive. You don't argue."[69]

In the North, support for civil rights buckled wherever whites considered the prospect of blacks moving into their neighborhoods or sending their children to all-white schools. Alabama's governor, George Wallace, demonstrated that racism, if not boundless, was unconstrained by sectional borders when in 1964 he garnered 34 percent of the vote in Wisconsin's Democratic presidential primary and then 30 percent in Indiana's and 43 percent in Maryland's. Although Wallace could not seriously challenge Johnson's hold on the nomination, he nonetheless exposed how raw white feelings were on the matter of race. By summer, when Wallace's campaign faded, many of his followers turned to a still more powerful champion of the Right, the Republican senator Barry Goldwater.

Unlike Wallace, the handsome, gray-haired senator from Arizona was less a demagogue than an ideologue. During the Republican primary campaigns early in 1964 Goldwater shunned divisive appeals to race, instead hitting hard at the evils of Johnson-size government. He claimed to favor neither an integrated nor a segregated society but one that permitted blacks and whites freedom of choice. Yet in practice he aligned squarely with the white South on civil rights issues, blending a near-antebellum enthusiasm for states' rights with a determined obliviousness to the reasons for black protest. In June the senator voted against the civil rights bill as violating rights of private property and individual preference, while scarcely noting the routine trampling of Negro rights that had prompted the legislation. By the time he captured his party's presidential nomination, with the backing of its most conservative elements, Goldwater had become a national rallying symbol for those who believed blacks were "moving too far too fast."

Black leaders recognized the stakes in the election campaign of 1964 and were virtually unanimous in preferring Johnson to Goldwater. Yet they divided on how fully to merge their cause with that of the President. Although most leaders continued to favor a coalition with white liberals as the best hope for further change, younger activists expressed suspicion of the Johnson administration and its allies. These strains in the civil rights movement peaked during the presidential campaign, when Lyndon Johnson called on Negro leaders to set aside all protest activities for the sake of his liberal candidacy.

Bayard Rustin, a longtime proponent of mass action but also an advocate of coalition politics, had no doubts about the wisdom of Johnson's call for a cessation of racial turmoil. Rustin feared that a Goldwater presidency would reverse civil rights gains and liberal economic programs. He also shared the President's dismay at an outbreak of rioting in Harlem and several other ghettos in July, which alienated many Americans and helped solidify Goldwater's conservative base. To counter this trend, Rustin and the CORE strategist Norman Hill, who had helped plan the March on Washington, arranged a conference of civil rights leaders in late July to plan a moratorium on demonstrations. Rustin urged them to face political reality and renounce further protests that might help propel Goldwater to the White House.[70]

The result was an accord by the most eminent civil rights figures to keep their movement aligned with a broader liberal consensus. For the NAACP and the Urban League, groups that had worked closely with the administration,

Roy Wilkins and Whitney Young praised Rustin's acceptance of a moratorium as the only sane political course. Martin Luther King, Jr., shied from a categorical ban on protests, in part because he knew that blacks were going to express their anger and frustration whatever their "leaders" pronounced. Yet he, too, endorsed a carefully worded statement that "the present situation" required a "temporary alteration in strategy" and that "the greatest need now" was for "political action." The three signatories further agreed to call on their "members voluntarily to observe a broad curtailment if not total moratorium of all mass marches, picketing and demonstrations until after Election Day, November 3."[71]

Yet the conference also registered signs of discord. SNCC's chairman, John Lewis, refused to submerge the civil rights revolution beneath Lyndon Johnson's electoral ambitions and spurned the demand for a moratorium on protests. James Farmer at first followed Rustin's lead, then under pressure from other CORE members sided with Lewis. Both Farmer and Lewis in fact accepted the premise underlying Johnson's demand for a moratorium: that the Democratic party, for all its flaws, represented the best hope for further reform. They cautioned, however, that if black leaders tried to stop the protests, "the kids in the street who were demonstrating would laugh at us."[72] They also questioned whether aiding Johnson's election prospects justified four months of studied inaction by all civil rights forces. SNCC leaders in particular believed that their most important task lay in augmenting the voice of blacks in the liberal coalition, rather than in simply avoiding offense to any segment of the electorate. Accordingly their one concerted protest in those four months involved an attempt by the Mississippi Freedom Democrats to integrate thoroughly, not a city, but the Democratic party itself.

The Freedom party challenge to Mississippi's regular Democrats was an offshoot of the freedom summer project that extended all the way to the 1964 Democratic National Convention in Atlantic City. Sixty-eight Freedom party delegates reached the August convention by bus, train, dilapidated cars, and persistent hitchhiking. They represented a fair cross section of rural and urban blacks in Mississippi, comprising some relatively educated and well-to-do local leaders as well as small farmers who had only months earlier handled a registration form for the first time. The delegation included four white activists, among them the Reverend Edwin King, a native Mississippian who had risked his safety to help found the Freedom party in 1963. Bob Moses, among other COFO staffers, doubted whether the insurgents stood much chance in the coming struggle over credentials. Still, the tenacity of these new politicos in planning their trip to the convention had surprised many. It raised hopes that if they were supported by liberals, greater surprises would lie ahead.

Freedom party delegates counted ample legal and political grounds to contest the legitimacy of Mississippi's regular Democrats. The regular party organization in the state had systematically excluded blacks from voting and office holding. Its treatment of Lyndon Johnson was scarcely warmer, as the party resolved at its state convention in July to "oppose, condemn and deplore the Civil Rights Act of 1964" and to "reject and oppose the platforms of both national parties and their candidates."[73] Surely, the Freedom party delegates told each other, the convention would recognize a delegation on record as loyal to the President and the ideals of the national party rather than a delegation that spurned both.

The confident mood of the insurgents stemmed also from their newly stimulated belief in the promise of American life, even for Mississippi Negroes. The former sharecropper Fannie Lou Hamer conveyed the enthusiasm of many fellow delegates when she explained why the Freedom party's challenge had to succeed: "When we went to Atlantic City, we didn't go there for public-ity, we went there because we believed that America was what it said it was, 'the land of the free.' " She therefore believed "with all of [her] heart" in the triumph of her delegation, "because if the Constitution of this United States means something to all of us," the convention would unseat the segregated Mississippi delegation in favor of the Freedom party's representatives.[74]

Hamer's exuberance soon wilted in the thin moral atmosphere of conven-tion politics. Battle-hardened civil rights professionals like Roy Wilkins treated her with barely disguised disdain. Hamer remembered the NAACP leader accosting her in the hall: "Mrs. Hamer, you people have put your point across . . . [but] you don't know anything about politics. I [have] been in the business over twenty years. You people have put your point across, now why don't you pack up and go home?" "That," said Hamer, "was blow number one."[75] Blow number two was more dispiriting: the discovery that the Freedom party might be challenging not only the Mississippi Democratic organization but also the President of the United States.

Lyndon Johnson at first inclined toward a compromise proposed by Jo-seph Rauh, head of the liberal Americans for Democratic Action (ADA) and now also representing the Freedom party to other Democrats. Rauh publicly insisted on the ouster of Mississippi's regular Democrats but privately tem-pered his demand with the suggestion that both delegations be seated. But Governor Paul Johnson of Mississippi personally informed the President that neither he nor any other regular Democrats would ever share their convention seats with the Freedom party. At the same meeting Governors John Connally of Texas and Carl Sanders of Georgia elaborated on the repercussions if the President ratified such a compromise: they would lead their delegations out of the convention, and other Southern delegations would follow suit.[76] After the President heard these prominent spokesmen for the "moderate" South, his initial resolve to seat the Freedom party collapsed as if shelled by a Thompson tank. The prospect of a Southern walkout was abhorrent to Johnson, whose love of consensus shaded easily into an effort to dominate the left, the center, and the right. From that moment, Johnson decided that the Freedom party lacked the legal standing to merit inclusion as a legitimate delegation.

Johnson picked Senator Hubert Humphrey from Minnesota for the un-welcome task of checking the Freedom party's challenge. Humphrey could be expected to influence Joseph Rauh, a longtime political ally. Both had been among the handful of young men who founded the ADA in 1947 as the liberal activist wing of the Democratic party. A year later Rauh had helped Humphrey precipitate a floor fight at the Democratic convention that led to the adoption of a strong civil rights plank and to the walkout by Southern Dixiecrats. In recent years Rauh, as counsel to both the ADA and the United Auto Workers Union, had depended on Humphrey's support. However sympathetic to the Freedom party's cause, Rauh felt the stronger pull of Hubert Humphrey's rising star.

At first glance an ultraliberal civil rights champion like Humphrey might have seemed a poor choice for a mission to dispatch the Freedom party delegation. Yet it fit Lyndon Johnson's style to try to co-opt potential opposition and to emphasize his control of people regardless of their stated beliefs. To ensure his cooperation Johnson sent word that Humphrey was his leading choice for a running mate, but that his selection would depend on how well he handled the convention challenge. The senator, in some anguish, agreed to do his best.[77]

Early in the convention several delegates and supporters of the Freedom party met with Humphrey to present their case. Fannie Lou Hamer had come "delighted even to have a chance to talk with this man," who she had heard was an eloquent defender of racial justice. But by this point the tantalizing possibility of the vice-presidential nomination, which Johnson had dangled in front of him, held Humphrey fast in near-hypnotic responsiveness to the President's wishes. Instead of a flaming reformer Hamer saw only "a little round-eyed man with his eyes full of tears" while Rauh chided the delegates that their pressure could cost Humphrey the vice-presidency. Hamer started in amazement, saying, "Well, Mr. Humphrey, do you mean to tell me that your position is more important to you than four hundred thousand black people's lives?" Humphrey responded weakly, and Hamer walked out weeping. Later she encountered him again and declared, "Senator Humphrey, I been praying about you . . . you're a good man, and you know what's right. The trouble is, you're afraid to do what you know is right." Hamer told him she understood that he wanted "this job" as vice-president, but she knew others who had lost jobs— alluding to people like her who had registered to vote and been fired for their trouble—and she knew God would care for them all. "But Mr. Humphrey, if you take this job, you won't be worth anything. Mr. Humphrey, I'm going to go pray for you again."[78] Her words apparently touched a nerve deep in Humphrey's psyche; he made it clear to Freedom party representatives that he did not want to deal with Fannie Lou Hamer again.

Despite Johnson's opposition the Freedom party continued to bid for acceptance at the convention. Joseph Rauh dismissed as insulting an offer from the administration to welcome the delegates as "fraternal members" without voting privileges. Rauh told presidential aides and newsmen that the Freedom party commanded the necessary support among members of the credentials committee to file an official minority report objecting to the Mississippi regulars. He added that there were enough friendly state delegations to guarantee a debate over the issue on the convention floor—a tactic that the unity-hungry President wanted to avoid at almost any price.

The Freedom party's chances further brightened with the televised testimony of delegates and supporters at hearings conducted by the credentials committee. Artless tales of suffering at the hands of callous politicians and brutal law enforcement authorities led American memories back to the horrors of Birmingham and galvanized public opinion in favor of the Freedom party delegation. By all accounts the main presence at the proceedings was Fannie Lou Hamer, who told how she was evicted in 1962 from the farm where she had worked for eighteen years as a sharecropper, just after she registered to vote. She recounted, too, how she was jailed for encouraging others in Mississippi to register and how state highway patrolmen ordered other black prisoners to beat her as punishment for her organizing efforts:

The first Negro began to beat, and I was beat until I was exhausted. . . . After the first Negro . . . was exhausted, the State Highway Patrolman ordered the second Negro to take the blackjack. The second Negro began to beat . . . I began to scream, and one white man got up and began to beat me on my head and tell me to "hush."

One white man—my dress had worked up high—he walked over and pulled my dress down and he pulled my dress back, back up. . . . All of this is on account we want to register, to become first-class citizens, and if the Freedom Democratic Party is not seated now, I question America.[79]

Even as the program aired, Johnson could see the handwriting defacing his wall of consensus. Fannie Lou Hamer was still testifying when Johnson suddenly discovered a pressing need to speak on national television. He hurriedly called a press conference preempting television coverage of the remaining credentials committee testimony. Among those whose statements were bypassed by the networks was Rita Schwerner, widow of the murdered civil rights worker. As the hearings ended, Johnson wound down his own remarks. Yet if he had hoped to keep the Freedom party's cause hidden from the public, his maneuver had limited impact. That evening the networks rebroadcast the hearings in prime time, including Hamer's powerful witness in its entirety.[80]

As telegrams piled up in the office of the credentials committee demanding the seating of the Freedom party delegates, Johnson arranged for a postponement of any decision. Pressure was now building in favor of a proposal by Congresswoman Edith Green of Oregon to seat all Mississippi delegates who took a loyalty oath to the national Democratic party. They would then share the delegation's sixty-eight votes equally whether they belonged to the regular Democratic organization or to the Freedom party. Publicly the Freedom party balked at the compromise, but privately its counsel Joseph Rauh barely concealed his glee while indicating that the proposal was not altogether beyond consideration. Paul Johnson was more consistent in representing the Mississippi regulars. If the convention accepted the Green compromise, his delegation would not even be there to comment.[81]

Preoccupied with averting a walkout, Lyndon Johnson still had to make some concession to the Freedom party's unexpected strength in public opinion and on the convention floor. Through Hubert Humphrey the President conveyed his willingness to accord the new organization two delegate seats, and sixty-six honorary, nonvoting seats with Northern and protectorate delegations. There was also a somewhat general promise to revise the convention rules so that the 1968 Mississippi delegation would be chosen without discrimination. But there were limits to this show of goodwill. Johnson's aides specified that the two official delegates would be "at large" rather than members of the Mississippi delegation, thus undercutting the Freedom party's claim to constitute the legitimate representatives of the state party. Nor could the Freedom party select its two delegates. Johnson had decided that the white minister Edwin King must be one, to show that the state delegation was interracial. Aaron Henry of the NAACP was to be the other delegate, as the best-known member of the Freedom party and the most flexible toward the administration. Johnson specifically listed one person who would never be allowed to grace the choice of delegates—the one most identified with the cause of poor blacks—Fannie Lou Hamer.

As an overtly emotional advocate of racial justice without regard for the delicate wheels and cogs of coalition politics, Fannie Lou Hamer struck the administration as plainly unsuited to represent the Freedom party's cause. Johnson reportedly declaimed that he would not let that "illiterate woman" become one of the delegates-at-large.[82] Although this may simply have reflected his paternal concern that she first pass through the purifying filter of his Great Society programs, it is likely that Johnson was less concerned with her limited education than with her limitless indignation at political expedience. If that outrage should spill over within range of a radio or television microphone, who knew how much damage control the administration might require to repair the breach with the white South? There was room for only one moralist in the Johnson political universe, and the President alone would determine when to thunder in the role.

The Freedom party turned down the Humphrey compromise, but if it had shown surprising skill in the battle of public opinion it now had to contest rules and procedures in an arena composed of back rooms and corridors. The delegates found that Lyndon Johnson, as usual, was doing his best work behind the scenes. He browbeat Governor Edmund G. Brown, Sr., of California for failing to take a tough line against signs of pro–Freedom party sentiment in his state's delegation. A delegate from the Canal Zone received a call from the secretary of the Army, informing him that if he voted to seat the Freedom party he would be fired from his job. The Johnson treatment was so intense that in Washington, D.C., where Joseph Rauh chaired the Democratic delegation, only Rauh's last-minute importuning kept a majority of delegates from deserting the Freedom party's cause.[83]

When intimidation did not dissuade delegates from taking the Freedom party's position, Johnson found ways to keep their votes from being tallied at all. Rauh had counted on delegates from several territories—Puerto Rico, the Virgin Islands, and Guam—to promote the Green compromise. The President therefore had Carl Sanders, in his role as head of the rules committee, ensure that only state delegations be permitted to participate in certain votes crucial to the Freedom party challenge.[84] In such ways, without winning the hearts and minds of these delegates, Johnson nonetheless effectively blocked their support for the insurgents.

In the committee on credentials Rauh's support was whittled away until on Tuesday, August 25, Johnson felt confident enough to encourage a formal vote on the two compromise measures. Only four of the eighteen members who had earlier pledged to vote for the Green proposal actually did so. Rauh himself, warned by the UAW chief, Walter Reuther, that a wrong vote would cost him his lucrative post as UAW counsel, saw his quest turning quixotic. He sought to caucus with his Freedom party clients, but the credentials committee bruskly approved the Humphrey compromise without his endorsement.[85]

The Freedom party delegates overwhelmingly rejected the offer that same evening. But at ten the following morning they convened at a black church in Atlantic City at Aaron Henry's request, to hear varied friends of the administration who planned to speak on behalf of the Humphrey offer. The presence of eminent leaders in government, civil rights, labor, and the clergy bespoke Lyndon Johnson's determination to straighten out these sixty-eight mavericks and their supporters. And it left them, in James Forman's words, "amazed—dumbfounded—at the array of power that the administration had dished up."[86] There was Bayard Rustin, who believed that a united Democratic party was vital to advance justice at home and peace abroad, and whose own ties to liberal leaders like Walter Reuther kept him from pledging unreserved support for the Freedom party insurgents. Martin Luther King also came to discern merit in the offer of two delegate seats as the most the Freedom party could win, after talking with Rustin and with Reuther, whose UAW was a major benefactor of the SCLC.[87] James Farmer of CORE and the Freedom party's own counsel, Joseph Rauh, added to the roster of conciliators presented by Aaron Henry and the Johnson forces.

Addressing a skeptical group of delegates and supporters, some of these speakers elicited little more than chuckles, as when the white, blond-haired lawyer for the National Council of Churches hailed the decision of the credentials committee as the greatest thing that had happened for the Negro since Emancipation.[88] But it was a more serious matter when Bayard Rustin, tutor to Martin Luther King, Stokely Carmichael, Bob Moses, and other movement leaders, strode to the rostrum to announce his embrace of the administration's two-delegate offer.

Rustin stood before the delegates a forceful veteran of reform campaigns, now burdened with concern for the wider repercussions of every political act. He seemed the very embodiment of coalition politics as he tried to bring his listeners to accept not simply the compromise at issue but also the necessity of compromise generally in the interest of a larger struggle. "There is a difference between protest and politics," he lectured them. "The former is based on morality and the latter is based on reality and compromise. If you are going to engage in politics then you must give up protest. . . . You must be willing to compromise, to win victories and go home and come back and win some more.

. . . That is politics." Amid angry murmurs and a white SNCC member's shouts of treason, Rustin urged the Freedom party to proclaim the Humphrey offer a "symbolic victory" and to look toward larger victories ahead. When he finished, Stokely Carmichael and others pointedly questioned not only the wisdom of the compromise but also the reliability of Rustin's valued "friends" in liberal-labor circles.[89]

Martin Luther King, Jr., was the next speaker, and the commotion in the church gave way to admiring attention. In a softer echo of Rustin's catechism on coalitions, he conceded that there remained many wrongs in the country, there remained a long road to travel, and indeed neither he nor his listeners could travel that road alone. Despite the segregationists in the Democratic party it was the only party that had helped the Negro. While he could not counsel acceptance or rejection—that was the decision of the delegates—Hubert Humphrey had assured him that acceptance would help bring a new day in Mississippi's Democratic politics, free of segregation. The delegates applauded King far more vigorously than they had any other speaker. Yet he had not moved the audience with his usual emotional power. Edwin King recalled that SNCC staffers had been "terrified" of King's eloquence, fearing that he would stampede delegates into cheering for the compromise; but the white minister had already learned in private conversation that King's heart was not in such an effort. The civil rights leader confided that as a national figure he would find it helpful if the Freedom party accepted Johnson's offer because the symbolism might inspire blacks in other states to register and try to displace lily-white delegations. But if he were a member of the Freedom party, King added, he would be unable to accept that offer. "So," Edwin King realized, "he understood."[90]

James Farmer, too, understood. His speech seemed both to support and to oppose the compromise, but in the end it was interpreted as a subdued plea for acceptance.[91] Joseph Rauh spoke for the offer with less ambivalence but equal deference to the Freedom party's wishes.[92] Yet the ongoing battery of speakers never hit the central concern of the delegates, until Bob Moses rose to condemn the operating principles—or lack thereof—behind the compromise.

Moses rejected the notion that there was a choice to be made between politics and morality. The Freedom party delegates, he said, had come to put morality into politics, not to trade one for the other. Moses noted acerbically that he did not want anyone telling him about Walter Reuther's needing help; Reuther had not come to Mississippi.[93] James Forman followed with a detailed analysis of the flaws in the compromise proposal, which Fannie Lou Hamer later distilled in a private session with the other delegates. "We didn't come all this way for no two seats!" she said.[94] With near unanimity the delegates once again rejected the administration's offer.

The delegates further departed from the administration's carefully scripted convention scenarios by using passes provided by Michigan and Massachusetts delegates to enter the convention hall. During their first attempt, on Tuesday evening, a guard threw out one such infiltrator. But Lyndon Johnson stayed abreast of the situation and hurled orders at the convention security detail to desist from further action against Freedom party delegates. His aim, after all, had been to avoid embarrassing melodrama at his convention. On Wednesday, August 26, the Freedom party members occupied en masse the seats reserved for Mississippi's regular Democrats. By then all but three of the regulars had already walked out, unable to digest even the pallid offering of two delegate seats to the insurgents. (So, too, had most of Alabama's delegates, rather than abide by the party's insistence on a loyalty pledge to the national ticket.) But delegates from Georgia, Texas, and other Southern states remained to support the President for reelection, satisfied that he had done everything possible to keep Mississippi's black delegates from tainting the party of the South.

Johnson was well pleased with the results, and he reached deep into his store of patronage prizes in the belief that to the genuflectors belonged the spoils. Senator Humphrey, who had passed his loyalty test, was rewarded with the vice-presidential nomination; he would go on to gain that office and pass still greater, more tormenting tests of personal loyalty in succeeding years. Walter Mondale, a young attorney general from Minnesota who chaired the subcommittee on the Mississippi challenge in accord with the administration's wishes, was appointed Humphrey's successor in the Senate. Then there was the counsel for the Democratic party committee, Harold Leventhal.[95] This eminent liberal attorney had denied the Freedom party counselors use of the records of previous conventions so that they would not know how to proceed with their challenge. Six months later the President named Leventhal to the U.S. Court of Appeals for the District of Columbia Circuit, a judgeship second in prestige only to a place on the Supreme Court.

In his memoirs Lyndon Johnson recalled the convention as a place of unbroken harmony. The unpleasantness of the Freedom party challenge vanished amid memories of cheering throngs, unanimous votes, and a strengthened candidacy.[96] There was consistency in this, for as President he had brooked no disharmony from any quarter, whatever the ideological or moral cavils. In July, he had driven the liberal bandwagon roughshod over Senator Russell's segregationist forces to produce a historic civil rights measure. In August, as Johnson felt a chill political wind on his right, he fed the agenda of integrationist leaders into the omnivorous maw of consensus politics.

The Campaign of 1964

The presidential election campaign of 1964 witnessed sharp exchanges over the issues of nuclear arms, federal spending and authority, American involvement in Southeast Asia, and relations with the Soviet Union. Both major party nominees, however, resolutely avoided the issue of race for most of the campaign, viewing the subject was too volatile for them to risk inflaming national tensions or undermining their own candidacies. Yet, even unspoken, the race question hovered over the campaign, a silent specter, casting doubt on the leadership of both candidates and on the nation's commitment to an integrated society.

Goldwater early belied liberal caricatures of him by resisting the temptation to exploit a potential white "backlash" against black protests and ghetto violence. Out of principle and a desire to reassure Northern Republicans, he refused to pursue a "Southern strategy" of appealing openly to segregationist sentiment, as some aides advised. Moreover, in the wake of Harlem's rioting, he proposed that, for the sake of national stability, both candidates refrain from appeals to race. Johnson publicly finessed the offer but privately accepted it, pleased that his opponent was tossing aside a lever with which he could pry away conservative Democrats.

Goldwater's candidacy was nonetheless more than the sum of his own principles. From the beginning his base of support had been top-heavy with right-wing extremists, including arch-segregationists such as Wallace and Eastland. Moreover, his speeches denouncing the "soul-less" monster of expanding government were at odds with the idea of benevolent federal leadership to which black leaders were committed. Rejecting the middle ground that politicians generally cling to with unfailing determination, if not conviction, Goldwater trumpeted his motto "Extremism in the defense of liberty is no vice; moderation in the pursuit of justice is no virtue." All elements of the liberal coalition took careful note of this declaration, and no group was more attentive or responded more energetically than Negroes. They saw themselves as prime victims of Goldwater's crusade to undo half a century of American political reform.

Although black leaders still whispered complaints about Johnson's inconsistencies as a reformer, they saved their public tirades for Goldwater, whose consistency they found frightening. Roy Wilkins ended the NAACP's long tradition of neutrality in presidential races by warmly siding with Lyndon Johnson. Martin Luther King, Jr., declined to endorse Johnson directly, but at campaign rallies in every major city he found a negative word to say about Goldwater, the candidate who "fawned on the segregationists." Even the Mississippi Freedom Democrats, headed by the Johnson loyalist Aaron Henry, returned to their native state to barnstorm for the President. Everywhere civil rights leaders acted on the fear that a victory for Goldwater, as Martin Luther King, Jr., warned, would mean the destruction of America "as we know it."[97]

Johnson was in fact vulnerable to a challenge from the Right. To many Americans he appeared a shadowy manipulator. His record of legislative legerdemain had done more to win awe than popular affection even among liberals. A different Republican adversary, one chosen by the party's moderate wing, might have effectively tapped the unease over the President's character and his vast expansion of government power, which included concern over how far enforcement of black rights would extend. But Goldwater offered voters little assurance that he would be a steady guardian of the status quo. When the candidate spoke of nuclear weapons, which he did often, he appeared less concerned with arms control than with suggesting that he had no unseemly fears about pressing the button. On the domestic front he assailed not only new, untested liberal programs but also Social Security and other hallowed bipartisan landmarks of reform. With each campaign salvo Goldwater tore gaping holes in his own credibility and helped enable Lyndon Johnson to present his liberal leadership as the safe, middle road for the nation.

Johnson offered a soothing silence on race issues, but by mid-October he felt emboldened to work civil rights fully into the framework of consensus politics. Brushing aside the cautioning of aides, he chose to give his one major speech on the subject in the Deep South city of New Orleans. "There are men down there," Johnson told a Northern Cabinet officer in explaining why he carried the civil rights banner unfurled on both sides of the Mason-Dixon line. "They may not like it, but at least they would like it straight." Johnson gave it straight, but in a political dialect pleasing to the Southern ear. Knowing that Southerners were "brought up on Constitution, Constitution, Constitution," Johnson spoke the language of reverence for the nation's sacred legal charter, "which happens to include equality for the Negro." He talked economics, too, with equal fluency, evoking Populist yearnings for development of the land and security for the farmers—all the farmers. Talking to audiences on this subject invariably reminded him of what an Alabama friend had said to his wife, Lady Bird. The man was troubled by "a lot of stories" about what had happened in race relations. After much thought the man concluded, "I would rather have a Negro beside me on a job than beside me in a soup line." Johnson hammered home the moral: it was time for the South to hear "a real Democratic speech" about helping the common people, instead of hearing only "Negro, Negro, Negro!" at election time. The crowd, deep in the heart of Goldwater country, marveled at Johnson's bluntness and rose for a long round of cheers, whistles, and clapping. However well Goldwater could reach the South's fears, no one could rouse the hopes and pride of the region like Lyndon Johnson, the President from Texas.[98]

On November 3, 1964, Goldwater's "hidden supporters," the legions of citizens he believed secretly shared his conservative views, failed to materialize. Instead a popular avalanche, precipitated by Goldwater's own campaign incantations, returned Johnson to the White House with a record 61 percent of the vote. Outside the South, Johnson won every state except his opponent's home base of Arizona. In the Deep South the race issue helped Goldwater capture five traditionally Democratic states—Mississippi, Alabama, Louisiana, South Carolina, and Georgia. Yet Johnson handily won Texas, while overwhelming black support for the President in Virginia, North Carolina, Tennessee, and Arkansas outweighed white majorities for Goldwater.[99] Thus even the dreaded white backlash proved more apparent than real. Combined with Democratic gains in the House and the Senate, the election results emphatically confirmed Johnson's liberal course, including his push for civil rights. They encouraged the President to hasten preparations for bolder reform measures.

In their zeal to blunt Goldwater's right-wing challenge, Negroes cast over 95 percent of their ballots for Lyndon Johnson. That figure held for urban and rural areas, North and South, making blacks the staunchest Democratic supporters of any ethnic, regional, or religious group. The journalist Theodore H. White noted, "Some urban Negro precincts approached 99 percent for Johnson—which can only be interpreted as meaning that several people, by mistake, pulled the wrong handle in voting booths in several big-city ghettos." It was, in White's view, "the most nearly unanimous expression of will in any community free of political surveillance anywhere in history."[100]

For all that, the celebration of Johnson's landslide victory was subdued among key elements of the black protest movement. This was particularly true of the younger activists, whose memories remained fixed on the embittering experience in Atlantic City. Charles Sherrod, known within SNCC for his religious moralism, announced after the convention that SNCC was now "demanding power" and that the only question was whether blacks would share power "in reconciliation" or seize power "in rioting and blood."[101] Stokely Carmichael reflected on the Freedom party episode as showing "not merely that the national conscience was generally unreliable but that, very specifically, black people in Mississippi and throughout this country could not rely on their so-called allies."[102] Two Freedom party officers—its chairman, Lawrence Guyot, and its Washington spokesman, Mike Thelwell—described the trust blacks had placed in federal goodwill as

a simplistic faith somewhat akin to that of the Russian peasants under the Czars. Caught in the direst kind of oppression and deprivation, the peasants would moan, "If the Czar only knew how we suffer. He is good and would give us justice. If only he knew." The fact was that he knew only too well.[103]

Even hardened political veterans like Bayard Rustin paused to acknowledge the moral costs exacted by coalition politics. After the Democratic convention battle over credentials, Rustin visited the Freedom party delegates to apologize for his role in backing Johnson's efforts and in opposing their own. He had not been proud of some things he felt compelled to say and do at the convention, but he was deeply proud of the delegates who had fought for their beliefs at any price. He encouraged them to continue their protests, not to keep the nation's leaders honest but to make them "less crooked."[104] For a brief moment the novice politicians of the Freedom party understood why Rustin had been revered by so many activists in the movement. Then Rustin moved on to resume his political labors, helping the Great Society take root while lamenting the passing of a more fragile vision, the Beloved Community.

Chapter 5

The Voting Rights Campaign

THE 1964 ELECTION eclipsed the forces of racial extremism in American politics, but it also highlighted persistent barriers to Negro suffrage in many parts of the South. Privately Lyndon Johnson acknowledged a need to strengthen voting rights legislation, but he planned to defer such proposals for a year or more, to give the South time to digest the Civil Rights Act of 1964.[1] Once again, however, black protests disrupted racist traditions and reform timetables alike, as movement leaders launched a nonviolent campaign against the last legal pillar of Jim Crow.

Southern Resistance

The catalyst for the new campaign was the failure of existing voting rights laws to deter the familiar legal and extralegal harassment of Negroes. Enforcement of these laws relied on judicial remedies that could not keep pace with state and local violations. In 1963 the Justice Department completed a three-year struggle to end arbitrary voter qualifications in Louisiana, whose legislature then quickly passed new statutes similar to those just voided.[2] Moreover, most lawsuits brought by the Justice Department targeted individual registrars, requiring hundreds of man-hours from government attorneys to win cease-and-desist orders of minimal scope. Even these cases held no guarantees, for they seldom reached the liberal Warren Court. Instead they typically went before Southern district judges like Harold Cox, who in 1961 flexed his powers of obstruction by first denying the Justice Department a registrar's records and then dismissing the case for lack of evidence.[3]

As a result of these tactics only two million of the South's five million voting-age blacks were registered in 1964. In Louisiana the proportion dropped to 31.8 percent, in Alabama to 19.4 percent, and in Mississippi to 6.4 percent. The numbers formed a persuasive argument for black leaders: the judicial approach to enforcement of voting rights was ineffective, and the government would have to make good its guarantees in some new, more powerful way.

The Movement in Selma

The campaign for voting rights centered on Selma, Alabama, a city in which Negroes made up a majority of the 29,000 inhabitants but only 3 percent of the voting rolls. Situated on a bluff overlooking the muddy Alabama River, some fifty miles west of Montgomery, Selma in antebellum days had been a market for cotton and slaves. One hundred years later wagons laden with cotton still lumbered down Selma's streets on mule power, and among the town's stately buildings was a three-story house where in antebellum times four to five hundred slaves might have been auctioned off on a brisk business day. Here in Selma, Bull Connor was born and raised, and here Alabama's White Citizens' Council first met. In late 1962 a SNCC field secretary scouted the city, hoping to find signs of a Negro community ready to demand its rights. He returned glumly to SNCC's headquarters in Atlanta, went to the wall map showing sites for community organizing, and scratched an X through Selma.[4]

Shortly after this unpromising episode, the Nashville protest veteran Bernard Lafayette found himself between project assignments. He requested Selma as a tempting challenge, requiring patient cultivation of local black morale and unity. Lafayette also welcomed the long odds, which spared him pressure from SNCC coworkers to produce instant confrontations:

Sometimes in our organization, they would say, "Well, what's going on down there?" You know, [if] you don't have any action going, then, you know, maybe, you're not doing anything. And it was hard to explain to people your justification for being there and there was no action. Because movement was getting people *moving.* Visible movement in the streets. . . . [But] because they didn't expect anything to happen, it was a good opportunity for me to get some work done.[5]

Early in 1963 Lafayette and several other SNCC workers spent months canvassing black homes in Selma to discuss voting rights and the way Dallas County officials had limited black registrants to 335 out of a voting-age population of 15,000. They learned that the registration board met only two days a month and rejected black applicants who failed to cross a *t* in registration forms and for other, equally immaterial failings. If applicants managed to submit a letter-perfect form, registrars probed their "basic" command of the Constitution with such questions as, "What two rights does a person have after indictment by a grand jury?" Sometime later the black applicants received letters tersely informing them that they had failed the tests, with no further explanation. By that point, however, it was clear that to the registrars administering the tests, one constitutional right a dark-skinned American did not have was the right to vote.

A local judge sized up the SNCC students, many of whom sported overalls and hailed from outside Alabama, and pronounced them "Communist agitators" controlled by Moscow, Peking, and Havana. But black residents welcomed the students. They accompanied SNCC workers in small numbers to the downtown courthouse to protest the treatment of Negro applicants. A black dental hygienist named Marie Foster began evening citizenship classes for her neighbors. Soon came weekly mass meetings to explain how the ballot could help overcome the daily humiliations that blacks suffered in Selma.

Those humiliations worsened as blacks tried to register to vote at the Dallas County courthouse. Thirty-two teachers lost their jobs for daring to show up at the courthouse; John Lewis went to jail for leading a picket line at the forbidden building; the SNCC worker Worth Long was beaten by a deputy sheriff in the county jail. SNCC's executive secretary, Jim Forman, addressed a voter registration meeting at the Tabernacle Baptist Church, then waited with his audience until a posse of several hundred whites armed with clubs and cattle prods grew tired of staking out the site.[6]

That posse belonged to strapping Jim Clark, the best- dressed sheriff in the Black Belt. Clark was one of the South's abler lawmen, a college graduate who had early made his mark as a reform-minded politician in the mold of his uncle, Governor "Big Jim" Folsom of Alabama. In the mid-1950s Clark had quietly courted Alabama's modest Negro vote for Folsom; in return the governor showed his avuncular generosity by appointing Clark to a vacant sheriff's post in Dallas County. Soon afterward the Negro bus boycott in Montgomery tinged Clark's populism with a streak of racial belligerence. To poor rural whites, Clark railed against Negro agitators, Yankee meddlers who pushed for race mixing, and smooth-talking rich white city folk who might just let it happen. Nor was this mere bluster. Clark armed and deputized scores of supporters, leading his loosely disciplined battalions throughout Alabama and as far as Oxford, Mississippi, wherever Negroes challenged the social order. When not at the fore of his paramilitary outfit, Sheriff Clark strove to maintain cordial if not close ties with the local black community, scrupulously respecting the myth that "his" Negroes were content. In 1963, blacks in Dallas County nonviolently shattered that myth, and a hurt, angry Jim Clark rushed to meet them with his helmeted posse.

October 7, 1963, was "Freedom Day" for SNCC workers and several hundred Negroes who marched to the Dallas County courthouse hoping to find safety in numbers. James Baldwin, Dick Gregory, and other celebrities were also on hand, the better to draw network news teams. Justice Department officials and FBI agents were present as well, for the Dallas County courthouse stood opposite a federal building. But Clark was there, too, a towering presence bedecked in gold braid and sporting a button in his lapel that answered Negro hopes in one word: "NEVER."[7]

Clark ignored the passive federal officials; if they had a higher sovereignty, he had his posse and the grit to use it. He arrested SNCC workers on the courthouse steps, to cries of "Get 'em, Big Jim! Get 'em!" and kept others from bringing food and water to the 350 blacks waiting outside the courthouse to register. Jim Forman and Amelia Boynton, a local black leader, approached Clark in a doomed attempt to create a bond of reason:

FORMAN: We'd like to bring food to these people on line. They've been waiting all day.

CLARK: They will not be molested in any way.

MRS. BOYNTON: Does giving them food mean molesting them?

CLARK: They will not be molested in any way. If you do, you'll be arrested.

FORMAN: We'd like to talk to them; they're standing on line to register to vote, and we'd like to explain registration procedure to them.

CLARK: They will not be molested in any way, and that includes talking to them.[8]

SNCC then tried a more direct approach. One bold "molester," Chico Neblett, wheeled a shopping cart filled with sandwiches and food toward the line outside the courthouse. Immediately state troopers knocked him down, pounded him with their clubs, and seared him with cattle prods. Four troopers then each took a limb and threw Neblett into the green arrest truck at the curb. The offending sandwiches never reached the people waiting to register.[9]

Voter registration efforts continued in Selma but with little visible progress against Clark's possemen and the equally intransigent registrars. In July 1964 a state judge, who during his off-hours wrote tracts on African inferiority, formally banned all marches and black meetings in Selma. With the law behind them Clark's deputies swung their nightsticks more freely than ever before, and by November the movement in Selma was nearly inert. In desperation Boynton and other local black activists urged Martin Luther King to help their voter registration drive, a plea that coincided with King's own thoughts of launching a voting rights crusade in Alabama.

King's planning staff, pushed by a seasoned Alabama-based organizer, James Bevel, agreed that Selma offered a more promising target for nonviolent direct action than their campaign to desegregate St. Augustine, Florida. Blacks in Selma were better organized, and the focus on voter registration fit well with King's own priorities. Even more enticing, in St. Augustine police sanctioned but seldom joined white terrorist actions, while in Selma, Sheriff Clark's deputized roughriders held sway. The SCLC counted on Clark as a man of proven inability to rein in his rage, who might draw the nation's attention to racist violence much as Bull Connor had done before him. King told Bevel that if Selma's Negro leaders united in seeking his aid, he would make their campaign his own. Fifteen major black groups in Selma responded with a joint invitation, and the minister began charting a nonviolent campaign directed not only at Selma's sheriffs and judges but also at the leaders of the nation.[10]

Not every Negro group welcomed King's decision with equal enthusiasm. SNCC found this development part of a familiar and frustrating pattern in which its young volunteers would build the groundwork for a campaign only to find a well-known civil rights figure, usually King, taking command and receiving credit. This resentment had an ideological component as well. SNCC had come to favor deliberate efforts to develop local black initiative as a long-range answer to white racism. By contrast the SCLC seemed inclined to under-cut this painstaking community work by staging high-profile marches centered on the Reverend King's leadership, in order to win national publicity.

At a SNCC executive meeting early in 1965, shortly after King's move to Selma, all but one person favored withholding support from SCLC activities. That one, however, was John Lewis, who remained an advocate of nonviolent direct action and still followed King as a prophet of the movement. The executive board reluctantly permitted Lewis to assist the campaign, adhering to the rule that each member of SNCC must follow his own conscience; the board also observed a second dictum known to SNCC veterans, that no one could tell John Lewis what to do.[11] With SNCC thus neutralized by Lewis, King projected an aura of united black support as he prepared to bring his "soul force" to bear on the white folkways of Dallas County.

King's plan of provocation was an open secret to Selma's officials. In October 1964 the minister's briefcase had been stolen in Anniston, complete with detailed strategy papers on "Project Alabama," and soon every law en-forcement officer in the state was poring over these documents.[12] They were therefore aware that the SCLC intended to exploit Jim Clark's violent tenden-cies—indeed, during the early 1960s Clark and his paramilitary posse had torn through much of Alabama hitting or taunting civil rights workers. The only question was whether Clark, and Selma's leading citizens, would display the unbridled racist behavior that King expected and counted on.

Moderate whites in Selma trembled not only at the prospect of new dem-onstrations but also at the thought of Sheriff Clark overreacting and creating a public relations nightmare for the city. These concerns added new worry lines to the nervous-looking mayor of Selma, thirty-five-year-old Joseph Smither-man. This former appliance salesman had risen in politics by pledging to up-grade the city's image and attract new industry, a goal that racial turmoil could wreck. Smitherman therefore created the post of public safety director and filled it with a professional lawman, Wilson Baker, to keep the irascible Sheriff Clark in check. The hefty Baker conceded little to Clark in brawn, but in temperament he fit more the mold of a Laurie Pritchett. At the University of Alabama he had instructed classes in the techniques of modern law enforce-ment that minimized the use of force. In Selma, Baker could expect to test those principles fully against both black protesters and white hard-liners who venerated Jim Clark and favored bumper stickers that showed a tattered Con-federate soldier saying, "Hell No, I Ain't Forgettin'!"

King made Selma his primary headquarters in January 1965, and it did not take long for the expected violence to erupt. On January 18, as King entered the Hotel Albert, a twenty-six-year-old member of the National States Rights party leaped at him, punched him twice in the head, and kicked at his groin. John Lewis saved his mentor, stretching the code of nonviolence far enough to wrap King's assailant in a peaceful bear hug until Wilson Baker could subdue the man. While Baker angrily dragged the culprit off to jail, King moved into a room at the hotel, the first Negro ever to do so.[13] Later that night at a church rally King looked past Selma to a national audience, exhorting blacks to fill the jails and "arouse the federal government" to assure the ballot.[14]

Wilson Baker worked overtime at his new job of protecting Selma from the effects of any violent misstep against King. When the Nazi party leader George Lincoln Rockwell headed for King's church rally with two henchmen, Baker's police spirited them off to the city jail. Baker also quieted Jim Clark, whom he regarded as "an intelligent man" though easily "swayed by the last people that talked with him."[15] As a result the rally went smoothly; by the SCLC's media-conscious standards, it was a severe disappointment.

King's staff held a midnight meeting to discuss the looming crisis of an uneventful campaign. The ministers doubted that they could maintain press coverage in the absence of some conflict. They would try one more day to provoke someone in the possee or Jim Clark into committing some violent act. If this did not work, then Dr. King would make a face-saving out and find another community in Alabama to try again. Baker kept apprised of these plans through an informant at the meeting, an obscure civil rights worker blackmailed for homosexual behavior. The sheriff drawled to his police force, "Let's control the posse and Clark one mo' day, and we'll be through."[16] Then he received a phone call from an anxious Mayor Smitherman. Jim Clark was furious at Baker's soft policy toward King, swearing he would arrest anyone who tried to register the next day.

On the morning of January 19, blacks found Jim Clark barring their way to the Selma courthouse. When Amelia Boynton was slow to move aside, Clark seized the tall, stout woman by the back of the collar and shoved her halfway down the block into a waiting police car. In all, Clark found sixty-seven aspiring registrants guilty of "unlawful assembly" and had them arrested also. Mayor Smitherman and Wilson Baker watched Clark's antics in dismay. The sheriff was "out of control," they lamented to newsmen, who seemed more interested in recording Clark's latest outrages for national consumption.[17]

On Wednesday, January 20, Clark determined to face down Negro leaders and his white critics alike. "You are here to cause trouble, that's what you are doing," he barked at John Lewis, who was leading fifty Negroes toward the courthouse. The sheriff then issued Lewis an insult and a warning: "You are an agitator, and that is the lowest form of humanity. If you do not disperse in one minute or go in as I have directed you, you will be under arrest for unlawful assembly."[18] After Lewis, his followers, and a second wave of fifty registrants were all taken to jail, Clark warned a third contingent that he would brook no attempt to enter through the front door. This was too much for Wilson Baker, who countermanded the order. But Clark's deputies loyally blocked the entrance, and for the next several minutes Selma's two rival lawmen glared at each other from a distance of several yards while aides shuttled between them. Clark ended the standoff by warning the marchers that they had one minute to move and by then having them all arrested.

Clark was only now hitting his stride. On Friday, January 22, 105 Negro teachers—representing one of the most conservative elements in the black community—donned their best Sabbath-day clothes and marched slowly around the courthouse in silent protest. They were routed with clubs and electric cattle prods by Clark and his deputies. Three days later blacks marched to the courthouse under protection of a federal court order forbidding city and county officials to impede the "orderly process" of voter registration. Clark did not care. He swaggered up and down the line, bullying people with threats and shoves. When one Annie Lee Cooper defiantly told Clark, "There ain't nobody scared around here," Clark pushed her off balance. But Cooper, at 226 pounds, was even larger than Clark, and now she was also angrier. A single punch dropped Clark to his knees, and a second sent him to the ground. one of Clark's deputies grabbed the woman from behind, but she dispatched him by stepping on his foot and elbowing him in the stomach, freeing herself long enough to fell Clark once again. At last three deputies pinned her to the ground, and Clark faced a moment of truth. Newsmen were looking on, ready to report and photograph any improper move. Without hesitation Clark sat astride her stomach and clubbed the woman senseless. Several blacks began to interfere, but King stopped them despite his own intense anger. The sound of the clubbing could be heard throughout the crowd that had gathered in the street. By the next day the political echoes of the beating had resounded through the country.[19]

Before King entered Selma, Lyndon Johnson had expected the civil rights issue to lie discreetly fallow for a year while he cultivated bills for Medicare and aid to education. But in January 1965 the President instructed Nicholas Katzenbach, who had replaced Robert Kennedy as attorney general, to accelerate his work on a voting rights bill. Johnson recognized that King—and Clark—had made civil rights once again the nation's most urgent domestic issue.

Clark's roughhouse tactics could not even quell the movement locally. On February 1 King personally led a mass march toward the Selma courthouse. He was arrested, along with his aide Ralph Abernathy and 770 demonstrators, most of them schoolchildren. The next day Clark's deputies sent 550 more, largely young black marchers, to prison. The sheriff seemed not to recognize his part in King's pageant of reform symbolism, in which every arrest became an indictment of the police, every beating a way to conscript new civil rights supporters among the mass of citizens.

From his prison cell, with its steel-gray walls and acrid facilities, King continued to guide the Selma protest, sending covert notes that revealed a grasp of minute detail and an instinct for protest as national theater. He instructed the SCLC's executive director, Andrew Young, to try to involve Leroy Collins, now a federal mediator in racial conflicts. He requested that Young urge Lyndon Johnson to send an emissary and appeal to Selma's officials in a White House press conference. Above all, Young should try to arrange for a congressional delegation to investigate conditions in Dallas County. Now, King emphasized, was the time to keep the pressure on: "By all means don't let them get the offensive. They are trying to give the impression that they are an orderly and good community because they integrated public accommodations. We must insist that voting is the issue and here Selma has dirty hands." King ordered new mass marches as well, until Dallas County's jails packed in some three thousand blacks. Still, King found the campaign too lax. When one of his lieutenants let a day lapse without a major demonstration, King dashed off a rebuke to Young from his makeshift prison office: "Please don't be soft. . . . In a crisis we must have a sense of drama."[20]

King displayed that dramatic sense in abundance as he penned a letter to the American people that urged them to support federal protection of the franchise and that pointed out, "THERE ARE MORE NEGROES IN JAIL WITH ME THAN THERE ARE ON THE VOTING ROLLS."[21] Once again the acoustics of a Southern jail cell proved ideally suited to carry his message to the public. Sympathy demonstrations took place in numerous cities, and a bipartisan congressional group of twelve Democrats and three Republicans led by Michigan's Charles Diggs arrived in Selma to study the racial situation.

While King's aides stirred the caldron of discontent to their leader's specifications, other black leaders favored a more vigorous boil. SNCC organizers invited Malcolm X to visit a church rally in Selma on February 3, to the dismay of SCLC officers who feared his mesmerizing diatribes. As the ministers winced, loud cheers greeted Malcolm's warning that "the white man should thank God that Dr. King is holding his people in check, because . . . there are other ways to obtain their ends." If King's tactics failed, Malcolm added, those "other ways" would be tried.[22] Andrew Young and other ministers frantically pressed a reluctant Coretta King to give a calming follow-up speech on the nonviolent ideals of the movement. She too drew cheers, confirming only that Selma's Negroes would move down any path that promised an end to white domination.

If the Negro rank and file had not fully decided what road to travel, the leadership was groping as well. After his speech Malcolm confided to Coretta King his regret at not being able to visit her jailed husband. He wanted to let Dr. King know, "I didn't come to Selma to make his job difficult. I really did come thinking that I could make it easier. If the white people realize what the alternative is, perhaps they will be more willing to hear Dr. King."[23] Eighteen days later he was assassinated by his former Black Muslim colleagues, an act that generated countless conspiracy theories and endless speculation on where his search for a strategy of black protest would have led.

Close associates reported that King, too, was struggling with doubts about the political wisdom of his course. Yet he continued to thread a path between the critics of direct action and those of nonviolence. On February 9, four days after bailing out of jail, the minister traveled to Washington to court and prod the white liberals critical of his campaign. Vice-President Humphrey, Attorney General Katzenbach, and finally Lyndon Johnson all pledged to submit a voting rights bill to Congress "very soon."[24]

While King tightened the movement's claim on federal support, the Reverend James Bevel assumed the burden of raising local tensions. On February 8

Bevel and a small group of Negroes trying to register at the Dallas County courthouse found Jim Clark "shaking with anger" at this latest incursion against his authority. The sheriff jabbed Bevel in the abdomen with his billy club, then grabbed his shoulders and forced him backward down the courthouse steps. In a low voice, taut with fury, Clark accused Bevel of "making a mockery out of justice." Bevel began to tell Clark of his constitutional rights but was cut off by the sheriff's repeated use of his club. When Bevel still refused Clark's command to leave the courthouse, two deputies arrested him. During his imprisonment Bevel became feverish and had to be transferred to an infirmary. But there was no mistaking that this act of humanity occurred in Sheriff Clark's domain—despite doctors' protests, a deputy secured Bevel to his sickbed with leg irons.[25]

The rougher Clark's tactics, the more he unwittingly inspired his victims to embrace nonviolent resistance. On February 10, Clark's men arrested 165 protesting youths, then chased them out of town, lashing out with electric cattle prods as they drove alongside. "You wanted to march, didn't you?" the deputies called out. *"Now march!"* After a three-mile forced run the youths stumbled into the countryside, crying, vomiting, still burning from the shocks of the cattle prods.[26] Yet two days later, when Clark checked into a hospital with chest pains (complaining that the blacks were giving him a heart attack), 200 young Negroes knelt before the courthouse to pray for Clark's recovery "in mind and body." Two children, aged seven and fourteen, carried signs that read from one to the next: "Get well fast sheriff—we miss you."[27] Some whites may have been moved, though others accused the blacks of "putting on an act." But Rachel West Nelson, nine years old when she joined the prayer vigil, remembered this as a sincere gesture, explaining, "When we prayed for something it wasn't a joke. . . . We didn't joke with the Lord."[28] Another black youngster felt that demonstrating "just wasn't the same without Jim Clark fussing and fuming": "We honestly miss him."[29] It was as if Clark's blustering, by showing blacks in raw form the evils they were resisting, had strengthened their sense of moral mission.

Clark soon returned to guard the courthouse against new registrants, and he clearly had not spent his convalescence rethinking his ways. On February 16 the Reverend C. T. Vivian brought two dozen people to the courthouse steps, and with the élan of a much larger man he engaged Clark in a one-sided Socratic examination, peppering the sheriff with sharp questions about his conduct and the Constitution. As Vivian became more openly disdainful of Clark's behavior, the sheriff suddenly wheeled around and with a swing of his club sent the minister reeling down the steps. Indifferent to the news cameras rolling nearby, Clark pointed to Vivian and ordered his arrest. The event, a reporter understated, "made vivid television."[30]

As Alabama Negroes heeded the Reverend King's call for night marches in nearby towns, the hostility of whites flared into armed violence. In the rural community of Marion, Colonel Al Lingo's state troopers ambushed a group of marchers. One trooper assaulted a woman and her infirm father. When her son, twenty-six-year-old Jimmy Lee Jackson, interceded, the trooper shot him in the stomach at close range. Jackson died two days later. His funeral drew two hundred mourners and an angry eulogy from Martin Luther King. Who killed Jimmy Lee Jackson? He was killed, King declared, by every lawless sheriff, every racist politician from governors on down, every indifferent white minister, every passive Negro who "stands on the sidelines in the struggle for justice." No sermon by King lacked a note of hope, and this one, too, urged blacks to work "passionately and unrelentingly to make the American dream a reality."[31] King had already concluded, though, that Alabama's white citizens would not soon share that dream of their own accord; that would require federal force. More than ever, King the dreamer thought and acted in terms of harsh political facts.

"Bloody Sunday"

As at Birmingham in 1963 the excesses of uniformed vigilantes now drew the President into the vortex of racial conflict. On Friday March 5, 1965, King spent over an hour conferring with Lyndon Johnson at the White House and received assurances that a voting rights bill would soon be introduced in Congress. Moreover it would bear the support of Senate Minority Leader Dirksen, all but guaranteeing an early end to a Southern filibuster. It remained for civil rights leaders to solidify popular opinion in favor of rapid federal action on the voting rights issue. For this King planned a fifty-four-mile march from Selma to Montgomery to petition Governor Wallace of Alabama for protection of black registrants. King did not imagine that this act would affect the stance of Alabama's premier spokesman for Jim Crow. But such a march, uniting blacks and whites as in the pilgrimage to Washington nearly two years before, might stir the country in a way that would overwhelm any opposition Wallace or others could mount.

White Alabamans reacted to the proposed march with the usual hostility and more than ordinary fear. Governor Wallace publicly announced that he would take all measures to prevent the march as a hazard to public safety. Privately he instructed Sheriff Clark and Colonel Al Lingo of the state troopers to halt the marchers with a minimum of adverse publicity, and he assured Mayor Smitherman that Selma would remain peaceful. The prospects were not promising, however. Wilson Baker began his rounds at the courthouse, where he broke up mob assaults on seventy white professors, liberal ministers, and their wives who had gathered from across the state to rally for black voting rights. He then visited Smitherman to argue for the second time in as many days that Clark and Lingo would never restrain their forces. In disgust Baker declared that he wanted no part of a massacre, and he urged the mayor to have city police halt the marchers before they reached Lingo's state troopers or Clark's county deputies. But not even Baker's threats to resign could shake Smitherman's sanguine insistence that all would be well. At last, several city council members, more concerned to preserve peace in the office than in the street, arranged a compromise: Baker's city police should do nothing, either to stop the marchers or to cooperate with Clark and Lingo. In short, if the marchers were heading for a bloodbath, only two of three law enforcement groups would perpetrate it.[32]

Six hundred blacks gathered outside Brown Chapel African Methodist Episcopal Church on Sunday morning, March 7, 1965, to begin the trek to Alabama's capital. At the head of the march were King's bold grass-roots organizer Hosea Williams and SNCC's John Lewis. King himself did not stay to lead the march, chiefly because his staff had caught rumors of a plot on his life more serious than most. King also favored delaying the march until Tuesday, the ninth, long enough, he hoped, for the federal judge Frank Johnson to void Wallace's ban against it. He tried to persuade Hosea Williams to wait, but the crowd and Williams's own impatience permitted no postponement. King therefore blessed the fait accompli and returned to Atlanta by plane to preside over his congregation. Then Williams and Lewis led their flock toward the Edmund Pettus Bridge, where Wilson Baker, Jim Clark, and Colonel Al Lingo were waiting.[33]

State troopers' cars with Confederate insignia lined the sides of Highway 80, and troopers wearing gas masks beneath their blue helmets stood with billy clubs ready as the six hundred blacks toted their sleeping blankets across the bridge. The march codirectors had just time enough for a whispered exchange over the prospects for survival: "John, can you swim?" "No." "I can't either, and I'm sure we're gonna end up in that river."[34] From the other side of the bridge, Major John Cloud represented Colonel Lingo, in tone as well as in delegated authority. "Turn around and go back to your church," the major shouted into a bullhorn. He gave the marchers two minutes to disperse. Hosea Williams requested "a word with the major," but Cloud snapped back, "There is no word to be had." The Negroes bowed their heads in a prayerful manner but did not retreat. Within a minute Cloud ordered the troopers to advance, and they rushed forward in a flying wedge, clubs poised to strike.[35]

Almost alone among the marchers, John Lewis held his ground. He fell from the first blow of the onslaught, his skull fractured in the exact spot where he had been struck during the freedom rides. Further blows sent other Negroes to the ground screaming, clutching their heads, while white onlookers cheered the troopers' efforts. While most blacks ran for their lives, five women remained unconscious at the site of the original attack. One was a prime mover in the voting rights campaign, Amelia Boynton. A trooper had clubbed her in the back of the neck, and she had fallen by the roadside. As she began to stir, a trooper ordered her to get up and run or she would be teargassed. A canister of gas soon afterward exploded near her head as troopers began the second wave of their assault on the marchers. Then with blacks running or limping in all directions, Sheriff Clark loosed his mounted possemen on the fleeing Negroes. The deputies charged with a rebel yell, swinging bullwhips and rubber tubing wrapped in barbed wire. Hosea Williams and the injured John Lewis eventually created a semblance of order among the bleeding, confused, and terrified refugees, and they retreated to Brown Chapel with Clark's lawmen close behind.

Wilson Baker stepped in at this point to try to prevent further bloodshed, but Sheriff Clark shoved past him, shouting that his patience was wearing thin. "I've already waited a month too damn long about moving in!" he said.[36] His deputies rioted in the Negro quarter that same day. At a black Baptist church they seized a young man and threw him through a stained-glass window depicting Christ as the Good Shepherd. Wilson Baker finally brought Clark under control with a sharp warning that blacks were going to start shooting soon unless the sheriff got his men out. But by this point the posse's random assaults had already exacted a heavy toll. Seventy Negroes were hospitalized and an equal number treated for lesser injuries.

That night the ABC network interrupted its feature film *Judgment at Nuremberg,* in order to broadcast footage of the assaults. By Monday evening all three major television networks had repeatedly stunned viewers with scenes of Selma in the throes of police fury. One California couple watching the six o'clock news found that the staccato editing of the carnage gave these electronic images an impact at once riveting and repellent:

> A shrill cry of terror, unlike any sound that had passed through a TV set, rose up as the troopers lumbered forward, stumbling sometimes on the fallen bodies. The scene cut to charging horses, their hoofs flashing over the fallen. Another quick cut: a cloud of tear gas billowed over the highway. Periodically the top of a helmeted head emerged from the cloud, followed by a club on the upswing. The club and the head would disappear into the cloud of gas and another club would bob up and down. *Unhuman.*

The scene shifted quickly to Brown Chapel, with "the bleeding, broken and unconscious" victims passing across the screen, "some of them limping alone, others supported on either side, still others carried in arms or on stretchers." At this point in the broadcast the wife turned away sobbing, unable to look any more. The images were still haunting the husband several hours later when he abruptly scheduled a midnight trip to join the Negro demonstrators in Alabama. Several thousand other Americans did the same.[37]

In the halls of Congress leaders on both sides of the aisle responded to the violence in astonishment and anger. The Republican senator Jacob Javits appraised law enforcement in Selma as an "exercise in terror," a fair summation of the fifty congressional speeches denouncing the city within two days of the assaults. These legislators were swept forward by a deluge of telegrams and letters, many from people normally conservative, even apolitical. William Proxmire of Wisconsin read to his Senate colleagues a message from the publisher of the *Chippewa Herald Telegram,* a journal that in Proxmire's view showed how events in Selma affected people who held "careful and stable" attitudes and were "certainly not characterized by emotional reaction." The publisher wrote that community leaders and working people alike had bombarded his journal with letters as "never in our experience." Was it not possible, he implored, to send federal marshals to stop "this bloody disregard of

Americans' constitutional rights"? He concluded by stressing the extraordinary character of this proposal: "Please understand, we and the many citizens who have contacted us, are generally not advocates of this type of intervention, but we see no other recourse in this situation. It is not a time for words; it is a time for action."[38]

The *Chippewa Herald Telegram* knew its middle American readers. The national mood now clearly favored federal action to guarantee voting rights, as was confirmed by surveys and the outpouring of letters and telegrams to newspapers and congressmen.[39] Demonstrators also crowded the sidewalk in front of the White House, imploring President Johnson to intervene against the rampaging Alabama police.

Predictably Governor George Wallace issued a public defense of the state and local forces at the march; less predictably he summoned Jim Clark to the governor's mansion for a harangue that contained few homilies but a good many references to political stupidity. Clark's impulsiveness had played into the most ambitious plans of King and his aides.[40] Yet the governor's tirade missed the heart of his problem, which was not Clark but a whole system of race relations that could no longer be kept from public view.

While the civil rights movement had exploited the accident of history that made Jim Clark sheriff of Dallas County, still the movement thrived because Jim Clark was by no means a rare species of Southern lawman. Before the movement arrived in Selma, he was known as a competent, well-liked peace officer, and by the standards of the region not especially severe toward blacks. Though Clark displayed a short temper in coping with protests, he nonetheless fit a common mold of Southern lawmen, given to proud self-assertion and raised to equate the public welfare with the maintenance of a caste tradition. Had Clark somehow controlled his anger, King would quite likely have found another sheriff steeped in the same folkways, and for whom the unfamiliar deterrent of national television exposure would exert less force than a lifetime of social habit.

King's next challenge was to maintain the drama of Selma without permitting his followers to react in anger, or in defiance of federal authority. Already tensions in the black community were building. Hosea Williams told seven hundred marchers who had taken refuge in Brown Chapel after the assault, "I once was captured by the German Army, and I want to tell you that the Germans never were as inhuman as the state troopers of Alabama." And just before leaving for a hospital, swathed in bandages, John Lewis assailed federal inaction: "I don't see how President Johnson can send troops to Vietnam . . . [and] the Congo . . . and can't send troops to Selma, Alabama." He added a bitter coda: "Next time we march, we may have to keep going when we get to Montgomery. We may have to go on to Washington."[41]

King had no intention of going that far, however; he was still less interested in besieging the President than in beseeching him. Returning to Selma a day after learning of the violence there, King reassumed command of the campaign and prepared to lead a new march on Tuesday, March 9. But before he could do so the minister discovered that Judge Frank Johnson was about to issue a temporary injunction against further efforts to march to Montgomery, pending his decision on Wallace's request for a permanent ban. Despite rising black anger—against Governor Wallace, President Johnson, and "de Lawd" himself—King decided he could not risk national support for federal action or his own ties with the administration by defying a federal injunction.

On Monday morning SNCC's young men refused to wait for King to catch up to the masses. Many blacks in Selma appeared eager for a confrontation with the troopers, echoing the claim of one middle-aged man: "If they gonna be violence, that's okay. They caught us by surprise yesterday. Next time, we gonna give as good as we git." SNCC's Willie Ricks tried to provide the final push. Marching a crowd of schoolchildren back and forth in front of Brown's Chapel, he encouraged them to overrun two lines of troopers on either side. Ricks ignored the SCLC ministers who tried to stop him from "inciting the people." Other SNCC workers refused to ask Ricks to withdraw. After watching a few shoving matches between the children and the troopers, Ricks realized that his plan would not work and he dispersed his young cohorts. By then the SCLC leaders were furious, and Martin Luther King most of all.[42]

Dr. King had over the years abided criticism from every faction of the movement with nearly unfailing modesty and courtliness. But Willie Ricks had appeared to endanger the children, the movement, and King's authority all at once. At a closed meeting in the back room of Brown Chapel the minister was in a hellfire-and-brimstone mood. Cleveland Sellers remembered King as "visibly angry" as he summoned Ricks before him:

"Come here son." Ricks moved forward and stood in front of Dr. King.

"I've been out here fighting for a long time and I know what I'm doing. I'm in charge here and I intend to remain in charge. You can't hurt me. Remember that. You are not Martin Luther King! I'm Martin Luther King. No matter what you do, you'll never be a Martin Luther King."[43]

Ricks did not reply. The meeting soon ended, with positions clear and no differences resolved. Still, if King failed to convert the unbelieving, his words did seem to curb SNCC's open heresies. Following the showdown at Brown Chapel SNCC leaders decided to move their base of operations to Montgomery, provide token support for the campaign in Selma, and avoid public criticism of the SCLC.

On Tuesday morning King prepared to lead fifteen hundred blacks and whites to the Edmund Pettus Bridge, hoping, as he acknowledged afterward, to give them an outlet for their pride and resentment. King never told the enthusiastic crowd that he had already agreed to a compromise devised by the federal mediator Leroy Collins, whereby King would turn back after a token march. The throng outside Brown Chapel erupted in cheers when King emerged with Abernathy and declared, "We march." Aside from a few trusted aides, only King knew, as he said softly to Harris Wofford, "But we may not march very far."[44]

Once more Colonel Lingo's troopers leered at the marchers just beyond the bridge. This time, though, they planned insult rather than injury. Apprised of King's agreement to turn back, they suddenly wheeled out of the way, leaving a clear path to Montgomery. This intensified the pressure on King to lead his cohorts on or risk humiliation. Already SNCC staffers in the group, like Cleveland Sellers and James Forman, were charging him with timidity and implying cowardice. But King had set his course all along on the goal of federal support, and he would not jeopardize it for ephemeral cheers from SNCC's young militants. As Lingo's men sneered from the roadside, King abruptly ordered the marchers back to the church. SNCC youths looked ahead at the clear expanse of road and exchanged bitter gibes at "de Lawd." Many other marchers, though, sighed in relief not to find themselves pitted—some for a second time—against the people they referred to as "Alabama's storm troopers." To cushion any discord or disappointment Andy Young broke into a freedom song, "We Love Everybody," that soon had the marchers joyfully chanting—back to Brown Chapel. They began adding verses in the nonviolent tradition as they went: "We love Governor Wallace in our heart." The song embraced even Colonel Lingo's henchmen: "We love the state troopers in our heart."[45] But one song may have been better left for another occasion. SNCC youths must have winced when the returning marchers began a spirited rendition of "Ain't Gonna Let Nobody Turn Me Around."[46]

No violence marred this second march, but back at Brown Chapel James Forman argued that here, too, lay proof of white racism. Why was no one attacked? "You know the answer. They don't beat white people. It's Negroes they beat and kill." But his harsh words did not carry the crowd. A Selma Negro answered him, "That's right. They didn't beat us today because the world was here with us. But that's what we want. Don't let these white people feel that we don't appreciate their coming. We've paid our dues, all these years, and it's too late for us to keep paying them all by ourselves."[47]

In the aftermath of the march Selma once again tore its way into the nation's headlines. Four white Unitarian ministers were assaulted as they left a black soul food restaurant, while customers in a white restaurant across the way passively observed the scene. Among the victims was the Reverend James J. Reeb, a welfare worker in Boston's black slums. He rose slowly but remained dizzy, his eyesight unfocused. Two days after the incident he died from the blows. An integrated march and service on March 15 commemorated Reeb's sacrifice. Then as Jim Clark peered from a window of the city jail, Martin Luther King placed a wreath at the sheriff's door.[48]

From the White House, Lyndon Johnson monitored the events in Selma with growing fury. He had already determined to press for a voting rights act, but he now felt that "Bloody Sunday," as blacks spoke of the March 7 brutality, called for more than a routine request to Congress. Johnson considered a nationally televised address on voting rights before a joint session of Congress. Before acting, he consulted the Senate leaders Mansfield and Dirksen, heard their objections that such a course might convey an impression of rash, impulsive conduct to the public, and as usual remained firm about his plans while convincing both senators of his correctness. Monday evening, March 15, Johnson entered the House of Representatives to make his case for a powerful new civil rights law.

The President began slowly, amid a hush so complete that even the clicks of photographers' cameras sounded clearly in the chamber. Johnson became more animated as he warned the legislators and the public: if America defeated every enemy, doubled its wealth, conquered the stars, and yet failed to resolve this issue, "then we will have failed as a people and as a nation." Selma, he continued at a quickened pace, marked a turning point in American history equal to Lexington and Concord, equal to Appomattox. What happened there was "part of a far larger movement . . . the effort of American Negroes to secure for themselves the full blessings of American life." Then, thumbs raised, fists clenched, radiating determination, Johnson lifted consensus politics to its full moral height: "Their cause must be our cause, too. Because it is not just Negroes, but really all of us who must overcome the crippling legacy of bigotry and injustice. And," he concluded with a pledge that brought tears to Martin Luther King, Jr., "we shall . . . overcome."[49]

Johnson's speech was punctuated by nearly forty ovations from the floor of the Congress. While his specially invited guest, the Reverend King, watched in absentia—having just hours before eulogized James Reeb in Selma—Negro leaders united in unreserved tribute to Johnson's commitment. One Negro lawyer whose references to federal leadership generally ranged from unpleasant to unprintable told Harris Wofford, "When I heard him saying, 'We shall overcome,' I just couldn't believe it. Why, if he had asked me, I would even have advised him, 'You better not say that. That's going too far.' He's with us—he's really with us!"[50]

Two days later Judge Frank Johnson decided that he, too, was with the civil rights forces. Johnson had grown up in Alabama and had once accepted its segregationist ways. Since their college days together George Wallace had esteemed Johnson as a valued friend. But Johnson's growing liberalism on race issues led the governor to emend his view of the judge, whom he now discerned as a "low-down, carpetbaggin', scalawaggin', race-mixin' liar."[51] It was an appraisal that Johnson's next ruling could only have deepened.

Against a backdrop of continued white vigilante actions, Johnson first ruled that Clark and Lingo, "while acting under instructions from Governor Wallace," were not enforcing any valid laws but deliberately trampling on the right to assemble peacefully and petition for the redress of grievances. It was true, Johnson observed, that the general public also held a right to unimpeded transit, and therefore "the extent of the right to assemble, demonstrate and march peaceably" on the highways and streets in an orderly manner "should be commensurate with the wrongs" at issue. "In this case," Johnson concluded, "the wrongs are enormous."[52] The judge then struck down the governor's request for an injunction. There would be one more march, with state and local officials forbidden to interfere, and with the Justice Department conveying through Frank Johnson its intent to assist. King and his lieutenants celebrated Johnson's decision by planning a nonviolent demonstration beyond anything Selma—or the South—had ever experienced.

Marching to Montgomery

A successful march depended on continued black solidarity, and King worked quickly to repair the frayed edges of his coalition. Although federal leaders now fully backed King's endeavor, the minister found that winning over the firebrands in SNCC was more difficult. While "Bloody Sunday" had acted as a lure for SNCC's risk-oriented volunteers, the retreat two days later reminded SNCC workers of their doubts about the federal government, coalition politics, and "de Lawd" himself. King's lieutenants Andrew Young, James Bevel, and Hosea Williams spent four days conferring with James Forman and other SNCC leaders, trying to salvage some show of unity for the voting rights campaign. What made this difficult task possible was that there remained within SNCC a faction committed to the goals and methods of the SCLC, eloquently represented by Chairman John Lewis. SNCC finally promised to permit individual members to march to Montgomery, though without endorsing the event. In return SCLC leaders pledged to join a SNCC-sponsored march in the nation's capital to protest the seating of five newly elected Mississippi congressmen.[53] As in the agreements before the March on Washington, once again black leaders subordinated their disputes and resentments to the common task of winning federal reform action.

As King fixed plans for a third demonstration, on March 21, George Wallace continued to parade along the ramparts of segregation, warning that there could be no guarantees of safety for demonstrators. The governor's threats posed a painful dilemma for Lyndon Johnson. He knew he could not permit a repeat of the "Bloody Sunday" massacre, yet he worried that sending troops into Wallace country might only provoke violence. In a last bid to forge consensus out of conflict, he summoned Wallace to the White House for an emergency application of the "Johnson technique."

For three hours Johnson played to the complex figure that was George Wallace, whom he sized up as "a nervous man; a rough, shrewd politician." Johnson easily matched Wallace in his rougher qualities. In the course of earthy, often profane exchanges the President told the governor that he would tolerate no misunderstanding such as occurred between Eisenhower and Orval Faubus over Little Rock. If state and local authorities did not protect the marchers, Johnson "would not hesitate one moment to send in federal troops." Yet Johnson also played to Wallace's pride and ambition, seeing in the man not merely a stick-figure racist but also a scrapper who had risen from dirt farmer's poverty to become a champion of the masses—Alabama style. When not fretting that other politicians might appear to be more staunchly segregationist than he, this former Sunday-school teacher had worked to increase the number of Alabama's public schools, hospitals, and roads, and to provide free textbooks to all the state's children. Johnson played to those flashes of social vision in urging his visitor to "stop looking back to 1865 and start planning for 2065." Blacks were eventually going to vote in Alabama, and there could be no limits to the national aspirations of a Southern governor who became a symbol of racial harmony by supporting universal suffrage.

Wallace was noncommittal but apparently not unmoved by Johnson's alternating currents of firmness and flattery. Returning to Alabama, he said privately that he understood how Johnson got his legislation through Congress. Asked how the new President compared with JFK, Wallace replied, "Johnson's got much more on the ball," and then decided that even this did not adequately convey the President's powers of persuasion. "If I hadn't left when I did," the governor added, "he'd have had me coming out *for* civil rights."[54]

Not even three hours of close-range reasoning by Lyndon Johnson, however, could prevail over years of reflexive race baiting. Once back in Montgomery, Wallace inveighed against the upcoming march and fired off a telegram to the President, claiming that his state could not bear the cost of mobilizing the forces needed to defend the demonstrators. That money, he explained in his most presentable populist rhetoric, could better be used to help needy Alabamans, a category that tacitly excluded blacks seeking the ballot. Johnson now saw his chance to send in federal units without appearing to violate state authority. The Alabama National Guard would be federalized by executive order, the President replied; the governor would have all the "assistance" necessary to ensure the safety of the marchers. Johnson later wrote of this dextrous stroke, "So the troops went in after all. . . . But they were not intruders forcing their way in; they were citizens of Alabama. That made all the difference in the world."[55]

On March 21, for the third time in two weeks, demonstrators gathered at Brown Chapel to begin their journey to Montgomery. This time there were some notable changes in the scene. State troopers kept a low profile, while federal marshals and Alabama guardsmen flanked the roadside, and helicopters scouted for signs of danger. The assembly outside the chapel had also grown from the original band of some five hundred to several thousand, including many from outside Selma. It was a diverse army of white and black, fresh Northern volunteers and veterans of many nonviolent campaigns, ministers of all faiths, and even small children.

Standing in front of the chapel, King extended a special welcome to poor blacks who might have felt out of place among the many affluent, educated marchers:

> Those of us who are Negroes don't have much. We have known the long night of poverty. Because of the system, we don't have much education and some of us don't know how to make our nouns and verbs agree. But thank God we have our bodies, our feet, and our souls.[56]

Ralph Abernathy as usual expressed mass sentiment with matchless clarity. Surveying the crowd through sunglasses, he urged it on with the promise "Wallace, it's all over now."[57] Following these brief speeches Highway 80 filled with people stepping toward Montgomery, eager to bring Wallace the news.

The sweep of humanity en route to Alabama's capital fairly embodied the liberal coalition for civil rights. Black ministers directed the march, with Andrew Young roaming the ranks, tending the sunburned, tendering encouragement to all. White clerics were prominent as well, none so much as Rabbi Abraham Heschel, whose tall figure, massive beard, and flowing hair inspired the awestruck comment "Why, there *is* the Lawd!"[58] Assistant Attorney General John Doar came to see that the marchers enjoyed full safety, in accord with Judge Johnson's order and President Johnson's will. Uncelebrated white citizens found a model of determination in one-legged James Letherer of Michigan, who pressed forward on crutches, lamenting his real handicap—that he couldn't "do more to help these people." Seventeen-year-old Joe Boone, arrested seven times in the Selma campaign, explained that his mother and father never thought this day would come. "But it's here and I want to do my part." So, too, did the seventy-eight-year-old grandfather of Jimmy Lee Jackson, Cager Lee, who could march only a few miles a day but always returned the next, saying, "Just got to tramp some more."[59]

At the head of the massive, joyous assemblage was the Reverend Martin Luther King, strolling in shirt-sleeves, chatting now with Coretta, now with John Lewis or some other aide, joking easily with newsmen, clearly relishing the event. Although he did not march the entire fifty-four miles, having left for a fund-raising engagement on Tuesday amid new rumors of an assassination plot, his presence dominated the event. As the black journal *Ebony* noted, cameramen and reporters strained to catch "every twist of the mouth and wrinkle of the forehead of leader King." To many Negroes who joined the march or lined its path to Montgomery, he appeared set apart for a heaven-sent mission of deliverance. As he led the burgeoning throng past one ecstatic woman, she cried out to all around her that she had kissed "the Martin Luther King!"[60]

Like most crusades for brotherhood, this one contained its share of sibling rivalry. In particular the artless piety of many older Negroes strained the patience of better-educated and often more cynical youths. At one stop a clique of Selma high school students snickered at an old minister on the roadside who loudly thanked God for sending King and the Reverend "Abernickel" to deliver them from Egypt land. But the exuberance of the march never permitted such squabbling to submerge the feeling of kinship that bound the participants together. The same Selma students meekly accepted a rebuke from the local activist Marie Foster. "Don't you make fun of him!" she said, in defending the wizened preacher, and further doused their elitism by observing, "It isn't pronunciation that counts." Then Foster and Amelia Boynton hastened to praise the students—and all the young—to a white onlooker, their voices warm with pride: "These kids are the great ones. . . . They were ahead of their parents and their teachers."[61] The generational divide still tested the movement's strength, but at least for these festive days the road to Montgomery seemed to span the gap.

The marchers similarly took in stride the displays of hostility by local whites. Under great pressure, segregationists contented themselves with relatively low-level harassment. A lone plane marked "The Confederate Air Force" buzzed overhead, but neither it nor Clark's possemen nor Lingo's troopers made any threatening maneuvers. Lyndon Johnson had made the federal presence felt throughout the march with an array of army vehicles and patrols.

Opponents of the march did assume an aggressive verbal stance: a number of hand radios in the crowd broadcast the news that the Alabama state legislature formally resolved to charge the marchers with free love, constant fornication, and a trail of sex orgies. This led several nuns in the march to offer good-humored laments over their lost reputations. Others complimented each other on their stamina—slogging through exhausting terrain day and night yet still finding the energy for endless debauchery. In the same light tone they greeted further charges that the march was Communist inspired. "There are as many Communists in the civil rights movement," King told a reporter, "as there are Eskimos in Florida."[62] Throughout the march he and other spokesmen reiterated that the movement was not about sex, communism, or any other irrelevancy introduced by its opponents. It was about equal constitutional rights.

The road to Montgomery led the marchers across flat farmlands, rough cotton patches, freshly plowed red fields, and pine thickets. Their lively singing kept up even when the blacktop lanes veered into ghostly swamps, where the still waters and dead tree stumps were enveloped by gray Spanish moss. Rain drenched the marchers on the third day but failed to dampen the spirit of the crowd. A black man boomed out a chant like an old spiritual—"Lift 'em up and lay 'em down, we are coming from Selma town!"—and people pushed forward to the beat. Along the roadside spectators answered the call-and-response greetings from one or another of the marchers:

What do you want?
Freedom!
When do you want it?
Now!
Where are we going?
Montgomery![63]

On Wednesday, the fourth day of the march, Montgomery came into view, about four miles in the distance. An array of celebrities now rewarded the crowd with an evening of entertainment, and their buoyant performances reflected the civil rights forces at the zenith of their confidence. Peter, Paul, and Mary, whose sweet-voiced renditions of protest songs had much in common with Dr. King's velvet phrasing of black demands, sang "The Times They Are a-Changin'." It was a softer, more widely palatable version of Bob Dylan's angry prophecy of social turmoil, yet it still caught the heady mood of a revolution in the making.

The King had his court jesters as well. Mike Nichols and Elaine May turned their satiric talents on George Wallace's telegram to Lyndon Johnson, which had lamely denied responsibility for the marchers. (Nichols, as Wallace: "I cannot afford to call the National Guard." May, as switchboard operator: "I don't see why not, it only costs a dime, you know.") The black comedian and activist Dick Gregory was more openly mordant in his mockery of both Cold War chauvinism and racism, as he discounted recent news that a Soviet cosmonaut had climbed out of his rocket in a heroic scientific experiment. That was mere "Communist propaganda," Gregory assured his audience. "What really happened," he elucidated, "is that they had engine trouble and the radio told them they were to make an emergency landing. 'We're going to put you down in Selma, Alabama,' their radio orders said. That's when that Russian decided to climb out."[64]

On Thursday the muddied but unbowed assemblage sang spirituals under raised umbrellas, then followed King through a misty drizzle into Montgomery. One of the marchers described the expectant mood as the crowd moved the final four miles toward a tense, defiant city:

[We advanced] past cheering Negro homes, then the business section of town with stony-faced, camera-clad whites peering hostilely from windows and balconies. We marched six abreast while helicopters buzzed over us. There was an amazing amount of restraint on both sides.

Then Montgomery's capitol came into view, the dome displaying the Alabama flag above the stars and bars of the Confederate banner. "The only American flags visible were those [the marchers] had carried."[65]

That final phase of the march offered one more test of black unity. Some three hundred largely young blacks who had walked the entire distance from Selma refused to let newly arriving "dignitaries" lead the way into the capital. "There's no mud on those shiny shoes," one youth said of a man who was pulled out of the front ranks. "I didn't see you fellows in Selma and I didn't see you on the road to Montgomery. Ain't nobody going to get in front of me but Dr. King." Such treatment risked displays of wounded vanity, but the sixty-three-year-old Roy Wilkins set the tone among civil rights leaders by politely walking from the front lines to a place behind the youths. Although some people urged the NAACP dean to return to the front, Wilkins declined, telling the young marchers, "You fellows deserve to go first."[66] His gesture, yielding the stature of "dignitary" but maintaining full dignity, said much about the spirit of the day.

That mood of harmony was equally evident in the greatest gathering of civil rights leaders since the 1963 March on Washington. Joining Dr. King and John Lewis of SNCC on the speakers platform were Wilkins, Whitney Young of the Urban League, A. Philip Randolph, and Bayard Rustin, all intent to show the black protest movement still united in its moral vision for the nation. The UN diplomat Ralph Bunche also made a rare political appearance, defying half a dozen serious ailments in order to lend his international prestige to the cause of black voting rights.

March 25, 1965, was a day for testimony, by prominent orators and by black townsfolk who had tried to register but could not. The crowd responded knowingly to these discouraging tales but remained exuberant through the last speech of this long day, which Ralph Abernathy introduced with a rapturous injunction: "As God called Joshua to lead His people across the Jordan, so also He called Martin Luther King to go to Montgomery and tell Pharaoh Wallace, 'Let my people go.' "[67]

As the sun slowly disappeared behind the capitol, King assured his listeners that despite the desperate acts of their antagonists they were "standing before the forces of power in the state of Alabama saying, 'We ain't goin' let nobody turn us around.' " Behind him the Reverend Bernard Lee grinned in affection and respect for the master orator, while booming out, "Tell it, Doctor!" and "Yessir!" in precisely timed counterpoint to King's rhythmic phrases. "We are on the move now," King promised, and no wave of racism, no burning of churches, no bombing of homes, no clubbing and killing of clergymen and young people would deter the march for freedom. "Let us march on to the realization of the American dream," a march until racism is annihilated and "the Wallaces of our nation tremble away in silence." There was a somber reflection on the costs yet to be paid for these advances: "I must admit to you there are still some difficult days ahead. We are still in for a season of suffering." But he assured them, in a catechism of faith,

> It will not be long, because truth pressed to earth will rise again.
> *How* long?
> *Not* long, because no lie can live forever.
> *How* long?
> *Not* long, because you will reap what you sow.
> *How* long?
> *Not* long, because the arc of the moral universe is long but it bends toward justice.

And for the pious listeners who drew their fortitude from hymns of God's righteous wrath: "*How* long? *Not* long, 'cause mine eyes have seen the glory of the coming of the Lord." King concluded in thundering tones:

> Glory, glory hallelujah!
> Glory, glory hallelujah!
> Glory, glory hallelujah![68]

The audience, now swelled to twenty-five thousand, sang the movement's anthem—modified to express the sense of triumph wrought by the march and all it represented—"We *Have* Overcome Today."

That same evening an act of violence marred the day's joyous mood, as the season of suffering claimed another martyr. Four Klansmen, racing along Highway 80, tracked a housewife from Detroit who had driven several blacks back to Selma and was returning for a second group. On a lonely stretch of road the Klansmen pulled even with the woman's car and, as she turned toward them, shot her to death. A young black SCLC worker also in the car, Leroy Moton, lay still as the murderers inspected the wreckage, and thus he escaped alive. The crime was solved within hours because one of the four men was the FBI informant Gary Rowe (who claimed he fired in the air).[69] But the death of Viola Liuzzo continued to haunt the national memory. While George Wallace scoffed that Americans were killed every day, Mrs. Liuzzo's fate became as much a symbol of the voting rights campaign as the march she had aided.

The Voting Rights Bill

Following the march to Montgomery, attention shifted to the voting rights bill beginning its own, sinuous journey past the gauntlet of Southern legislators. The measure the administration sent to Congress on March 19, 1965, authorized the attorney general to send federal examiners to supersede local registrars and regulations wherever discrimination occurred. A provision to trigger federal intervention included counties where fewer than half the adults had voted in the 1964 presidential election and where literacy tests or similar restrictions were then in force. The bill, in short, radically streamlined the Justice Department's efforts in disenfranchisement cases by providing an alternative to the cumbersome machinery of the courts.

Johnson lined up a powerful bipartisan convoy for the bill in the Senate, partly by directing his attorney general to work closely with the Republican minority leader, Everett Dirksen, in drafting the legislation. With a favorable political wind blowing toward Capitol Hill from Selma, Johnson's strategy reaped a harvest of sixty-six Senate cosponsors of the voting rights bill, just one vote shy of the two-thirds needed to end the expected Southern filibuster. The Senate's civil rights bloc also apprised Mississippi's James Eastland of the changing times by voting to instruct his Judiciary Committee—graveyard of many earlier bills for black rights—to report the voting rights bill to the Senate floor within fifteen days.

The fortnight of hearings before the Judiciary Committee brought forth the full spectrum of Southern objections to black suffrage. They ranged from the subtle legal obscurantism of North Carolina's senior senator, Sam Ervin, Jr., to fears of Communists and "immoral" Negroes voiced by the stocky, cigar-chomping Democratic boss Leander Perez of Louisiana's Plaquemines Parish. The hearings also elicited some troubling testimony about the mechanics of the bill, which, for example, categorized Alaska as guilty of disenfranchisement because snowfalls had kept election day turnout below 50 percent. At the same time, the formula for pinpointing disenfranchisement excluded Arkansas, Florida, Tennessee, and Texas, states where job reprisals and other extralegal measures, rather than literacy tests, kept Negroes from the polls. On April 9 the committee observed its fifteen-day deadline and reported the bill favorably, but left disputes over its complex provisions unresolved. Senator

Eastland claimed that a long period would be needed "to explain this bill to the American public."[70] Discussion promised to be intricate, extended, and, as Eastland and like-minded lawmakers hoped, interminable.

Debate did follow, but at a crisp pace not at all consonant with Southern plans to lay a verbal shroud over the voting rights bill. The bill carried too much momentum, a crucial quality that, as Johnson once observed, was "*not* a mysterious mistress" but "a controllable fact of political life."[71] In this case momentum came from the sustained national pressure for an effective voting rights measure, from the rare harmony between Senate leaders Mansfield and Dirksen, and from the President's precisely calibrated supervision of the legislative process. Johnson took care to indulge the tirades of Southern legislators against the bill and advised his allies in the Senate not to press for a vote on cloture too quickly.

On May 21 the cloture vote finally came, with Everett Dirksen ornately expressing "regrets" that he had to cut off the voices of his distinguished colleagues, "but with some measure of assurance that in the long veil of history, over the transient concerns of this fleeting day, they will find [him] not too far wrong."[72] He then brought strong Republican support behind the motion, and the Senate ended the filibuster by a vote of seventy to thirty. Roy Wilkins, by now a connoisseur of filibusters, found this one "lame" from the first. "In a way," he wrote, "I think the cloture vote saved face for the Southerners. That year they had neither their old energy nor the sympathy of the country behind them."[73]

Opponents of the bill seemed to weather their isolation better in the House of Representatives, where the Virginia Democrat Howard Smith kept the measure imprisoned in his Rules Committee for five weeks. Once remanded to custody of the full House, the bill came under fire for its method of classifying counties as guilty of disenfranchisement. Howard H. ("Bo") Callaway, Republican from Georgia, ridiculed the formula's arbitrary features and obvious Southern focus. Why not refine the formula still further? he inquired. It would advance the purpose of the legislators much more, he said, to select

all states which have an average altitude of 100 to 900 feet, an average yearly temperature of 68 to 77 degrees at seven A.M., average humidity of 80 to 87 percent, and a coastline of 400 miles. With this formula we encompass all the southern states attacked by . . . [the Administration bill], but have the added advantage of including all of North Carolina and excluding Alaska.[74]

Northern Republicans, hoping to share in the credit for a voting rights bill, eschewed Callaway's sardonic ways but also criticized the administration's measure. William M. McCulloch of Ohio, the party's ranking member of the Judiciary Committee and a proven civil rights advocate, castigated the bill's "punitive tone" toward the South and its unreliable triggering formula that did not cover all areas in which blacks were disenfranchised. He offered instead a bill that provided for federal action in any county upon receipt of twenty-five "meritorious complaints" of discrimination. The measure had the advantage of evincing no sectional bias. It also offered a way to encompass discriminatory areas such as Texas, which lay outside the curiously defined bounds of the administration's measure. Yet the McCulloch bill contained weaknesses that made it anathema to civil rights leaders. Although fair on the surface, the requirement of filing twenty-five complaints that the Justice Department found "meritorious" placed the burden of proof back on the longtime victims of discrimination, while multiplying the administrative problems of enforcement. Those very weaknesses acted like a magnet to draw Southern congressmen to the substitute bill, while partisan loyalties led all but ten Republicans, by the administration's gloomy count, to stand behind McCulloch's measure. If this Republican-Southern bloc remained firm, the administration's own bill had no chance of passage.

Here momentum proved more mysterious and benign than even Johnson could foresee. During the House debate over the rival voting rights bills, William M. ("Genial Big Bill") Tuck of Virginia delivered "the plain, unvarnished truth" that the McCulloch bill was "milder" and therefore "far more preferable." Tuck had hoped his speech would expose the administration's bill as an "unconstitutional monstrosity," but its main effect was to assert publicly that its opponents preferred a weaker bill. The historian and Johnson aide Eric Goldman noted that the Republican minority leader, Gerald Ford, "sat listening with the look of a man betrayed." Ford insisted that the McCulloch bill should be passed because it was a "better bill," not because it did less to guard the voting rights of blacks. But the next day the House voted to reject the McCulloch substitute bill by a wide margin, with twenty-three congressmen from Florida, Georgia, Louisiana, and Texas backing the administration.[75]

Verging on a decisive victory, civil rights leaders now prudently retreated enough to ease the bill through an impasse over the poll tax, a Southern mainstay for keeping poor Negroes (and whites) from voting. In 1964 the Twenty-fourth Amendment to the Constitution had banned poll taxes in federal elections. The House version of the voting rights bill sought to complete the amendment's work by abolishing the poll tax in state and local elections. The Senate, with Johnson's backing, had avoided such language as controversial and possibly unconstitutional, instead simply directing the attorney general to challenge all remaining poll taxes in the courts. A House-Senate conference resolved a protracted debate only after the attorney general brought assurances from Martin Luther King that he preferred the Senate wording to deadlock on the entire bill.

The congressional conferees concluded their work of smoothing the bill's passage with acts of homage to two powerful senators. They accepted, in modified form, an amendment earlier proposed by Everett Dirksen for improving the bill's trigger formula. The final bill, in Eric Goldman's words, "preserved the original formula as the basis of the law but added a provision so complex that it is impossible to determine its effect, if any, except in terms of the senator's personal and political needs."[76] The conferees also incorporated an amendment sponsored by Robert F. Kennedy of New York, designed to facilitate voting eligibility for the one million Puerto Ricans in his state, many of whom were literate in Spanish but not English. Some claimed that Kennedy's advocacy ensured special treatment for this amendment, but Kennedy had received no more than the standard courtesies accorded any freshman senator and likely future President.

On August 3, 1965, the House of Representatives passed the voting rights bill by 328 to 74, better than a four-to-one margin. On the following day the Senate followed suit with nearly equal decisiveness, 79 to 18. For the signing ceremonies on August 6 the President invited the major civil rights leaders and two less heralded pioneers of the movement: Rosa Parks, whose quiet pride had sparked the Montgomery bus boycott, and Vivian Malone, who had enrolled at the University of Alabama in 1963 after federal marshals escorted her past Governor George Wallace.

The White House ceremony, for all its grandeur, could not wholly conceal signs of wear in the civil rights coalition. While Johnson handed out eighty-nine pens in all, he consistently overlooked the bearlike figure of James Farmer. The CORE leader's earlier rejection of a moratorium on protests had deprived him of all access to the White House. Now it also placed him outside the President's peripheral vision. Roy Wilkins repeatedly called out, "Mr. President! Farmer!" but the President's hearing suddenly failed as well. Farmer finally walked over and virtually plucked a pen out of Johnson's hand.[77]

Johnson's conduct was more thoroughly presidential in projecting the symbolic importance of the new law. The signing ceremony took place in the President's Room, where, on August 6, 1861, Lincoln had signed a law freeing slaves impressed into the Confederate army. "Today," Johnson said of the new, peacetime measure, "is a triumph for freedom as huge as any victory that has ever been won on any battlefield."[78]

Both the sponsors and the opponents of the Voting Rights Act agreed that the new law bid fair to change race relations in the South more radically than at any other time since Reconstruction. Yet despite its far-reaching implications, the legislation enjoyed broader, more sustained public support than any previous civil rights measure. Less than four months elapsed between its formal introduction in Congress and its final passage, barely half the time needed to deliberate over the civil rights bill of 1964. Unlike many controversial bills that were whittled down in conference, this measure emerged more clearly and strongly worded than in its original draft. And both the House and the Senate gave the bill a mandate that approached unanimity outside the South and included several Southern legislators casting their first vote ever for a civil rights bill. Never before had the civil rights movement exercised so commanding or prestigious a position in national politics.

As in the passage of the Civil Rights Act of 1964, legal change found its catalyst in social disorder. The historian David Garrow has argued persuasively that at Selma, Martin Luther King refined to new sophistication the tactic of precipitating racist violence in order to win media coverage and, in turn, public support that could translate into legislation. The spasm of one-sided violence at Selma helped solidify a stronger, more quickly formed consensus for civil rights action than had occurred in 1963, when violence in Birmingham involved black rioters as well as rampaging white police.[79] The nation had also traveled far in those two years, becoming more sensitive to the indignities as well as the dangers blacks endured in seeking their rights.

King and his allies in protest also benefited from a political climate that continued to breed an astonishing variety of liberal programs. Far from standing as an isolated landmark of progressive legislation, the Voting Rights Act joined an extraordinary parade of reform bills entering the law books during this session of Congress. Between March and July of 1965 Congress targeted $900 million for Appalachia, extended the manpower training program, granted $1.5 billion in additional federal aid to public schools, and enacted Medicaid and Medicare to provide federally subsidized health care for the poor and the elderly. Following the Voting Rights Act there came, in September, the creation of a Cabinet post in Housing and Urban Development; in October, various antipollution measures and additional antipoverty programs; and in November, $2.4 billion for higher education. When President Johnson drew from his abundant storehouse of superlatives to term this Congress "the greatest in American history," liberals unreservedly concurred. From the other side of the aisle Barry Goldwater sniped at Johnson's unexampled domination of the legislative process with a contemptuous reference to the "Xerox Congress." With greater detachment, James Reston of the *New York Times* observed of Johnson, "He's getting everything through the Congress but the abolition of the Republican party, and he hasn't tried that yet."[80]

The voting rights campaign marked, in short, the convergence of two political forces at their zenith: the black campaign for equality and the broader movement for liberal reform. The struggle to assure blacks the ballot fit perfectly with the liberal call for expanded federal action to protect the rights of all citizens. At the same time the emphatic rise of the voting rights bill to the top of the liberal agenda attested to the impact of nonviolent direct action in dramatizing racism to the nation. Die-hard racists remained to cry "Never!" even after Selma. But under the insistent prodding of Negro demonstrators and liberal spokesmen, most Americans resolved that in the matter of legalized discrimination, it was indeed past time to overcome.

Chapter 6

The Ghettos Erupt

Black Life in the North

IN THE SUMMER of 1963 a Negro picketer at New York's City Hall raised a sign, "I'd eat at your lunch counter—if only I had a job."[1] His protest attracted little attention at a time when television crewmen were fanning across the South to cover rallies against Jim Crow. Yet that placard summed up the resentments of Northern Negroes, who by the sixties formed nearly half of America's black population. No Jim Crow laws advertised their agony or stirred protests that aroused national concern. Instead racism worked in subtler ways to make ghetto residents the forgotten people of the Negro revolution.

The black migrants who began streaming north in the early twentieth century received separate and unequal treatment from the time of their first efforts to find housing. Their concentration in ghettos bore a limited resemblance to the pattern of other ethnic arrivals, who also clustered in certain districts for economic reasons and because of cultural and kinship ties. Yet seldom did Irish, Jewish, Polish, or Italian enclaves long exist before developing a vital economic life of their own and local political muscle at least commensurate with their numbers. With rising prosperity, moreover, immigrant groups tended to disperse across cities and into suburban developments. By contrast the black urban experience had a character all its own.

White ethnic groups that jockeyed for status among themselves found a common sense of mission in repelling blacks who tried to enter their neighborhoods. Although the Supreme Court in 1948 outlawed racially restrictive housing covenants, these private pledges not to sell or lease to blacks remained widespread and retained the force of public policy. Through 1950 the Federal Housing Administration openly advised that neighborhoods preserve "the same social and racial classes"[2] in order to assure stability. Realtors also continued to shunt blacks into overcrowded ghettos, obliging them to pay premium prices—often a third or more of their income—for dilapidated tenement apartments.

When on rare occasions Negroes slipped past these racial barriers into suburbia, they found that Northern liberal hospitality seldom functioned well at close quarters. In 1957 a Negro family that purchased a home in the inexpensive suburb of Levittown, Pennsylvania, moved in to a hail of rocks and obscenities. Forgoing the convention of a welcome wagon, white neighbors instead formed a betterment committee to evict the newcomers. Their hostility fed in part on fear that racial tolerance might bring financial ruin. One home-owner conceded that the Negro father was "probably a nice guy," but he added, "Every time I look at him I see $2,000 drop off the value of my house."[3]

Whites did not often have to resort to such open displays of prejudice, for poverty alone confined the mass of blacks to the same slum areas. Only 15 percent of all black workers in 1960 held professional, managerial, clerical, or sales positions, compared with 44 percent of all white workers. Nearly half of all black families lived below the federal poverty line of $3,000 for a family of four. Black median family income stood at 55 percent of white income, and the rate of unemployment for black adults (10.2 percent) and teenagers (24.4 percent) hovered at about twice the rate for whites.[4]

At first glance blacks were simply partaking of the same harsh process of economic adjustment common to other ethnic groups, each arriving at the bottom of the economic pyramid, each rising over generations through hard work, education, and enterprise. Low wages, difficult working conditions, lay-offs, and chronic unemployment seemed, like death, no respecter of persons or pedigree. Yet in fact white racism set blacks apart, affording them little more than the shell of opportunity around a core of persistent discrimination.

Blacks seeking lucrative jobs in the North soon discovered that migration did not change the basic facts of American race relations even in the "free market." Color lines excluded them from many expanding industries, channel-ing them instead into low-paying "Negro" jobs with little prospect for ad-vancement. Most urban blacks worked either as domestics, who lacked a ca-reer ladder to ascend, or as unskilled industrial laborers, subject to frequent layoffs and seldom rewarded with the privileges of seniority. Operating in the absence of Jim Crow statutes, these barriers proved resistant to civil rights pressures. In New York State, known for its laws barring racial discrimination, applicants for licenses as barbers, beauticians, boxers, and notaries public were required until 1962 to specify their race.[5]

Organized labor extended an uncertain hand of friendship to Negro work-ers, and sometimes only a closed fist. Industrial unions might accept Negroes with relatively little discrimination, but among local craft unions, which guarded a limited number of high-paying jobs, Negroes were much less wel-come. A five-year NAACP investigation reported in 1960 that unions virtually excluded blacks from apprenticeship training programs for plumbers, pipe fitters, boilermakers, operating engineers, iron and steel workers, plasterers and lathers, sheet metal workers, electrical workers, and other craftsmen. In the construction trades, where union members selected trainees and vouched for them, organized labor effectively barred blacks from employment.[6]

Where Negroes were already entrenched in an industry, unions com-monly recruited them as members with limited status. The Brotherhood of Railway and Steamship Clerks featured over 150 all-Negro lodges North and South, complete with segregated seniority rosters that limited promotions of

Negroes. In 1957 the New York State Commission against Discrimination gestured at a remedy by ordering a merger of the lily-white George N. Harrison Lodge with the black Friendship Lodge. The white union ignored the directive with impunity for years.[7]

The AFL-CIO under President George Meany vowed to police racism in its own ranks. This policy had little influence on union locals, nor did Meany care to force the issue. NAACP investigators concluded that the AFL-CIO civil rights department aimed "to create a 'liberal' public relations image rather than to attack the broad pattern of anti-Negro practices within affiliated unions."[8] Meany testified before Congress in 1964 on the need for legislation against union discrimination, which he hoped would strengthen his appeals for fair treatment. The Civil Rights Act included such a provision, but to limited effect. Among many examples of recalcitrance, the home local of Meany's own union continued to reject black plumbers.[9]

Northern blacks did improve their overall position in the postwar decades. Government statisticians brandished charts to show that the 1960s in particular marked a banner period for Negroes. By 1967 rapid economic growth and falling color barriers enabled a substantial majority of all black workers to attain middle-class status in white-collar or higher-paying blue-collar jobs. At decade's end fully two-thirds of all black Americans were living above the federal poverty line, still far behind the level of white prosperity (90 percent), but reflecting a rise of nearly three million blacks out of poverty since 1960.[10] For the most impoverished blacks, however, the gains registered by the most fortunate ghetto dwellers did little to check their own declining prospects.

The climate of race relations changed too late to revive the economic prospects of the hard-core black poor. Progress in civil rights coincided with broad social forces that fixed millions of blacks—and whites as well—in a permanent urban underclass. The share of industrial jobs in the central cities plummeted from two-thirds at the end of World War II to less than 40 percent in 1970, as manufacturing plants followed the general exodus of whites to the suburbs.[11] At the same time, the Negro revolution failed to keep pace with the revolution in automation, which required skills that many urban blacks could not provide. During the sixties, thousands of unskilled jobs disappeared every year, steadily closing the one road to upward mobility that every earlier immigrant group had relied on.

Despite vanishing opportunities over one million blacks moved to crowded Northern ghettos during the 1960s. As Southern agriculture became ever more mechanized, landowners evicted sharecroppers and fired wageworkers, pushing them into the cities. These black newcomers often replaced upwardly mobile Negroes who had just escaped the ghetto's poorest neighborhoods. Their arrival further concentrated the areas of chronic Negro unemployment, while the country as a whole was enjoying unexampled prosperity.

The broader effects of permanent economic depression bred a multitude of other ills among the two and a half million poor blacks in the central cities. Of 59,720 drug addicts known to the U.S. Bureau of Narcotics at the end of 1966, just over half were Negroes.[12] The incidences of juvenile delinquency, welfare dependency, school truancy, dropouts, and illiteracy all were markedly higher in black ghettos than in surrounding areas. Crime of every kind devastated the black slums, and homicide was the primary cause of death among young black adult men. A study of five Chicago police districts in 1965 showed that one low-income black district had thirty-five times the rate of violent crime of the safest, white neighborhood.[13]

Black families frequently crumbled under these social pressures. Fathers were absent from nearly one-fourth of all black families in 1966, nearly three times the rate among whites.[14] Desertion of families occurred most frequently among black men who could obtain only sporadic and menial work, and whose inability to fill the role of family provider eroded their self-esteem. Limits on welfare payments to two-parent households provided further, inadvertent encouragement for many black men to "assist" their families by staying away. Two-parent families remained the rule for upper-income blacks, but of poor black families in 1966, 42 percent were headed by women.[15]

All the crippling tendencies of black slum life together destroyed or distorted youthful ambitions. With fathers often absent and mothers at work, children looked to gang leaders, hustlers, dope peddlers, and numbers runners as models for survival on the ghetto's streets. Before reaching young manhood, they had absorbed the cynicism and despair of older males, who felt cut off from opportunity in a nation that measured a man's worth in dollars and suburban luxuries. This deep-rooted "culture of poverty" endured as a legacy of white racism even as civil rights laws declared an end to formal discrimination.

The nation's urban leaders generally did little to reverse the downward spiral of ghetto conditions and aspirations. Slum congestion, for example, demanded greater attention to the problems of inadequate sanitation, roaches, and rats yet seldom called forth more than symbolic efforts from fiscally pressed communities. In January 1964 New York City's mayor, Robert Wagner, pledged a million-dollar campaign to eliminate rats from six thousand buildings with 100,000 residents.[16] The Wagner administration departed the following year in favor of a still more liberal mayor, John V. Lindsay, but the rat infestation remained. In 1967 the city heightened an advertising campaign that offered techniques for keeping rats at bay. One health department poster informed mothers in slum tenements,

Don't Let a Rat Kill Your Baby. Keep Your House Clean. Keep Your Garbage Pail Tightly Covered. Keep Your Food In Covered Jars Or Cans. Keep Your Baby's Crib Clean. . . . [in large red lettering] RATS FOLLOW THE SMELL OF MILK. WATCH YOUR BABY BEFORE PUTTING HIM TO BED. WATCH HIM AFTERWARD.[17]

Such meaningless mandates to slum dwellers largely substituted for more comprehensive municipal services. The inadequacy of these policies could be seen in the substantially higher mortality rates for black men, women, and children. In 1950 infant mortality was 66 percent higher for blacks than for whites; in 1964, with a greater proportion of blacks living in cities, the infant mortality rate of blacks was 90 percent higher than that of whites.[18] This widening gap coincided with a general deterioration of the ghettos, despite the widely heralded success of a minority within them.

Violence erupted frequently amid squalid ghetto conditions, and friction with white police patrols increased the possibility many times over. Complaints about police abuses—racist remarks, arrests on dubious grounds, beatings of unresisting residents—were part of daily conversation in the ghettos. James Farmer described New York's police in 1965 as "a para-military organization of 28,000 heavily armed men who killed 95 people last year."[19] If this seemed to ignore the work of numerous humane officers, Farmer's words expressed a common black view that police were there not to protect them but to suppress them. James Baldwin explained,

The only way to police a ghetto is to be oppressive. None of the Police Commissioner's men, even with the best will in the world, have any way of understanding the lives led by the people they swagger about in twos and threes controlling. Their very presence is an insult, and it would be, even if they spent their entire day feeding gumdrops to children. They represent the force of the white world. . . . [A policeman] moves through Harlem, therefore, like an occupying soldier in a bitterly hostile country; which is precisely what, and where, he is, and this is the reason he walks in twos and threes.[20]

The task of policemen was not merely thankless but largely hopeless, for their presence could provoke as often as pacify ghetto dwellers. Even the smallest spark could set off a chain reaction of rage, as happened in the Los Angeles ghetto of Watts on August 11, 1965, a day that began in ninety-eight-degree heat and gave way to a week of flames.

Watts

Marquette Frye, a twenty-one-year-old black, was driving drunk down a busy Los Angeles street, indifferently sampling parts of each lane, when the police officer Lee Minikus waved him over to the side and asked for his driver's license. By all accounts Minikus was unfailingly courteous, smiled at Frye's banter, but found the youth intoxicated and unable even to produce his license. The event diverted residents already gathered in the street, seeking relief from a heat wave in its fourth day. They watched the proceedings with some amusement and good-naturedly joked with Minikus and his suspect. Even Frye's mother, Rena, took the officer's side, scolding her son for driving drunk and urging him to go quietly and make it easy on himself.[21] But in the ghetto, where policemen were viewed as intruders rather than as peace officers, the mood of bystanders could turn suddenly.

Marquette Frye began to panic at the thought of jail. He pulled away from

Minikus, then released his feelings in a stream of obscenities. Backup police and local residents multiplied on the street, the atmosphere souring amid muttered curses of the "blue-eyed" cops. Frye suddenly lunged for the nightstick Minikus carried, while his older brother Ronald, fearing a general police assault, remonstrated with an officer nearby. The newly arriving patrolman John Wilson surveyed the near chaos, decided that his brethren in blue needed rescue from 150 angry blacks and charged straight on. One blow of his riot baton doubled over Ronald Frye, and two more sent Marquette to the ground. Rena Frye desperately clutched at Minikus to get him to stop the beatings but instead found herself herded, along with her sons, into police squad cars. An onlooker screamed, "We've got no rights at all—it's just like Selma!" Another black raised the stakes: "Come on, let's get them!"[22]

Twenty-year-old Joyce Ann Gaines was standing a few yards from the line of police, bedecked with pink hair curlers and a hairdresser's smock, chatting with another young woman until she realized that this once amusing scene was getting out of hand. She began to walk away, just as a policeman felt a spray of saliva strike his neck and wheeled around to see Gaines fading into the crowd. He yanked on her left arm while a woman friend defiantly yanked back on her right. As Gaines struggled for balance, her curlers sailed into the crowd and her smock billowed in front of her, making her appear pregnant. Then she disappeared into yet another squad car. Within minutes the ghetto grapevine was embellishing the incident with ugly details that confirmed popular suspicions of the police force. In one version, a cop struck a pregnant woman in the belly with his club. In another, the cop pushed the woman against a patrol car and tried to choke her.[23] Reaction was swift. Stones and bottles rained down on the officers as blacks avenged the woman of these imaginary tales, and a history of sullen submission to ghetto police.

Had this been a middle-class area like Striver's Row in Harlem, where lawyers, doctors, and businessmen upheld a "model neighborhood," rage might have melted away amid concern for property values. But this was Watts, a district fifty miles square that lay beneath the approaches to the city's international airport, a dense, squalid ghetto where more than 250,000 Negroes were crammed into faded stucco buildings. Four times as many people per square block lived in Watts as in the rest of Los Angeles. Trash collection was a rare event, so a stroll along any street in Watts meant an encounter with broken glass, rusty cans, rotting food. Two-thirds of the residents were on welfare, unemployment among adult males was 34 percent, yet $20 million in federal antipoverty funds went unused while local politicians jockeyed for control. Complaints about racist police resounded throughout Watts, where the population was 98 percent black yet 200 of the 205 officers were white.[24] These conditions afforded little incentive for "keeping cool" after the arrest of Marquette Frye. Instead residents went about the cathartic business of destroying their neighborhood.

Within two days of the first disturbance five thousand blacks were smashing everything in a 150-block area. Dick Gregory appealed to the higher sentiments of the crowd and was shot in the leg. Rioters hurled Molotov cocktails at buildings and sniped at firemen answering the alarms, killing one of them. Looters followed the light of a hundred fires to carry away guns, appliances, liquor, jewelry, and anything else of value from ghetto stores. Frantic merchants posted signs in their store windows declaring "Soul Brother," "Negro owned," "Owned by a Brother." But while looters often targeted white-owned shops, some seized the good life with a single-minded frenzy that did not admit distinctions of color, ownership, or law. The black writer Louis Lomax confronted one enterprising man carrying a sofa from a burning furniture store by balancing it on his head and shoulders. "Brother, brother," Lomax implored, "do you realize what you're doing?" "Don't bother me now," the man replied; "I've got to hurry back to get the matching chair."[25]

Fourteen thousand national guardsmen and several thousand local police needed six days to stop the arson, rock throwing, theft, and sniping. The violence left thirty-four people dead, including a sheriff's deputy and a fireman who had been shot in the first days of the riot, before fire fighters were routinely issued bullet-proof vests. Nine hundred blacks suffered injuries, and four thousand were arrested for violence, vandalism, looting, loitering, or simply happening upon a policeman at an inopportune moment. Hundreds of families were left homeless, while businessmen found their stores charred and plundered. The damage, after inflated insurance claims were discounted, came to some $45 million. Amid the wreckage of Watts, civil rights leaders like Roy Wilkins left behind their hopes of ending "all the years of oppression" and instead realized that they "were just beginning a new ordeal."[26]

Even after the riot had burned itself out, the embers of hostility continued to smolder. "The riots will continue," a young black man said, "because I, as a Negro, am immediately considered to be a criminal by police and, if I have a pretty woman with me, she is a tramp even if she is my wife or mother."[27] Los Angeles police chief William Parker set the tone for his officers by explaining the violence in Watts as simply the work of a "criminal element,"[28] ignoring the fact that the majority of those arrested had no police record and that residents widely approved the acts of defiance. At bottom Parker expressed the prevalent urban approach to race relations, which was to downplay black grievances and to pacify the ghettos chiefly through police vigilance.

Bayard Rustin, Andrew Young, and Martin Luther King, Jr., saw firsthand the desperation that had fueled this violence as they toured the ruins of Watts. When a group of youngsters told them joyously, "We won," the civil rights leaders asked, "How can you say you won when thirty-four Negroes are dead, your community is destroyed, and whites are using the riots as an excuse for inaction?" "We won," the youths insisted, "because we made them pay attention to us."[29]

King and his companions ruefully confessed that the carnage pointed not only to the failures of the wider society but also to the limits of their own movement. It seemed more than grim coincidence that Watts exploded five

days after black leaders had jubilantly hailed the passage of voting rights legislation. Residents of Watts, Harlem, or Chicago's West Side slums could read
about Southern Negro triumphs in their local papers and watch Lyndon Johnson declaim about new laws against discrimination. Yet their own lives remained as bleak as before the Greensboro sit-in.

The Limits of Federal Programs

The ghettos did not lack for programs dedicated to helping blacks enter
the economic mainstream. In August 1964 the liberal tide carried through
Congress a training and employment bill that held special promise for black
families, more than 37 percent of whom lived below the federal poverty line of
$3,000, compared with just over 15 percent of white families.[30] Yet unlike the
recently passed Civil Rights Act, the new economic program originated with
white reformers and developed largely independently of black demands and
pressures. Once more, Negroes found their hopes for change resting on leaders
who dispensed federal favors with a warm, but heavily paternal, hand.

Black activists had anticipated the national drive against poverty with
campaigns and speeches linking economic issues with more general demands
for equality. At the 1963 March on Washington for Jobs and Freedom, Martin
Luther King appended to his dream of brotherhood a reminder that millions of
Americans were living "on a lonely island of poverty in the midst of a vast
ocean of material prosperity."[31] Earlier that summer Whitney Young, Jr., of
the Urban League, had called for a "domestic Marshall Plan" for the central
cities, inspired by the country's generosity in spending $12 billion to rebuild
European economies after the Second World War.[32] Black spokesmen widely
endorsed Young's proposal, thrusting the issue of deprivation into the public
spotlight more boldly than at any other time since the Great Depression.

These indictments of economic injustice nonetheless carried limited
weight. Black leaders were hampered by the political quiescence of most poor
people in the early sixties, as well as by their own, marginal position in American society. Moreover, to a movement dominated by middle-class Negroes
seeking basic constitutional rights, poverty was a concern but not a priority.
Most economic demands focused on ending discrimination rather than on
more ambitious plans to reshape the economic order. Even the March on
Washington, which Bayard Rustin had originally conceived as a way to lobby
for a federal jobs program, instead emphasized passage of a civil rights law. It
remained for others in the liberal coalition, less absorbed in civil rights campaigns and more attuned to traditional economic concerns, to generate federal
efforts to end poverty in the nation.

The idea for a massive antipoverty effort germinated in the Kennedy
administration, but for reasons that had little to do with either black political
pressure or economic need. President Kennedy's tutors on the problem of
poverty were neither black nor poor, but a professional elite of writers and

social scientists who pushed for bolder federal intervention in the economy. The Council of Economic Advisers stoked the President's activist temperament with reports of persistent widespread poverty and with predictions of burgeoning federal surpluses that could fund new social programs. While blacks formed a natural constituency for such a drive against poverty, this was not a primary consideration for Kennedy, who by mid-1963 already assumed nearly unanimous Negro support in the next presidential election. Keenly aware that several million poor whites lived in the rural South, Kennedy viewed the issue of poverty as an opportunity to transcend racial and sectional lines. He planned to dramatize the subject by returning to Appalachia, the chronically poor white region he had visited during the 1960 campaign. This strategy accorded with the advice his chief economic adviser, Walter Heller, gave at a fall Cabinet meeting, that "disadvantaged groups other than Negroes now deserve our attention."[33]

Impelled in part by the special problems of black Americans, Lyndon Johnson expanded Kennedy's commitment to an antipoverty program. Like many Southerners, Johnson believed that the race issue was at heart economic and that with the chance for good jobs and decent incomes Negroes would gain the respect of white people and race tensions would subside. At the same time, Johnson acted from a cluster of other motives, detached from race issues, which fortuitously converged with the hopes of civil rights leaders to aid poor blacks.[34]

From the outset of his presidency Johnson viewed the issue of poverty as an opportunity to prove himself as a reform leader of national breadth and independent vision. He hoped, first, that a campaign to help the poor could unify the country by mending the bruised feelings of his fellow Southerners over civil rights issues. As a man with strong memories of his days teaching poor Mexican-Americans in Texas, Johnson also believed that compensatory programs in education could salvage both the pride and the ability of disadvantaged citizens. This concern to help deprived Americans took on added importance as Johnson came to view poverty as an intolerable drain on national strength, contributing to the failure of one-fifth of all young men—nearly three-quarters of them white—in their selective service examination. Finally, the new President wanted to move beyond the Kennedy legacy and establish his own identity in the White House. Civil rights as well as proposals for tax reform, medical insurance for the aged, and federal aid to education were already associated with the late President. But a program to end poverty, looking beyond race, would be known as Johnson's creation. The issue enabled him to don liberal apparel cut in the fashion of his idol Franklin Roosevelt but perfectly tailored to his need for a distinctive reform image. Just after taking office, Johnson approved Walter Heller's plans for a major government initiative against poverty, then asked Heller to assure his liberal friends that the new President was "no budget slasher." "To tell the truth," Johnson said, letting the word go forth to partisans of the New Frontier, "John F. Kennedy was a little too conservative to suit my taste."[35]

Johnson's call for "an unconditional war on poverty" in his State of the Union Message in early January 1964 certainly did not strike many listeners as too conservative. Opposition quickly surrounded the economic opportunity bill he sent to Congress in mid-March, with its provisions for a billion-dollar program of special education and job training. Conservative Cassandras marshaled the usual doomsday predictions: the bill would trigger a massive bureaucratic buildup, threaten state and individual liberties, undermine the work ethic with government handouts, and spend the nation into devastating debt. None of these possibilities, however, so alarmed key opponents of the bill as its potential to further unsettle the racial status quo. "Judge" Howard W. Smith, chairman of the House Rules Committee, who for decades had been a hanging justice for dozens of civil rights bills, led the campaign to frame debate over the poverty program in terms of black and white. "Any Southerners who plan to vote for this bill," he lectured, "are implementing the civil rights bill that you opposed." Johnson's provision for a job corps to train youths for gainful employment was a way to establish "integrated camps," and the federal funds released under the legislation, Smith hinted, would go to the NAACP. In all, the President's economic opportunity bill was a "blueprint for mongrelization of the races."[36] Johnson had met such race-baiting bluster head-on in pushing the civil rights bill through a Southern filibuster; but he did not want to entangle his economic program in controversy. He preferred to neutralize the issue by moving through the familiar backways of Capitol Hill, taking pains not to alienate Southern supporters by publicly linking poverty and race.

First to feel the brunt of Johnson's Southern strategy was the Reverend Adam Clayton Powell, Jr., the most powerful black politician in the country. The administration denied Powell floor leadership of the antipoverty bill, outraging the Harlem congressman but avoiding further identification of the legislation as a "Negro" measure. It is possible that Powell would have met the same fate regardless of his race or constituency, for his aggressive manner and love of overstatement made him a strong competitor for media coverage with a President who did not share adulation lightly. Powell would also have been a dubious defender of greater federal spending. He was best known for using taxpayers' money in a highly personal crusade for better living standards, centered on frequent junkets to the Caribbean isle of Bimini. Still, Johnson's choice of a floor leader in place of Powell—the conservative Phil M. Landrum of Georgia, chairman of the committee that considered the bill—fit his plan to court white Southern support for the antipoverty measure while keeping black involvement safely out of public view.[37]

White integrationists fared no better than Powell in the President's legislative maneuvers. Johnson originally picked a talented administrator in the Pentagon, Adam Yarmolinsky, as deputy director of the poverty program. Yarmolinsky was uncommonly devoted to the cause of aiding the poor: his first words on recovering from serious surgery in the summer of 1964 concerned the progress of the economic opportunity bill during his time under anaesthesia. But in the eyes of many Southern congressmen, Yarmolinsky could never merit a clean bill of health as an agency head, because of rumored Communist leanings and his actual efforts to expose and end discrimination in the armed forces. When Johnson learned that eight representatives from North Carolina would support his antipoverty measure only if the "security risk," Yarmolinsky, were dropped from the program, the President agreed. After designating Sargent Shriver, the Peace Corps director, to head the War on Poverty, Johnson denied to reporters that he had ever considered Yarmolinsky as Shriver's assistant.[38]

The modest scope of the economic opportunity bill compounded the misgivings of Negro leaders, none of whom played a significant role in drafting its provisions. The bill did not include plans to provide decent-paying jobs or transfer payments to the millions of hard-core poor; instead it focused on small-scale projects to tutor and "rehabilitate" them. President Johnson rejected, as politically unrealistic, programs that would do more to relieve immediate hardships and afford employment, but which would also appear fiscally reckless and perhaps force an unpopular rise in taxes. When Sargent Shriver lobbied at a Cabinet meeting to expand the War on Poverty by adding a $1.25 billion public works program, the plan died with the sound of his voice. "I have never seen a colder reception from the president," a participant in the meeting recalled. "[Johnson] just—absolute blank stare—implied without even opening his mouth that Shriver should move on to the next proposal."[39]

Johnson's legislative strategy worked—the Economic Opportunity Act passed comfortably—but it left key black leaders squinting at the poverty program from a distance rather than embracing it. The absence of Negroes in high-level posts at the newly created Office of Economic Opportunity (OEO) only furthered this remove. So did the fact that funding for the office—under a billion dollars, about half of which would be taken from existing programs—fell far short of a "domestic Marshall Plan" treating a national emergency. Martin Luther King privately mused that Johnson's actions seemed designed to buy time and quiet discontent rather than to eliminate the root causes of poverty.[40] But black leaders muffled their criticisms. It seemed a time for faith in an administration, as well as a program, that promised so much for the poor and outcast.

Federal agencies dotted the central cities beginning in 1965, heralding the imminent conquest of poverty. But basic flaws in their operation immediately appeared. Many programs never obtained congressional funding. Others received just enough money to cover the cost of office space, salaries, and sundry administrative expenses, while requiring drastic economies in the area of antipoverty work. The ghetto poor also discovered that when an agency did receive adequate funding, their problems had by no means ended.

The Job Corps was among the most highly touted antipoverty programs, an investment in vocational training that focused on youths considered unemployable and frequently in trouble with the law. Urban blacks formed the primary source of recruits but faced daunting adjustments after being removed to huge, barracks-like surroundings far from their homes. Arriving trainees exchanged complaints on the absence of young women in these centers, then moved on to other evidence of unrelenting dreariness: food that trainees described as "slop," overcrowding, inadequate recreational facilities. As in the ghettos, small incidents could spark riots in these bleak and volatile conditions. One center in rural Kentucky, which crammed 650 inmates (400 of them black) in an ex–infantry camp, witnessed a melee among several hundred youths that began in the hated cafeteria, then spread throughout the compound.[41]

Seldom did Job Corps personnel transcend their limited facilities. Recruited mainly from the public schools, these volunteers had teaching credentials but otherwise seemed as disoriented and defensive as their young charges from the ghettos. Observers of a camp in Edison, New Jersey, reported that administrators viewed corpsmen as culprits and favored authoritarian, paramilitary methods to control behavior and curb the high absentee rate. Teachers appeared secretive, angry, distrustful, and punitive, with no understanding of a poverty culture. Like the administrators, they seemed preoccupied with showing a "good front" and imparted little knowledge to their charges.[42] Curricula generally were no more impressive than the quality of instruction; in an age of developing technology the Job Corps tended toward molding a generation of janitorial aides.

Agencies in the War on Poverty on occasion drew field commanders from the ranks of the local poor, thus checking the deadening paternalism that afflicted the Job Corps. But these Community Action Programs, or CAPs, had their own rendezvous with futility. Although they afforded some blacks valuable administrative experience and political connections, the larger effort to mobilize slum dwellers seldom met expectations. Absorbed by the daily business of survival and unmoved by news of a coming panacea, over 95 percent of all poor people declined to vote for local representatives to neighborhood antipoverty boards. The board meetings themselves were often less than harmonious. At some conferences delegates from the ranks of the disadvantaged would sit in silent self-effacement while politicians and professionals dominated policy discussions. In cities like New York, where the poor used their new political voice to shout down programs planned and staffed by the middle class, old political realities intervened. Protests by largely Democratic mayors and city councils led Congress to restrict funding of CAPs, while Lyndon Johnson prudently stood aside. The specter of disadvantaged elements wielding real political power, and commensurate economic power, was thus exorcised before it could fully materialize.[43]

The War on Poverty registered some successes. Educational programs, notably operation Head Start, reached over two million children during the late sixties and boosted long-term achievement in school and employment. Food stamps reduced serious malnutrition among low-income children and adults, while Medicare and Medicaid increased their access to health care. Community Action Programs provided services such as legal aid that would otherwise have been unavailable to the urban poor. Even agencies like the Job Corps, which had lower rates of retention and placement of its charges, helped some youths who had been considered lost to the labor force and to society.[44] Still, these and other efforts formed, at best, a frail prelude to an "unconditional" assault on poverty. The Office of Economic Opportunity spent, on the average, no more than seventy dollars a year for each poor person, and little of that money actually reached the poor as income. A former assistant director of the OEO concluded in 1970, "Most poor people have had no contact with [the War on Poverty], except to hear the promises of a better life to come."[45]

The Limits of Private Programs

The limits of federal action left the burden of ending ghetto poverty largely to private groups that shared the Great Society's integrationist aims. Foremost among these was the National Urban League, an interracial agency formed in 1911 to help the black poor and migrants unable to adjust to life in the cities. For fifty years the league had embodied the precepts of Booker T. Washington, a leading black advocate of self-help who believed in walking softly and carrying away big donations from Northern philanthropists for education and job training. This approach required a careful balance between accommodation of white corporate leaders and delivery of tangible services to urban blacks. With the student sit-ins that fine line snapped under growing black criticism of the league as obsequious toward whites and unresponsive to the changing times. In 1961 the aging trustees brought in the forty-year-old Whitney Young, Jr., as executive director, to adapt Washington's legacy of self-help to a new age of black assertiveness.[46]

Young stoically inherited the image of "Uncle Tom" that awaited anyone who took charge of the Urban League while CORE, SNCC, and the SCLC were shaking the South. Despite his six-foot-two-inch, two-hundred-pound frame, Young remained a nearly invisible man during the media's focus on nonviolent Southern protests. Reporters considered the Urban League a weak fifth sister among civil rights groups, and younger blacks scorned Young's dismal arrest record. Unlike Lewis, Farmer, King, and even Roy Wilkins, he had never been held on any charge, and was not even ashamed of it. "I do not see," Young once said, "why I should have to go to jail to prove my leadership."[47] Instead he worked at keeping black youths out of jail by lowering the long odds against their gainful employment.

As former dean of Atlanta University's School of Social Work, Young had ample experience gliding between white power brokers and black rebels. Soon after arriving at the Urban League in 1961, Young stepped up requests for corporate employment of Negroes, identified his organization with civil rights protests, and urged greater federal aid to the central cities. When a member of the Urban League's gerontocracy cautioned, "We don't work this fast," Young politely corrected, "From now on, we will. We've got to, or we'll be left behind."[48]

The sixties witnessed a vast expansion of Urban League projects to reclaim the unemployed, the unlettered, the untrained. The National Skills Bank found positions for jobless or underemployed blacks with marketable skills. On-the-Job-Training, under contract from the Department of Labor, apprenticed unskilled workers to private firms. A variety of specialized employment services, such as the Broadcast Skills Bank, catered to blacks with more novel aspirations. The league also encouraged education through tutoring and fellowships, provided family counseling, helped finance homes, and provided a range of other services designed to strengthen the black community.[49]

The revitalized Urban League showed like no other agency the power of private initiative to aid poor urban blacks. But the very energy of the league also indirectly revealed the limits of such initiative. It was not simply that the league reached only a small percentage of the urban poor. Like the government's antipoverty programs, the Urban League tended to help those closest to the poverty line, those with relative confidence, ambition, and the knowledge to take advantage of a social agency. Its human-reclamation projects amounted, in practice, to a system of reverse triage, aiding the people most likely to succeed anyway in a rapidly expanding economy. But while the league plucked some fortunate souls from destitution, it left intact the ghettos themselves and the conditions that bred chronic misery for the great majority.

Where the Urban League relied on black self-help and white goodwill, other groups preferred a more confrontational approach. Often led or abetted by local chapters of CORE or the NAACP, they aimed to apply to the ghettos the techniques of nonviolent direct action, which Northern blacks had tried only sporadically in previous decades. Although overshadowed by King's Southern campaigns, these ghetto-based coalitions challenged even more fundamentally the merchants, landlords, administrators, and politicians who kept down the black urban underclass.

CORE's Northern chapters accepted James Farmer's admonition in 1961 that they "could not survive merely on sympathy with the South."[50] With tactics that ranged from picketing to more innovative obstruction, they protested discrimination in hiring and housing, school segregation, and police brutality in the ghettos. CORE's job campaigns registered the greatest results, as a succession of companies chose to develop a social conscience after some nonviolent prodding. St. Louis CORE, for example, singled out the Jefferson Bank for a day of disturbance in August 1963. Members sat on the floor, at the entrance, and in front of the tellers' windows. The tactic brought jail sentences for fifteen CORE members—Alderman William Clay spent nearly four months behind bars—but it also brought jobs for eighty-four blacks in the Jefferson Bank and fourteen other financial centers. That November, Newark CORE showed Western Electric the need for a more enlightened employment policy by picketing and jamming switchboard lines with a "phone-in." New York CORE threatened a selective buying campaign that led a dozen corporations to begin making integrated television commercials. In these and other ghettos CORE carried a diversified protest portfolio, including such targets as the construction trades, the Howard Johnson's restaurant chain, Bell Telephone, and the Bank of America.[51]

Desegregation of schools also absorbed CORE's Northern leadership, with Cleveland's Reverend Bruce Klunder giving his life in this effort. A young white minister, Klunder had aided CORE's lobbying for a fair-housing law by conducting a one-man vigil at the House chamber in 1963. The following year, Klunder helped lead CORE's campaign to stop construction of three ghetto public schools that were being built to avoid the busing of black schoolchildren into white neighborhoods. Some demonstrators lay down in front of vehicles on the construction site in order to halt the work. A bulldozer driver backed up to avoid a protester, and Klunder, who had crouched behind the vehicle, was crushed to death. Nearly all black students—some 75,000—boycotted the Cleveland school system several weeks later in memory of the minister's sacrifice.[52]

CORE's ghetto campaigns pointed the way north for other nonviolent protest groups still fixed on the former Confederate states. But the ghettos took the measure of CORE's tacticians. Efforts to form coalitions foundered, not simply from bickering between local ministers and civic leaders, but also from tensions with the NAACP. In the South, danger from racist whites inhibited public squabbling among black spokesmen, while civil rights groups tended to avoid places where other activists were present. In the North, disunity had no such natural enemies, and CORE chapters disputed with NAACP branches over tactics and territory.

CORE workers tended to view NAACP leaders as well-intentioned persons deserving an honorable retirement. They envied the NAACP's ties with religious and fraternal organizations, politicians, and middle-class blacks. But their dominant sentiment was the disdain expressed by the CORE worker Genevieve Hughes, who described a local chapter as so inactive that it reminded her of the NAACP.[53] This was not fully fair, because the character of NAACP chapters varied widely with leadership and location. But in many cases CORE chapters had to prod their NAACP counterparts to participate in boycotts, sit-ins, and picketing. In some locales this resulted in ad hoc alliances or in friendly rivalries that invigorated job and housing campaigns. Often, however, the groups revealed little sense of common cause, as in Philadelphia, where CORE and NAACP branches produced a rivalry with no discernible friendship and little hint of civility.

CORE's Philadelphia story revealed the pitfalls of operating two aggressive civil rights organizations in the same Northern city. In Cecil Moore the NAACP had a leader who so relished confrontation that he unsettled even seasoned Philadelphia CORE members, as well as local whites and his own group's cautious national headquarters. Moore staunchly supported Gandhian measures, on his terms. He was piqued, however, that after he halted a supermarket boycott in exchange for concessions on hiring, CORE insisted on continuing the protests. CORE members informed Moore that they were not bound by his agreements and that they would stage a "lie-in" to tie up traffic near the store. No one showed up for the event, however, perhaps because members bore in mind Moore's threat to run over CORE protesters in his own car and mash their bodies into the ground.[54] Relations between Moore and local CORE leaders remained chilly for some time thereafter.

No more success marked CORE's efforts to win over the broader public with its Northern protests. It could not compete with the drama of the Southern campaigns—or with King's charismatic leadership—for national publicity. It also failed to win consistent cooperation from federal, state, or local governments, which shrank from interfering with store owners or realtors except in specific cases of blatant discrimination. Lacking such support, CORE at best secured piecemeal victories, mostly in employment, but more typically suffered unmitigated defeats. In Cleveland, for example, CORE's intensive pressure for a fair-housing law failed in 1963; and several months after the Reverend Klunder's death a segregated public school opened on the site where he was killed.[55] By the end of 1964 CORE's Northern activities had sharply declined, having done more to bankrupt the organization than to change the lives of ghetto residents.

CORE's most basic failure in the North was apparent to anyone who observed a typical picket line, which was likely to be staffed by white volunteers and perhaps one or two middle-class blacks lending a token "ghetto" presence. The conspicuous absence of the masses from CORE's mass action campaigns suggested a fundamental flaw in its approach, even apart from its meager results. Like the NAACP and the Urban League, CORE brought with it a philosophy of integration that had moved Negroes in Birmingham and Atlanta, but did not travel well outside the South.

Integration as a means to full citizenship meant little to Northern blacks, who already had the ballot and exercised a multitude of other civil rights for which Southern Negroes were still struggling. "The black cat in Harlem wasn't worried about no damn bus—he'd been riding the bus for fifty years," snapped a disgruntled Urban Leaguer in New York. "What he didn't have was the fare."[56] Integration into the larger economic system had greater potential appeal, but it remained a remote abstraction for most ghetto dwellers. Such gains as they experienced involved crumbs of opportunity doled out by white-owned businesses, benefiting chiefly a narrow segment of ghetto society. Unsurprisingly, then, among the black urban poor the term "integration" often stirred greater suspicion of middle-class Negroes than faith in reform-minded whites.

Integration as a spiritual ideal, rooted in the goal of the Beloved Community embracing all people, occasioned a further split in the priorities of Southern and Northern blacks. In the South blacks and whites were bound in an organic relationship that was conceived at the time of slavery and that, however exploitative, exerted a complex emotional pull on both groups. If Martin Luther King, Jr., called on Negroes to love whites partly as a sage tactic, he also tapped a yearning to overcome the pathology of Southern race relations. Northern blacks could share the goal of a unified society up to a point, but as a group they had less contact with white people than Southern Negroes did, the absence of Jim Crow laws notwithstanding. Whites in the North might appear less blatantly repressive than those in the South, but they also tended to emerge as more shadowy, less fully human. Ghetto dwellers therefore showed less urgent interest in transforming the ties between the races, or even in cultivating those ties. They gravitated instead to leaders who preached black pride, black solidarity, black independence from the wider society. These voices of the ghetto pointedly dismissed the aims of black integrationists, and they rose to power on the failures of civil rights reform.

The Nation of Islam

Black separatist ideologies found expression in numerous ghetto sects and cults, the most powerful of which was the Lost-Found Nation of Islam. Popularly known as the Black Muslims, this group directly contradicted the ideals of mainstream black spokesmen. Under its leader Elijah Muhammad the Lost-Found Nation swept across the ghettos in the sixties, rooting its appeal in assertions of black superiority and rejection of all things white.[57]

Elijah Muhammad looked less the part of a black nationalist cult figure than that of a Negro "first" trying gingerly to mingle in a white corporation. Eurasian in features and complexion, dressed in dark business suits, he moved with a refinement bordering on fragility. His soft voice and slight lisp further handicapped his venture as a preacher to the masses. Yet to his devoted following across the urban North, Elijah Muhammad's faltering speech mattered little beside his unerring grasp of black resentments, which he developed as an early victim of the great northward migration.

In the twenties the man christened Elijah Poole had left a sharecropper's plot in Georgia for the auto factories of Detroit, then joined the multitude of last-hired, first-fired Negroes at the start of the Depression. In 1930, while languishing on the unemployment rolls, he listened to an Arab silk peddler named Wali Farrad teach that white schemes lay behind black misery. As authority for his claims Farrad drew out hidden meanings in Eastern texts and, in time, identified himself as the Mahdi—"the one the world has been expecting for the past two thousand years."[58] The Mahdi's stay was considerably shorter than the vigil for his coming; after four years of imparting his singular mixture of Islamic and racial doctrines, Farrad disappeared, repairing to Mecca, according to his followers. He left behind his most intent disciple, Elijah, who took the surname Muhammad in place of his American "slave" name. Inheriting the master's teachings, 104 sacred books, and a set of symbolic puzzles, Elijah Muhammad continued to initiate slum dwellers into the mysteries of black history, torment, and coming redemption.

Muhammad's worldview was a negative image of Martin Luther King's, indeed, of all black Christianity's. He preached to scattered followers that white "blue-eyed devils" had imposed Christianity on black people to keep them submissive. He largely dismissed the ancient biblical tales as so much ammunition for white supremacists, who were particularly fond of citing

Noah's curse on the sons of Ham as proof of divinely ordained black inferiority. Muhammad fostered a rival genealogy. In the beginning, he taught, all people were created black. Whites were merely a bleached, artificial creation of the evil black geneticist Yacub. They had seized power and wealth through treacherous means, but blacks remained God's chosen. They must strive to restore their original glory, until one day Allah would complete their triumph by overturning all white civilization.

Muhammad's message of racial solidarity and self-help reached down to the most disadvantaged elements of ghetto society: criminals, ex-convicts, derelicts, those living on the margins of the law or the border of subsistence. He imposed a strict, transforming discipline on his adherents that infused pride in place of despair. Followers renounced drugs, tobacco, liquor, excessive talk and sleep, emotional display, and sexual activity outside marriage. They observed dietary proscriptions that included traditional Islamic taboos such as that against pork but also extended to fried chicken, black-eyed peas, collard greens, and other pleasant reminders of life in the region of greatest segregation. Disciples heeded injunctions to work diligently, further their education, and pursue economic success through business ventures in the ghetto. Here, then, was a practical plan for the meek to begin inheriting a fair share of the earth through small-scale capitalism, powered by a sense of racial and religious mission.

The Nation of Islam shot up from obscurity in the late fifties, on the edge of a larger black rising and during a time of worsening ghetto conditions and prospects. In this volatile setting the Black Muslims did not attract notice so much for their reform of ex-convicts, improvement of family life, or thriving shops that adorned depressed blocks. Rather they came to symbolize racial hostility—a threat to white America and to the civil rights leaders who wanted to conciliate and change it. Bestriding this controversy with grim humor was the Nation's chief recruiter and its acid emissary to white America, Malcolm X.

A copper-skinned Negro, with hair tinged slightly red, Malcolm was a walking allegory of black rebirth from self-hatred and degradation in the slums. He was born in Omaha, Nebraska, in 1925 to the Reverend Earl Little, six feet four inches of jet black militancy and a follower of the pan-African crusader Marcus Garvey. Little took young Malcolm to local meetings of Garvey's Universal Negro Improvement Association, which the minister would personally conclude by chanting a Garveyite litany, "Up, you mighty race, you can accomplish what you will!" Malcolm remembered an old lady at one meeting, grinning and saying to his father, "You're scaring these white folks to death!"[59] Years of Ku Klux Klan harassment led the Little family to relocate to Lansing, Michigan, where in 1931 local whites threw Earl Little under the back wheels of a streetcar, causing injuries from which he died after several hours of agony. A sizable life insurance policy never reached his widow, for the white managers claimed that his death had been a suicide.

White society destroyed Mrs. Little more obliquely, through the progressive disintegration of her independence, family, and morale. Though she worked as a domestic and seamstress, the Depression reduced her to accepting relief so that she could feed her seven children. Malcolm recalled that their food all bore a special stamp designed to keep recipients from selling it: "It's a wonder we didn't come to think of Not To Be Sold as a brand name."[60] Welfare investigators visited the home repeatedly, despite frosty greetings by Mrs. Little. Persistent efforts to break up the family and find foster homes for the children contributed to Mrs. Little's gradual lapse into withdrawn melancholy. Investigators had her committed to a mental institution in 1937 and made the children "state wards." To Malcolm this was more than tragedy; it was atrocity: "A white man in charge of a black man's children! Nothing but legal, modern slavery—however kindly intentioned." The family, Malcolm recalled, "wanted and tried to stay together. Our home didn't have to be destroyed. But the Welfare, the courts, and their doctor, gave us the one-two-three punch. And ours was not the only case of this kind." Years later, filled with anguish over the fate of his mother, he felt "no mercy" toward "a society that will crush people, and then penalize them for not being able to stand up under the weight."[61]

The teenage Malcolm still hoped, for a time, to find a niche within that society. After a period of truancy and petty thievery (apples were a favorite quarry) he pulled back from the road to reform school and began to excel in his studies. He relished every token of white favor, including election as seventh-grade president by his all-white classmates. The euphoria of being an honorary white survived until an English teacher he admired counseled Malcolm that a career in the law was unrealistic for a Negro and that he should develop his promise as a carpenter. Shaken awake from his American dream, Malcolm "began to change—inside" and "drew away from white people."[62]

A year more and Malcolm left school, left his foster parents in Lansing, and moved first to Boston, then to Harlem. He also chased the successful life as refracted through white expectations of Negroes. Fortified by cocaine and harder drugs, he hustled, bussed tables at Boston's Parker House, sold reefer, ran numbers slips and bootleg whiskey, steered white johns to brothels, and, not quite twenty-one, went to jail for attempted burglary.

In prison Malcolm Little took correspondence courses in English, Latin, and German, devoured the large prison library, pondered history, philosophy, philology, and etymology. Through his younger brother he also discovered the Black Muslim teaching that there was no God but Allah and that white people were His enemy. For Malcolm, who had been socialized to think, act, and admire white, the message transformed his view of the world with the force of revelation. Prison now appeared as the most recent stage in a lifetime of locked doors. This one gave him time to reflect upon who had constructed the walls around his life. He corresponded with Elijah Muhammad, converted to the Lost-Found Nation, and took the surname X as a marker for that African family name whose knowledge had been ripped from him. Malcolm X emerged from prison in 1952, after serving seven years. He was filled with religious zeal, grateful to the Honorable Elijah Muhammad for lifting him up and eager for the chance to save other blacks from the white, blue-eyed devils.

A powerful symbiosis operated between Mr. Muhammad, the protective, paternal tutor, and his devoted, brilliant student Malcolm X. Entrusted with editing the Black Muslim journal *The Messenger,* Malcolm peppered his racial polemics with reverent allusions to "the Honorable Elijah Muhammad." Heading the movement's mosque number 7, in Harlem, he drew thousands to hear him tell how Mr. Muhammad opened his eyes to the evils of white America.

In addressing urban slum dwellers, Malcolm ignored the usual amenities toward whites that marked the language of civil rights leaders. Instead he cut to the deep nerve of pain and anger in his listeners, praising Elijah Muhammad's *"greatest* greatness" as "the *first,* the *only* black leader to identify, to you and me, *who* is our enemy! . . . Our *enemy* is the *white man!"*[63] For those who criticized his reference to all whites as devils he shifted from theology to history: "We are speaking of the collective white man's cruelties. . . . You cannot find *one* black man, I do not care who he is, who has not been personally damaged in some way by the devilish acts of the collective white man!"[64]

The judgment rang true to fellow ghetto dwellers. Although the Nation of Islam would not divulge its membership, careful estimates in the late fifties and early sixties showed between 5,000 and 15,000 registered followers, at least 50,000 believers, and a much larger number of sympathizers.[65] As the movement gathered strength despite civil rights gains in the South, Malcolm X became a subject of scrutiny in *Time, Reader's Digest, Cosmopolitan,* the *New York Times,* and diverse other pillars of Americana. His ability to transfix white people with fear, guilt, and revulsion buoyed the Nation of Islam to an almost undreamed-of notoriety.

Malcolm's catalog of white injustices did no more than match the bills of indictment drawn up by James Baldwin, Roy Wilkins, and Martin Luther King, Jr. Unlike these figures, however, Malcolm extended no hope of collective white salvation through reform. Nor did he have any use for would-be white allies. His harangues on television and to racially mixed audiences moved some white listeners to painful self-examination; but even toward these people he could envision only an adversarial relationship. Lacking the smallest faith in white goodwill, Malcolm curtly dismissed the aspirations of civil rights leaders as fantasy. Instead he embraced the idea of black nationalism: the need for blacks to unify and assert control, by any means necessary, of their own land, livelihood, and culture. Black nationalists did not want "to *integrate* into this corrupt society, but to *separate* from it, to a land of our *own,* where we can reform ourselves, lift up our moral standards, and try to be godly."[66]

Malcolm's antagonism toward the civil rights movement sprang as much from its conciliatory style as from its integrationist solutions. He could not abide the indignity of having to importune whites for basic human rights, and he did not believe that the country's leaders would in any case voluntarily accord them. Blacks needed a revolution, and those Negro leaders who talked of nonviolence simply did not "know what a revolution is." Malcolm intended to clarify the real stakes: "Revolution is bloody, revolution is hostile, revolution knows no compromise. . . ."[67] Thus, the absurd predicament of civil rights leaders:

> Who ever heard of angry revolutionists all harmonizing "We Shall Overcome . . . Suum Day . . ." while tripping and swaying along arm-in-arm with the very people they were supposed to be angrily revolting against? Who ever heard of angry revolutionists swinging their bare feet together with their oppressor in lily-pad park pools, with gospels and guitars and "I Have A Dream" speeches?
>
> And the black masses in America were—and still are—having a nightmare.[68]

With the same caustic precision he cast doubt on the wisdom, if not the integrity, of black civil rights leaders. After Dr. King received the Nobel Peace Prize in 1964, Malcolm observed, "He got the peace prize, we got the problem. . . . If I'm following a general, and he's leading me into battle, and the enemy tends to give him rewards, or awards, I get suspicious of him. Especially if he gets a peace award before the war is over."[69]

What to do about Malcolm X was a regular topic of conversation among civil rights leaders. They believed it tragic, and not simply accidental, that this bête noire of the movement commanded more publicity from the white-controlled media than any other black leader except King. It was as if American society preferred Malcolm's polarizing racial rhetoric to their own demands for reform. Whitney Young once complained to a *Newsweek* editor that Malcolm X had never gotten anyone a job or decent housing, "but you could find his name in the *TV Guide* program listings more times than Johnny Carson's."[70]

Despite their indignation few civil rights leaders dared to challenge Malcolm X directly. Young, Wilkins, and King agreed never to publicize the Muslim spokesman by any joint appearances, and King once warned that he would withdraw from a television panel if Malcolm were invited. There was reluctant admiration in this. Malcolm came into such encounters with several advantages—a quicksilver mind, a gift for artful exaggeration, and unshakable confidence in the truth of Elijah Muhammad's doctrines. His erect, almost military bearing accented his tall frame and gave his sharp-edged delivery added authority. "He was a mesmerizing speaker, the toughest man in debate that I've ever seen," Roy Wilkins said. "None of us could touch him, not even Dr. King."[71]

Malcolm had one more advantage in debate that particularly alarmed Wilkins and other Negro leaders. When he pounded at white America, blacks openly or silently applauded, and any Negro who tried to soften the accusations appeared a pawn or a fool. Middle-class Negroes who defended their white colleagues as genuinely respectful (always, Malcolm noted, at interracial forums, never in wholly black gatherings) struck him as symbols of black self-deception rather than status and elicited his special scorn. One "token-integrated" black professor who branded Malcolm a "divisive demagogue" and "reverse racist" led the Muslim minister to apply some improvised shock therapy. "Do you know what white racists call black Ph.D.'s?" he asked. As Malcolm recalled, the man "said something like, 'I believe that I happen not to be aware of that'—you know, one of these ultra-proper-talking Negroes. And I laid the word down on him, loud: *'Nigger!'* "[72]

Negro leaders who tried tossing Malcolm into the category of "extremist" also risked their own credibility when he waved back from the briar patch of black resentments. "Yes, I'm an extremist," he exploded to the writer Alex Haley, after King had condemned his speeches as irresponsible. "The black race here in North America is in extremely bad condition. You show me a black man who isn't an extremist and I'll show you one who needs psychiatric attention!"[73] When Bayard Rustin charged him in a debate with indulging in emotionalism, Malcolm fired back, "When a man is hanging on a tree and he cries out, should he cry out unemotionally? . . . When a man is on a hot stove, he says, 'I'm coming up. I'm getting up.' Violently or nonviolently doesn't even enter into the picture—'I'm coming up, do you understand?' "[74]

Not even Malcolm's debating prowess could conceal, however, the essential conservatism of the Lost-Found Nation. White and black students were risking their lives in the South, Bayard Rustin tartly informed Malcolm at a Harlem church forum in 1962, adding that the Nation of Islam had yet to do anything concrete to help the fight against Jim Crow.[75] James Farmer learned to press his Muslim opponent in debate, "Brother Malcolm, don't tell us any more about the disease—that is clear in our minds. Now, tell us, physician, what is thy cure?" On first broaching this line, Farmer watched amazed as Malcolm rose slowly for the microphone, began speaking in subdued tones, and "floundered around for a few minutes with some unaccustomed inarticulateness, obviously searching for a speech." He settled briefly on the goal of a separate black homeland, before shifting to a familiar set piece against nonviolence as undignified and ineffective. Later at the Muslim restaurant in Harlem, Malcolm advised Farmer that they stop debating. "All we're doing," he said, "is conducting a circus with two black guys belting each other's brains out verbally for the amusement of a largely white audience." Farmer agreed to this "verbal non-aggression pact," both men leaving unspoken that Malcolm's polemic neither admitted rebuttal nor afforded a map for change.[76]

The limits of the Black Muslim approach did not escape Malcolm himself. Privately he had begun to doubt that either integrationists or separatists alone could solve the problems of black people. One group had an active program, but it did not meet the needs of most blacks and was, in any case, dependent on white allies of limited reliability. The other group fully grasped the need for black self-esteem and solidarity, but otherwise it had scarcely any program, preferring to leave to Allah the burdens of political liberation.

Malcolm beseeched Elijah Muhammad to sanction a greater protest role for the Nation of Islam, but his mentor preferred that the movement continue in isolation from white authorities. Seething with the contradictions between Muslim polemic and Muslim passivity, Malcolm nevertheless deferred on this point, as on all others, to the man he revered as infallible and virtually divine. Then, in late 1963, personal tensions between the two men corroded the loyalty that their political differences had largely spared. Two paternity suits by young black women exposed Mr. Muhammad to high Muslim officials as more than a spiritual father to his flock, and as less than the ascetic divine he had seemed. While Malcolm reeled from the shock, he also found his role as movement spokesman suspended by Mr. Muhammad, who had grown jealous of his protégé's greater fame and fearful of his penchant for antagonizing white society. In March 1964 a chastened Malcolm X drifted away from his former savior and away from all previous certitudes.

"Moral reform it had, but beyond that it did nothing."[77] This judgment on the Nation of Islam might have come from the NAACP leader Wilkins, but the speaker was Malcolm X, who reappraised his own past with the same unsparing candor: "I did many things as a Muslim that I'm sorry for now. I was a zombie then—like all Muslims—I was hypnotized, pointed in a certain direction and told to march. Well, I guess a man's entitled to make a fool of himself if he's ready to pay the cost. It cost me twelve years."[78] Now he was ready to consider any strategy, any kind of movement that could bring a revolution in race relations.

Malcolm's whirlwind pilgrimage of ideas encompassed many black nationalist paths, while revealing no clear destination. He began employing Marxist terms and insisted, "You can't have capitalism without racism."[79] Yet Marxism remained a secondary motif in his speeches, and at other times he praised black capitalism as a route to economic independence.[80] Similarly his growing interest in Africa as a source of black power, pride, and culture contained ambiguities as vast as the continent. He took as role models leaders like Egypt's Gamal Nasser and Ghana's Kwame Nkrumah, who blended vaguely socialist programs with unmistakably defiant nationalism. Yet he recognized the limits of pan-Africanism as a strategy for Afro-American uplift, warning, "We have to be realistic and flexible. Africa is a long way off and there's a lot of water in between."[81] He still inveighed against one-sided nonviolence, but he no longer excluded the possibility, however scant, of peaceful revolution. At the founding rally of his Organization for Afro-American Unity, in March 1964, he predicted that the true ideology of black liberation would emerge spontaneously, like riffs at a jam session, and that it would be something nobody ever heard before.[82] Privately he confided that he had "no idea" where his path was leading, beyond a determination to win freedom for black people "by any means necessary."[83]

Not even Malcolm's ingrained racism could withstand the volcanic flow of experience and ideas following his break with the Black Muslims. As he met whites in African countries and on American college campuses who shared his commitments to racial justice, he gained "a new insight— . . . that the white man is *not* inherently evil, but America's racist society influences him to act evilly."[84] To change that system Malcolm now looked not to one race but to a new generation: "The young whites, and blacks, too, are the only hope that America has. The rest of us have always been living in a lie."[85]

Symbolic of his changing views was a trip to Mecca, holiest of Islamic cities, which helped him reclaim his religious faith from the racial doctrines wrapped around it. At the end of his hegira an epiphany awaited him, though it was a vision of mankind rather than of divinity that gripped Malcolm's prophetic sense. He saw pilgrims of every color gathered together, praying and conversing in harmony, something that in earlier years he would not have believed possible. The experience did not lessen his revulsion toward American society, but the gap between whites and blacks no longer seemed foreordained. Hatred, he now understood, was the only devil.

Openness toward whites, toward "anybody who will help get the ape off our backs," coexisted with Malcolm's old yearning for revolution. "I haven't changed," he told a *Village Voice* reporter early in 1965. "I just see things on a broader scale. We nationalists used to think we were militant. We were just dogmatic. It didn't bring us anything. . . . If you attack [a man] because he is white, you give him no out. He can't stop being white." Malcolm concluded with brushstrokes from both his Black Muslim period and his newly evolving style: "We've got to give the man a chance. He probably won't take it, the snake. But we've got to give him a chance."[86]

Malcolm also reached out to black integrationist leaders, whom he had once condemned out of hand. He openly drew on aspects of their doctrine, notably the importance of the ballot, though he looked to a cohesive black voting bloc rather than to entry into two-party politics as usual. He was perhaps the least likely observer at the NAACP's annual convention in 1964, which he attended in hopes of respectfully pointing out new directions to leaders who epitomized the integrationist approach. Malcolm did not come to endorse integration, but he no longer exalted separatism. In one of his last interviews a Canadian host asked if he still believed in a black state. Malcolm answered, "No, I believe in a society in which people can live like human beings on the basis of equality."[87]

While Malcolm's horizons were expanding, his search for a broader coalition afforded less encouragement. Civil rights leaders shrank from his ideological embrace out of resentment at past slanders, fear of another charismatic rival, and suspicion that Malcolm would always be anathema to most whites. There remained, as well, profound differences over integration, nonviolence, and liberal reform, the bedrock of civil rights activity that Malcolm still largely dismissed. On the left wing of the movement SNCC leaders occasionally spoke with Malcolm, in Africa and in America, but they too pulled back from his overtures, uncomfortable with his harsh treatment of their Gandhian, integrationist ideals. SNCC's executive secretary, James Forman, denied to a reporter that any joint enterprise with the Muslim leader was possible or that he was even a force to be reckoned with: "Look, man, nobody's worried about Malcolm X."[88]

Malcolm meanwhile became the subject of criticism among poor urban blacks. Many had revered him for his unqualified condemnation of whites and for his equally unreserved praise of blacks. Now he was drifting from that core wisdom as well as from his tutor Elijah Muhammad. "He doesn't know *what* he believes in," came the complaints in Harlem's bars and restaurants. "No sooner do you hear one thing than he's switched to something else." And he still had no clear plan of action: "All he's *ever* done was talk, CORE and SNCC and some of them people of Dr. King's are out getting beat over the head."[89] The political trapeze act was falling short; Malcolm's main base of support was slipping away, but no new, let alone larger, constituency was coming into view.

Worse still for Malcolm's embryonic movement, much of his energy went simply into steeling himself against the risk of assassination. Black Muslims followed him everywhere, murder plots narrowly missed, and he strongly hinted that his old movement was responsible. On some days the threats visibly drained him. He looked harried and prematurely haggard, his usual lithe gait replaced by leaden slowness. Still he continued to appear in public, and in moments of reflection he seemed strangely liberated. Even during his days as a Black Muslim he had impressed individual white reporters as innately humane, responsive, even friendly within the bounds of an austere demeanor. Now those qualities could emerge unrestrained by ideology. To his friend the photographer Gordon Parks he expressed relief that he had escaped his old mind-set: "That was a bad scene, brother. The sickness and madness of those days—I'm glad to be free of them. It's a time for martyrs now. And if I'm to be one, it will be in the cause of brotherhood. That's the only thing that can save this country. I've learned it the hard way—but I've learned it. . . ."[90]

Malcolm had also mentioned to Parks that there were two attempts on his life that week. Three days later, on February 21, 1965, he appeared at a Harlem rally, its ranks thinned by knowledge that Malcolm was a hunted man. As he started his talk, three Black Muslims in the front rows fired revolvers and a sawed-off shotgun, killing him almost instantly. Black Americans speculated intently on how high up the Muslim hierarchy the order went, and whether the CIA, the FBI, or even the Mafia had had a hand in the plot.[91] Some six thousand Harlemites viewed his casket. Yet by then Malcolm had few friends and not many more followers. On the streets and in night spots of the ghetto one could hear the harsh folk wisdom that he had deserved his fall from popularity, whether for his desertion of Elijah Muhammad, his changeable views, or his budding ties with whites. The cynicism overhanging every ghetto was fast descending on the late Muslim leader, enshrouding his memory.

King in Chicago

If poor urban blacks were going to reshape public policy and their own lives, someone of Martin Luther King's stature would have to overcome their doubts and the nation's indifference. Until 1965 this was an unlikely prospect, but the conclusion of the voting rights campaign and the catastrophe in Watts turned King's attention north. The Reverend James Bevel was already in Chicago laying the groundwork for King to try his brand of consciousness-raising in a major metropolis. Most of King's aides warned against a Northern campaign. Bayard Rustin argued that King had no organizational base in Chicago and no conception of the ghetto's daunting problems. He would only wreck his reputation on a doomed campaign. But King was going on moral instinct and could not be dissuaded, despite Rustin's fear that King was never in worse trouble than when he went solely on "inspiration."[92]

Chicago presented a novel challenge to King. Mayor Richard Daley ran a Tammany-style machine that ground down potential opposition through modest accommodation and massive patronage and corruption. His approach to race relations was characteristic: he offered enough to co-opt black politicians like the aging congressman William Dawson, while ignoring the 800,000 Negroes crowded into the city's South and West Side slums. Most of Chicago's blacks lived below or close to the poverty line, and although they composed nearly 30 percent of the city's population they played little part in governing their communities, let alone the larger metropolis. "I have never seen such hopelessness," Hosea Williams said after a month in the city. "The Negroes of Chicago have a greater feeling of powerlessness than any I ever saw. They don't participate in the governmental process because they're beaten down psychologically. We're used to working with people who want to be freed."[93]

Al Raby, a thin, balding young teacher with a heavy mustache, was one Chicago black who wanted passionately to be freed. To assert Negro rights in the city, Raby cofounded and presided over a network of thirty-four civil rights, religious, and civic groups called the Coordinating Council of Community Organizations (CCCO). The council did little coordinating, however, racked as it was by schisms between groups pressing for confrontation with Daley's machine and those favoring more discreet routes to reform. Raby himself tilted toward the militant minority faction, and in July 1965 he persuaded the council to request King's help during a protest over the city's segregated school system. On July 26 King led 30,000 people to City Hall at the peak of rush hour traffic. This was nearly 29,000 more people than had ever protested against racism in the city. "Chicago will never be the same now that the people here see what he brought," declared the local Urban League director. Knowing that King would soon depart, Daley adroitly hailed the march as a "tribute" to the minister and preached that "all right thinking Americans" shared his position on poverty and segregation. When King returned to organize a fair-housing campaign there, in January 1966, he found Daley as adroit as ever but not nearly so cordial.[94]

King planned to move to Chicago's West Side and expose the inadequacy of ghetto housing. His aide Bernard Lee leased an apartment on South Hamlin Street, located in a black neighborhood formally known as North Lawndale but more often called "Slumdale." Alerted just before King's arrival, the landlords urgently dispatched four plasterers, two painters, and two electricians to upgrade the facility. Despite the hasty repair work, few could have mistaken this renovated residence for anything other than a slum tenement. On entering the apartment in late January, Coretta King found the smell of urine overpowering, since drunks came in from the street past the unlocked door and relieved themselves in the hallway. She found, too, that the old refrigerator was not working and that the heaters were scarcely up to the challenge of a Chicago winter.[95] Several days later Dr. King guided newsmen through the facility, which was reminiscent of jail conditions he had known, and declared that if landlords did not drastically improve housing maintenance tenants would nonviolently take matters into their own hands.

Mobilizing black Chicago occupied King's time in the weeks ahead. One day he held a "hearing" in a Lawndale church, where people complained of high rents, collapsing houses, and the ever present rats. King assured them, "We're going to organize, to make Chicago a model city. Remember, living in a slum is robbery."[96] The next day King toured "Slumdale" with six members of a youth gang. Poorly dressed children playing in the subzero weather grinned as he passed, and chatted with him in delight. In succeeding days more speeches and essays hit at one basic point—the ghettos mocked the notion that racial justice was a reality. At the University of Chicago, King discoursed on the interlocking problems of ghetto dwellers; at a local church he evangelized on the need for community action:

> *What* is our problem?
> Tell us!
> It is that we are powerless—how do we get power?
> Tell us, Martin!
> By organizing ourselves. By getting together.
> That's right!
> We are *somebody* because we are *God's* children.
> That's right!

King reminded his audience to shun the example of Watts residents. "You don't need to hate anybody," he told his cheering listeners. "You don't need any Molotov cocktails. A riot can always be stopped by superior force. But they can't stop thousands of feet marching nonviolently!"[97] More cheers and applause, and then King was off to see the leaders of Chicago's black street gangs to make sure that the marching thousands would indeed remain nonviolent.

Members of the Vice Lords, the Cobras, and the Blackstone Rangers followed James Bevel, James Orange, and other SCLC lieutenants to meet "the leader." The gang members, proud veterans of switchblade scraps and occasional gun battles, approached King with deference and even awe. "Is that really you? Is that really Martin Luther King?" one asked. When King confirmed his identity, the young man exclaimed, "You don't mean to tell me I'm sitting here with this cat who's been up there talking to Presidents!"[98]

King heard the youths complain about the bleakness of street life, the feudal force of mobsters, the run-ins with police. He sympathized with their desire for respect and power but offered a new way: "Power in Chicago means getting the largest political machine in the nation to say yes when it wants to say no." Would the gangs experiment with putting away their guns and knives? If so, King wanted them as march marshals. James Bevel showed the gangs a film of the Watts riot, noting that almost all the victims of violence the past August had been black and that the police were still in control. But in Selma, where Negroes were nonviolent, the sheriff had been discredited and later replaced. "That's the difference between a riot and thinking," Bevel told them. Two hundred gang members eventually gave their word to try Dr. King's way. He was the one person they trusted, and they would march, nonviolently, "as soon as Brother Martin gives the word." "Maybe," said one youth, "we will get a better deal now."[99]

King began his challenge to Chicago on a small scale. On February 23, 1966, he and CCCO representatives persuaded four families in a tenement slum to withhold their rents, and declared the building in indefinite "trustee-ship." The money, King explained, would be used to finance basic repairs. He parried questions about the law by categorizing his action as "supralegal" rather than illegal. "The moral question," he stressed, "is far more important than the legal one."[100]

For Daley the crucial question was political, and he directed a skillful public relations campaign to undermine King's leadership. The mayor spoke of Chicago's slum-clearance plans in grandiose terms, stating that by 1967 there would be no more substandard housing in the city. He also instructed high-ranking political debtors, both white and black, to express their gratitude for Daley's patronage favors by condemning King's seizure of rents. One black federal judge obliged with the obiter dictum "I don't think [King's action] is legal; it is theft." Daley profited, too, from some negligent staff work by the SCLC. The landlord targeted by the rent strike turned out to be aged, very ill, and nearly as poor as his tenants, a revelation that further checked public sympathy for the protest. In early March a court officially ruled that King's action was indeed illegal but that the apartment owner must make repairs on the building. With that the movement stalled for lack of public drama, and from disorientation. King confessed that Daley was far shrewder than he had realized, and no one in the SCLC quite knew how to proceed.[101]

When King addressed a rally in July 1966, calling for a "Freedom Sunday" march to City Hall, some black youths booed him. This was the first time King had faced such a reception, even in audiences filled with hostile whites. For a man of his powerful dedication and equally strong ego, it was a bitter experience. He brooded through the night, wounded and indignant, wondering why these people would boo one so close to them. Before morning King's feelings had softened toward his detractors, as he considered the disillusioning limits of civil rights activity:

For twelve years I, and others like me, had held out radiant promises of progress. I had preached to them about my dream. I had lectured to them about the not too distant day when they would have freedom, "all, here and now." I had urged them to have faith in America and in white society. Their hopes had soared. They were now booing because they felt that we were unable to deliver on our promises.[102]

King's ability to empathize with these youths came partly from his new, firsthand experience of ghetto life. He could see the effects of "Slumdale" on his own children after just a few days: "Their tempers flared and they sometimes reverted to almost infantile behavior." Their apartment was "just too hot, too crowded, too devoid of creative forms of recreation." It was not long before King saw that the stifling environment he had entered "was about to produce an emotional explosion in [his] own family."[103]

Freedom Sunday, July 10, arrived in a ninety-eight-degree swelter that drove half a million people to the Lake Michigan beaches and kept attendance at King's rally far below the 100,000 he had predicted. About a third that number appeared in Soldiers Field stadium to hear King urge blacks and another aggrieved minority, the city's Puerto Rican population, to boycott all banks and companies that discriminated against them. Alongside these economic concerns King offered the old-time religion of moral confrontation. As he had declared in Albany and Birmingham, so in Chicago: this day we must decide to fill up the jails of Chicago, if necessary, to protest the injustices of ghetto life. He added a message for Richard Daley: "We must make it clear that we will purge Chicago of every politician, whether he be Negro or white, who feels that he owns the Negro vote." Then with thousands trailing him, the man whom aides had begun calling the Pied Piper of Hamlin Avenue set out for City Hall. He posted on the City Hall door a modern version of Martin Luther's ninety-five theses. The twelve-page document demanded an end to housing discrimination, greater employment of blacks, creation of a civilian review board to curb police brutality, and improved education in black neighborhoods.[104]

This was too much for Richard Daley, who had always ruled Chicago with only one thesis: do what I say. Red-faced with anger, the mayor spurned King's demands, claiming that Chicago already had a "massive" antislum program. He remained intransigent even after violence broke out on the West Side several times in the week after Freedom Sunday. Instead Daley blamed the disorders on anarchists, Communists, and King's staff, who he claimed taught Negroes "how to conduct violence" by showing them films of Watts. Daley's main gestures to the West Side, and to King, were to have the city bring in ten portable swimming pools and attach sprinklers to fire hydrants so that children could more easily endure the July heat. This did not strike King as an adequate program of social reconstruction, and he vowed there would be a march against segregated housing, which would venture into the lily-white neighborhoods that ringed the ghettos.[105]

As in the Selma campaign, King was elsewhere when Andy Young, Al Raby, and others led the first group of interracial marchers into an Irish and Lithuanian blue-collar neighborhood adjoining the southwest side. When aides later reported to King that whites had jeered and harassed them, he seemed even more determined to lead a second march. On August 5 six hundred blacks and whites followed him to Marquette Park, located in a neighborhood of second-generation Poles, Lithuanians, Italians, and Germans who had fled the West Side years earlier as blacks streamed in from the south. In front of the marchers strode 960 police, on the flanks a nonviolent guard of Roman Saints, Cobras, and Vice Lords. At the park a thousand whites stood on a knoll overlooking the demonstrations, waving Confederate flags, sporting Nazi insignia, and cursing the marchers. Suddenly they hurled bottles and rocks at the marchers; a brick struck King just above his right ear, and he fell to the ground. As reporters clustered around him, he assured them that the march would continue—it could not be stopped. What of his own condition? King casually observed, "Oh, I've been hit so many times I'm immune to it." The march continued as another barrage of hand-thrown missiles rained down upon marchers and police alike.[106]

News cameras caught the unusual sight of white police pummeling white neighbors with nightsticks to protect a group of Negro marchers. But the rock-throwing vigilantes were sparing no one, and police grimly proceeded with their law-and-order tasks despite their own fears and wounds. Al Raby could scarcely believe the rage reflected in "that terrible noise of people shouting at" the marchers: "Women are among the most vicious, screaming 'you monkeys' at the blacks and 'you white trash' at the others. They called all of us *apes* or told the blacks to go back to Africa." With police providing what protection they could, King and his followers knelt in prayer while white teenagers screamed, "Hate! Hate! Hate!" One man threw a knife at King. He missed his target and instead wounded another heckler. Afterward King reflected on this dispiriting example of Northern racial bias: "I've never seen anything like it. I've been in many demonstrations all across the south, but I can say that I have never seen—even in Mississippi and Alabama—mobs as hostile and as hate-filled as I've seen in Chicago." His one spark of consolation: the young gang members had weathered the assault without retaliating. In an era of rioting, King found it heartening that "even very violent temperaments can be channeled through nonviolent discipline."[107]

King was becoming ever more of a puzzlement to Richard Daley, who could neither flatter nor bully him away. On August 17, just days after blacks marched in three white neighborhoods, Daley staged a "summit meeting" with King and several dozen local civic leaders, including black activists. There the mayor pressed a squirming spokesman for Chicago's Real Estate Board to affirm a clear commitment to open housing. Yet Daley's overriding aim remained a quiet city, not a desegregated one. On August 19, while a subcommittee of the summit group debated the steps needed to end racism, Daley secured a court injunction drastically limiting demonstrations in Chicago. King promptly countered with a plan to march through Cicero, the most volatile of all-white suburbs, a neighborhood where four whites had recently caught a Negro looking for a job and beaten him to death. "Not only are we going to walk in Cicero," King promised, "we're going to work in Cicero, and we're going to live in Cicero."[108]

The prospect of several thousand Negroes walking to Cicero conjured up visions of race war that unnerved the sheriff of Cook County, who called the march plan "suicidal"; the governor of Illinois, Otto Kerner, who put the National Guard on alert; white liberals, who implored King to stop the madness; and Richard Daley, who did not want his city to become the next Selma. On August 26, 1966, Daley again met with King and other summit delegates, and coaxed their unanimous approval of a ten-point accord to combat residential segregation. City officials agreed to intensify enforcement of Chicago's open-housing law, disperse low-cost public housing, and assign housing to welfare recipients without regard to race; financial leaders promised mortgages on a non-racial basis; and Chicago's Real Estate Board grudgingly—and somewhat abstractly—endorsed "the philosophy of open occupancy." King in turn called off the march to Cicero, though he added a pointed postscript to the compromise: "If these agreements aren't carried out, Chicago hasn't *seen* a demonstration."[109]

Ever intent to wring maximal symbolism out of an ambiguous settlement, King hailed the summit for producing "the most significant program ever conceived to make open housing a reality in the metropolitan area."[110] Yet the pact contained no specific timetable for achieving progress; while an ongoing summit committee, formed to help implement the accord, never commanded the consensus or the authority to act effectively even as investigators exposed the policies of city agencies, realtors, and banks as largely unchanged. Once again, King's critics charged, the minister had settled for a token gain and, perhaps, a face-saving route out of his Chicago blues. It seemed to many blacks, as King's biographer David Lewis wrote, that the "Selma bridge syndrome"—referring to the march King had halted under federal pressure—once more prevented him from following through on a confrontation with authority.[111] Chester Robinson of the militant West Side Organization added another reason for opposing the agreement: "We're sick and tired of middle-class people telling us what we want."[112]

Chicago's black residents found little change in their lives as King left for Atlanta with his executive staff. They could point only to "Operation Breadbasket," an SCLC program that showed unforeseen energy in winning jobs for Negroes, as a tangible legacy of King's campaign. This spin-off of a program begun in Atlanta had been a secondary venture in the Chicago movement. Its surprising progress could be traced mainly to the efforts of a charismatic, twenty-five-year-old aide to Dr. King, Jesse Jackson, who used a network of churches to negotiate with white firms and conduct selective buying campaigns. Yet even this program, a sympathetic observer commented in the *Nation,* might truly be called "Operation Drop-in-the-Bucket," given the extent of black poverty in Chicago. In many respects the Chicago freedom movement had emerged as a debacle to rival the Albany movement.[113]

There was blame to go around for everyone, beginning with King. He had focused narrowly on an issue, open housing, that had little practical meaning to slum dwellers unable to afford homes in white neighborhoods even had townsfolk welcomed them and realtors sought them out. Local blacks, for their part, expected far too much of one man. It was not King so much as his followers who harbored a messiah complex over his leadership, and it invited disillusionment.

If the Chicago campaign taught King and his allies a central lesson, it was that the task of improving ghetto conditions in the North was going to be vastly more difficult than earlier struggles for desegregation in the South had been. Al Raby, returning to college for graduate study, concluded that neither he nor King "realized what a tough town this is and how strong the Democratic organization is." Chicago revealed "that we are in for a much larger and longer fight than any of us thought it was ever going to be." And worst of all, *"there may never be an answer!"*[114]

Raby's pessimism reflected nonviolent direct action's meager impact on the Northern slums. It was as if a curative once hailed as a wonder drug had encountered a hardier strain of virus and was no longer potent, at least at that dosage. In Chicago the old tactics had failed to personify for the public the evils of institutional racism. Unlike the campaigns in Birmingham and Selma, the one in Chicago brought no dramatic villains to the nation's television screens. The occasional news footage of police violence showed angry whites as victims. Nor was racism easily exposed in Northern municipal laws. Even in Albany, Georgia, where Laurie Pritchett posed a mirror image to King's nonviolent leadership, the minister could point to segregationist statutes that confined the town's black residents. But racism moved through Northern cities like Chicago in so many faceless, impersonal forms as to escape detection by a society inclined to ignore it.

One powerful by-product did emerge from the Chicago protests. While the campaign scarcely changed the ghetto, it did much to transform the larger black protest movement. In the early sixties it had been a Southern-based drive narrowly intent on eliminating blatantly racist laws and practices. With King's Northern commitment the movement sharpened its critique of the social and economic order. It demanded concrete sacrifices from the nation as well as symbolic affirmations of a commitment to equality. Still seeking direction in the wake of its legislative triumphs, the civil rights movement was becoming more thoroughly egalitarian than the first college demonstrators had ever imagined.

Chapter 7

Reformers at the Crossroads

The Southern Movement in Crisis

VIOLENCE in the ghettos shook the morale of civil rights leaders just as the Southern-based protest movement appeared to be succumbing to its own success. Passage of voting rights legislation in August 1965 had largely vanquished the formal barriers to equality, leaving no clear markings on the path toward further reform. A malaise crept over the movement, which—like the women's movement after it won the ballot earlier in the century—suddenly lacked an overriding goal to unify and inspire it. As black activists groped for a new agenda, they began to look more carefully, and cynically, at the values of nonviolence, coalition, and integration that had sustained their efforts.

The ethic of nonviolent protest had exalted civil rights campaigns beyond the realm of politics as usual, and led Americans to admit the moral enormity of racism. Yet that ethic had also demanded extraordinary courage, discipline, and goodwill in the face of repeated savagery. By 1965 it was evident that people were tired of professing love for brutal sheriffs and racist mobs. The mass saintliness that had sustained the nonviolent revolution was at last giving way to more common if less admirable human responses—frustration, blind rage, and, perhaps inevitably, racial hate.

Occasional scuffles between black youths and white toughs marred the remarkable decorum of the sit-ins in 1960. So did the conduct of some freedom riders the following year. Overtaxed by prison life, several riders broke into fist fights, pledged hunger strikes they could not carry out, or broke down in solitary confinement and screamed to be let out. These lapses in nonviolent discipline prompted James Farmer to confess privately that CORE and other groups had not given the freedom riders sufficient training.[1] Two years later incidents of rock throwing in Birmingham violated King's nonviolent strictures. No one was immune to the pressures of the field: in 1964 John Lewis, SNCC's gentle symbol of nonviolence, reportedly fought with policemen as they dragged him to a patrol wagon.[2] Such episodes marked rare departures from the exacting standards of restraint that civil rights workers had set for themselves. Yet they hinted at resentments that sermons and strategy sessions might submerge but could never wholly dispel.

These resentments germinated as the years of nonviolent direct action ground down the physical and emotional reserves of the movement's Christian soldiers. Ulcers, headaches, and nervous disorders struck young civil rights workers in the Deep South, often for the first time in their lives. Many SNCC staffers needed to leave the movement after prolonged exposure to conditions they likened to those of a "war zone." For organizers in Mississippi such incapacitating battle fatigue was as commonplace as a jail record.[3]

The most disciplined activists might, through superhuman will, press back the ill effects of constant activity, responsibility, and danger. There was, of course, the example of Bob Moses to guide them. Privately churning with doubts and fears, he nonetheless remained SNCC's quiet master of emotion. One evening Moses confessed to a morbid fear of dogs as he and the Yale law student Marian Wright gingerly passed a growling canine. The two friends next saw each other during a march to the Leflore County courthouse in Mississippi, a rally that police greeted by unleashing attack dogs. One grunting animal sprang for Moses and tore a long gash in his trousers. "And there was Bob," Wright marveled, "refusing to move back, walking, walking towards the dogs."[4]

By winter 1965 five years of walking toward the dogs had caught up with Robert Moses. He formally withdrew from SNCC, dropped his last name, and returned to the North. As Robert Parris, he claimed that his departure and change of name were essential to prevent others from becoming more dependent on his leadership, which would contradict SNCC's democratic spirit. There were also signs that the burdens of such leadership were growing unbearable. Connie Curry, one of the first white members of SNCC's executive committee, remembered "watching the changes in Bob Moses" since 1960:

See, we used to have argument after argument of whether or not nonviolence was a technique or a way of life, and that was probably one of the biggest debates in the early days of SNCC. Because I maintained, as did other people, that nonviolence as a way of life was good as an ideal, but it was something that was absolutely alien to all of our backgrounds and the way that we were raised. . . . That's why being beaten and thrown into jail and trying to love everybody while they did it to you . . . was bound to mess you up. . . . I mean, look what it did to Bob Moses. It just made him into a—it broke his heart. . . . He used to get hurt everytime anybody would look mean at him, literally. I mean, he would feel it, and you could imagine that kind of sensitivity in Mississippi where people wanted to kill him.[5]

Curry found that disillusionment was inevitable for the SNCC youths who "really believed that they were going to win." She added,

It was the whole thing of "We Shall Overcome." They really sorta thought there was an end in sight, and when they would sing "God is on our side," I would never sing that verse. . . . I don't think that anybody ever envisioned the long years of struggle and violence and everything—anguish. I don't think they were really aware of it. And as it emerged I think it was just a terrible, terrible toll.[6]

That toll was often greatest for Negroes who attempted to suppress their anger toward white tormentors. The Harvard psychiatrist Alvin Poussaint frequently commented to victims of assault during civil rights protests, "You must feel pretty angry getting beaten up like that by those bigots." The typical marcher denied all: "No, I don't hate those white men, I love them because they must really be suffering with all that hatred in their souls. Dr. King says the only way we can win our freedom is through love. Anger and hatred have never solved anything." Dr. Poussaint would nod, and silently wonder, "Now, what do they really do with their rage?" In time he learned:

> Violent verbal and sometimes physical fights often occurred among the workers on the civil-rights projects throughout the South. While they were talking about being nonviolent and "loving" the sheriff that just hit them over the head, they rampaged around the project houses beating up each other. I frequently had to calm Negro civil-rights workers with large doses of tranquilizers for what I can describe clinically only as acute attacks of rage.[7]

Apart from suffering the strains of adhering to a philosophy of nonviolence, civil rights workers in some areas were coming to doubt whether turning the other cheek served any purpose except to give their abusers symmetrical targets. So long as Gandhian confrontations had produced victories in the Upper South and even in Alabama and Georgia, there was widespread acceptance of the sacrifice. But Dr. King's doctrines found little nourishment in the harsh facts of Negro life in Mississippi. Instead local blacks like the grizzled farmer Hartman Turnbow, who several times dissuaded whites from trespassing by using his Remington automatic shotgun, became role models for SNCC youths. Turnbow was a pillar of the young Freedom Democratic party, and his forceful nature scarcely permitted any civil rights workers to preach the way of peace. "Ain't but one," Turnbow marveled. "He used to git on me a whole lot 'bout it, and that was Martin Lufus King. I went to a meetin' in Frogmore, South Carolina, and he were there, and he'uz against that shootin' back. He believed in nonviolent. I told him, 'Well, I never, never make a nonviolent man.' "[8]

At the Democratic National Convention in 1964 Turnbow met King again and told him about a firebombing and rifle attack on his home. They might have killed his wife and his fourteen-year-old daughter, but Turnbow had shot it out with the marauders and driven them away. King repeated his dedication to nonviolence, but Turnbow was stunned. Dealing in the simple currency of Mississippi's Negro population, physical survival, Turnbow told King, "This nonviolent stuff ain't no good. It'll get ya killed. . . . If you follow it long enough, it's gon' get *you* killed." A young Negro woman cut in, "If nonviolent ain't no good, what's good?" "It ain't but one thing that is good," Turnbow replied. "[Whatever] the Mississippi white man pose with, he got to be met with. . . . If he pose with a smile, meet him with a smile, and if he pose with a gun, meet him with a gun." As Turnbow recalled, everyone in the room, white and black, agreed with him, with one exception: "[King] said that's just his way, say he gon' finish up with nonviolent. I told him, 'Well you finish up in a cemetery you just keep a followin' it.' "[9]

Civil rights workers who renounced nonviolence were often signaling a broader disaffection with their political tactics and partnerships. Despite the array of laws issuing from President Johnson's liberal consensus, the majority of blacks still lived in segregation and poverty. Therefore, while traditional Negro spokesmen continued to urge alliance with the Democratic party, younger activists were resolving that blacks must win bolder changes in policy than their liberal allies dared to contemplate.

The Broadening Protest: Civil Rights Leaders and Vietnam

American military intervention in South Vietnam aggravated black misgivings about the priorities of white liberals. By 1965 the war against Vietnamese Communists was siphoning funds from programs just beginning to aid the ghettos. Late in the year another barometer of commitment to the Great Society dropped sharply: Vice-President Hubert Humphrey was relieved of duties coordinating civil rights policy and reassigned to supervise all matters on Vietnam. Although the President insisted that his domestic programs remained vital, it appeared to some black leaders that social reform might soon become a casualty of war.

Dissent on Vietnam did not come easily to blacks, who shared with other Americans the conviction that national security demanded a global military presence. Negro and white military trainees alike received indoctrination that Vietnam was a testing ground of American resolve against Communist invaders. In the ghettos, as in white working-class districts, support for "our boys" was the rule, and the sight of a green beret on a uniformed young man occasioned deep respect. Civil rights groups also hesitated to break their own longstanding rule during the Cold War, never to risk a consensus for racial equality by playing with foreign policy fire.

In addition to feeling indebted to the President, civil rights leaders shared the widespread fear among liberal Democrats that any criticisms of American military commitments would risk weakening their anti-Communist credentials. All but two Democratic senators in August 1964 had voted for the Gulf of Tonkin resolution, which gave the President wide latitude to conduct war in Vietnam. The anxiety to appear firm against communism gripped Johnson himself, who believed that a precipitous withdrawal from Vietnam might provoke a storm of right-wing indignation and cost him his consensus on domestic issues. In turn, most other liberals suppressed doubts about Johnson's policies because they prized the health of the Democratic coalition—as well as their own political well-being—over fine points about the proper limits of America's global role. Black leaders in particular realized that their hold on the President's support depended on reciprocal loyalty to his administration, a quality that Lyndon Johnson was not inclined to measure in degrees. The silence enveloping the civil rights movement on Vietnam persisted largely unbroken until August 1965, when Martin Luther King, Jr., felt he could no longer swallow Johnson's assurances whole without damage to his own, nonviolent philosophy.

Although King did not belong to any pacifist group, he had a deep aversion to war that was strengthened by what he saw as the racist arrogance of American policy toward Vietnam. By ignoring widespread Vietnamese resentment of American military intervention, the United States had once more shown, in King's view, an indifference to the rights of nonwhite peoples. King also feared that escalating the war would divert money and political attention from urgent domestic tasks. His decision to speak out came when the voting rights campaign was safely behind him, ghetto unrest on the rise, and the American presence in Vietnam fast expanding. The year 1965 had witnessed the first sustained American bombing of the North, an increase in U.S. troop strength to 75,000, and acceleration of draft notices. Viewing racial injustice, poverty, and the war in Vietnam as "inextricably bound together," he concluded that his message of peace must extend to relations between nations as well as between races.[10]

King's musings on Vietnam left his inner circle alarmed at the prospect of a breach with the national government, just months after federal forces had hovered protectively over his every step between Selma and Montgomery. Bayard Rustin, himself a pacifist, preferred to view King's position as a realist: criticism of the war might alienate the President and the Congress. Stanley Levison, a white attorney who advised King on financial matters, warned that the SCLC would lose its donors and have to abandon its campaigns against poverty in the North. But King felt compelled to speak out against "the madness of militarism" and plunged ahead toward every available forum.[11]

On the stump, in press conferences, and later on the CBS program "Face the Nation," King urged a halt to the bombing of North Vietnam and a negotiated end to the conflict before it imperiled "the whole of mankind."[12] King offered to mediate personally—he was, after all, the Nobel Peace Prize recipient for 1964—and try to bring the Americans, Russians, Chinese, and Vietnamese to the conference table. The minister's statements formed the most forthright condemnation of the war by a leader of his national stature. Yet as Rustin and other SCLC aides had feared, his principled stand dragged the civil rights movement into unfamiliar political terrain, leading uphill against the President of the United States.

Black leaders, especially those in government posts, repulsed King's diplomatic aspirations. Assistant Secretary of Labor George Weaver treated the annual Masonic convention as an occasion to censure civil rights figures who presumed to pass foreign policy judgments. King was the unnamed but unmistakable target of his message. Among the articulate middle class, reaction ranged "from cool to bitter." King later told the journalist David Halberstam that many of the more privileged blacks were hoping that "the war will win them their spurs" by establishing their patriotism. He added, "That's not the way you win spurs."[13] The civil rights leaders Roy Wilkins and Whitney Young, concerned with avoiding Johnson's spurs, privately suggested to King that he, more than the country, should withdraw from Vietnam in order not to upset the President's consensus on civil rights.

The President himself was already explosively upset—who in the hell did King think he was? he demanded of his aides, then settled the question by opining that the minister was an amateur diplomat and, worse, an ingrate. Behind the scenes he moved to silence his new critic. UN Ambassador Arthur Goldberg and other presidential emissaries assured King that the war would soon be over and that he should have more faith in the President's judgment. "They told me I wasn't an expert in foreign affairs," King later said in regard to the administration's warnings, "and they were all experts. I knew only civil rights and should stick to that." King smarted under this patronizing treatment and marveled that he had never fully understood Johnson's "ego thing."[14]

SNCC youths for once lagged after Dr. King, the "establishment" black leader, as they spun in uncertain orbit between the demands of conscience and of coalition. At first glance antiwar dissent should have poured forth easily from SNCC headquarters, considering the group's roots in nonviolent philosophy and its hair-trigger responses to perceived moral wrongs. But SNCC was then under attack in the media and in Congress as a Communist-infiltrated organization. Such charges had long been standard fare in the South, but now Northerners were joining in and that augured fewer donations to SNCC's always malnourished treasury. Most members therefore avoided public comment on the war or else made disclaimers that their views in no way represented SNCC. When a white SNCC member, Howard Zinn, urged support for the fledgling antiwar movement early in 1965, the black activist Dona Richards countered, "While we care a great deal about both Vietnam and civil rights, we can't do anything to help the Vietnam situation, and we can hurt ourselves by trying."[15]

Apart from trying to withstand the mudslinging and arrows of Red-hunting columnists, SNCC refused to permit the war issue to deflect its focus from the black poor. The SNCC veterans John Lewis and Marion Barry were trying to secure a role for poor blacks at the White House Conference on Civil Rights planned for June 1966, and they would not risk severing ties with Johnson over the war. Other staffers simply wanted to focus on organizing the black community, without diffusing their energies in white-dominated antiwar protests.[16] Whereas black militants of earlier periods had sometimes counseled withholding support from a white man's war, SNCC in 1965 hesitated to join an unpopular white man's dissent. SNCC members had not lost their stomach for martyrdom, but as their problems multiplied they were becoming more selective about the ends and the circumstances.

A murder broke the policy deadlock. On January 3, 1966, Samuel Younge, a twenty-two-year-old veteran of both the U.S. Navy and SNCC, was shot dead as he tried to enter the "white" rest room at a gas station in Tuskegee, Alabama. Earlier that day Younge had led forty blacks to the Macon County courthouse, where he was threatened by a knife-wielding registrar. Jolted by news of the killing, SNCC's executive committee asserted "a right and a responsibility to dissent" against the war in Vietnam. Just as a black Navy veteran was slain because U.S. law was not being enforced, so Vietnamese were being murdered because the United States was "pursuing an aggressive policy in violation of international law."[17]

Johnson met SNCC's dissent with a battery of political attacks, coordinated by black aides. Louis Martin spoke with Roy Wilkins, who needed little encouragement to excoriate SNCC in his nationally syndicated newspaper column. The White House counselor Clifford Alexander advised Johnson to "have the six Negro Congressmen issue a statement expressing the wholehearted support of the Negro people for our actions in Vietnam." He also expressed his concern over King's possible response and planned to talk with the minister's aide Andrew Young "to impress upon him the seriousness of the [SNCC] statement and the over-all negative consequences of it for the civil rights movement."[18]

Alexander might have done better to reach Julian Bond, just elected a state assemblyman from a predominantly black district near SNCC's Atlanta headquarters. Four years of service as SNCC's public relations director had given Bond a reputation for radicalism, and even after he resigned in early 1965 his views continued to draw avid media scrutiny. Bond shared the pacifist leanings common to the early SNCC membership, and he replied matter-of-factly to a reporter's question that, yes, he found the group's antiwar statement reasonable. The next day, Bond became a household word in Georgia, and not a pleasant one. White liberals joined hands with white conservatives to brand his comments treasonous. On January 10, 1966, his colleagues in the statehouse barred Julian Bond from taking the oath of office.

In fact, Bond was guilty of something almost equal to treason in the eyes of the legislators: he had committed an act of independence from those white politicians who expected to act as his permanent tutors. Although there were obligatory denials of racist sentiment—had the legislature not seated five other black assemblymen?—Bond alone had taken a controversial stand without first consulting the white establishment. It was bad enough to appear a pacifist in a state that solidly backed the President's policy in Vietnam. It was still worse for this Negro, coming from an upstanding family that had surely taught him better racial etiquette, to act "uppity" in public. Bond himself understood that he could yet reclaim his seat with an abject plea for forgiveness, but instead he affirmed his position.[19]

Knowing that Johnson was monitoring reactions to the Bond imbroglio, most civil rights leaders declined to comment. But the coalition continued to buckle when King defended Bond's dissent. Even some SCLC stalwarts decided that they had had enough. The president of the Chattanooga, Tennessee, branch and his assistant both resigned, explaining that King's antiwar pronouncements had gone too far.[20]

President Johnson thought so, too. His aides refused King an invitation to the June 1966 White House Conference on Civil Rights, citing FBI reports that branded him a subversive. Later Johnson relented when many whites and blacks in the movement informed the White House that there would not be a conference without Martin Luther King. But Johnson took care to minimize King's role at the event. King's biographer David Lewis observed that King was so thoroughly ignored that "his wife came nearer to making a contribution to the proceedings when she was asked to sing."[21] Johnson's message was clear: King could choose honor as a civil rights leader if he ceased to meddle in foreign policy. But wretched were the peacemakers who flouted their President's will.

Not content simply to humble King before the assembly of civil rights leaders, Johnson orchestrated the conference to show black support for both his domestic and his foreign policies. He made an unscheduled appearance as, quite literally, a master of ceremonies, introducing the federal judge Thurgood Marshall in glowing terms. It was the first time, Johnson pointed out, that an American President had introduced a speaker who was not a head of state. Marshall reciprocated this tribute with an enthusiastic report of the civil rights gains made under Johnson's benign oversight. Whitney Young assured reporters at the scene, "The people are more concerned about the rat tonight and the job tomorrow than they are about Vietnam."[22] Because SNCC sent no representative to the meeting, only Floyd McKissick of CORE challenged Johnson directly on Vietnam. His resolution condemning the escalation was sharply rejected in a committee chaired by the Negro educator and UN official James M. Nabrit, Jr., whom Johnson had designated for just such a contingency. Nabrit was the president of Howard University, whose last commencement ceremonies had featured as its keynote speaker President Lyndon Johnson.[23]

Although King declined his aides' advice to walk out of the conference, he and other black leaders realized that the President was less interested in gathering their suggestions than in administering an object lesson to dissenters. Moreover, Johnson's widely reported, expletive-filled warnings that King should tend his own civil rights garden seemed tainted by patronizing racial attitudes. It was as if Johnson were directing the Nobel laureate away from the protest line for national issues, and onto a separate protest line, marked "Integration." The President's display of political muscle temporarily restrained antiwar sentiment among Negroes, but the White House Conference on Civil Rights scarcely ensured the desired harmony. The conference showed rather that the bonds of the civil rights coalition were fragile, subject to stress not only on "race" issues but along the whole range of administration policies.

Closing Ranks: Black Politics in
Lowndes County

SNCC, alone among civil rights organizations, boycotted the White House Conference on Civil Rights. This act formalized a breach with the President, most white liberals, and the Democratic party—a breach that had been years in the making. SNCC's political journey from faith to cynicism had led through Mississippi in the summer of 1964, through the maze of Democratic politics in Atlantic City, and into the halls of Congress. After the tepid welcome of Mississippi's black delegates at the 1964 Democratic National Convention, young black activists shifted their focus from moral entreaty to a quest for power. That resolve deepened in September 1965 when the Democratic-controlled House of Representatives upheld the election of five Mississippi congressmen despite evidence of black disenfranchisement in every district. The House vote (228 to 143) was closer than expected; yet it further persuaded SNCC youths that blacks had to organize outside the framework of major-party politics.

Rather than accept token participation at the next Democratic National Convention, Robert Moses pointed early in 1965 to a separatist solution in the Deep South based on the assertion of black power: "Why can't we set up our own [state] government? So that in 1967, if we get organized enough between now and then, we can . . . declare the other one no good. And say the federal government should recognize us."[24] In March 1965—one day after the killing of Viola Liuzzo—Stokely Carmichael arrived in the Black Belt county of Lowndes, Alabama, to set about making a prophet of Bob Moses.

Negro residents found Lowndes County, located between Selma and Montgomery, to be like most of the Black Belt, rich in farmland but desperately poor in opportunity. The income of whites averaged five times that of Negroes, with most wealth going to the eighty-six families who owned 90 percent of the land and who controlled all elective and appointed offices. Although blacks formed a clear majority in the county, none was registered to vote. This contrasted with the official registration of 130 percent of the eligible white voters. SNCC's mission in Lowndes was simple, as Cleveland Sellers related: "We intended to register as many Blacks as we could, all of them if possible, and take over the county."[25]

Carmichael, Sellers, and a few coworkers showed once more what SNCC could achieve with a minimum of funds and tireless enthusiasm for door-to-door persuasion. At Carmichael's insistence SNCC canvassers avoided discussing differences between themselves and the SCLC despite temptations to challenge King's leadership. Carmichael explained to more pugnacious SNCC leaders like James Forman that local residents simply did not distinguish between groups of civil rights workers, but saw them all as just "freedom fighters." It made more sense, Carmichael realized, to exploit the enthusiasm that King inspired:

People loved King. . . . I've seen people in the South climb over each other just to say, "I touched him! I touched him!" . . . I'm even talking about the young. The old people had more love and respect. They even saw him like a God. These were the people we were working with and I had to follow in his footsteps when I went in there. The people didn't know what was SNCC. They just said, "You one of Dr. King's men?" "Yes, Ma'am, I am."[26]

For months SNCC workers aimed simply to convince blacks that they had, as Carmichael put it, "the *right* to fight racial oppression and exploitation."[27] Half a year passed, and perhaps sixty blacks had dared to appear at the courthouse and register to vote. Then in August the Voting Rights Act made its presence felt in Lowndes when federal registrars entered the county. Suddenly literacy tests no longer barred blacks from the ballot, nor were blacks rejected because of imperfections in penmanship. The courthouse soon received Negro registrants by the hundreds.

Whites reacted to the surge in black voter registration by jailing more civil rights volunteers and murdering one of them. The Reverend Jonathan Daniels and Father Richard Morrisroe, both white activists, were accompanying two black women to a grocery store in Hayneville, in Lowndes County, when a man with a shotgun shouted at them and took aim. Daniels pushed one of the women to the ground, out of the line of fire, as the assailant, a deputy peace officer, pulled the trigger. Daniels was killed on the spot. Father Morrisroe also fell, wounded by a second shotgun blast. Witnesses attested to the crime, but white residents widely approved the lawman's firm stance toward "outside agitators," and he escaped conviction.

The murders did not deter members of the black community from pressing their claim to political power. In March 1966, Negro farmers and domestic servants created an independent political party called the Lowndes County Freedom Organization (LCFO). It aimed to serve the poor people of the county and displace the Democrats who had ruled uncontested for generations. To those who argued that blacks should try to reform Alabama's Democratic party rather than sever all ties with it, Carmichael answered that this was akin to counseling Jews to reform the Nazi party from within.[28]

SNCC organizers seldom invoked racial separatism in describing the aims of the new party, but their actions bespoke the recent black disillusionment with coalition politics. "We want power, that's all we want," Carmichael told residents. "After we get power we can talk about whether we want all black or not."[29] In practice, though, this was an all-black endeavor. Unlike the Freedom party in Mississippi, the LCFO was organized entirely by blacks and fielded only black candidates. The new group further differed from Mississippi's insurgents in that from the outset the LCFO showed little interest in consensus politics except as it tried to unite the black masses whose votes it sought. For those who might still overlook the signs of changing black attitudes, the new party chose as its symbol the head of a snarling black panther.

In May, the month in which residents of Lowndes County selected candidates for their new Freedom Organization, SNCC experienced a watershed election of its own. John Lewis stood for reelection as chairman, but support for his leadership had been steadily eroding. Some complaints stemmed from his inattention to organizational rivalry—he continued to serve on the SCLC's board of directors and to work closely with Martin Luther King. Lewis had also flouted rank-and-file opinion by helping the Johnson administration plan its White House Conference on Civil Rights, though he withdrew when it became clear that Johnson's forum had less to do with public policy than with public relations. Perhaps most important, though, were the attitudes Lewis represented, rather than any specific misstep. He was the perfect embodiment of SNCC's original devotion to religious nonviolence and interracial coalition. By May 1966 such values were an embarrassment to many SNCC members, a reminder—along with Lewis himself—of an earlier, more naïve time.

Lewis defeated Stokely Carmichael by a wide margin in the 1966 election, but a former SNCC field-worker named Worth Long challenged the results that same evening. There was no technical basis to sustain his protest, but there soon proved to be a powerful emotional basis. Vehement argument over whether Lewis truly personified SNCC's values churned on through the night and into the dawn. At last the exhausted remnants of the SNCC convention held a new election, in which they overwhelmingly chose Carmichael as chairman, his friend and ally Cleveland Sellers as program secretary, and another young veteran with black nationalist leanings, Ruby Doris [Smith] Robinson, as executive secretary.

John Lewis was bitter. The machinations to overturn his reelection had hurt his pride and revealed little of SNCC's professed commitment to creating a harmonious community. Partly to heal the wounds from the acrimonious debates and maneuvers, staff members selected Lewis to be on a new, ten-member central committee to direct policy. Considerable guilt and remorse accompanied this action. Even the catalyst for the coup, Worth Long, felt a deep ambivalence toward the episode. "John would not just follow you into the lion's den," Long said; "he would lead you into it."[30] By this point, however, SNCC staffers were not about to follow anyone into the lion's den of the Deep South with only the spirit of Christian love to deliver them.

Marching toward Black Power

James Meredith, whose presence at a Mississippi college in 1962 had drawn white mobs and federal marshals, revived the spirit of nonviolent direct action with a solitary protest in June 1966. Meredith planned a 220-mile march through rural Mississippi to show blacks that they could confidently assert their right to vote. Death threats against him proliferated, reminiscent of his undergraduate days. But on June 5 Meredith set out from Memphis, Tennessee, marking each step with an ebony walking stick topped with ivory, the gift of an African chieftain. Imbued with a sense of destiny, he expressed the belief that he would be spared on this journey through backlands that had known more than their share of racial murders.

The next morning a sniper lurking in the bushes fired at Meredith from a dozen feet away as he crossed the border between Tennessee and Mississippi. Meredith collapsed, writhing on the ground, sixty birdshot pellets lodged in his back, neck, legs, and head. The assailant, who entered a police car with hands uncuffed and puffing on a pipe, was a thirty-year-old Klansman and unemployed steelworker who freely confessed to the shooting. When asked why he had tried to assassinate James Meredith, he could only mutter that he did not know.[31]

From his hospital bed Meredith began to revise his ideas about nonviolence. He expressed regret that he had not carried a gun, and vowed that never again would he walk that way unarmed. A sympathetic white companion joked, "That's not in keeping with the nonviolent philosophy, Mr. Meredith." "Who the hell ever said I was nonviolent?" Meredith snapped. "I spent eight years in the military and the rest of my life in Mississippi."[32]

The march Meredith had started was by no means over. As he slowly recovered, the heads of the five major civil rights groups traveled to Memphis to continue his journey. Stokely Carmichael, the new CORE leader Floyd McKissick, and Martin Luther King, Jr., gathered at Meredith's bedside to offer sympathy and to obtain the patient's blessing for a sympathy protest. They braced for objections, for Meredith was known to be a temperamental loner; but basking in the homage of these three eminent civil rights leaders, he approved their plans to carry on the "James Meredith March against Fear."

Carmichael, McKissick, and King found it a more difficult task to agree on the aims of the march. As they retraced Meredith's route from Memphis, together with aides and field-workers, young Negroes from SNCC and CORE exchanged words foreign to King's vocabulary of Christian love. "I'm not for that nonviolence stuff any more," one said. Another was still more pointed: "If one of these damn white Mississippi crackers touches me, I'm gonna knock the hell out of him." Some objected even to the presence of friendly whites, insisting, "This should be an all-black march. We don't need any more white phonies and liberals invading our movement. This is our march."[33]

King heard these militant murmurings in deep sadness. His spirits rose once, when the column "stopped to sing 'We shall overcome.' The voices rang out with all the traditional fervor, the glad thunder and gentle strength that had always characterized the singing of this noble song." But at the stanza "black and white together," a few marchers became silent. Later King asked them why they had refused to sing that verse. "This is a new day," they replied; "we don't sing those words any more. In fact, the whole song should be discarded. Not 'We shall overcome,' but 'We shall overrun.' "[34]

At night the marchers repaired to Memphis to continue their impassioned debates. Roy Wilkins and Whitney Young were also present, having paid their respects to Meredith but now finding only disrespect from young blacks in CORE and SNCC. Filling out the spectrum of black opinion were several proud Deacons for Defense from Louisiana, whose views were symbolized by their snub-nosed .38's and semiautomatic rifles. Coming at the invitation of SNCC, they added a rare immediacy to the question of whether the march should remain true to the principles of nonviolence.

Not since the Selma march had so many key civil rights leaders convened in one place, and never before had the movement seen such internal conflict. King and several members of the Deacons for Defense earnestly talked past each other on the issue of nonviolence. King spoke of pacifist values while the Deacons stood by the necessity of self-defense in a dangerous region. King also distinguished between individual acts of self-defense, which few people discouraged, and the proposal to arm demonstrators, which would cloud the moral issues and hand hostile whites a pretext to slaughter marchers. But the Deacons did not appreciate the subtlety in permitting individual retaliation while moving helpless and unarmed as a group. Floyd McKissick, a former NAACP attorney from North Carolina, turned the Deacons' aggressive common sense into ideology by telling King that nonviolence had outlived its usefulness in this racist country. Negroes, he said, ought to break the legs off the Statue of Liberty "and throw her in the Mississippi," for all the respect people paid to her. Carmichael added that blacks should seize power wherever they outnumbered whites: "I'm not going to beg the white man for anything I deserve. I'm going to take it."[35]

The objection of SNCC and CORE leaders to white participation in the march struck Wilkins and Young as the final foolishness. Wilkins had expected the march to "mobilize revulsion over Meredith's shooting and turn it into support for the 1966 Civil Rights Bill," which would afford federal protection for civil rights workers.[36] But Carmichael instead promoted an all-black march and drafted a manifesto to "put President Johnson on the spot."[37] Wilkins deplored this "personal attack" on the President, prompting Carmichael to accuse the NAACP leader of selling out the people. This merely confirmed for Wilkins his suspicion that Carmichael and McKissick were spouting nonsense and that King was an ineffectual mediator between the young Turks and reality. Together with Whitney Young he left in disgust to catch a predawn plane for New York.[38]

Carmichael and his supporters became more circumspect when Dr. King warned that he would also leave unless they agreed to a nonviolent, interracial march. Although King frequented the same establishment circles as Wilkins and Young, he impressed SNCC and CORE workers as an authentic folk hero of the movement. They realized, too, that without the minister's presence they would find it much more difficult to draw either local crowds or national coverage. Floyd McKissick yielded first, then Carmichael; the march would go on according to King's terms.

Carmichael further agreed to soften his original manifesto as a gesture to King and the absent heads of the NAACP and the Urban League. Reminiscent of the previous SNCC chairman's speech at the March on Washington, Carmichael's amended document still bristled with radical ideas. The manifesto began, "This march will be a massive public indictment and protest of the failure of American society, the Government of the United States and the state of Mississippi to 'fulfill these rights.' "[39] It called on the federal government to endorse A. Philip Randolph's proposed antipoverty budget of $185 billion and to require states and counties to employ blacks as police officers and jurors in proportion to their numbers. Wilkins and Young still refused to endorse the manifesto, but King cast his signature with SNCC and CORE. With that commitment the three groups composing the hard core of the nonviolent direct-action movement set out from Memphis on June 9, 1966, in a show of unity unseen, and scarcely hoped for, since the march to Montgomery fifteen months before.

Charles Evers, brother of the slain NAACP leader and his successor as head of the Mississippi state chapter, observed this parade through his territory with a jaundiced expression. He took exception to Carmichael's criticism of Johnson and wondered about the march's value for local residents: "I don't want this to turn into another Selma where everyone goes home with the cameramen and leaves us holding the bag." He kept up this barrage of skepticism in the coming days, grumbling, "I don't see how walking up and down a hot highway helps. I'm for walking house to house and fence to fence to get Negroes registered."[40] This struck the march leaders as sound advice, however cantankerous the source. The pilgrimage soon turned into a mobile voter registration program whose popularity quickly burgeoned.

If one could gauge the impact of a march by the crowds drawn to it, Meredith's emissaries seemed destined for one of the movement's great triumphs. At every town large and enthusiastic crowds greeted King, Carmichael, and McKissick, who stood at the head of several hundred supporters. The three leaders walked along the hot Mississippi roads, pledging their common aim of registering blacks in defiance of all threats. Casting a wary eye toward nearby reporters, they spoke respectfully, even cordially, to each other. But the values that had once bound them together—nonviolence, integration, coalition—had long since eroded beyond repair. As they marched south toward Greenwood—SNCC territory—their displays of solidarity gave way to arguments that exposed the deep antagonisms within the movement.

Short, strident Willie Ricks knew how to inflame crowds. As SNCC's combination rabble-rouser and advance man, he discovered that the cry "Black Power!" could whip an audience into a frenzy. Carmichael at first doubted his claims but then saw Ricks in action, screaming for Black Power and having local blacks scream back in approval. Here was a chance to challenge King's hold on the movement. At Greenwood, police briefly deferred Carmichael's bid by arresting him with numerous other blacks at a rally on June 16. But that seemed to provide just the sense of outrage that Carmichael needed to turn the crowds to his rougher brand of protest.

That evening Carmichael emerged from jail to find three thousand blacks eager to hear him lash out at white society. He felt the anger building in his audience and let their energy lift him to dizzying heights of hyperbole. "This is the twenty-seventh time I have been arrested, and I ain't going to jail no more!" he told the cheering, clapping crowd. Then he buried his past as a civil rights worker, in effect dismissing the trials of nonviolent protest and coalition politics as a well-intended mistake: "The only way we gonna stop them white men from whuppin' us is to take over. We been saying freedom for six years— and we ain't got nothin'. What we gonna start saying now is 'Black Power!' " As the crowd roared, "Black Power!" Ricks jumped back on the platform, shouting, "What do you want?" The answer came back with deafening unanimity:

"BLACK POWER!"

"What do you want?"

"BLACK POWER!!"

"What do you want?!"

"BLACK POWER!! BLACK POWER!!! BLACK POWER!!!!"[41]

The hostility fanned by Carmichael and Ricks reached even to King's entourage. At the Greenwood courthouse Hosea Williams spontaneously cried out, "Get that vote and pin that badge on a black chest. Get that vote . . . Whip that policeman across the head." Stunned by this dereliction, King hastened to explain, "He means with the vote." But Stokely saw blood and triumphantly informed King in front of the charged crowd, "They know what he means."[42]

King knew he was preaching against the grain of black resentments, but he remained determined to wrest the movement away from SNCC's angry young men. On June 22 at Yazoo City, some fifty miles south of Greenwood, he watched Willie Ricks warm up the crowd with a litany of hatred against police, whites, Democrats, and society. As Ricks yelled, "Black Power!" and warned of "white blood flowing," King strode through the crowd toward the back of the flatbed truck where Ricks was perched. All the while elderly women tried to touch him and pressed to shake his hand. In his turn King ascended the makeshift platform and made it clear that he was not going to let Willie Ricks turn him or anyone else around. He was *tired* of hearing about violence and Black Power, he intoned, and the crowd's rage against whites began to melt away. He would never let any man pull him so low as to hate anyone. This was old-time civil rights religion, and coming from King it could still jolt the emotions. Awed murmurs of "Speak on!" and "Can't he talk, Lord, can't he talk!" formed a constant counterpoint to King's admonitions. Finally a frustrated SNCC staffer pointed at the minister from the edge of the crowd and shouted in his most derisive manner, "Blessed Jesus!" To his acute embarrassment no one in the crowd laughed. Some nodded approvingly at the hapless SNCC agitator for having recognized King's saintliness aloud.[43]

Though King had jabbed effectively against the young champions of Black Power, he realized that the escalating verbal war between civil rights leaders threatened to undo any gains from the march. Some of his aides urged him to renounce the march altogether in order to insulate his moderate image from the taint of Carmichael's oratory. King resisted the temptation, preferring to salvage a common front between the SCLC, CORE, and SNCC through an airing of their differences. At his invitation the staffs of the three groups met in a small Catholic parish house in Yazoo City the morning after King's public criticism of Black Power. Their impromptu summit meeting came as a last chance to avoid a prolonged factional struggle that would undermine hopes for either Black Power or Freedom Now.

Carmichael, stating the case for Black Power, brushed aside the question of violence or nonviolence as irrelevant. "Power is the only thing respected in this world," he said, "and we must get it at any cost." Looking King squarely in the eye as if to stare past the minister's images of brotherly love and address him realist to realist, Carmichael went on, "Martin, you know as well as I do that practically every other ethnic group in America has done just this. The Jews, the Irish and the Italians did it, why can't we?"[44]

Yes, King agreed, get power, economic and political power, and build racial pride that will stand against the prejudice that black is evil and ugly. But this will come through programs rather than slogans: "No one has ever heard the Jews publicly chant a slogan of Jewish power, but they have power. Through group unity, determination and creative endeavor, they have gained it. The same thing is true of the Irish and Italians." Carmichael and McKissick protested, "[But] how can you arouse people to unite around a program without a slogan as a rallying cry? Didn't the labor movement have slogans? Haven't we had slogans all along in the freedom movement? What we need is a new slogan with 'black' in it."[45]

Here the real difference between King and Carmichael emerged. Both sought to mobilize the energies of black people, but King alone aimed at sustaining a broad national coalition. Black Power was a legitimate objective, King explained, but the connotations were wrong. The press had already seized on the slogan's implications of violence, and the rash statements of a few marchers had fed these sensational reports. Slogans were necessary, King conceded to Carmichael. "But why," he asked, "have one that would confuse our allies, isolate the Negro community and give many prejudiced whites, who might otherwise be ashamed of their anti-Negro feeling, a ready excuse for self-justification?" King suggested "black consciousness" or "black equality," which were tactically less vulnerable. By contrast, he held, "the words 'black' and 'power' together give the impression that we are talking about black domination rather than black equality."[46]

But Carmichael was adamant: "Black Power" had an appeal to Negroes unequaled by any other slogan. He had not wholly rejected coalition politics, but he was not going to let anything confine his efforts to stir black people. And he wanted King to make that same decision: "Martin, I deliberately decided to raise this issue on the march in order to give it a national forum, and force you to take a stand for Black Power." King laughed. "I have been used before," he answered Carmichael. "One more time won't hurt."[47]

When the laughter subsided, King got down to the business of making sure he was not used again. He pressed Carmichael and his CORE ally Mckissick to refrain from using the cry "Black Power" for the rest of the march. In turn the SCLC leader would forgo the favorite cry of the nonviolent direct-action movement, "Freedom Now." In order to ensure King's continued presence, Carmichael and McKissick agreed. But this ban on rhetorical devices that could poison the civil rights atmosphere came too late to end the controversy over Black Power. Carmichael's slogan had already colored news reports of the march and opened a public breach among civil rights leaders. Soon another, more imminent danger loomed as well when Neshoba County's white residents took notice of the civil rights "outsiders" with a traditional, menacing welcome.

Trouble came first in Philadelphia, Mississippi, during a memorial service for the three slain civil rights workers of the freedom summer. As the Reverend King eulogized Michael Schwerner, Andrew Goodman, and James Chaney, local whites surrounded the marchers and shouted taunts at the minister's every phrase. "Sometimes," the journalist Renata Adler observed, "they listened and screamed so carefully that Dr. King appeared to be leading them in a responsive reading."[48] Then they clubbed the marchers with hoes and ax handles. Police sent the whites away only after blacks began to retaliate. That night white vigilantes and some marchers exchanged gunfire.

Desperate to keep the march from turning into a massacre, King wired a request for Lyndon Johnson to send federal marshals before "civil war" ensued. But King's recent statements against the country's escalation of the war in Vietnam had dissolved his influence at the White House, while Carmichael had blunted public sympathy for the marchers with his Black Power rhetoric. The President failed to comply, or even reply. King had greater sway over his colleagues in CORE and SNCC, who recognized that the slaughter of all marchers was imminent. When King announced that there would be another march to Philadelphia but that only those committed to nonviolence could participate, Carmichael and McKissick supported him "100 percent."[49] In crisis, King's unswerving moral authority still prevailed, though his hopes had now been pared to one—simple survival for the marchers.

On June 23 two thousand marchers reached Canton, within twenty-five miles of the state capital. They pitched their tents at the town's segregated elementary school and found a line of state and local lawmen advancing against them. When the blacks refused to leave their tents—they were in the midst of a driving rain—police fired tear gas canisters and then flailed the marchers with whips, gun butts, and sticks. The carnage brought the most battle-hardened survivors of Birmingham and Selma to unpredictable extremes. Carmichael watched blacks falling all around him and sobbed, "Don't make your stand here. I just can't stand to see any more people get shot." Meanwhile the amiable, nonviolent Reverend Andrew Young (seen as an "Uncle Tom" by King's radical aides and trusted as a voice of restraint by King himself) looked at the gleeful horde of policemen and longed to hold and fire a machine gun.[50] King and McKissick finally led the marchers to a Negro church, where drenched in rain and blood they shared their considered opinions of nonviolence, whites, and American society. King later managed to telegraph the President, urgently requesting federal marshals before the next assault on unarmed Negroes led to murder. Again the President dismissed the telegram. The Justice Department scolded the marchers for trespassing on school grounds.

On June 24 the victims of the preceding day's teargassing and clubbings rallied once more at the school grounds. Morale had disintegrated as the ex-SNCC chairman John Lewis "rose on a shaky box" to exhort the dispirited marchers. "Fellow freedom fighters," he said. "The whole man must say no nonviolently, his entire Christian spirit must say no to this evil and vicious system." Once, such words had stamped Lewis as the implacable militant among civil rights leaders, but at Canton, in the summer of 1966, listeners walked out unmoved even before Lewis finished. "I felt like the uninvited guest," Lewis recalled.[51] The sole speaker to win applause was a local black woman who said, "We accuse the Governor, the Justice Department and President L. B. Johnson for the trouble that took place here last night."[52]

Three hundred marchers accompanied the civil rights leaders back to Philadelphia on June 24. Once in the city King and Ralph Abernathy walked toward the courthouse to pray, but Sheriff Lawrence Rainey barred the way. "You can't go up these steps," he told them. "Oh, yes," King eyed him, "you're the one who had Schwerner and the other fellows in jail." Rainey beamed that he was the one. "I believe the murderers are somewhere around me at this moment," King whispered as he and Abernathy knelt to pray. "You damn right," Rainey replied; "they're right behind you."[53]

The service took place amid flying bottles and taunts from the crowd. Stokely Carmichael had had enough. He waved his arms at the jeering whites and shouted at them, "The people that are gathered around us represent America in its truest form. They represent a sick and resisting society that sits in the United Nations and gives lip service to democracy." King in his turn promised, "We are going to build right here a society based on brotherhood and understanding," prompting an onlooker to scream, "Go to hell." Unlike Carmichael, King saved his appraisal of the situation for a private session with his aides. He had been certain they were going to be killed by the mob. "And *brother,*" he said, "I sure did not want to close my eyes when we prayed." He added, grinning, "Ralph said he prayed with his open."[54]

The marchers then moved in full force to Jackson. King, McKissick, and Carmichael arrived together, still cordial, still seeking to show their basic unity. But neither Carmichael, McKissick, the Freedom Democratic party, nor Mississippi's "Delta Ministry" of black preachers would permit Charles Evers to speak, for he had not signed or endorsed the manifesto of the marchers. The decision had little to do with Evers himself, but aimed to ruffle the NAACP national office, which had directed Evers not to sign.[55] Roy Wilkins expressed his sympathy to Evers over this "petty act," but Evers assured his chief, "It's all right. I'll be here when they're all gone."[56]

Few white marchers were among the fifteen thousand people present at the final rally on June 26 in the state capital. There, Carmichael called on blacks to "build a power base . . . so strong that we will bring [whites] to their knees every time they mess with us."[57] But the rally clearly showed a movement in disarray, with rival contingents chanting, "Black Power!" and "Freedom Now!" Dr. King's assistants showed their continued faith in national values by dispensing hundreds of American flags, but the sight of the Stars and Stripes enraged SNCC workers. Willie Ricks rushed at one marcher and snarled, "Give me those flags. That flag does not represent you." Others in

SNCC handed out placards depicting a black panther above the warning "Move on Over or We'll Move on Over YOU."[58]

James Meredith, who originated this march against fear, revealed how far it had strayed off course by joining SNCC's bid to silence Negro ministers singing for freedom. Shaking his ebony stick at the Reverend James Orange, Meredith commanded, "Shut up!" "Big Jim" Orange gently inquired, "You mean you can say 'Black power' but we can't say 'Freedom'?" A tight-lipped Meredith glared in reply.[59]

At the end of June 1966 John Lewis left SNCC, feeling hurt and bewildered at the apparent rejection of his deepest values. Only later could he clearly perceive the worsening crisis of faith among many black Americans since the memorable triumphs of the civil rights coalition:

> It's hard to accept when something is over even though you know things have to change. In the beginning, with the sit-ins and Freedom Rides, things were much simpler. Or we thought they were. People just had to offer their bodies for their beliefs and it seemed like that would be enough, but it wasn't. By the time of Canton nobody knew what would be enough to make America right, and the atmosphere was very complicated, very negative.[60]

The still, small voice of nonviolence continued to move some individuals at these rallies. But most of them could no longer hear it above the din of angry, defiant crowds.

Black Power, White Backlash

Like most slogans, "Black Power" could mean all things to all people. As carefully explained by spokesmen like Floyd McKissick, it referred to racial pride, solidarity, and black leadership of institutions for Afro-American progress[61]—a tribute of sorts to American pluralism and ethnic identity. Here was a term to inspire both Northern and Southern Negroes to organize politically. Yet as King had foreseen, whites and conservative blacks fixed on the slogan's hints of reverse racism and occasional revolutionary overtones. Calls to Black Power therefore tended to divide blacks from whites and from each other, undermining one of the main pillars of actual black progress toward national influence.

Following the march to Jackson SNCC remained on the cutting edge of black protest, but in a way far removed from its origins as a force for American unity and universal love. The late Malcolm X, with his defiant manner and revolutionary concerns, became the role model for black activists in place of the Reverend King. It was still fashionable to carry at least one volume by a French-speaking philosopher reflecting on the Algerian struggle for independence. But the popularity of Albert Camus had fallen since the days when Bob

Moses expounded on his injunction to be neither victim nor executioner. Instead SNCC youths exchanged quotations from the black psychiatrist Frantz Fanon's *Wretched of the Earth,* a tract exalting Third World revolutionary struggle. Fanon prescribed violence not only as a means of political liberation but also as a way for the oppressed to assert their courage and thus become fully human.[62] With 150 full-time staffers, SNCC leaders did not seriously consider Fanon a guide for imminent assault on American society. As a symbol, though, Fanon, like Marx, denoted a radical change in the character of black protest. For SNCC, "Black Power" was merging with beliefs that contradicted the organization's founding charter, even its very name, and moved it beyond the pale of liberal respectability.

By the summer of 1966 SNCC's ability to shock white society gave it the high visibility it had long coveted. Chairman Stokely Carmichael became a magnet for media attention, his every pronouncement recorded as a barometer of Negro anger by newsmen who once had raised their microphones only for Dr. King. Lanky, sharp-eyed, with a smile that gleamed mischief, he parried interviewers with casually alternating assurances and threats to white society. Depending on when a television viewer tuned in to the news, he might learn from Carmichael's glosses on Black Power either that Negroes were banding together for progress or that armed revolution was at hand.

The NAACP's chief, Roy Wilkins, tore into Carmichael and other proponents of Black Power as if they were a cancer in the movement for racial equality—a group of once vital cells now growing in a dangerously distorted way. At his organization's national convention in July 1966 Wilkins claimed, "No matter how endlessly they try to explain it, the term 'black power' means anti-white power." The slogan might offer many blacks "a solace, a tremendous psychological lift," but "the quick, uncritical and highly emotional adoption of the slogan [by] some segments of a beleaguered people can mean in the end only black death."[63] As for the man who popularized Black Power, Wilkins viewed Carmichael as a brilliant but shortsighted provocateur: "If Stokely had not joined S.N.C.C. he would have made a wonderful Madison Avenue sloganeer. . . . [But the] phrase couldn't have been more destructive if Senator Eastland had contrived it. I imagine [Eastland] sat there saying to himself, 'Now, why didn't I think of that?' "[64]

The unshakable sage of coalition politics, Bayard Rustin, produced the most trenchant critique of the new black nationalists in the liberal journal *Commentary.* Although Rustin conceded that the explosive acclaim for Black Power had "roots in the psychological and political frustrations of the Negro community," he argued that the idea not only lacked "any real value for the civil rights movement" but was "positively harmful":

[SNCC's] perspective is simultaneously utopian and reactionary—the former for the by now obvious reason that one-tenth of the population cannot accomplish much by itself, the latter because such a party would remove Negroes from the main area of political struggle [the Democratic party] . . . and would give priority to the issue of race precisely at a time when the fundamental questions facing the Negro and American society alike are economic and social.[65]

Defenders of Black Power who locked pens with Rustin returned his charges, tarring him as a reactionary and alleging that he had slid to the right in order to accept a comfortable niche as an administration house servant. Yet the democratic socialist Rustin and his antagonists on the front lines of Black Power advocacy occupied essentially the same place on the political spectrum. The real source of their conflict was a matter less of ideology than of temperament and tactics. Rustin was a self-described "social engineer,"[66] the quintessence of a rational strategist. He believed that blacks should temper their resentments in order to forge broad alliances that would advance their social and economic interests. But few people ever confine their view of self-interest to purely rational aims, least of all people who have long suppressed deep anger and frustration. To many blacks the chance to express their feelings to each other and to the wider society was in fact a vital facet of their self-interest. Whether or not Rustin's strategy of coalition building was radical or conservative, bold or cautious, mattered less than that it demanded an emotional sacrifice millions of blacks were no longer prepared to make.

Age divided the two camps more consistently than any other factor. Critics of Black Power such as Roy Wilkins, Whitney Young, A. Philip Randolph, and Rustin varied widely in their ideology and tactics, but all were veterans of civil rights protest. They considered Kennedy and Johnson, with their stirring initiatives and expedient retreats, as part of a long procession of liberal achievements and follies. These civil rights leaders were, in Rustin's words, in there "for the long pull."[67]

No stoic vision of perpetual struggle tempered the young men and women of SNCC. Nurtured on the faith that racial justice was near, these youths transformed the movement with their willingness to risk everything, every day, to complete the quest for equality. But if their zeal speeded civil rights progress, their utopian expectations also ensured frustration. The new generation that swept into leadership of the movement was emotionally unprepared for the shock of defeat or for prolonged exposure to both physical danger and political cynicism. The persistence of black poverty further discouraged many youths who had trusted that the early protests against segregation would bring full equality of opportunity. Perhaps these reformers were least prepared to cope with the discovery that the Beloved Community, if it existed at all, was much farther off than they had believed.

Black Power was therefore more than a political strategy; it was an alternative utopianism for embittered idealists. In place of universal love the new rhetoric of protest narrowed the band of brotherhood to those of darker complexion. For the goal of American unity it substituted racial pride through appeals to black nationalism. The millennial tone and the hope of group salvation remained, but adjusted to express black anger toward a society still per-

Robert Moses, SNCC worker, in Mississippi, July 1964. *AP/Wide World*

Slain civil rights workers in Mississippi. *From left:* Michael Schwerner, James Chaney, Andrew Goodman. *AP/Wide World*

Martin Luther King, Jr., with Ralph Abernathy on his right, at the funeral of the martyred demonstrator Jimmy Lee Jackson, in Marion, Alabama, March 4, 1965. *AP/Wide World*

Troopers attack black marchers in Selma, Alabama, March 7, 1965. *Charles Moore, Black Star*

Mourners for the slain civil rights marcher the Reverend James Reeb, in Selma, Alabama, March 15, 1965. *From left, in foreground:* **Archbishop Iakovos of the Greek Orthodox Church, Martin Luther King, Jr., Ralph Abernathy, Andrew Young.** *AP/Wide World*

Catholic nuns resting along Route 80 on the third march from Selma to Montgomery, Alabama, March 21, 1965. *AP/Wide World*

LBJ signing Voting Rights Act, August 6, 1965. Directly behind the President is the Reverend Martin Luther King, Jr. *Lyndon Baines Johnson Library*

Below left: **Malcolm X addressing convention of Black Muslims in Chicago, February 27, 1963.** *AP/Wide World*

Below right: **Martin Luther King, Jr., and the former Black Muslim minister Malcolm X smile during their sole, fleeting encounter, in Washington, D.C., March 26, 1964. King had just announced plans for direct-action protests if Southern senators filibustered against the civil rights bill. Malcolm predicted another march on Washington if a filibuster dragged on.** *AP/Wide World*

Stokely Carmichael, June 1966. *Flip Schulke.* **Julian Bond, 1966.** *AP/Wide World*

Symbol of the Lowndes County (Alabama) Freedom Organization, 1966. *AP/Wide World*

ONE MAN -- ONE VOTE

Confederate flags greet marchers on the outskirts of Greenwood, Mississippi, during the "James Meredith March against Fear," June 17, 1966. *AP/Wide World*

A deputy sheriff shoves the Reverend Hosea Williams at the front of a group of blacks attempting to cross a courthouse lawn during a voter registration rally in Greenwood, Mississippi, June 17, 1966. Stokely Carmichael, on Williams's right, gave his first speech on "Black Power" that evening. *AP/Wide World*

Martin Luther King, Jr., is pelted with a rock while leading a civil rights march through a South Side Chicago neighborhood in August 1966. *AP/Wide World*

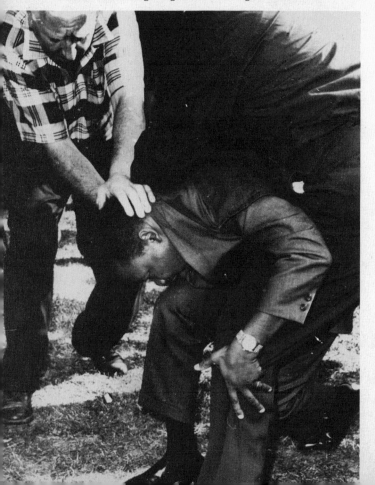

National guardsmen and state police collar suspected looters along Newark's Springfield Avenue during rioting, July 14, 1967. *The Bettmann Archive*

Michigan's national guardsmen force rioting Negroes from a burning building on Detroit's west side, July 26, 1967. *The Bettmann Archive*

vaded by prejudice and complacency. Black Power, in brief, shifted black activism away from its preoccupation with government policy toward the development of group identity, expression, and independence.

The apostles of Black Power paid a high price for devaluing coalition politics. Excommunicated by civil rights leaders, they also became anathema to liberal politicians. Vice-President Hubert Humphrey appeared at the July 1966 NAACP convention to declare, "We must reject calls for racism whether they come from a throat that is white or one that is black." From the White House, Lyndon Johnson stated that there was a need not for black or white power but for "American democratic power." Even Robert Kennedy, who was increasingly prone to flick left jabs at the President's policies, agreed that "black power could be damaging not only to the civil-rights movement but to the country."[68]

Stokely Carmichael had no doubt about why Black Power provoked shivers and curses: white racism was reasserting itself. But the public was reacting in part to the volatile summer mood in the ghettos, which erupted in a nearly constant backdrop to calls for Black Power. While the inner cities needed no slogans to burst into rioting, ghetto violence conveyed to the public a more vivid notion of Black Power than any reassurances Carmichael or even King could give.

Thirty-eight "civil disorders" in the summer of 1966 destroyed ghetto neighborhoods in cities ranging from San Francisco to Providence. No single episode approached the carnage of Watts—a landmark of destruction that became imprinted in the nation's memory as emblematic of all racial turmoil— but the cumulative toll of these riots included seven lives, four hundred injured, three thousand arrests, and $5 million of property looted or burned.[69] Like earlier outbreaks of violence these were sparked by conflicts with police. But compared with that in Watts the fuse in each ghetto had become shorter and more exposed to any chance provocation. It was as if the slum dwellers in South Central Los Angeles had broken some emotional barrier, making violence first thinkable, then attractive, then, perhaps, inevitable. Watts had triggered the resentments of ghetto residents as powerfully as four college students had stirred the hopes of Southern blacks in 1960.

Richard J. Daley, who left few things in Chicago to chance, determined that there would be no riot in his city, however hot the summer of 1966 became for the rest of urban America. The mayor's "modern" police force, under the command of the former army colonel Orlando W. Wilson, "developed elaborate counterinsurgency tactics—flying squads, special weaponry, and a Task Force of trained shock troops." The mayor readied carrots as well as nightsticks, ladling into ghetto neighborhoods an extra helping of antipoverty funds from the city's dwindling reserve. And the word went forth to police: no incidents. "It won't be me," they all said. Accustomed to control, Daley did not grasp that in the West Side slums incidents were not simply the result of occasional lapses in police behavior. Rather they formed part of the fabric of ghetto life in a city where police had made a quarter of a million gratuitous stops the preceding year in hopes of spotting fugitives or illegal weapons. A minute slip in judgment brought this point home one day in late June:

> Presumably, the officers who turned off a fire hydrant one sweltering afternoon had no idea that that was "the incident." Then, somehow, all the plans fell apart. No one cared about the Neighborhood Youth Corps centers, the pre-schools, or the Foster Grandparents program. The police Task Force couldn't begin to cope with 5,000 rampaging slum-dwellers. The frightened, cautious cops turned into storm troopers, beating Negroes, smashing bars, cursing the mob. A white Chicagoan who stayed as an intermediary in a precinct station one night reported the pep talk given departing squads: "the bounty is a buck a head."[70]

Four thousand policemen quelled the disturbance, which cost two lives and left hundreds wounded and four hundred jailed. Still, Chicago escaped lightly compared with other cities. Although Mayor Daley applied only superficial balms to an organic ghetto illness, this policy contrasted favorably with the racist truculence of many big-city governments. Cleveland's white officials virtually declared the city's black districts enemy territory, as if daring the ghetto's denizens to try something. It proved a potent formula for racial violence.

On the surface residents of Cleveland's main black neighborhood, known as Hough (rhyming with "tough"), knew no more than the ordinary desperation of inner-city slum dwellers. Black unemployment in Cleveland for 1966 exceeded by a factor of four the jobless rate for the city as a whole, and the usual private and public barriers to Negro advancement stood firmly in place. There were only 13 Negroes among 11,500 workers in the five major construction trades, and Negroes filled less than 4 percent of the 1,350 apprenticeships in federally sponsored training programs. Antipoverty funds were dispensed with strict parsimony, with 38,000 Negroes receiving Aid to Families with Dependent Children payments that were pegged far below the poverty level— seventy-three cents a day after rent.

Hough itself presented a textbook example of unchecked urban decay. The neighborhood had hosted Cleveland's most affluent families in the late nineteenth century, then a middle-class mix of immigrants and Negroes, until destitute blacks poured in from the South after 1915. Over the decades Hough's fine shops were displaced by shabby markets, its elegant turn-of-the-century mansions subdivided into egg-crate cubicles, and its spacious streets obscured by slum tenements. City administrators gave up trying to enforce the housing code in Hough. The housing commission budget in 1966 fell short of the allotment to the city's shade tree department; its small staff was over fourteen thousand inspections behind schedule and required years to uncover even flagrant violations.

On the fringes of Hough stood Cleveland's most imposing cultural landmarks: to the north the Cleveland Play House, the oldest professional resident theater in America; to the east Severance Hall, home of the world-famous Cleveland Orchestra, and the Museum of Art. Together these monuments attested to Cleveland's self-proclaimed image as "the best location in the nation"; they also unwittingly accented the blight of the ghetto, a place where Langston Hughes found that "the pressure of the blood is slightly higher/due to smoldering shadows that sometimes turn to fire."[71]

Failure to provide blacks with adequate housing, jobs, or economic security did not distinguish Cleveland from other cities, but its white elite seemed more than usually callous toward inner-city residents. Mayor Ralph Locher shunned local and national Negro leaders, including the "extremist" Martin Luther King. The police department ignored Negro complaints of abuses, such as the common practice of telling persons held without arrest to sign a "waiver" by which they forfeited their right to sue the city for unlawful arrest and detention. When the black director of the city's Community Relations Council sought to meet Police Chief Richard Wagner, Wagner refused, effectively shutting off any safety valve for racial tensions. The inevitable "incident" finally inflamed Hough's residents to violence in July 1966, engulfing Cleveland in the most destructive rioting of any city in the nation.

Police Chief Wagner reacted to the riot by riding into Hough with his personal hunting rifle, which he used against snipers. When a woman was killed by gunfire while searching for her children, Wagner explained this with a farrago of fantasy and racism. "There was a similar occurrence in the Chicago riots," he told reporters. "They sacrifice one person and blame it on police brutality."[72] Local police were unable to control the riot, and in the end several thousand Ohio guardsmen restored order after five days. Four lives were lost, none of them taken by blacks: law enforcement officers were responsible for two of the deaths, a white man firing from a car for a third, and a group of young white vigilantes for a fourth.[73]

As the nation's racial turmoil worsened, the administration's liberal civil rights and antipoverty bills underwent repeated disfigurements. Like the portrait in Oscar Wilde's *Picture of Dorian Gray,* which changed to reflect the sins committed by its subject, Johnson's legislation degenerated with every riot. In July 1966 the House passed a measure to strengthen federal protection of civil rights workers and to ban racial discrimination in housing. Yet it added provisions that President Johnson had neither requested nor wanted: a mandate to punish rioting as a federal crime, and a disclaimer of federal concern about racial imbalance in public schools. Even in its conservative guise the bill moved through the Senate without the usual bipartisan escort. Senate Minority Leader Dirksen, whom public pressure and White House entreaties had once made a reluctant hero of the civil rights movement, understood that a "hot summer" of ghetto rioting was no time to press for residential desegregation. While accepting most of Johnson's proposals, he solemnly denounced the bill's housing clause as "absolutely unconstitutional."[74] This time civil rights lobbyists realized that Dirksen occupied unassailable political ground. The bill appeared to have a majority in the Senate, but in the absence of Dirksen's support it died under a hail of speeches from Southern filibusterers.

Backlash continued to stalk the corridors of Congress in the debate over antipoverty legislation, as talk of law and order crowded out discussions of destitution in the ghetto. In September 1966 the House passed a bill renewing funds for antipoverty programs, with a rider forbidding the Office of Economic Opportunity "to provide payments, assistance, or services, in any form, with respect to any individual who incites, promotes, encourages, or carries on, or facilitates the incitement, promotion, encouragement, or carrying on of, a riot or other civil disturbance," or who "assists, encourages, or instructs any person to" incite, promote, etc. or to facilitate the incitement etc. This was a blunt effort to transform a Johnsonian bill into one with a Goldwater stamp, and the Senate version was yet more ambitious. In a line recalling the peak years of the House Un-American Activities Committee, it denied poverty funds to any member of an organization that the attorney general listed as "subversive."[75]

The scope of this Senate amendment, proposed by the Democrat Harry Byrd of Virginia, promised a more unconditional war against the restive poor than the President and Congress had yet launched against poverty. Liberal senators such as the Republican Jacob Javits of New York and the Democrat Albert Gore of Tennessee asked what limits, if any, might restrain the punitive intent of the provision. Would the children of a man who refuses to inform on rioters be excluded from the preschool educational program Head Start? Would someone who seemed to condone a riot by explaining its causes fall into the category of a person who "encourages" or "facilitates the incitement" of a riot? One senator noted that a fight between two boys in a school yard might well qualify as a "civil disturbance" in violation of local law. The thrust of the amendment, some liberal senators charged, would so burden the administration of the poverty program as to bring it to a dead halt.[76]

A mildly sanitized version of the Byrd amendment, still crammed with undefined catch-all terms such as "assist" and "encourage" (and retaining the provision about membership in organizations listed by the attorney general) passed by a vote of 39 to 32. Twenty-nine senators, including many Northern liberals, found more pressing business away from the Senate chamber that day. Some other liberal stalwarts, such as Birch Bayh of Indiana, Thomas Dodd and Abraham Ribicoff of Connecticut, and Daniel Brewster of Maryland, voted for the amendment. Most Republicans also did so, though not the unpredictable Dirksen and two or three others. In all, more than two-thirds of the Senate supported or abstained from voting on a measure that withheld aid from many of the most desperately needy. The *New Republic* marveled at the logic inherent in the Senate's handiwork:

> Riots in this mood are not something to be dealt with at the root, but a barking dog to be silenced. Riots are nasty, and every effort must be made to control them when they occur. But what sense is there in trying to insulate rioters from . . . a poverty program

aimed at preventing riots; to insist that vocational education or youth employment "benefits" be withheld from participants in a riot, so that they shall remain—they of all people!—untrained, unemployed, on the streets?[77]

The conservative tide continued to rise during the congressional election campaigns in the fall of 1966. For the first time since 1962, when Dr. George Gallup began polling Americans on the pace of civil rights reform, a majority (52 percent) believed that the administration was moving "too fast." Republican party elders urged candidates to press this point and cited their own survey findings that voters cared more about racial unrest than about inflation or any other domestic issue.[78]

"Backlash" campaigning was strongest in the South, where Republicans contested for right-of-way on the segregationist paths Democrats had regularly traveled to public office. Pressure to appear strong on race issues raised up such unlikely candidates as the Georgia Democrat Lester Maddox, who won nomination for the governorship on the basis of his reputation for uncompromising bigotry. The pudgy, bald restaurateur had first amazed the nation in 1964 by brandishing a pick handle at Negroes seeking to eat at his Pickrick diner in Atlanta. Negroes may have won the right to have coffee at Woolworth's lunch counters, but Maddox vowed to repel their bid for more solid fare. "You're dirty Communists and you'll never get a piece of fried chicken here," he shouted at blacks who tried to enter his establishment. Maddox often purchased space in the *Atlanta Constitution* and the *Journal* for advertisements that denounced the civil rights movement and asked, "Why go to Africa . . . when Atlanta could bear considerable hunting?" Maddox had little to offer voters beyond this single note of segregationist truculence, which he expressed in code during the campaign through attacks on Lyndon Johnson and Martin Luther King, Jr. In 1966 these slim credentials enabled him to finish in a dead heat with his nearest opponent, a Goldwater Republican. The state legislature resolved the impasse by choosing Maddox as Georgia's next governor.[79]

Nationally the white backlash struck hardest at the issue of ghetto violence. House Minority Leader Gerald Ford caught the national mood with a campaign plea to rise above misplaced compassion in dealing with rioters: "How long are we going to abdicate law and order—the backbone of civilization—in favor of a soft social theory that the man who heaves a brick through your window or tosses a fire bomb into your car is simply the misunderstood and underprivileged product of a broken home?"[80] Democrats answered with a refrain that two years before had been the most popular chorus in Washington: education, jobs, better housing, and an end to discrimination would set all right. By November 1966, however, these words had lost much of their appeal. The Republicans displaced forty-seven incumbents in the House and three in the Senate, chiefly at the expense of President Johnson's liberal supporters.

The election results provided some comfort to civil rights leaders. Blacks doubled their presence in state legislatures and secured their first U.S. Senate seat since Reconstruction with the victory of the Republican Edward Brooke in Massachusetts. Patches of racial moderation also shone through the demagogic haze covering the South, thanks to the registration of 2.6 million Negroes. In Arkansas, Maryland, and Tennessee, Republicans won key races with black support, while Alabama's Macon County, the site of Tuskegee Institute, elected its first black sheriff despite a white voter turnout exceeding 100 percent.[81]

Black voters nonetheless failed to halt the nation's turn away from liberal reform. Senate Majority Leader Mike Mansfield, who had helped enact the Great Society agenda, observed that the time had come for "tightening up" liberal programs, including those related to race. From the other side of the aisle Minority Leader Everett Dirksen concurred: "I should judge that the scalpel will be wielded rather freely."[82] The earlier consensus to promote social change was clearly receding before a growing national anxiety to preserve social order.

Chapter 8

The Radical Movement

SELDOM had a political slogan received such intense abuse in so short a time as "Black Power," or influenced national policy with such unintended results. Yet the term remained a potent rallying cry at a time when Negroes were widely turning inward, away from the tarnished politics of integration. To the advocates of Black Power, persistent racism disproved the liberal notion that civil rights laws would now let blacks rise in a fair and open society. It seemed more consistent with the harsh facts of black life to conclude that one's status depended on one's ethnic identity and that society rewarded group strength more than individual striving. Jews, Italians, Irish, and other immigrant groups had already shown the advantages of community ties in forming unions, controlling local patronage, and funding self-help societies, philanthropies, and lobbying campaigns. To Black Power strategists the lesson was clear: blacks had to forge their own institutions for ethnic influence if they were to move beyond formal civil rights to a position of genuine equality with other Americans.

The Black Power movement explored diverse paths to racial uplift: development of a distinct cultural identity, organization of ghetto neighborhoods, and demands for new federal policies to end Negro poverty in the city slums. On the surface these paths diverged from earlier reform campaigns mainly in their open pursuit of ethnic interests rather than of universal principles. But in each case a deeper contrast soon became clear. Unlike liberal reformers, who had always depicted the society as essentially just, Black Power spokesmen focused on evidence of a fundamentally racist and largely closed system. Even many activists who cheered the strategy of group advancement doubted whether this alone could overcome entrenched inequalities. The rise of Black Power politics therefore served as a radicalizing influence on Negro protest, shifting it away from the goal of assimilating into American society and instead calling into question that society's deepest values and commitments.

Black Cultural Nationalism

Basic to Black Power politics were the efforts by artists and intellectuals to cultivate a sense of shared values—in the words of an earlier black nationalist leader, Marcus Garvey, "one God, one aim, one destiny."[1] While this cultural mission actively engaged a relatively small elite within the black community, it spoke to millions of Negroes who, in every aspect of life, were taking racial solidarity as their proud first principle.

The concern with black identity fed on disappointment with the limits of liberal reform, but also on unprecedented advances by Negroes during the years of civil rights ferment. Although many blacks still found their lives blocked at every turn, a fortunate few were scaling barriers to wealth and national acclaim. Their achievements raised the image—and the self-image— of black Americans, who no longer felt their worth to be so dependent on white acceptance.

Athletics had long provided one of the few routes out of the ghettos, and during the fifties and sixties it accommodated a small exodus of Negroes. Jackie Robinson's spikes-high slide into major-league baseball stardom opened the base paths to dozens of gifted Negro players. "You'll never know what you and Jackie and Roy [Campanella] did to make it possible to do my job," Martin Luther King, Jr., told the retired pitcher Don Newcombe, one of Robinson's black teammates.[2] Other sports leagues also concluded that integration was the best box-office policy; among their drawing cards were football's Jim Brown, whose herculean physique suggested Black Power incarnate, and basketball's Wilt Chamberlain, who showed that grace could inhabit a seven-foot-two-inch frame. Coinciding with an age of televised sports coverage and soaring sports salaries, the rise of black athletes provided a group of strong, successful male role models for the vast majority left behind in the ghetto.

Black musicians, too, entered mainstream culture, and more than ever they helped define it. Whereas white performers once made millions of dollars singing the compositions of unknown, penniless Negroes, blacks were now stepping onto stages and into recording studios to claim the rewards of music stardom. Black executives of Motown Records in Detroit marketed dozens of artists by blending Negro rhythm and blues with the softer sounds popular with white audiences. Motown-groomed musicians shunned race-related lyrics as socially off-key, adhered to dress codes that were flamboyant but always formal, and in all ways projected images that would not unsettle white America. The decade's most popular American singing group, Diana Ross and the Supremes, polished this approach to dazzling smoothness. Raised in a low-rent Detroit housing project, these three young female singers cast musical roots that extended as deeply into Las Vegas glitter as black gospel. Onstage, resplendent in furs, wigs, sequins, and smiles, they seemed worlds removed from black urban poverty, or even the daily drudgery of most whites. In an era hungry for evidence of black upward mobility these women served as glamorous, inviting icons of ghetto-based success.

The times were also changing for television's portrayal of black Americans, which became more respectful with each report of Negro boycotts and rallies. NAACP protests ended the long syndicated life of "Amos 'n' Andy," the popular comedy that offered stereotyped images of conniving or ineffectual Negro men and gratingly domineering Negro women. In its place came shows featuring Negro characters who were clean-cut, capable, courageous. "I Spy" debuted in 1965 as the first network series to highlight a black actor. Bill Cosby's engaging performance casually upended racial stereotypes and won three consecutive Emmy Awards, the first such honors for a Negro. Accepting his first Emmy, Cosby mentioned his white costar Robert Culp in a voice trembling with emotion, "He lost [the award] because he extended his hand to me."[3] Not every black role was so finely drawn as Cosby's, but the trend toward heroism was unmistakable. On CBS a rival spy program appearing the following year also featured a Negro: he played an electronics genius, a role originally written with a Nordic blond character in mind.

Black women fared less well on television but evolved far beyond the mammies and mistresses who once represented nearly the full range of black female roles. The science fiction program "Star Trek," debuting in 1966, featured a Negro woman lieutenant, a position of unprecedented authority for any black (or female) television performer. In this liberal vision of an equal opportunity universe, black and white personnel mingled in highly technical tasks as well as in the small screen's first interracial kiss. And if the program's able black officer seemed too often absorbed in transmitting messages between white male commanders, this likely pertained less to racial than to sexual stereotyping, the final frontier of American prejudice. Two years later the same network risked a ground-breaking program, "Julia," whose central character was a black woman very much in control of her life. Concessions were made to fashion and fantasy, with elegant Diahann Carroll cast as a widow struggling to survive on sheer grit and an extensive wardrobe by Givenchy. Still, the popular series showed its protagonist in an unfailingly positive light, appealing to both black pride and white middle-class sensibilities.

Hollywood kept pace with liberal sentiment by featuring more starring roles for blacks. Sidney Poitier headed the small list of Negro performers suddenly in great demand for dramatic parts. His work in *Lilies of the Field,* a film whose humanity wholly transcended racial issues, won him an Academy Award as best actor in 1963. He was better known, however, for films about race relations, including one that touched on the ultimate torment in liberal parlor rooms, "Would you want your daughter to marry one?" At length the costars Katharine Hepburn and Spencer Tracy, as the afflicted white parents, cast off all doubts and give Poitier their blessing. Their anguish is assuaged by their tolerant instincts and by the fact that Poitier's character is affluent, highly educated, and a surgeon—a product less of Watts than of nearby Hollywood. *Guess Who's Coming to Dinner* nonetheless marked a major step forward for the image of blacks in American film, even if Hollywood advanced in largely crablike fashion.

"Any writer, I suppose, feels that the world into which he was born is nothing less than a conspiracy against the cultivation of his talent," observed the Harlem-seared author James Baldwin.[4] The sixties made the country more attentive to the talent and the anger of Negro writers, Baldwin first among them. Raised in the nation's largest ghetto, Baldwin etched in his work a bleak portrait of American society, a picture of "sterility and decay" framed by racist deeds and dogmas. In his politics Baldwin was quick to spurn the slightest hint of patronizing conduct, "from Bobby Kennedy's assurance that a Negro can become President in forty years to the unfortunate tone of warm congratulation with which so many liberals address their Negro equals."[5] It was Baldwin whom Black Power advocates honored by repeating one of his retorts to white liberals, "Do I really *want* to be integrated into a burning house?"[6] Black Muslims encouraged him: "We'll soon be addressing you as Mr. James X."[7] But Baldwin's passions could not be confined to anger and despair. For this former preacher, and son of a preacher, societies as well as sinners could still be saved. That salvation depended on "the most radical and far-reaching changes in the American political and social structure."[8] Baldwin believed against all the evidence he encountered that it could yet happen:

> Everything now, we must assume, is in our hands; we have no right to assume otherwise. If we—and now I mean the relatively conscious whites and the relatively conscious blacks . . . do not falter in our duty now, we may be able, handful that we are, to end the racial nightmare, and achieve our country, and change the history of the world. If we do not now dare everything, the fulfillment of that prophecy, recreated from the Bible in song by a slave, is upon us: *God gave Noah the rainbow sign, No more water, the fire next time!*[9]

The list of "firsts," of Negroes entering areas long barred to them, extended beyond the ranks of a famous few. Americans reading or watching advertisements saw that blacks, too, wanted the finest laundry detergent imaginable, and would walk a mile for a Camel cigarette. Soul singers Aretha Franklin and Ray Charles harmonized on the virtues of Coca-Cola for radio audiences.[10] The notion that capitalism was now a black concern also spread to business personnel offices and college admissions boards. Corporations sought out black employees in response to rising social and legal pressure as well as to a tight labor market. Affirmative action unfolded most strikingly at liberal social gatherings, where the appearance of blacks on a guest list now certified an event as fashionable and, even more, as significant. "The invisible man," as the black writer Ralph Ellison had described Negroes in the 1950s, had become a vivid presence in American society.

A decade earlier these achievements would have lit up campaigns for integration with a dazzling burst of racial breakthroughs. By the mid-sixties, however, each announcement of racial progress seemed no more than pallid tokenism to Negro cynics. The advancement of blacks therefore did at least as much to spur racial pride as to renew their faith in the promise of American life.

The limits of white acceptance frustrated the sprinkling of visible, apparently successful Negroes as well as those who watched the parade of precedents from their slums. Discontent marked the lone black corporate employee searching vainly for a career ladder; the solitary black television panelist questioned only on civil rights issues; the black athlete who, no matter how gifted, was never permitted to quarterback or coach. Frustration followed even the Negro able to glide past the color line into a white party, where he might be readily embraced as a symbol of white tolerance, yet not gain full notice as a person.

Stung by continued discrimination, black role models in the sixties did not always play the roles white society assigned. Jim Brown, who in the 1964 football season rushed for fifteen hundred yards and over fifty thousand dollars, stunned the white sports world by refusing to appear grateful for his fame and wealth. "I am not thankful to be here," Brown insisted. "If anything, I am more angry than the Negro who can't find work." One Cleveland sportscaster warned that Brown was on the wrong track with his criticisms of American society and his expressed sympathy for the Black Muslims. The announcer later explained to Brown that he admired him as a football player and never looked at him as a Negro. It was the sort of color-blind palliative that might have soothed many Negroes just a few years before. It did not mollify Brown, who snapped, "That's ridiculous! You have to look at me as a Negro. Look at me, man! I'm black!"[11]

Cassius Clay, too, insisted on being seen as a black man. Handsome, glib, with a genius at self-promotion and the fastest hands and legs of any heavyweight boxer in memory, Clay won an Olympic gold medal in 1960 at the age of nineteen. Four years later he moved exuberantly into a championship match with the much larger Sonny Liston and, true to his boasts, carried away the heavyweight title. Clay stood on the threshold of a long, brilliant career, ready to claim the special awe America held for its heavyweight boxing kings.

Yet almost immediately after dispatching the seemingly invincible Liston, Clay went on to more protracted matches with the white public and the U.S. government. He announced his conversion to the Nation of Islam the day after becoming champion, taking as his Muslim name Muhammad Ali. Most sportscasters condemned the new champion's actions and continued to call him by his old name. The public rooted wildly for Ali's opponents, most of whom were also black but more in keeping with white images of Negroes. In 1967 Ali defied the military draft, though he need only have spent a tour of duty fighting exhibitions for the armed forces, much as Joe Louis had done in World War II. Instead Ali declared, "I ain't got no quarrel with the Viet Cong,"[12] and claimed exemption from the draft as a conscientious objector and minister of religion. His stand resulted in a conviction for draft evasion, with the threat of five years in jail and a $10,000 fine shadowing him through years of legal appeals. The World Boxing Association, wasting no time investigating Ali's status as a conscientious objector, stripped him of his title and effectively denied him a major ring bout until 1971. Ali remained buoyantly unrepentant. Although he was a pariah to many Americans, his stature in the ghettos—and in much of the world—approximated his expansive self-image. He was simply "the Greatest."

Only a minority of black athletes overtly rebelled, but these received intense scrutiny by whites and blacks. The young basketball star Lew Alcindor, who enjoyed a small height advantage over Wilt Chamberlain, was among the athletes who openly praised the Nation of Islam; in 1971 he took as his Muslim name Kareem Abdul-Jabbar. Others dared greater ostracism. In the 1968 Olympics, Tommie Smith and John Carlos finished first and second in the 100-meter dash, then raised their fists in a Black Power salute during the hoisting of the American flag. The U.S. Olympic Committee confiscated their medals as punishment.

While black sports figures were individually defying convention, other Negroes were laying down a broader challenge to American cultural and social values. Looking beyond the growing presence of blacks in the media, they emphasized that white executives, writers, and directors still exclusively shaped black images. Stokely Carmichael observed in 1965 that one could spot black faces on American television programs yet glean nothing about distinctive minority problems or points of view:

> One actor brother points out that on every television show where they got black people now, he's a cop. . . .*NYPD,* he's a cop; *Mission Impossible,* he's a cop; *I Spy,* he's an international cop. What they're doing to us is they're trying to make us identify with a black man who fights for law and order—*their* law, and *their* order.[13]

Holding few executive posts in network television, radio, or print journalism, blacks found their own cultural voice in personal writings that spoke to Negro pride rather than to white tolerance. Black authors rising in the white literary world stepped back, like the poet and critic LeRoi Jones, to explore more fully their Afro-American roots. Jones had been a young "beat" writer in New York's Greenwich Village during the late 1950s, mingling with such white cultural rebels as Allen Ginsberg and Jack Kerouac. In the mid-sixties Jones felt the pull of black cultural nationalism and set an emphatic example for other artists: he divorced his white wife, took the African name Imamu Amiri Baraka, and, in novels, plays, poems, and essays, celebrated his racial heritage. His lyrical work invited blacks to explore old cultural bonds and to invent new incantations of communal power:

> We are beautiful people
> with african imaginations
> full of masks and dances and swelling chants
> . . . .
> We have been captured,
> brothers. And we labor
> to make our getaway, into
> the ancient image, into a new
> correspondence with ourselves
> and our black family. We need magic
> now we need the spells, to raise up
> return, destroy, and create. What will be
> the sacred words?[14]

Baraka was, perhaps unconsciously, retracing earlier calls for black pride. In the 1920s Negro writers were uncommonly prolific, inventive, and defiant. Their literary achievements cut against bitter memories of white racial violence in 1919, the displacement of black workers by returning white veterans of the First World War, and a national surge of political conservatism. Blacks channeled much of their frustration into one of the few available outlets, artistic expression, often subsidized by white patrons hungry for "exotic" ethnic culture. Langston Hughes epitomized the mood of the resulting "Harlem Renaissance" with a poem encouraging blacks to wrest their identities away from white image makers:

> You've taken my blues and gone
> . . . .
> And you fixed 'em
> So they don't sound like me
> . . . .
> But someday somebody'll
> Stand up and talk about me,
> And write about me—
> Black and beautiful—
> And sing about me,
> And put on plays about me!
> I reckon it'll be
> Me, myself!
> Yes, it'll be me.[15]

Writers of the 1960s black renaissance built on this theme even more ambitiously than their artistic forebears had done. To a greater extent than in the 1920s, the new burst of black cultural activity was a mass movement, as much the property of the populace as of a handful of Negro literati. In Watts, where residents celebrated every anniversary of the riot, the thrill of defiance inspired a mass outpouring of artistic and literary reflections. The Rhodes scholar Stanley Sanders returned from Oxford to his native Watts in August 1965 to find the ghetto's squalor unchanged but its residents jolted into a new awareness:

The new intellectual climate in Watts was hard-wrought. It was rich enough to support even a communist bookstore. Writers, poets, artists flourished. I was handed full manuscripts of unpublished books by indigenous writers and asked to criticize them. I have not seen during eight years of college life as many personal journals kept and sketches written than in Watts since the 1965 riots. A new, rough wisdom of the street corner was emerging.[16]

The Watts riot had a singular effect on twenty-four-year-old Ronald Everett, a native of Los Angeles and president of the black student body at his junior college. Taking the African name Maulana Karenga, he urged blacks to recover their cultural and historical roots. To help the search along, Karenga revealed the ornate rituals of "Kwanzaa," a holiday bringing a touch of rural

African tradition to America's urban ghettos. Word of mouth soon brought the celebration into thousands of black households from Watts to Harlem, as a festive sign of their African heritage.

Karenga's single-minded missionary activity kept him from noting several facts about Kwanzaa that he felt might inhibit its appeal. Contrary to his assertions, Kwanzaa had never been celebrated in Africa, or anywhere else in the world, but rather began as Karenga's own brainchild in 1966. "I said it was African," he explained years later, "because you know black people in this country wouldn't celebrate it if they knew it was American. Also, I put it around Christmas because I knew that's when a lot of people would be partying."[17] Notably, Karenga's admissions scarcely affected Kwanzaa's burgeoning popularity, a tribute to the larger truths beneath his shrewd merchandising. For although he had taken broad liberties in promoting his festival, Karenga had drawn knowledgeably on elements in African culture. He had also tapped, at precisely the right moment, a widely felt need among Negroes to renew their sense of African identity. Whatever Karenga's role as midwife to this tradition, Kwanzaa became, as he had always hoped, a vital reminder of black American roots.

Far more than earlier periods of Negro artistic awakening, the 1960s black renaissance helped shape bold political protest. Writers who cultivated distinct black values often glided into arguments for separate black institutions, denunciations of white liberals, and, at their most militant, calls to revolution. A common rebellion against integration provided a busy ideological thoroughfare linking the emerging realms of cultural nationalism and Black Power politics.

"There can be no real black revolution in the United States without cultural revolution," Harold Cruse summed up the militant credo of the new politics of identity.[18] After long obscurity as a critic and playwright Cruse burst onto center stage among black cultural rebels carrying a 600-page critique of virtually all paths to black advancement through 1967. *The Crisis of the Negro Intellectual* was part historical analysis, part social commentary, part political polemic, and 100 percent iconoclasm. The central task of Negro thinkers, Cruse argued, was to expose the myths that had misshaped black activism—and there was scarcely a comforting tradition or ideal about American society, race relations, and civil rights leadership that looked quite the same after several pages of the author's intense glare.

Cruse marveled first at the credulity of liberal civil rights leaders in chasing a mirage of racial integration, as if there existed "a great body of homogenized, inter-assimilated white Americans" with whom Negroes could integrate. In reality, Cruse observed, whites belonged to distinct ethnoreligious groups that neither wanted nor needed "to become integrated with each other."[19] Blacks alone had been mesmerized by the melting-pot ideal, and their integrationist hopes were therefore doomed to defeat "beyond token levels."[20]

The quest for equality through constitutional guarantees struck Cruse as similarly sheltered from the harsh facts of ethnic life. The Constitution explicitly conferred only individual rights, but was otherwise silent in favor of those groups with the resources and organization to seize the lion's share of status, wealth, and power. Like a latter-day Charles Beard, the historian who spied vested economic interests behind every clause and comma of the Constitution, Cruse depicted a document that was of, by, and for the privileged. In the name of liberty but for the benefit of an Anglo-Saxon elite, the Constitution permitted "the most profligate economic exploitation, . . . crypto-legal crime and extortion, widespread poverty and illiteracy, [and] waste of human material."[21] Promises on parchment carried little weight with Cruse, who found that "the individual in America has few rights that are not backed up by the political, economic and social power of one group or another."[22] Amid this enduring ethnic competition, "those Negroes, and there are very many of them, who have accepted the full essence of the Great American Ideal of individualism are in serious trouble trying to function in America."[23]

Black nationalism, Cruse concluded, was the only sensible course for Negroes, in order for them to rise as a community from "the bottom of the ethnic totem pole."[24] This, however, would require a rebirth among the Negro intelligentsia, who for half a century had betrayed their roles as creative tribunes for the black community. Unsupported by the small Negro middle class, which above all sought white acceptance, Negro intellectuals drifted toward outside sponsorship. In the 1920s the Harlem Renaissance artists revolved in orbits preset by affluent white hostesses and impresarios; during the Great Depression white Communists "coddled" and controlled black intellectuals such as Richard Wright and Claude McKay, crowding out indigenous black nationalist aims with Marxist dogmas. In later decades the Negro intelligentsia, under the heavy wing of white liberals, "sold out their own birthright"[25] for the folly of racial integration. While James Baldwin and Kenneth Clark, among other Negro thinkers, gained renown in the sixties for assailing white liberal hypocrisy, this merely confirmed to Cruse their own lack of direction. Instead, Cruse asserted, "now would be the time for Negro intellectuals to start thinking for themselves as truly independent and original radicals."[26]

Even as Cruse wrote, artists were experimenting with ways to shape black culture, politics, and economics into a "dynamic synthesis."[27] For Imamu Amiri Baraka, helping to set black literary standards formed part of a more ambitious, separatist challenge to American society. As director of the Black Arts Repertory Theatre School in Harlem, Baraka called on ghetto residents to establish their own nation. This would involve black control of properties, politics, and above all a common culture, for "only a united Black Consciousness can save Black People from annihilation at the white man's hands." The role of the black artist in this process was to render white evils and black potential so movingly as "to aid in the destruction of America as he knows it."[28]

New literary talents pressed Baraka's fusion of art and activism still further. Black writers just coming of age amid calls for nationalist rebellion often viewed literature as a branch of political theory. The aesthetic test for such writers and their burgeoning readership was simple: did their work bring America closer to revolution?

The ex-convict and unrepentant rebel Eldridge Cleaver had spent much of his life at war with white America before turning his pen to the black nationalist cause. As an eighteen-year-old resident of Watts in 1954, the year of the *Brown* decision, he served his first jail term, for possession of marijuana. Released in 1956, Cleaver began assaulting white women, acts he considered "insurrectionary" rape aimed to avenge white males' abuse of black women by "trampling upon the white man's law." But Cleaver's fury was too hot for him to shape into a clear revolutionary mold even by his own, savage standards; he also repeatedly attacked black women in the ghettos, "to refine [his] technique and *modus operandi.*" In 1957 Cleaver went back to prison, where he had ten years to reflect and decide that his crimes were not justified.[29] But his personal revolt against society burned on in writings that thrust at startled whites an image of black rage unfiltered by Christian, Gandhian, or liberal faith.

The publication of *Soul on Ice* in 1968 brought Cleaver's meditations from the Folsom state penitentiary in Los Angeles to best-seller status. His subject matter included his own, misspent and malformed youth, compared with which Malcolm X's ghetto origins seemed sheltered and his crimes petty. Beyond this surface sheen *Soul on Ice* also offered a penetrating psychological profile of young black men whom white racism had stripped of opportunity, self-esteem, and the full respect of black women. From these portraits of individual anguish Cleaver pushed his readers—black and white—to realize that Negroes in America had only one way to recover their dignity, and that was through unrelenting rebellion against white domination.

Soul on Ice allowed for the possibility of coalition and even friendship across racial lines, but nonviolence and love were decidedly minor themes. As an early disciple of Malcolm X and at one time a minister in the Nation of Islam, Cleaver scorned the "self-effacing" approach of civil rights demonstrators.[30] In August 1965 Cleaver thrilled to the news of rioting in Watts and boasted to fellow black inmates of his roots in the Los Angeles ghetto. "The tired lamentations of Whitney Young, Roy Wilkins, and The Preacher notwithstanding," those ghetto fires warmed his soul.[31]

Cleaver's politics of virility, which exulted in black male pride, heterosexual aggressiveness, and violent revolution as inseparable virtues, placed him at odds with his main black predecessor in the literary limelight, James Baldwin. Cleaver faced this squarely with a chapter that damned Baldwin as little more than an Uncle Tom who could turn a phrase. "There is in [his] work," Cleaver fulminated, "the most grueling, agonizing, total hatred of the blacks, particularly of himself, and the most shameful, fanatical, fawning, sycophantic love of the whites that one can find in . . . any black American writer of note in our time."[32] Cleaver's animus fed on the discovery that his one-time hero Baldwin was a homosexual, which in Cleaver's scheme of masculine values was akin to racial treason. For Baldwin's sexual and social leanings seemed to Cleaver two facets of the same effeminate, passive Negro mind-set that had proven unequal to the "power struggle" at the core of American race relations.[33]

A few years earlier, at the height of national good feeling, Cleaver's literary standing might have succumbed to the venom oozing from his own prose in the form of lingering misogyny, racial bitterness, and virulent homophobia. But in the late 1960s, when black rage in any form widely passed as ethnic authenticity, even white critics excused or minimized the intolerance that permeated *Soul on Ice.* Eminent liberal journals such as the *Nation* and the *New Republic* gauged the polarizing racial climate and hailed Cleaver's "beautifully written" book as one that stood "at the exact resonant center of the new Negro writing."[34]

Poets, too, caught the spirit of black nationalist politics, with writings that left no verse ideologically blank. Prominent among the new breed of bards who preferred manifestos to sonnets was a slight, intensely energetic young woman, Nikki Giovanni. Intellectually precocious, she was long politically adrift, like many young Negroes of the day. At Fisk University she cofounded her campus chapter of SNCC; yet she read avidly from the fountainhead of conservative thought, Ayn Rand, and in 1964 declared her support for Barry Goldwater. The wave of black militancy in the mid-sixties swept her into an active role promoting black cultural consciousness: editing a campus literary magazine, organizing a black arts festival and the New Arts Theatre in Cincinnati, forming a black history group in Wilmington, Delaware, and lecturing at various black nationalist centers. And there were the poems, which hurled vengeful darts at white sensibilities and stirred blacks to pride, anger, and hatred. She warned, "We have tried far too long to ally with whites," and exalted the goal of a violent black revolution. What of the hope that whites could change, could reform themselves? All charades:

> It is still a circus we are watching
> Barnum and Bailey are the minds
> behind president Johnson
> You would not trust your life to a wolf or tiger
> no matter how many tricks they can learn

Giovanni pursued the rhythms of her revolutionary verse with unhesitating candor:

> All honkies and some negroes will have to die
> This is unfortunate but necessary[35]

Giovanni took these grim prophecies to college campuses and other centers of youthful black activism, where her impassioned readings drew warm applause and grateful shouts of encouragement. Not long before, these admirers had devoured the anguished writings of James Baldwin, who saw race relations not alone in black and white but in tortured shades of gray. If Baldwin told of the fire next time, he did so in fear, trembling, and stubborn hope. But by the late sixties black writers were garnering plaudits for asserting that white society had passed the point of prophetic warnings, that the divine fire was already consuming the nation. By comparison Baldwin seemed dated by his expressions of love and, for some, by his confessions of ambiguity. To fervent apostles of the new literature, the black revolution had few enough resources without sacrificing fervor to the quest for a more complex, or magnanimous, moral vision.

Religious thinkers also began reinterpreting their Christian mission—and the movement for racial justice—according to the militant canons of black nationalism. Such writings as *Black Theology and Black Power* brought James Cone to prominence in the late sixties among the biblical exegetes who looked equally to Saint Paul and to Stokely Carmichael for inspiration. The God of James Cone was interested primarily in liberation, and, since black people were the victims of society, Black Power was "Christ's central message to twentieth century America."[36] Freedom was the star of Bethlehem guiding the true Christian, and there could be no freedom independent of a fight for justice. Black theology, he wrote, *"confronts* white society as the racist Antichrist."[37] As for Christian love, Cone found that "love without the power to guarantee justice in human relations is meaningless."[38] Neither could a Christian be nonviolent in an unjust society. Cone anticipated that some might point to Jesus' turning the other cheek, but Cone asserted, "If the system is evil, then revolutionary violence is both justified and necessary."[39]

A young pastor in Detroit, Albert Cleage, pressed black theology to its limit. Shepherding his congregants at the Church of the Black Madonna, Cleage also wrote *The Black Messiah* (1968) to root his ideas within a biblical framework. Cleage's work maintained that Christianity (like Buddhism, Judaism, and Islam) originated with black people. Those not fully persuaded by his historical claims, Cleage admonished, "Black people cannot build dignity on their knees worshipping a white Christ."[40] Nor a passive, otherworldly Christ. "The Black Messiah Jesus did not build a Church, but a Movement."[41] This Messiah "was a revolutionary black leader, a Zealot, seeking to lead a Black Nation to freedom."[42] Theology therefore was the work of divining the Lord's path for black rebellion.

To the black militants who spurned Christianity, Cleage made a special appeal reflecting pain as well as sympathy for their position: "To Stokely and the young men in SNICK, I would just say briefly that the Christian religion you are rejecting, that you are so opposed to, is a slave Christianity that has no roots in the teachings of the Black Messiah."[43] All political dissent and all deeds were permitted within the black Christian revolution.

Cleage's extreme formulation of Christian duty converted few Negroes. Yet the broader tide of black nationalism swept up staunch integrationists among ministers and theologians, depositing them in unfamiliar ideological settings. In 1963 the eminent Negro scholar Joseph R. Washington, Jr., published a magisterial volume, *Black Religion,* that pronounced black churches as devoid of Christian purpose; segregated, imitative institutions, they had no better hope for the future than to merge with the rest of American Christendom. Three years later, amid shifting black attitudes toward integration, the much criticized Reverend Washington produced a new volume in which he tacitly recanted his earlier paean to assimilation. In its place *The Politics of God* offered glistening predictions for a separate black church as a vital force for the nation's moral renewal.[44]

While black nationalists diverged widely over specific programs, they found a nearly universal sacred text with the the posthumous appearance, late in 1965, of *The Autobiography of Malcolm X*. In this powerful volume the black novelist Alex Haley wove Malcolm's story together from interviews recorded between 1963 and 1965. Graphically recounting his doomed bid for white respect, his zealotry as a Black Muslim, and his final, free-floating year trumpeting revolution "by any means necessary,"[45] the *Autobiography* immediately raised Malcolm to a higher level of influence in death than he had known in life. Events had belatedly prepared audiences for Malcolm's legacy: Negro disaffection with the civil rights movement gave him prophetic stature, his assassination (though coming at the hands of blacks) conferred martyrdom, and Malcolm himself served as a wellspring of ideas that activists seeking legitimacy could draw from and claim as their own. *Newsweek*'s Peter Goldman, who had seen firsthand the Muslim leader's shifting complexity, observed a frenzied, many-sided contest to monopolize his memory:

> Integrationists assured me that Malcolm was becoming an integrationist. Nationalists told me that he never left home. Marxists were sure he would have been a socialist had he lived. White liberals wanted him to be a black liberal. His special affection has been claimed by Trotskyists, Maoists, Nkrumists, Garveyites, orthodox and unorthodox Muslims, civil-rights organizations from the Urban League to CORE and SNCC, and Adam Clayton Powell. And out of that mystery of becoming that was Malcolm's last year . . . all of them could produce evidence to prove it.[46]

Malcolm's image never quite succumbed to these partisan raids that aimed to strip and repackage his thought in more convenient form. For he had tapped the genius of black American culture precisely by rescuing it from any one dogma, pursuing instead a more fluid search for human dignity. "The greatest mistake of the movement," he told a *Village Voice* reporter just before his murder, "has been trying to organize a sleeping people around specific goals. You have to wake the people up first, then you'll get action." The reporter tried to assist her subject by tendering some stock revolutionary wordage: "Wake them up to their exploitation?" But Malcolm had fastened onto a more basic revolution. "No," he explained, "to their humanity, to their own worth, and to their heritage."[47]

The Politics of Black Nationalism

Racial pride stirred Negroes in the late 1960s to assert control of local schools, police, and other public services, hoisting the flag of Black Power above the fraying banner of integration. In practice, however, these campaigns seldom followed the paths to power foreseen by black activists. More often they exerted their greatest impact by polarizing relations between blacks and whites, many of whom had been staunch supporters of the drive for racial equality.

The politics of black nationalism touched the South mainly in places where local civil rights organizers were already active. It was a short jump from seeking the ballot to understanding that the power to choose a black sheriff might help end police brutality, or that a tax assessor from the ranks of black sharecroppers would take a dim view of levies on the poor. In Lowndes County, Alabama, Negroes rallying around the Black Panther symbol scarcely looked to white, mainstream approval in mounting a challenge to the Democratic and the Republican tickets. In November 1966, candidates from the all-black Freedom Organization defied growing harassment to run for sheriff, tax assessor, tax collector, coroner, and three seats on the board of education. On election eve an ebullient, overflow crowd of 650 gathered at Mount Moriah Baptist Church near Hayneville, the seat of Lowndes County, to hear seven homegrown champions talk about plowing under the old social system. The nominee for tax assessor admirably compressed the new party's aims into a single-sentence oration. "My platform," she declared, "is to tax the rich and feed the poor."[48] She sat down to thunderous applause. Stokely Carmichael spoke later in the evening. Surrounded entirely by black faces, he omitted traditional odes to racial tolerance and instead fired staccato warnings at old oppressors:

We have done what they said we could not do. Colored people have come together tonight! Tonight says that we CAN come together and we can rock this country from California to New York City! When we pull that lever we pull it for all the blood of Negroes that the whites have spilled. We will pull that lever to stop the beating of Negroes by whites. We will pull that lever for all the black people who have been killed. We are going to resurrect them tomorrow. We will pull that lever so that our children will never go through what we have gone through.

Despite Carmichael's long interest in socialist thought, he drew less on Marx than on Moses in building rapport with his audience. Some were left behind during the crossing of the Red Sea, he said, and so the Uncle Toms would be left behind in this new movement for liberation. And if some whites were not ready to accept the new age of black assertiveness, "We say to those who don't remember—You better remember, because if you don't MOVE ON OVER, WE ARE GOING TO MOVE ON OVER YOU!"[49]

"We filed out of the church into the dark, clear night *knowing* we were going to win," wrote Carmichael's friend and fellow organizer Cleveland Sellers. But the local Democratic party resorted to the time-honored tradition of using all means to defeat candidates who enjoyed black support. As in the 1890s, when massive fraud sent Populist candidates to defeat in Alabama, Georgia, and other Southern states, white Democrats proved that the power of the ballot lay less with the individual voters than with those who counted the votes. Sellers described a range of fraudulent and coercive measures against blacks who went to the polls:

They stuffed some ballotboxes; they forced some blacks to use ballots that had already been marked for white candidates; they insisted on helping those blacks who couldn't read; they brought in truckloads of blacks who worked on their farms and told them who to vote for; they refused to allow several of our watchers to work at the polls.[50]

Every LCFO candidate lost, officially, but no amount of creative recounting at the polls could undo the growth of black pride in Lowndes County. In contrast to the dismay at the 1964 Democratic convention in Atlantic City, where the MFDP had at least wrung token concessions from the President of the United States, the complete rout of the Lowndes County Freedom Organization scarcely dampened the spirits of SNCC organizers and local residents. The Freedom Organization chairman had declared on election eve, "No matter what happens tomorrow night, I will hold my head as high as I have ever done. It is a victory to get the black panther on the ballot."[51] Uncompromising defiance of racism thus took on the aura of triumph, and the appeal of interracial coalition receded further behind memories of liberal hypocrisy and betrayal.

Although black nationalism found roots in the South, it remained above all a response to conditions in the Northern ghettos. Negro slum dwellers were mightily unimpressed by the "pie-in-the-sky" religion offered by civil rights proselytizers. Instead of looking to a distant day of residential integration, urban blacks increasingly demanded "community control" over ghetto neighborhoods where white merchants, police, social workers, and other "outsiders" appeared to monopolize the wealth and power.

The emerging campaigns for community control often flowed directly from the sea change in black cultural attitudes. Newark's Black Community Development and Defense group (BCD) typified the rise of urban separatist organizations. Formed in January 1968, six months after rioters had burned much of black Newark, the BCD instilled African cultural values, the asceticism of the Black Muslims, and the warnings of its founder Imamu Amiri Baraka against internalizing "the white boy's system."[52] In politics that meant opposing all ties with whites and biding time by working for local black candidates until the moment seemed ripe for a more cleansing armed rebellion.

Huey Newton and Bobby Seale, two college-educated ghetto youths in Oakland, California, aimed to speed the day of revolution. In October 1966 they formed the Black Panther Party for Self-Defense to combat police brutality in the ghetto. Armed patrols of young male Black Panthers accosted police in the act of mistreating local Negroes and recorded evidence of abuses, often narrowly avoiding shootouts with incensed officers. Although the Panthers fired instamatic cameras rather than rifles, they kept their weapons prominently in view, in homage to Premier Mao Tse-tung's motto for revolutionaries, "Power flows from the barrel of a gun."

Black Panthers spoke openly of armed revolt, seemingly innocent of the danger they courted from white authorities. While their reputation for fearlessness helped them recruit in the ghettos, it also turned them into virtual outlaws. FBI Director J. Edgar Hoover early declared open season on the Panthers, assigning agents to infiltrate, disrupt, and discredit the organization. Forged correspondence, posters, and leaflets assisted the FBI's efforts to sow suspicion between the Black Panthers and other California-based black groups, including Maulana Karenga's equally well-armed band known as US. Local police were understandably even less partial to the existence of avowed police haters in their city. The Panthers' flamboyant display of firearms, while not directly threatening, precipitated police raids on their offices that resulted in arrests and the shooting death of several members. In 1967 Huey Newton, the Panthers' "minister of defense," was sentenced to fifteen years in prison for killing an officer, though the circumstances of the shooting remained too hazy for Newton's claim of self-defense to be tested. Under this relentless harassment the Black Panthers proved unable to develop the following or funding to transform their revolutionary bravado into political power.[53]

Shorn of threatening slogans and displays of Remington rifles, black nationalist ambitions sometimes received a more receptive hearing from white liberals. Black activists in New York City drew white fellow travelers, if not converts, with speeches that reconsidered the merits of school desegregation along the nationalist lines foreshadowed by Malcolm X. Malcolm had denied that "a school is segregated because it's all black": rather it is segregated when it is "controlled by people who have no real interest in it whatsoever."[54] During the mid-sixties these sentiments merged with a broader drive by New Yorkers to streamline the cumbersome educational bureaucracy and "revitalize" local school boards. And at a time when even minor racial incidents were sparking riots across the urban North, white officials dared not ignore black and Hispanic demands for more responsive schools.

The cause of ghetto autonomy in education received a powerful boost from one of the nation's fastest-rising liberal lights, John V. Lindsay. In 1965, New Yorkers had elected Lindsay mayor in the belief that this Kennedyesque congressman, blessed with aristocratic charm and blue-eyed matinee-idol looks, would lead their metropolis ("Fun City," as Lindsay dubbed it) to new frontiers of glamour and good government. As mayor, Lindsay conveyed a special sympathy with nonwhite aspirations; and his widely publicized "walking tours" of Harlem helped keep New York calm during the long, hot summers of Northern rioting. Walking tours alone, though, would not be enough to defuse the rising anger over inferior ghetto education. The mayor's office therefore encouraged projects to give nonwhite residents control over neighborhood schools, as a test of citywide decentralization and, more urgently, as a salve for racial unrest.

As in the South, in New York the focus of the incipient experiment in black nationalism was a community that civil rights workers had already stirred from quiescence. Seventy percent black, 25 percent Puerto Rican, the decaying Brooklyn neighborhood of Ocean Hill contained all the indices of sociological gloom associated with ghetto life. Yet amid the poverty, high crime, drug abuse, and broken homes, residents were organizing for change. Some parents convened at the Church of Our Lady of the Presentation to hear the white priest John Powis preach the virtues of community-run schools. Others, inspired by a young white CORE worker and teachers' spokeswoman, Sandra Feldman, joined school picket lines to win removal of an unwanted junior high school principal in 1966. These instances of black, Hispanic, and white unity prompted the United Federation of Teachers to support Ocean Hill's drive for locally run schools as an extension of the union's own reform activism under its president, Albert Shanker.

"Al" Shanker was an invaluable ally for any liberal cause in city politics. At once bookish and tough-minded, Shanker had guided the local teachers' union during the sixties to unprecedented stature. Along with a readiness to pummel the city with strikes to upgrade teachers' salaries, Shanker gained a reputation as the foremost integrationist in the New York labor movement. His commitment to racial equality carried over to Ocean Hill, where local self-rule seemed to mesh with union goals of smaller classes, parent-teacher cooperation, and reduced power for a remote board of education. Shanker convinced executives at the Ford Foundation that Ocean Hill offered a model "demonstration district" for community control; and the foundation in turn provided this reform idea with funding and a healthy aura of corporate respectability.

In late spring of 1967 a neighborhood planning council set up a new school board in Ocean Hill with the support of the mayor's office, the United Federation of Teachers, the board of education, and a Ford Foundation grant of $44,000. Liberal architects of this experiment soon found, however, that giving black slum dwellers a sudden, ill-defined power over white, middle-class union workers was scarcely the design for racial peace they had imagined. Unlike the earlier civil rights campaigns, which rewarded leaders who could appeal to both Negroes and whites, the politics of community control raised up spokesmen who best evoked local anger toward all outside authority. The five parents on Ocean Hill's planning council, all nonwhite women dependent on welfare, gravitated toward two such polarizing orators: Father Powis, who openly sought confrontation with "a sick society," and the black nationalist Herman Ferguson (later convicted of conspiracy to murder Roy Wilkins and Whitney Young, Jr.). Under their strident tutelage, council members proclaimed in their first policy statement, "The ending of oppression and the beginning of a new day has often become a reality only after people have resorted to violent means."[55]

Even before the start of the school year in September 1967, Ocean Hill's loosely woven local coalition of teachers, parents, and diverse neighborhood leaders unraveled. The pipe-smoking, stocky Rhody McCoy, a black school official of eighteen years' service, emerged as the people's choice for unit administrator of Ocean Hill's schools although teachers complained that they had lacked any role in the selection. No one quite knew how far the new administrator's authority extended in the dimly lit realm of community control, and McCoy repeatedly tested the edges of his mandate during the fall semester. He bypassed the civil service list to appoint five Negro principals, and the teachers' union promptly disavowed their legitimacy and sued to remove them. McCoy heightened union suspicions by covertly issuing weekly payments to parents on the new school governing board, using Father Powis's church to dispense Ford Foundation funds. However well intended, this policy left the parent representatives financially dependent on the very staff they were supposed to monitor. To critics of the Ocean Hill project this did not represent local self-rule but a power grab by a small circle that thrived on militant agitation.

Amid these tensions Ocean Hill's normally fractious schools approached chaos. Riots broke out among students, harassment of teachers led nearly twenty to transfer out of the district, and arson leveled part of Intermediate School 178. In the spring of 1968 one final, overarching grievance swallowed up any lingering hopes for peace in the schools: parents in the Brooklyn school district pressed McCoy and the governing board to oust teachers they considered unqualified. This raised the sensitive issue of who was fit to teach Ocean Hill's children—were any of the white, middle-class employees who formed 90 percent of the teaching staff? And it exposed the still thornier question of just who was empowered to decide.

Everyone involved in public education, from Shanker to the city school superintendent, Bernard Donovan, knew that ghettos like Ocean Hill had often served as involuntary sanctuaries for the wretched refuse of New York's teaching staff. Because strict tenure rules guarded teachers from dismissal for any breach short of a felony, principals commonly banished unwanted personnel to districts where low expectations of student progress might camouflage incompetent, indifferent, and even mentally ill employees. With the advent of community control McCoy had to respond decisively to these cumulative frustrations or make way for others who sought confrontation with the union, the board of education, and any other "colonial" presence in Ocean Hill.

Anxious to avoid a possible scandal over the clustering of unfit educators in the slums, Shanker and Donovan assured McCoy that they would expedite the transfer of any teachers he reported to them as unqualified. This proposal assumed that McCoy, in the mold of liberal reformers, was primarily concerned with preserving a broad coalition for concrete change. But petitioning Donovan would have cast McCoy as a supplicant of the city and a partner of the teachers' union, credentials the unit administrator shunned as detrimental to his immediate political survival. Rather, he encouraged the governing board's public announcement, on May 7, 1968, which named nineteen teachers who had allegedly harmed children's educations and were no longer welcome in Ocean Hill.

Projected as a plan for autonomy, community control in practice was evolving into a racially charged test of wills between ghetto spokesmen and organized labor. Ten white teachers who were targeted for dismissal refused to transfer without first receiving a formal review of their records, and the white-led teachers' union supported them by striking the district schools for the remainder of the spring semester. In August the union secured its legal position with a court order to reinstate all ten teachers. When McCoy and the governing board vowed to resist, 54,000 of the city's 57,000 public school teachers struck all public schools on September 9, 1968, the opening day of the fall semester. Under pressure from an overwrought Superintendent Donovan, McCoy pledged the safe return of the ten teachers. But he shrank from admitting this pledge to the governing-board members he had earlier roused to fury, for fear that his militant image would collapse, and with it his stature in the community. Rather he acquiesced in an unnerving community reception for the unwelcome union workers.

On September 11 eighty-three teachers reported on McCoy's orders to a school auditorium to await class assignments but instead encountered fifty young black vigilantes, who trapped them inside. Sporting bandoliers holding bullets, helmets, and sticks, the blacks flicked the lights on and off, cursed the hostage educators, and warned that teachers who flouted the community's will by remaining in the schools would be carried out in a pine box. This rough exercise in direct democracy left Ocean Hill's teachers badly shaken but determined to stay at their jobs. It left Albert Shanker furious and poised to resume the strike. As for Ocean Hill's elusive unit administrator, whose confusing signals had encouraged union and ghetto militancy alike, he defended his tortuous course as the normal business of politics: "Everybody else seems to have a public posture and a private posture. Why shouldn't McCoy?"[56] The answer to this disingenuous question unfolded over the next several months as the community control experiment continued to veer out of control, threatening to destroy New York City's fragile hopes for racial harmony.

Mayor Lindsay stood as the last buffer on the collision course between the local governing board and the union. He had kept a nearly invisible profile during the fifteen months of festering troubles in Ocean Hill, until it became inescapably clear that time can aggravate some wounds, if they cut deep enough into the body politic. Still, as much as any big-city mayor, Lindsay had the political capital to coax an aggrieved minority like that in Ocean Hill back within the bounds of legality. Instead he vainly pressured the ten teachers to accept a transfer, while telling an angry meeting of mainly white parents' associations that the Ocean Hill governing board had lived up to its agreements "more or less." Lindsay's course was consistent with his profound commitment to black aspirations, of which the Ocean Hill governing board was becoming a symbol. Yet his policy risked leaving the fate of community control to the rougher touch of Albert Shanker's angry union.

Two more teachers' strikes, spanning seven weeks, gradually clarified the balance of urban power to Mayor Lindsay and his young aides. Lindsay fulminated on television that Shanker lacked "the moral authority" for his actions, but New Yorkers generally approved the strike and blamed the mayor for the growing inconvenience. Teachers' rallies swelled to five and ten times the size of crowds mustered by Ocean Hill's supporters. On November 16, 1968, a frantic Mayor Lindsay approved a pact with the teachers' union that resembled an unabridged list of Shanker's most ambitious bargaining points. It reinstated the ten dismissed teachers, suspended the governing board, barred its members from visiting the schools, and authorized union as well as city inspectors to countermand orders from McCoy and the principals. McCoy scorned the terms as "degrading and humiliating," but agreement no longer depended on his approval, public or private. By then, as the journalist Martin Mayer observed, Lindsay preferred to risk a race riot rather than let the strike continue.[57]

The "sick society" had proven more vigorous and vindictive under challenge than the ghetto's militant leaders had ever considered. Yet those agitators who stood in the ruins of the Ocean Hill project appeared more angry than abject. Father Powis, a prime mover in the debacle, joined other board members in denouncing the "sell-out," then called out to reporters, "Hey, baby, now we burn down Brooklyn!" Not all Negroes warmed to this nihilistic bravado, however. Whitney Young, Jr., who had helped mediate the conflict, caught the white priest's blithe prescription for Negro progress and snapped, "It's a pity—isn't it?—that there are only 2,000 blacks you can get killed on Ocean Hill."[58]

The struggle at Ocean Hill offered a cautionary lesson on the limits of liberal idealism on racial issues. Throughout this crisis Mayor Lindsay had shown a social vision that was long but narrow; attuned to the genuine grievances of ghetto residents, he had a less certain grasp of how to balance the competing factions that shaped urban politics. He had erred, first, in assuming that a policy of unbroken concessions would placate Ocean Hill's extremists. In fact it merely encouraged their intransigence and in turn buffeted Rhody McCoy down a militant path that permitted no graceful retreat. Lindsay also failed to summon the same generous impulses toward union leaders—whom he viewed as greedy, myopic, petty antagonists—that he volunteered to the inner-city poor. In this he seemed oblivious to a fact of urban life that towered like the city skyline above his one-sided overtures: the politics of community control in the 1960s could generate white as well as black militancy, and to ignore either was to invite disaster.

Fallout from the conflict at Ocean Hill poisoned race relations in New York City. The rise in tensions accelerated white flight to the suburbs, discouraged the entry of new businesses, and hastened the spread of violence throughout the public school system. Polarization of racial attitudes appeared most sharply, perhaps, in the dual image of Albert Shanker, the dominant personality in the strike. Negroes came to speak his name as a byword for racism and demagoguery, bent on thwarting black ambitions for independence. But many whites praised Shanker—often in language dripping with racial epithets—as a gritty labor hero of almost Churchillian stature who upheld due process against racially motivated job displacement.

The transformation of Shanker's image also spoke volumes about the effect of black nationalist politics on the coalition for liberal reform. Only a few years earlier the unsparing nemesis of Ocean Hill's governing board was rallying union support for the voting rights marches from Selma to Montgomery. But for New Yorkers, and Northerners generally, events like the Selma march were distant, clouded memories. Black protest was moving inexorably beyond the old issues of basic rights, to demands for substantive economic and political power. And in this harsh arena of open interest-group conflict, old partnerships and unifying moral tenets had little standing.

Nowhere else did the politics of black nationalism unsettle the civil rights coalition so sharply as in the relations between Negroes and Jews. Jewish donors had helped keep CORE and SNCC solvent, and numerous Jewish volunteers had shared the life-threatening displeasure of Southern vigilantes. But in the ghettos, where white civil rights workers were a rare sight, this history carried little credit. Jews there were known in other guises, as shopkeepers, landlords, perhaps corner pawnbrokers—in short, as part of the unwelcome white presence in black neighborhoods. In education, too, Jews were disproportionately represented in many cities; the cast of union characters in New York City's teachers' strike was largely Jewish, including Albert Shanker and all ten teachers dismissed by Ocean Hill's governing board. Ethnic jockeying for jobs and status was nothing new to the country's metropolitan melting pots, but for two groups as sensitive to prejudice as Negroes and Jews, no conflict appeared—or remained—routine.

Given the tense atmosphere of black-Jewish relations, almost any spark could set off outbursts ill-suited to consensus politics. In February 1966 Mount Vernon, New York, witnessed a vehement town discussion on de facto school segregation where the black CORE leader Clifton Brown shouted at a Jewish opponent, "Hitler made a mistake when he didn't kill enough of you." Brown later explained that he had merely tried to convey his frustration with white liberals who did not grasp his urgency on matters of racial justice; but this demurrer that he had simply overshot his mark calmed few people. CORE's initial reluctance to discipline Brown did not help matters. Will Maslow, executive secretary of the American Jewish Congress, quit CORE's advisory committee in protest. Angry letters poured into CORE's national and New York offices, each one echoing the terse declaration of a Jewish official: "There can be no compromise with ovens for Jews."[59]

A year later three SNCC workers tossed new incendiary rhetoric into this simmering ethnic conflict with a denunciation of Israel (just victorious in the Six-Day War) as an agent of American imperialism. Jewish activists reacted as if personally indicted by SNCC's polemic. The folksinger Theodore Bikel, who had strummed a repertoire of Israeli melodies at many fund-raisers for SNCC, resigned from the group with a parting charge that SNCC had "spit on the graves" of the Jewish civil rights martyrs Schwerner and Goodman, "who died for the concept of brotherhood" that SNCC was now "covering with shame." North Carolina's pamphleteering zealot for Jewish liberalism, Harry Golden, also resigned, asking how SNCC could echo ideas "found in the Ku Klux Klan and the American Nazi Party."[60]

Negroes alarmed that the tide of Jewish indignation could sweep through their own organizations' treasuries retreated to the high ground of philo-Semitic sentiments. A. Philip Randolph and Bayard Rustin led the way with an expression of distress at SNCC's "anti-Semitic" diatribe, which they believed fell beyond the pale of decency and liberal coalition.[61] SNCC workers, however, had reached a point of no return in their hardening attitudes toward white liberals. They saw no logic in equating attacks on Israel with attacks on all Jews, ridiculed Bikel and Golden as nonmembers who could not quit what they had never been a part of, and reiterated the charge that Israel and America were partners in white imperialism. "Rather than breaking our will," the program secretary Cleveland Sellers said of SNCC's state-of-siege view, "this made us more convinced than ever that we were correct when we accused the majority of America's whites of being racists."[62]

Donations to SNCC and CORE in 1967 sank to critical levels, while white volunteers moved on to antiwar activity or back to college. Black nationalist fervor continued unfazed, indeed unsated, by these developments. For in the protest groups themselves black leaders determined to purge all hints of white control, condescension, and, in some cases, simple cooperation. At a SNCC staff meeting repeatedly disrupted by arguments and tears, the executive committee voted in December 1966 to expel the five whites remaining in the organization. Whites who wanted to continue working with SNCC after this purge could do so only on a "voluntary contractual basis." Staff members believed this would eliminate contradictions between SNCC's integrated staff and its demand for unilateral black control in black communities. Not every white member left SNCC without dissent. The Alabama native Bob Zellner, the son of an itinerant Methodist minister (and repentant former Klansman), was among the few heroes remaining from SNCC's mythic early years. Senior to most black SNCC workers in service and scars, he had been on leave with his wife and co-worker, Dorothy, during the December purge. In May 1967 the Zellners petitioned for active status in order to organize poor whites in New Orleans. The executive committee welcomed them back, up to a point: the Zellners could rejoin SNCC so long as they agreed to exclusion from staff meetings. But the two veteran members refused to reenter their organization through the back door. Executive Secretary Jim Forman explained to other black staff members that Bob Zellner was his best friend. But in a rambling, anguished speech, Forman concluded that there could be no exceptions to SNCC's policy. "I think this is a mistake, but that is among us," Bob Zellner said on hearing that SNCC had chosen to fire both him and his wife, the last white members, as a matter of racial principle.[63]

CORE, freighted with a longer integrationist tradition, also navigated painfully toward black nationalist moorings. Since its founding, in 1942, it had enjoyed two decades of unity on the need for color-blind policies. But by 1963 this consensus was grating against the demands of organizing in the Northern ghettos. Members stirred uneasily when Congressman Adam Clayton Powell of Harlem charged in March, a few months before CORE's annual convention, that whites were dominating the major civil rights organizations. James Farmer countered that whites in the movement were "just as dedicated as Negroes and [had] just as much right and responsibility to share in this field." But CORE's founding father felt a storm of black resentment coming, and he moved to trim the organization's white sails. He cautioned a white associate, Alan Gartner, whom he considered "brilliant and dedicated" as well as "a close friend," not to seek the presidency of CORE. Otherwise the convention "might turn from the really able Negroes available to a rabid racist, who would raise the divisive racial issue on the floor." Farmer's account of a top-level staff meeting revealed the new, race-based facts of life in CORE:

We argued painfully and tearfully for hours. What of CORE's principles of interracialism and color-blindness? Some accused me of being a black nationalist, though the candidate did not. "Why can't he run? Is he competent or isn't he?" Well, Mr. Gartner agreed not to run and a floor fight was averted. . . . I was personally saddened by the cost of our decision. For, no doubt, we had denied this man categorically, because of color, and this was not at all like us. Yet I defend the compromise.[64]

The organization remained loath to surrender its interracial character. At the 1963 convention Gartner defeated a black man for the lesser post of treasurer, and the white chairman of Detroit CORE was elected secretary. Still, CORE was clearly moving to accord blacks primacy in a movement that, after all, was dedicated to expanding black rights and opportunity.

Farmer's own turn to relinquish authority came several years later. His softened integrationism never satisfied hard-line black separatists. Farmer's close ties to whites in the movement, the fact that his wife, Lula, was white, and his eloquent support of interracial unity all made him suspect to a growing faction of CORE's membership. By the end of 1965, when he resigned from CORE to work on a federal literacy program for black youths, Farmer's influence in CORE was in sharp decline.

Like SNCC, CORE chapters steadily phased out their white contingents during the mid-1960s, either through direct ouster or emotional pressure. At length CORE members felt they had no choice but to end the disparity between their founding principles and their color-conscious actions. On July 5, 1967, delegates to CORE's annual convention pruned from their constitution the term "multi-racial" in describing the group's membership.[65] The oldest of the three major Gandhian forces for integration was once more fully consistent, at the price of nearly complete isolation from white America and its own roots in civil rights activity.

Challenging the "Great Society"

To many citizens the spectacle of civil rights veterans spurning integration and white supporters appeared ungrateful and peculiarly ill timed. Television, radio, and journal accounts depicted Negroes as everywhere politically triumphant, gaining sweeping federal legislation and antipoverty programs with the aid of a thoroughly reconstructed Southern President. Few black activists, however, shared this roseate view of the movement's progress or prospects. Nor did they uniformly view the federal government as a benign, indispensable ally in the struggle for justice. Instead by the mid-sixties black activists—including some who still believed in integration—were coming to view Lyndon Johnson's Great Society as an insidious enemy of black America.

However perverse this antagonism toward Johnson may have struck most whites, it built on inescapable political logic. Civil rights legislation had exhausted the original demands of the movement, and its leaders had to expand their concerns in order to retain a constituency. Johnson's War on Poverty had anticipated the shift in black priorities and helped for a time to keep movement leaders within the Democratic fold. As disappointment with the antipoverty programs mounted, though, black critics increasingly doubted whether patchwork reforms could justify their faith either in the President or in the existing social and political system.

Blacks had muted their criticisms of federal antipoverty programs during the first year of disappointments. Then in late 1965 the White House selectively released a Labor Department study that attributed much of ghetto poverty to the absence of a strong male figure in many Negro families. Although some blacks cautiously commended the report's focus on urban problems, others scorched the study and the walls of the White House over the implicit blame of slum dwellers for their own misery. CORE's James Farmer wrote that he was "really angry," a mild flourish in a critique that excoriated white reformers:

> As if living in the sewer, learning in the streets and working in the pantry weren't enough of a burden for millions of American Negroes, I now learn that we've caught "matriarchy," and "the tangle of Negro pathology." . . . By laying the primary blame for present-day inequalities on the pathological condition of the Negro family and community, [the report] has provided a massive academic cop-out for the white conscience and clearly implied that Negroes in this nation will never secure a substantial measure of freedom until we learn to behave ourselves and stop buying Cadillacs instead of bread.

Farmer observed that the report might have done better to emphasize the benefits of an open job market than to offer "a documented basis for men in elected authority to divert practical anti-discrimination programs into an open season on 'pathological' Negroes."[66]

Apologetic footnotes followed from the Harvard sociology professor Daniel Patrick Moynihan, the much-maligned author of the White House study.

He had intended no denigration of blacks but only a portrait of urban crisis that would stimulate the lethargic federal bureacracy to take action. A close reading of the report, Moynihan added, would show that it plainly fixed white racism as the root of Negro family distress.[67] All this was true, but Moynihan also became a victim of his own flamboyant prose when he wrote that female-headed households posed "the fundamental problem" of ghetto life. Yet the report, which said little new in government or sociological circles, had the greater misfortune to appear when blacks were already whispering about the uncertainty of federal commitments to the poor. In this context Moynihan's treatise acted like a red flag to black activists poised to attack any sign of administration slackening.

Apprehension among Negroes turned into very public cynicism as the continued failings of Great Society programs pointed to a larger failure of federal concern. The inadequate sums spent during the first year of the War on Poverty diminished in real-dollar value in 1966 and 1967. Congress meanwhile tightened eligibility requirements for programs like Medicaid and began phasing out the Community Action Programs that had stressed self-determination for the poor. The assault on poverty, suspect at the outset, was proving unable even to sustain its own operations.

Black activists in SNCC and CORE sharpened their radical instincts against the grindstone of liberal belief in the social order's basic justice. During a 1966 appearance on the David Susskind show, a weekly forum in which "Liberal" was all but emblazoned on the television screen, Stokely Carmichael charged that the federal government had failed the poor. It was a disgrace, Carmichael advised his host, to let even a single child go hungry in America. The white-haired, gray-suited Mr. Susskind, a veteran intellectual moderator in every sense of the word, serenely trumped Carmichael's arguments with a single question. "Are you a *socialist?*" he asked, leaving his guest to evade the dreaded label, while deftly removing American society from the docket of moral criticism.[68] Such exchanges confirmed to already restive black leaders that the liberal drive for equal opportunity moved with a fatal complacency where poor and black people were concerned.

Martin Luther King, Jr., still seeking liberal allies, was also doing his utmost to clear away that complacent view of society's progress. Although he continued to reject communism because it denied individual liberty, King charged in 1967 that capitalism, even in its liberal guise, had "left a gulf between superfluous wealth and abject poverty."[69] Firing salvos from the left of the Great Society, he lamented the "fragmentary and spasmodic" reforms that had "failed to reach down to the profoundest needs of the poor."[70] Instead, King insisted, the federal government must either ensure full employment or provide guaranteed incomes "pegged to the median income of society, not at the lowest levels."[71] Late in 1967 King began planning a poor people's march on Washington to focus public attention on his call for "the total, direct and immediate abolition of poverty."[72]

As black leaders took stock of America's declining commitment to the disadvantaged, no single cause so outraged them as the continued escalation of Lyndon Johnson's other, undeclared war. By 1967 the federal government was spending $24 billion annually to maintain 450,000 troops in Vietnam. Absorbed by daily "body counts" of slain rebels, Pentagon spokesmen omitted from their array of numbers that it cost some $30,000 to kill an enemy soldier, or about three times what was spent to rehabilitate a Job Corps trainee. Such spending ratios seemed to black leaders more than coincidence. As Martin Luther King, Jr., told a *New York Times* reporter in April 1967, "In a real sense, the Great Society has been shot down on the battlefields of Vietnam."[73]

The ascendancy of Johnson's foreign war over his domestic one further angered civil rights leaders because racism threaded its way through every aspect of the war effort. On the basis of selective service exams blacks should have been among the groups least affected by the draft. Two-thirds of eighteen-year-old black males failed the exam, compared with less than one-fifth of white males, according to a study released in October 1966.[74] But this mattered little beside the failure of blacks to gain a voice on Southern draft boards or to match middle-class whites in following the maze of legal exemptions and deferments out of the line of fire. Lacking the same arsenal of defenses that whites employed against the draft, blacks made up 20 percent of the conscripts fighting in Vietnam, twice their percentage in the general population.[75]

The selective service considered black organizers especially fit specimens for military duty. Activists of whatever color and cause were vulnerable because they were less likely to be full-time college students, or those with the highest grades, and therefore could not easily obtain student deferments. But in practice it was an added risk to be black. In the South young Negro male protesters were virtually guaranteed involuntary admission into the armed forces. Even the epileptic James Jolliff found his classification upgraded from 4-F to 1-A after he became president of his county's NAACP chapter in Mississippi.[76] No disability, it seemed, was great enough to disqualify a civil rights worker from distant military service.

Racism followed black servicemen into the jungles of Southeast Asia. The heart of the American officer corps consisted of white soldiers, while Negro draftees figured prominently among the raw recruits who provided the mortar fodder. Bearing the brunt of fighting and dying, blacks proved better able to secure landing zones and fortifications than promotions. Saving a platoon might earn a Negro a bronze star, while the same heroism by a white soldier would qualify for a silver star and perhaps an extra stripe in rank. Familiar, personal forms of racism further reminded blacks of home, including segregated housing near some Army training bases. In all, the war effort belied the Great Society's promises of equality.

Black criticism of the war continued for a time to move in halting, tentative steps under the weight of Gallup and Harris polls showing support for the President and his Vietnam policy. Young activists, moreover, knew that the selective service considered antiwar dissenters among the most select potential draftees. As late as August 1966 SNCC circulated a leaflet on how to oppose the war circumspectly, conceding that the Negro masses were virtually as conservative as other Americans on the war. The writer discussed ways to avoid "a frontal attack on the draft," and instead approach the issue "in terms of certain acceptable American concepts." The leaflet warned that the wrong tactics could lead to black workers' "being charged legitimately with treason or even worse [sic], being un-American."[77] Black critics of the war became more strident, though, as the administration maneuvered to have them dishonorably discharged from the ranks of liberals, Democrats, and even loyal Americans. Lyndon Johnson showered praise on the NAACP and the Urban League, where a discouraging word on the President's policies was as rare as a south Texas frost; but he did not admit distinctions between black dissenters for peace and dupes of the Communist regimes in Hanoi, Peking, and Moscow. (Indeed, Johnson lashed out whenever a stray white "dove" like Robert Kennedy crossed his bipartisan foreign policy consensus.) Lacking any hope of conciliation with the President short of renouncing their position on the war, King and other black dissenters steadily moved beyond their soft-toned suggestions for curbing American commitment, to a sweeping condemnation of the country's foreign policy and the values behind it.

King matched the military escalation in Vietnam with a series of blistering jeremiads on the immorality of America's war effort. On February 25, 1967, a gathering of white liberals at the exclusive Beverly-Hilton Hotel in Los Angeles heard King berate the country's "paranoid anti-Communism" that led to involvement in "one of history's most cruel and senseless wars." In order to neutralize this war hysteria and the reflexive chauvinism behind it, King proposed to "combine the *fervor* of the civil rights movement with the peace movement," confronting the ills of American society "until the *very foundations of our nation are shaken.*"[78]

Long before King unsettled the nation's foundations, he completed the demolition of ties between the nonviolent direct-action movement and the President. Speaking at New York's Riverside Church on April 4, 1967, King fused his deepening criticisms of the war, the administration, and national priorities. He recalled a time of national promise for the poor, until the buildup in Vietnam:

I watched the [poverty] program broken and eviscerated as if it were some idle political plaything of a society gone mad on war, and I knew that America would never invest the necessary funds or energies in rehabilitation of its poor so long as adventures like Vietnam continued to draw men and skills and money like some demoniacal destructive suction tube.

Nor did the nation's war on the poor end there: "We were taking the black young men who had been crippled by our society and sending them 8,000 miles away to guarantee liberties in Southeast Asia which they had not found in Southwest Georgia and East Harlem." Americans watched on television screens the images of white and black soldiers "in brutal solidarity burning the huts of a poor village but we realize that they would never live on the same block in Detroit. I could not be silent in the face of such cruel manipulation of the poor."[79]

Although King saw himself ascending the moral heights of nonviolence, Lyndon Johnson consigned the vexing preacher to an abyss reserved for one-time allies who had fallen from his personal grace. Six days after King's Riverside speech the President turned for assistance to King's longtime nemesis FBI Director J. Edgar Hoover. The FBI had extensively spied on King since October 1963, when his renewal of ties with an alleged Communist, Stanley Levison, enabled Hoover to win approval for a wiretap from a reluctant Robert Kennedy. This surveillance failed to reveal any link between either Levison or King and the Communist party, though Hoover later charged that King was tied to the Communists, as well as being the "most notorious liar"[80] in America. But in April 1967 Hoover's personal vendetta was raised to the level of administration policy, as Johnson welcomed the circulation of FBI documents identifying King "as a traitor to his country and to his race." Congressman Joe D. Waggonner of Louisiana, deriving his insight into King from long talks with White House and FBI aides, meanwhile told colleagues on Capitol Hill that King's "earlier training" at alleged Communist bastions like the Highlander Folk School "called him on to another Communist end, mobilizing support for Peking and Hanoi in their war against South Vietnam."[81]

The public atmosphere outside the capital was nearly as uncomfortable for King. *Life* magazine suggested that King's sermonizing for surrender merited broadcast by radio Hanoi.[82] *Newsweek* pilloried the minister as a politically simplistic man, ready to sacrifice his dream of an integrated America for a country "in which a race-conscious minority dictated foreign policy."[83] "Dr. King's Error" was the headline of a *New York Times* editorial that in fact announced many errors, from his misjudging American policy to his fusing peace with civil rights and leaving the battleground of the ghettos for Vietnam.[84]

Black leaders who had hoped to avoid controversy over Vietnam now felt the hot breath of presidential exhortations to answer King's denunciations of the war. Carl Rowan, head of the U.S. Information Agency, virtually wore Johnson's banner as he jousted against the errant minister's "one-sided broadside about a matter on which he obviously has an abundance of indignation and a shortage of information." Rowan added the more revealing indictment that King had made himself "persona non grata to Lyndon Johnson." Ralph Bunche, too, analyzed King's foreign policy statements in light of needs closer to home: "I am convinced he is making a very serious tactical error which will do much harm to the civil rights movement. . . . [King's] anti-U.S. Vietnam crusade is bound to alienate many friends and supporters."[85] The chorus of black voices joining to censure King's flight from political respectability included those of sports legend Jackie Robinson; Massachusetts Republican Edward Brooke, the Senate's solitary symbol of integration; and heads of civil rights groups who refused to let qualms over a remote war destroy what remained of the liberal coalition.

Roy Wilkins and Whitney Young, Jr., understood that Lyndon Johnson's imperial presidency brooked no public corrections on Vietnam; and with or without clothes this emperor still shaped policies critical to Negroes. On April 12 the NAACP's sixty-member board of directors unanimously resolved to oppose any effort to fuse the civil rights and the antiwar movements. The Urban League's Whitney Young went further still, indeed all the way to Asia, as part of a presidential delegation to monitor (and approve) the 1967 elections in South Vietnam. Young dutifully reported that Vietnam was a showcase of democracy, a judgment at odds with widespread allegations of political murders, arrests, and ballot stuffing. Young's comments were consistent, though, with his repeated criticisms of King as rashly disloyal to the President, to the detriment of the civil rights movement.

King could not keep turning the other cheek at such rough treatment from his former colleagues. At a fund-raising dinner in Great Neck, New York, early in March 1967, he was fielding questions at the same podium with Whitney Young when the subject of Vietnam arose. Within minutes the affluent suburbanites in attendance heard more, much more, than they had bargained for.

Young told King that his position was foolish because it would alienate the President and get nothing from him. "Whitney," King retorted, "what you're saying may get you a foundation grant, but it won't get you into the kingdom of truth." Young did not appreciate the slap from King's impromptu pulpit. He asserted that his interest in the ghettos was greater than King's, slipping in a stiletto comment on the minister's robust appearance, "You're eating well." King shot back that he opposed the war precisely because of what it was doing to the ghettos. As guests riveted their gaze on the two men, the argument became so heated that King's lawyer broke it up. Afterward King felt disgusted with himself for descending to such a bitter personal exchange and telephoned Young to apologize. An hour later they exchanged good-byes, having bridged some of their personal differences.[86] In political terms, however, this remained from first to last a long-distance call.

Though King's outspoken antiwar views isolated him from both the White House and the mainstream civil rights leadership, his position elicited growing appreciation from Negroes, including the "grunts" who fought in Vietnam. This was not simply a matter of racial polarization, for by mid-1967 few Americans were wholly satisfied with a war effort whose character was murky, its aims shifting, its casualties mounting into the tens of thousands with no end in view. A decorated black paratrooper from San Francisco, Bob Sanders, expressed the mix of patriotism and frustration that seized Negroes and whites, in the ranks and on the home front: "I felt that if war broke out on the shores of America, hell, I'd fight my heart out. But we were half a world away. I couldn't see that we were accomplishing anything."[87]

Black soldiers carried an added ambivalence toward their military mission, which left them more receptive to King than to those blacks and whites trying to hound him into political exile. "We knew that Communists were supposed to be bad, and that they were trying to take the South Vietnamese's rice away from them, and that we were out there to stop them," Bob Sanders noted, in recalling his Army indoctrination.

But at the same time, the Black Panther organization, the Muslims, the Kings didn't feel that we should be out there participating in it. We didn't have nothing to gain from being there. . . . Black people were fighting with honor in Vietnam just like they did in other American wars. . . . [But] we felt they put us on the front lines abroad and in the back lines at home.[88]

King's radical critique of American policy scarcely represented all Negroes, who were no more united in their views on Vietnam than whites were. Black soldiers who had lived through assaults and jungle leeches and diseases, who took away memories of dying friends, villages destroyed by "friendly" American fire, and sanctioned platoon raids on South Vietnamese women, still spoke up for the American presence in Vietnam. Marine First Lieutenant Archie Biggers of Colorado City, Texas, thought that the nation's armed forces at least made the Communists pay for their actions, adding, "And personally I feel good about it." After returning home in 1968, Lieutenant Biggers refused to spend a hard-earned four dollars to see any film with the actress Jane Fonda, who had visited North Vietnam as an antiwar activist: "She's a sexy girl and all that other kind of stuff, but she's not the kind of girl that I'd like to admire." Still, Biggers was at odds with many younger blacks. At Howard University, where he traveled in uniform to help recruit officer candidates, students jeered him as "Uncle Sam's flunky." The women wouldn't speak to him. He felt he was "completely out of it."[89]

Whatever Negroes thought about Dr. King's antiwar stance, few—not even the radicals who once chided and mocked him—considered him "Uncle Sam's flunky," and by the late sixties that counted heavily in his favor with ghetto dwellers. Among blacks and Americans generally, King's stance shifted the notion of "moderate" protest further away from the approach of traditional civil rights groups. It also conferred more credibility on Black Power advocates who had already decided that the society needed some heavy, possibly violent, shaking. When King spoke at Riverside Church in New York on April 4, 1967, to deplore "the greatest purveyor of violence in the world today"—his own government[90]—he drew applause from white clergymen and pacifists. But at a later antiwar rally Stokely Carmichael sat in the front pew and cheered King's new mix of Christian love with fire and brimstone.

SNCC still set the outer limits of organized black dissent, with draft resistance the order of the day. Cleveland Sellers waited a day after receiving his draft notice in May 1967, then filed a legal petition to block his induction into the armed forces. Draft board officials had been so eager to punish him for his leadership in SNCC, he charged, that they disregarded medical documents proving the existence of a cardiac defect. Sellers went on to identify a greater villain—"a wealthy, hungry nation" ravaging the resources of his "brothers in Asia, Africa and Latin America." Sellers fashioned his antiwar critiques from much the same materials of indignation and dismay that led Dr. King to grieve at America's callous bombing of "little brown children." Yet King tempered his universality with a self-conscious patriotism, shunning the Third World romance of so many black radicals. No such considerations restrained Cleveland Sellers, who vowed to help Vietnam "fight to keep America from taking her tungsten, tin and rubber," and to stand with the people of other nations against American depredations: "I shall be prepared to back my brothers in the Congo when they tell the U.S. 'Hell, no! This copper belongs to me.' I shall stand ready when my brothers in South Africa move to overthrow that apartheid regime and say to the U.S. 'This gold, these diamonds and this uranium is ours.' "[91]

Stokely Carmichael's world tour of socialist states in the summer of 1967 reinforced Sellers's militant Third World perspective. In September, Carmichael declared that his fellow black activists shared a common cause with the North Vietnamese: "We are not reformers. . . . We do not wish to be a part of the Government of the U.S.A. or the American regime. We are revolutionaries." Like the Vietnamese, he added, "we want to stop cold the greatest destroyers of humanity, the American leadership."[92] Carmichael delivered this encouragement personally to dignitaries in Hanoi, capital of North Vietnam and the repeated target of American bombing missions.

Vietnam thus acted as both a catalyst and a symbol for the radicalizing of black protest. Opposition to the war helped awaken black pride and Third World solidarity. It also drove many blacks beyond the fringes of any mainstream coalition. Whereas SNCC youths had once spoken of capturing their share of the American way, lunch counter by lunch counter, now the vanguard of protest defined black integrity in opposition to national values. Concern to reform America yielded to the belief that the society was inherently too racist, imperialistic, class biased, and corrupt to be saved.

In Search of New Coalitions

To convert rage into revolution required, at the least, that black activists reach out to other groups in that sparsely settled wilderness of American politics—the far Left. Stokely Carmichael and other black radicals understood this and therefore never renounced coalition politics, only their old coalition partners. By 1967 they were seeking new allies, white as well as black. The test of fitness varied, but at a minimum every group in the alternative coalition had to accept Black Power—if black, with a respectful salute; if white, with an uncritical embrace.

Campaigns to organize in the Northern slums led to the first alliances among black radical groups. SNCC's coalition hunters tracked the Black Panthers for their base in the ghettos, while the young Panthers were similarly hungry for SNCC's fame and charismatic leadership. Contacts between Stokely Carmichael and the Panther leaders Huey Newton, Bobby Seale, and Eldridge Cleaver culminated in an announcement, in February 1968, that the two groups would merge. Carmichael became the Panthers' "prime minister," giving the two revolutionary organizations an interlocking directorate.

The allegiances linking black radical forces still left gaping holes in their revolutionary design. Their combined popular support and financial resources were far too small to let them do much more than theorize about revolution. Beyond the ghettos, however, radicalism in suburbs and college campuses was growing with each fresh account of American bombing raids and casualties. Among young whites, in particular, doubts about the war easily turned into shouts against "the system," and unconditional solidarity with black activist increasingly became a badge of white leftist commitment.

The "New Left," an amalgam of avowedly radical, mostly college-educated foes of racism, sexism, nuclear weapons, and the war in Vietnam, offered a hardy network of white support for black militants. Tom Hayden of the Students for a Democratic Society admired SNCC's pioneering efforts to create true "participatory democracy." So did Mario Savio of Berkeley's left-leaning "free speech" movement and other opinion molders of youth protest. As traditional sources of white aid eroded, SNCC and like-minded black groups probed the New Left's earnest, even imploring, overtures for unity.

Few black militants could wholly put aside their misgivings about accepting white hospitality under any circumstances. Maulana Karenga and other guardians of pan-African purity balked at entering the white radical tent, distrusting all whites too profoundly to associate even with pale-toned revolutionaries. Others warily stepped inside, in a mood of mistrust, belligerence, and cynicism. Stokely Carmichael, who moved during the late sixties from sour skepticism about white leftists to a more thorough going hostility, made the case for intransigence: "The history of Africans living in the United States has shown that any premature alliance with white radicals has led to complete subversion of the blacks by the whites, through their direct or indirect control of the black organization."[93]

Despite these anxieties, the logic of developing a broad political base kept alive black interest in an "open" revolutionary movement. Eldridge Cleaver, second to none in his perception of white evils, rose above his own, tortured feelings to rebuke Carmichael's "paranoid fear" of interracial activity. In an open letter, Cleaver dismissed as folly Carmichael's recruitment of revolutionary companions on the basis of color instead of progressive attitudes:

What you called for . . . was a Black United Front that would unite all the forces in the black community from left to right, close ranks against the whites, and all go skipping off to freedom. Within the ranks of your Black United Front you wanted to include the Cultural Nationalists, the Black Capitalists, and the Professional Uncle Toms. . . .

[What] seems to escape you, is that there is not going to be any revolution or black liberation in the United States as long as revolutionary blacks, whites, Mexicans, Puerto

Ricans, Indians, Chinese and Eskimos are unwilling or unable to unite. . . . Your talk and fears about premature coalition are absurd, because no coalition against oppression by forces possessing revolutionary integrity can ever be premature.[94]

The ideal of color-blind revolution still required some concrete incentives before militants who had clenched their fists in a Black Power sign would extend their palms in friendship toward whites. The inducements offered by New Left groups were generally limited by their upper-middle-class concerns and political weaknesses. Suffused by suburban affluence, white leftists often minimized the role of economic change in the coming millennium. Instead they struck out for goals of peace, freedom, and community that barely glanced against the immediate needs of ghetto dwellers. Worse still from the viewpoint of practical politics, their opposition to President Johnson placed them outside the party structures that controlled government funding, patronage, and legislation; in short, outside the circles of power that blacks sought to influence. Given such weak bonding material for an interracial alliance, black radicals often turned toward New Left networks only to spin vehemently away in disillusion and disdain.

The major leftist convocation of 1967, Chicago's Conference for a New Politics, revealed white activists at their most quixotic in building on the quicksands of black suspicion. At Chicago's Palmer House Grand Ballroom in early September, blacks were conspicuous—indeed dominating—among the representatives from two hundred New Left organizations. The antiwar movement offered a bond between white and black delegates that many hoped to seal by nominating Dr. King for president and a white pacifist physician, Benjamin Spock, as his running mate. But any thought that the New Politics might be spared the nation's racial agony perished even while King was delivering the keynote speech. As he invoked the ideal of nonviolence and welcomed all persons into this coalition of conscience, a hundred blacks outside the ballroom chanted to a bongo rhythm, "Kill Whitey!" They rather than King set the tone of the proceedings, turning the political convention into a racial melodrama enacted by twenty-one hundred delegates.

To project Negro unity blacks formed a separate caucus, whose conduct did not augur well for an alliance spanning the color line. An observer from the *Nation,* a journal sympathetic toward radical Negro protest, wrote that the caucus had the aura of a menacing cabal, "meeting continuously in secrecy, with shaven-headed bodyguards posted at the doors, shifting from one building and one room to another, staring fiercely at whites as they walked past them in the hallways, and taunting them as they solicited contributions for 'our black brothers in the jails.' "[95] A single caucus spokesman, Carlos Russell, represented two hundred fellow delegates in negotiations with white leaders. No one knew just how this tall, articulate, former antipoverty worker from Brooklyn had been called to preach to the unconverted rather than King or some other luminary. No Negro remembered ever having voted for Russell, though some claimed he had been selected through "African consensus." If so Russell rivaled Lyndon Johnson's skill at invoking consensus, by speaking for an assemblage that included black nationalists in African shirts and *faletas,* ministers from Dr. King's Southern Christian Leadership Conference, blue-jeaned ghetto youths defiantly staring through rimless tinted glasses, women from Mississippi's Freedom Democratic party, and SNCC members displaying Black Power T-shirts. Outsiders could only surmise what conflicts might have rent the black caucus within its private chambers. To white delegates the caucus formed a solid front of hostility as it demanded approval of a thirteen-point platform, including support for resolutions voiced at a recent Black Power conference in Newark. The Newark planks included approval of a black militia, recognition of the right of black people to revolt when they deemed it necessary, and "a national dialogue" for "partitioning the United States into two separate nations, one white and one black."[96]

Driven by guilt, white delegates passed over a substantive discussion of the thirteen points, delving instead into "their own responsibility for centuries of oppression"[97] and into the need for an atoning gesture. They went on to approve the resolutions by a three-to-one margin, also conferring on blacks sole power to amend them. The delegates then treated themselves to a standing ovation, only to be informed of the additional black demands for half the convention votes, as a matter of trust. This meant awarding complete sovereignty to a caucus that probably counted no more than a third of all delegates. But whites refused to permit crude notions of self-interest to intrude on their effort to repent a history of racism. Once again, defying conventional political logic and the usual imperatives of self-esteem, white delegates bowed to the occasion.

As blacks stood silently in wrathful waiting, whites took turns at the rostrum to concede the wisdom of granting the caucus full control. After all, they reasoned, white radicals lacked a broad base of support, whereas black delegates could presumably rally millions of their ghetto "brothers." A member of Ann Arbor Citizens for Peace caught just the mood of self-abasement that thrilled the delegates. "We are just a little tail on the end of a very powerful black panther," he said. "And I want to be on that tail—if they'll let me," he added, in a white flourish of black pride. Nor was this all. Once they surrendered power, the whites must "trust the blacks the way you trust children." Suddenly the speaker peered into the Pandora's box of white paternalism that he had tipped open, and rushed to shut it: "Now I don't mean to say it like that because these are very sophisticated people and they've taught the whites in here a hell of a lot."[98] The delegates agreed, voting more than two to one to hand full power to the black caucus. Surely now, the whites believed, they would be absolved of their tainted national past. Few were prepared emotionally or intellectually when, shortly afterward, most blacks stormed out of the conference in disgust, pronouncing whites unfit partners for coalition.

For all the language of abuse, substantial elements of the black caucus had hoped to ally with whites on the basis of mutual interests, only to hear white spokesmen proclaim that they had risen above mundane conceptions of self-interest. And if, as white speakers had freely admitted, they had no mass support to match that of black groups, what was the point of coalition? CORE's Floyd McKissick, among the Black Power advocates most receptive to ties with white groups, concluded in Chicago, "I don't believe black people are in a position to coalesce with anybody at this time and age. We have to build our own position."[99] Roy Innis of Harlem CORE was blunter in setting aside the politics of sentiment for unadorned calculation: "Why should I negotiate with the whites here? They've got nothing to deliver. I'd rather bargain with the power structure."[100]

In the aftermath some white delegates ruefully conceded that their own lack of realism had caused the conference to fail. More likely, though, whites were chiefly responsible for the elements of farce rather than failure, because the black caucus as a whole had shown little disposition to bargain with any group. Beyond their unbroken belligerence, which nourished the neuroses of white delegates, caucus members ignored warnings that some of their planks would damage any candidacy tied to the New Politics. A resolution condemning the "imperial Zionist war" drew the strongest objections. Martin Luther King, Jr., secretly delivered an appeal to the black caucus through his aide Hosea Williams. The caucus accepted only slight changes in the wording, with a parenthetical note that their hostility to Israel "does not imply anti-Semitism."[101] Much like SNCC's earlier disquisition on the Middle East, this resolution turned major contributors to the New Left, such as Martin Peretz and his wife, Anne Farnsworth, into contemptuous apostates. For most black caucus members it mattered little. The politics of emotional catharsis left little room in the Palmer House for a workable coalition with even the most serious white activists.

Antiwar rallies continued to feature joint appearances by white and black leaders, with Martin Luther King providing a central point of contact and inspiration. Yet in 1968, when protest against the war in Vietnam began to draw strong support from liberal Democrats as well as college youths, the ground swell had little connection to black interests or input. By that point the most forceful black critics of the war, once ardently courted by white radicals, had burned their bridgeheads to the New Left.

While racial animosity caused the grandly conceived coalition of black and white radicals to emerge stillborn, the alliance had already been weakened by exposure to other politically divisive ailments. The unruly diversity of New Left groups stretched the very notion of coalition beyond workable bounds. Within one organization, the Students for a Democratic Society, factions struggled and sometimes seceded over questions of terrorist violence, the correct line of Marxist thought, and charges of sexism against male officers. Black radical organizations were far fewer, yet they, too, proved capable of internal conflicts every bit as self-destructive as any seen on the fringes of American politics.

Feuds sapped the energies of SNCC, their nominal allies in the Black

Panther party, US, and other groups that each claimed to have discovered the one true path to revolution. Announcements of ideological breakthroughs by a Cleaver or a Carmichael alternated with reports of beatings and occasional murders of black activists by rival bands. Like a comet spending its force before reaching Earth, the coming black revolution was shooting into fragments unlikely to survive their own superheated trajectories.

Black radicals blamed much of their confusion on government efforts to divide and ultimately destroy them. They singled out the FBI as the chief instrument of federal repression, a charge propelled by constant suspicion but encased in hard fact. J. Edgar Hoover's minions were actively following his August 1967 directive "to expose, disrupt, misdirect, discredit, or otherwise neutralize the activities of black nationalist, hate-type organizations and groupings, their leadership, spokesmen, membership and supporters."[102] FBI infiltrators in SNCC concocted tales of a plot by Black Panther leaders to kill James Forman, which contributed to Forman's increasingly agitated and fearful state of mind. Blacks recruited by the FBI inflamed a rivalry of epithets and bullets between Maulana Karenga's cadres in US and the Black Panther party. Nor did the bureau confine its tricks to groups that spoke of armed revolution. In Hoover's expansive view, the nonviolent Southern Christian Leadership Conference exemplified a "hate-type" grouping, justifying efforts to discredit Martin Luther King, Jr., by any available fact or fabrication.

In a rare convergence of interests both Hoover's aides and black extremists attributed devastating significance to the FBI's intrigues—one side to arrogate all credit for the decline of black protest, the other side to avoid blame. In fact, however, the FBI's covert operations had little effect beyond straining the psyches of those in the movement. The bureau had routinely placed civil rights groups under surveillance in the early sixties, yet it could not keep the movement from maintaining unity, public support, and executive cooperation. If the FBI's disruptive tactics registered greater results later in the decade, by then black activists were already losing broader support and battering each other without need of a federal assistance program such as Hoover was providing.

Tactical disputes and petty jealousies were familiar vexations to a movement encompassing so many local and national organizations. Cross fire between SNCC, the NAACP, and the SCLC had become so acute by 1962, during the ill-conveived Albany campaign, that a representative of the liberal Taconic Foundation began hosting meetings aimed at easing suspicions between the major black groups. Although in 1963 the newly formed Council for United Civil Rights Leadership helped coordinate the disbursement of liberal donations, the "United" was, in James Farmer's words, "more a posture than a reality."[103] Roy Wilkins acerbically reminded other leaders at these sessions of the NAACP's preeminent role; SNCC's James Forman in turn bridled at the NAACP's political caution; Martin Luther King, Jr., politely accepted Wilkins's rebukes but maintained his independent ways. Such conferences revealed little impulse toward selfless harmony among civil rights leaders, only a precarious balancing of territorial interests and campaign strategies.

Until 1965, however, the underlying unity of aims among civil rights workers had withstood the pull of conflicting ambitions. Their joint demands, focusing on access to polling booths, schools, and public accommodations, had widely inspired Negroes or, at the least, seemed to them unexceptionable parts of a more ambitious program. This consensus gave leaders ample room to dispute the proper scope of nonviolent protest as well as their proper share of glory for its success. Yet in all essentials this competition usually proved mutually reinforcing, spurring each group to act more boldly on behalf of a common integrationist goal. Even Roy Wilkins, afflicted by obsessive envy of Martin Luther King's dominant image in the mass media, at heart understood their natural alliance. Heading toward one coordinating session, Wilkins turned to King and said without rancor, "Martin, I'm going to catch up with you yet."[104]

By the latter part of the decade that spirit of fundamentally friendly rivalry could hardly be found among Negro leaders, who no longer had a clear, unifying program. Instead, with new issues crowding their agenda, schisms developed along with calls for socialism, separatism, and armed insurrection. News coverage continued to focus on conflict between the emerging black radicals and those blacks and whites in the liberal coalition. Yet the actual lines of conflict atomized the younger black groups as thoroughly as they set them at odds with their elders in the NAACP.

As questions of economic justice absorbed black radical leaders, racial solidarity stretched and snapped from the pull of Marxist doctrine. A minority of black activists lauded Marxist ideology as a revolutionary alternative to the liberalism they despised. Rejecting the liberals' faith in the value of free enterprise and the conciliation of class interests, Marxists identified the exploitation of black (and white) labor as inherent in capitalism, disdained welfare measures as weak palliatives that did more to contain poor people than to uplift them, and advocated public ownership of all sources of production in order to ensure a fair distribution of wealth. Martin Luther King, Jr., who stopped short of embracing Marxist solutions, nonetheless concluded that Marxism offered a piercing critique of American capitalism. Other activists, including Eldridge Cleaver and Huey Newton, went further and proclaimed socialist thought as a key to the salvation of poor blacks. Some black dissidents found that Marxism offered even a sense of pan-African identity, when such rising states as Ghana and Tanzania were pursuing socialist paths. Despite all these attractions, though, Marxism ultimately acted as a point of sharp contention among black leaders.

Apart from the fragmentation of Marxist thinkers into followers of Lenin, Trotsky, Mao, and lesser doctrinal pioneers, Marxism could never unify black Americans, because it remained alien to their basic values. The great majority of blacks, including even those most contemptuous of liberal reforms, wanted a chance to attain wealth in the free-enterprise system rather than to overthrow that system. Word of the coming black socialist revolution carried little appeal to Elijah Muhammad's faithful, who continued to sharpen their small-business talents and middle-class ambitions. Nor did Marx, a white European sociologist, impress Maulana Karenga, who declared that the black revolution was not a class struggle but a battle to change "racist minds" and the patterns of black culture. "The international issue is racism, not economics," Karenga declared in 1967, taking aim at the Black Panthers, who were then embracing socialist ideals.[105] Most other black nationalist leaders, who shared Karenga's upwardly mobile, educated, middle-class status, also evinced little sympathy for the leveling zeal of a Marx or his latter-day Afro-American disciples.

Black radicals and nationalists enjoyed no greater cohesion on other questions of mutual concern. Was black cultural identity an end in itself, as Karenga claimed, or subordinate to political aims, as Newton asserted? Would blacks ignore the American government, in the tradition of the Nation of Islam, aim like Dr. King to alter national policy, or implement the threats of SNCC and Panther leaders to bring down the whole political structure? Under what conditions, if any, was "revolutionary violence" justified, and just who would act as revolutionary commander-in-chief? The rise of white and Hispanic radical groups posed a further complication regarding alliances and control within them; how many colors would the revolutionary banner display, and in what order? Avowed black militants wielded an array of conflicting certitudes on all these questions, which left little energy for protests or even community organization.

Creeping sectarianism fed on the decaying hopes of the movement. In the early sixties Negro groups were inclined to overlook differences for the sake of winning concrete reforms in a receptive political climate. But American society after 1965 was stepping away from its liberal enthusiasm of earlier years and looking complacently at the status of Negroes in the wake of civil rights legislation. The prospect of massive economic reconstruction seemed particularly frail, as the war in Vietnam pushed domestic reform further into a remote corner of the national agenda. In the absence of imminent triumphs to inspire black unity as in the past, ideological purity—and stridency—became important compensating virtues, displacing the openness needed to mobilize a mass movement.

The impulse toward arrogance in the cause of ideologically "correct" thinking afflicted Negro scholars and critics who might otherwise have helped interpret black factions to each other. Harold Cruse, the most gifted student of black protest in the 1960s, succumbed to the militant fashion of forgoing wider influence in favor of unrestrained invective. It was one thing for him to decry American society as a "deranged, tormented cultural wasteland,"[106] an observation that resembled many white critiques and in any case scored points with black cultural nationalists. It was a much different, and self-defeating, tack for Cruse to liken the progress of every other Negro intellectual to that of "a retarded child."[107] Wherever the precise dividing line lay between hard criticism and wanton vilification, Cruse had barged across it with unbecoming zeal.

Harsh and hyperbolic rhetoric was also becoming central to the leadership rites of radical Negro groups, which competed in verbally thrashing white society while lacking any real political influence. Black Panthers, decimated by police crackdowns and maintaining only a scant hold over the black urban masses, nonetheless spoke casually about killing "pig" policemen in the ghettos. CORE's director, Floyd McKissick, who tempered his black nationalism with a down-home North Carolinian amiability, stepped down in 1968 in favor of the volatile West Indian Roy Innis, who delivered harangues against integration to the few remaining members of his organization. The most dramatic infusion of angry rhetoric went to the group in sharpest decline, SNCC, increasingly derided as the Non-student Violent Non-coordinating Committee as its membership changed and dwindled. Twenty-four-year-old Hubert ("my friends call me 'Rap' ") Brown succeeded Stokely Carmichael as chairman in May 1967 and exceeded him as the nation's prime symbol of uncontrolled black anger.

Brown's transformation from a reliable, largely unknown SNCC worker into America's Negro ogre of choice owed much to the competition of black radical groups to feed reporters headline-grabbing comments. A tall, light-skinned man from Baton Rouge, Louisiana, Brown initially drew attention in SNCC only for his long, curled mustache and his flair for "rapping" with ghetto youths. His debut press conference was so halting and subdued that *Newsweek* certified him "far less flammable" than Carmichael, a judgment reinforced by his subsequent avoidance of microphones except to say, "SNCC is moving from rhetoric to program."[108] But SNCC's role as a mouthpiece of militant black America continued to draw flattering crowds of journalists, who would not let Brown rest on his obscurity. Instead they prodded him into making new, provocative, and disastrous revelations.

At subsequent press conferences the inexperienced and artless SNCC leader continued the organization's self-destructive bent for shock effect. Brown expressed his faith in guns as an answer to police oppression of blacks, urged returning black servicemen to turn their military skills against whites in the ghetto, branded the President "an outlaw from Texas," and warned Negroes trying to cool off rioting youths in Atlanta that they would be "dealt with as traitors."[109] This bravado came at a time when SNCC counted scant grass-roots support and only a few dozen full-time workers, a growing number of them in the pay of J. Edgar Hoover. These FBI moles in SNCC, and in other small, harried, and isolated black radical groups, were among the most vociferous advocates of revolution.

Sectarianism grew to the point where black extremist groups became intolerant of small ideological deviations even by their own members. As late as 1966 SNCC's participant-chronicler Howard Zinn praised its openness in welcoming "anyone who will work, regardless of affiliation or ideology."[110] SNCC members soon afterward repented in full their past indulgence of heretics. In August 1968 Stokeley Carmichael was fired from the organization, partly for failing to clear his speeches with SNCC's executive leadership. At the end of the year Cleveland Sellers and Willie Ricks refused to supervise a small black militant group in St. Louis, and for this infraction they joined the roster of SNCC legends drummed out for taking a wrong doctrinal turn. When Jim

Forman announced their dismissal, Sellers stared increduously at Ricks, overcome with surprise and embarrassment at the actions of "a group of posturing idiots" who were acting like SNCC veterans though most had joined after Carmichael's departure. As he left with his friend Ricks, Sellers asked himself, "What have we been reduced to?"[111]

No program to capture the mass imagination ever came into view for these assorted radical groups. Instead the emerging currents of black rebellion converged chiefly in their rejection of the existing order, whether expressed through the creation of new values, withdrawal into a separate ethnic universe, or attempts to wholly transform the wider society. In a period of gathering national reaction against all dissent, these currents were rapidly carrying many black activists beyond the outermost buoys of a coalition for equality.

Chapter 9

"Law and Order"

A Divided Society

IN JULY 1967, white youths rampaged through the town of Lake Geneva, Wisconsin, for no apparent reason. Police arrested two hundred unruly teens, and national guardsmen moved in for mop-up duty. Shattered windows, park benches, statues, and parking meters everywhere reminded residents of this high-spirited interlude.[1] Just a few years earlier this abrupt descent into anarchy might have been the stuff of which national television specials and Pulitzer Prize–winning reports were made. But Lake Geneva's violent seizures drew only passing outside attention, being too commonplace for surprise and too mild for alarm. SNCC's chairman, H. Rap Brown, may have overbaited white society in calling violence "as American as cherry pie."[2] Still, civil disorders were becoming the staple diet of national news, feeding as well neighborhood fears and the growing public hostility toward all forms of dissent.

As residents in Lake Geneva could attest, the breakdown of social order during the late sixties did not require racial animosity, or even the presence of black people in a community. America's first televised war sent nightly subliminal messages, in color, that violence was routine to national policy. The baby-boom generation entered college in record numbers, forming a new "ethnic" group many of whose members were detached from parental influence and disenchanted with corporations, racism, the war, and, ultimately, "the system." Their protests, through drugs, dress, long hair, sexual license, rock music, and campus politics, challenged the legitimacy of national values. Finally, Great Society programs stimulated the poor, Hispanics, native Americans, and other previously quiescent elements to organize and challenge authorities, from welfare supervisors to mayors. When even the federal government subtly encouraged assaults on current conditions, discontent could more easily lead to confrontation.

Americans who railed against lawlessness still tended to identify the face of disorder as that of a black urban male. Prejudice helped explain this tendency, but only up to a point. Blacks had been the first group to defy authority on a broad scale in the sixties, as well as to invest civil disobedience with political and moral value. By 1967 the logic of black protest acquired a harsher symbolism. Urban riots displaced nonviolent marches as the focus of media interest in blacks, with reporters vying to cover the worst domestic disorders since the Civil War.

Waterloo, Iowa, was 92 percent white, ran an integrated school system, and held black unemployment to 4 percent, but the small midwestern town suffered a race riot in mid-July 1967.[3] Wherever blacks crammed into ghettos, wherever unemployed youths encountered tight-lipped police patrols, no city or town could feel immune from sudden violence. In Buffalo, New York, the police habit of shoving young people off street corners and sidewalks cost $100,000 in riot damages. "And where else are you going to stand?" a riot leader asked. "You were probably pushed out of school and you can't get a job so you stand on the streets just hoping some money will come by or that you can get into some happening—something, something." Eyewitness accounts of a policeman firing tear gas at a busload of blacks added to Buffalo's racial tensions. The black riders were returning from City Hall, where they had discussed ways of keeping the city cool.[4]

In some cities only the uniforms clearly distinguished lawmen from riot-ers. Beleaguered police moved through the urban jungle as if in Vietnam, suspecting every civilian and tensing for ambush from any quarter. On July 15, 1967, a panicked national guardsman in Newark, New Jersey, fired at a man near an apartment window, and a hundred fellow guardsmen jumped, guns poised, looking for a sniper's nest. Police Director Dominick Spina harangued the soldier, "Do you know what you just did? You have now created a state of hysteria."[5] Spina remained on the scene for three hours to calm local and state units, and during that time the only shot fired was the one from the guardsman. No one filled this role as the voice of reason after Spina left. Two columns of guardsmen and state troopers began firing fusillades at apartments for fear of possible snipers, instead killing two people, both chatting in their homes: one was a grandmother and the other a mother of four. A block away from the main firing an apprehensive mother alertly plucked her two-year-old daughter away from a window. The woman was momentarily framed there, just long enough for a frightened young lawman to shoot her fatally in the back. Among the twenty-three lives lost in Newark's six-day riot, six were women, one was a seventy-three-year-old man, and two were children.[6]

Fear was not the only powerful emotion behind police excess. A Chinese laundry owner in Newark related how he had placed a sign saying "soul brother" in his window, to turn away black rioters. But he had not accounted for all lawless elements: from an upstairs room the store owner saw several jeeps from which soldiers and state troopers were firing into shops that indica-ted Negro ownership.[7] To these law enforcement officers the ghetto and all its inhabitants had become the enemy.

Black fury and white repression reached their respective peaks in Detroit, where a riot late in July 1967 lasted a week, leaving forty-three dead, hundreds injured, thirteen hundred buildings destroyed, and five thousand people home-less. Looting was more extensive than ever before; for the first time whites played a part, sometimes joining blacks to ransack stores in integrated teams.

Police did little, since they were greatly outnumbered by rioters and since, as one officer confessed, the lacked instructions as to what they were supposed to be doing. By contrast the National Guard acted aggressively, yet it failed to control rioters or even its own behavior. Most of the deaths during the disorders occurred when Negro bystanders moved in range of guardsmen looking for snipers. One unit of guardsmen exchanged rumors of sniper fire until a panicked soldier, "alighting from a jeep, accidentally pulled the trigger on his rifle," according to a federal report. "As the shot reverberated through the darkness an officer yelled: 'What's going on?' 'I don't know,' came the answer. 'Sniper, I guess.' "[8]

As the ghetto shot up in flames, outside authorities painstakingly discussed who had responsibility for preserving the remainder of the city. Detroit's mayor, Jerry Cavanaugh, and Michigan's governor, George Romney, agreed on the second day of violence to ask for federal aid. Lyndon Johnson was amenable but wanted Romney to admit publicly that state and local forces could no longer maintain law and order. Romney could hardly disagree that this was so, having earlier flown over the riot area by helicopter and observed, "It looked like the city had been bombed on the west side. . . ."[9] But he balked at the request to declare a "state of insurrection," for fear that insurance policies would not cover the losses incurred as a result of the riot. The governor and the mayor decided to reevaluate the need for federal troops. Hours went by, Detroit lost more blocks to fire, and a renewed request went to Lyndon Johnson. After further negotiation the first federal troops were dispatched. Their discipline and restraint were striking beside the performance of guardsmen and police, though disturbances lingered for five days. By then the damage to Detroit had surpassed that caused by any previous outbreak of urban violence since the New York draft riots of 1863.

However frightening, riots were by now half-expected by white Americans. Approving comments by middle-class blacks were more bewildering, and ominous. Although the old guard of the civil rights movement still signaled its revulsion toward urban violence, news coverage focused on blacks like H. Rap Brown of SNCC, who gloried in the destruction. In early August, Brown went to Cambridge, Maryland, site of white racist demonstrations and a vigorous Ku Klux Klan chapter, and urged three hundred furious Negro youths, "Burn this town down . . . when you tear down the white man, brother, you are hitting him in the money." The SNCC chairman had no patience for the old verities of nonviolent persuasion of the white man. "Don't love him to death," Brown demanded. "Shoot him to death." Later that night blacks rioted in downtown Cambridge.[10]

Among whites the riots pared away another layer of liberal support, while encouraging conservative speechmakers to warn that the violence stemmed from some larger devilish intrigue. Those professing sympathy with urban slum dwellers tended to limit their social prescriptions to placebos, taken with liberal doses of water: Detroit's Mayor Cavanaugh opened extra swimming pools in the ghetto, while Governor Romney suggested seeding clouds over the ghetto to bring down a cooling rain.[11] Conservatives viewed even these gestures as too generous. California's governor, Ronald Reagan, expressed a popular line among officials when he argued that the riots had little to do with intolerable social conditions. At most 2 percent of all ghetto residents were involved, he speculated, and they were nothing more than "lawbreakers" and "mad dogs."[12] Others, like Mayor Frank Sedita of Buffalo, opined that "out-of-towners" had instigated the disorders.[13] Governor Spiro Agnew of Maryland, though elected as a moderate in 1966 with strong Negro support, blamed H. Rap Brown as the root cause as well as catalyst of the Cambridge riot. Agnew hoped that authorities would jail the SNCC leader "and throw away the key."[14]

Congressional Republicans asserted that an alien plot best explained these explosions of native discontent. Senate Minority Leader Dirksen demanded an investigation to see if there was "a touch of Red" behind the riots. His counterpart in the House, Gerald Ford, denied that the riots sprang simply from conditions in the inner cities, and posited a far-flung conspiracy. "I can't help but believe," he said, "that there is in the background some national plan."[15] Ford's remarks proved him a poor sociologist but an astute politician. For the national mood was clear; in the upcoming election year, candidates who touted the virtues of law and order would be the country's most honored prophets.

Year of Reaction

Lyndon Johnson had always understood that his mandate for reform could not endure. At the height of his popularity, in November 1964, he confided that his fifteen-million-vote margin of victory in the presidential election was no match for shifting political currents:

> Just by the natural way people think and because Barry Goldwater scared the hell out of them, I have already lost two of those fifteen and am probably getting down to thirteen. If I get in any fight with Congress, I will lose another couple of million and if I have to send any more of our boys into Vietnam, I may be down to eight million by the end of the summer.[16]

By 1968 Johnson's margin of electoral safety had disappeared. Several of the most powerful corrosive agents directly threatened the civil rights movement: polarizing racial violence, disenchantment with Great Society programs, and worsening inflation, which spurred a pocketbook conservatism among the white middle class. Only a minority of Americans had opposed his reforms at the outset, but over the years even staunch liberals at least privately seconded the view of Congresswoman Edith Green that the Office of Economic Opportunity was "probably the worst administrative agency" she had ever seen in the government.[17] Worse still for Johnson's prospects of consensus was the turn in opinion among traditionally liberal, Democratic individuals who recoiled at what seemed the government's concern to aid ghetto blacks at the expense of working-class whites.

If Johnson wanted to glimpse where his once vast support for reform had gone, he need only have toured Newark's North Ward, an Italian-American enclave where voting Democratic was as much a tradition as hard work and close family ties. As rioting scorched the city, Anthony Imperiale formed a North Ward citizens committee to patrol streets and train its all-white members in karate. "Everybody says, 'don't bother 'em now,' " exclaimed Imperiale as he presented his two-fisted, and immensely popular, stance on liberal indulgence of urban black crime. " 'Leave 'em alone, and they'll calm down.' Well, it took riots that burned down half of a town before we learned." Imperiale's hard-line views did not slacken in response to reports of worsening poverty in Newark's ghettos, beside which even most lower-class whites lived in comfort. He was more concerned about urban blight in the deteriorating North Ward:

Are there no poor whites? But the Negroes get all the anti-poverty money. When pools are being built in the Central Ward, don't they think the white kids have got frustration? The whites are the majority. You know how many of them come to me, night after night, because they can't get a job? They've been told, we have to hire Negroes first.[18]

When critics cited Imperiale's "para-military" squads as destructive of legitimate government, he insisted, "I love the government and am trying to save it."[19] His continued lionization in the North Ward, where he won election to the city council, suggested that thousands of his white neighbors agreed.

While domestic issues eroded the President's stature, it was his foreign policy that finally exhausted public patience with Lyndon Johnson and all that his administration represented. The war in Vietnam quickly overextended the nation's fiscal resources, though it took some years longer to overtax the President's credibility. Throughout his escalation of the conflict Johnson had pointed to General William Westmoreland's assurance that victory was at hand, that there was "light at the end of the tunnel." Then in January of 1968 the Communists' massive Tet offensive rocked the South Vietnamese capital and showed the Pentagon to be laboring with tunnel vision of a different sort. Although Communist troops retreated with heavy losses, Washington did not weather the combat as stoically as Saigon. Antiwar demonstrations mounted, and liberal critics of Lyndon Johnson's foreign policy, including Robert Kennedy, ran well in early Democratic primaries. At the end of March, Johnson spoke to the nation about his desire for peace, then briefly noted that he would not again seek his party's nomination for the presidency.

For civil rights leaders, including those who deplored "Johnson's war," the President's fall posed more problems than it resolved. At best it blunted the trend toward escalation and denied another term to a man who had exhausted his mandate for change. Yet Johnson's withdrawal signified no new consensus to end the war, restore social programs, or heal the breach between black and white. His fate pointed instead to a society so intensely divided that even the most agile artists of consensus could lose their footing on the shrinking political center.

The middle ground was even more treacherous for black leaders, who saw the country reacting against all protests at a time when inner-city anger required that they assume a more militant stance. This paradox weighed upon the only remaining Negro spokesman who had wide interracial support, Martin Luther King, Jr. His solution, emerging more fully with each eruption of rioting, was to embrace the cause of the urban underclass, but as a radical critic of capitalism rather than as a black nationalist. Gandhian principles retained their central place in King's moral philosophy. He pledged, "If every Negro in the United States turns to violence, I will choose to be that one lone voice preaching that this is the wrong way."[20] Yet nonviolence could assume powerfully disruptive forms. Anticipating fierce resistance to appeals for redistribution of national wealth, King believed that protests might have to reach a higher level of mass civil disobedience. The minister noted approvingly that "to dislocate the functioning of a city without destroying it can be more effective than a riot because it can be longer-lasting, costly to the larger society, but not wantonly destructive." Such protests, King hoped, would "transmute the deep rage of the ghetto into a constructive and creative force." It meant, as well, a shift away from reliance on federal goodwill in favor of new tactics "to compel unwilling authorities to yield to the mandates of justice."[21]

Young urban blacks who had once scorned King as an "Uncle Tom" began to take the full measure of the man. "I'm not nonviolent myself," one youth said in giving his reaction to King's leadership. But King was "definitely in touch with the people because he had changed his stand, he had become more militant and everyone could see this."[22] Such ghetto dwellers accepted King for the first time, as they saw him moving—much like Malcolm before him—toward higher, revolutionary ground.

The question whether King's nonviolent techniques could reverse the nation's polarizing trends, let alone achieve his political goals, raised doubts even in SCLC headquarters. In the days surrounding Johnson's withdrawal from the presidential campaign King was barely sustaining his own leadership. Earlier in March 1968 he had joined the ranks of striking black sanitation workers in Memphis, Tennessee, who were seeking union recognition from the city government. King entered a crowded field of local and outside leaders, however, and found it difficult to unite the black community or to calm an atmosphere saturated with racial hostility. Violence marred a demonstration on March 28, and the press fixed on the actions of a few unruly black teenagers rather than on extensive excesses by the nearly all-white police force. Under the strain, feeling personal responsibility for the breakdown of nonviolent discipline, King lapsed into melancholic despair.

Close associates like Ralph Abernathy had grown accustomed to King's changes in mood, with periods of anguished questioning followed by a recovery of purpose and faith. Yet they had never seen his depression reach so low a point or persist so long. Their fears were not eased when King addressed a black rally in Memphis the night of April 3, offering glimmers of hope to his audience but also an acceptance of martyrdom. As often in the past, he reflected aloud on his own mortality. Longevity had its place, King told the crowd, but it really did not matter with him any more. Through God's grace he had seen the promised land of racial justice. "I may not get there with you," he said, while aides exchanged worried glances over King's tendency toward morbidity. "But . . . we as a people will get to the promised land."[23]

King astonished his entourage the next day by returning yet again from his descent into private torment to his role as uplifting minister to a movement. With relieved aides he spent the day at his motel going over details for a march to Memphis City Hall. That evening a bullet from a high-powered rifle shattered his jaw, leaving him dying on the motel balcony. The news carried through angry ghettos that Martin Luther King., Jr., the prophet of nonviolence, had been killed and that his assassin was a white man.

Blacks in Indianapolis heard the news from Robert Kennedy, who had spent the day stumping Indiana for votes in the state's upcoming Democratic primary. Like other white politicians he received sound campaign advice in the wake of King's death: stay clear of Negro neighborhoods. But the shock of the assassination, coupled with Kennedy's own memories of personal loss, drew him to his appointed rally in the Indianapolis ghetto. He found a crowd of smiling supporters uninformed of the shooting. "I have some very sad news for all of you," he began, and silenced stray shouts of joy with a request to "lower those signs, please." Shrieks covered the final words of his statement on King, then near silence as Kennedy struggled on. Discarding his prepared speech, he groped for answers to the killing and hatred seizing the nation, seeking solace for himself, for blacks, for the country:

In this difficult time for the United States, it is perhaps well to ask what kind of a nation we are and what direction we want to move in. . . . Considering the evidence . . . that there were white people who were responsible, you can be filled with bitterness and with hatred and a desire for revenge. We can move in that direction as a country, in great polarization, black people amongst blacks and white amongst whites, filled with hatred toward one another. Or we can make an effort, as Martin Luther King did, to understand and to comprehend, and replace that violence, that stain of bloodshed that has spread across our land, with an effort to understand, compassion, and love. For those of you who are black and are tempted to be filled with hatred and mistrust at the injustice of such an act, against all white people, I can only say that I can also feel in my own heart the same kind of feeling. I had a member of my family killed, but *he* was killed by a white man. But we have to make an effort in the United States . . . to go beyond these rather difficult times. My favorite poet was Aeschylus, and he once wrote, "Even in our sleep pain which cannot forget falls drop by drop upon the heart until in our own despair, against our will, comes wisdom through the awful grace of God."

Kennedy's intense, at times trembling phrases expressed faith that America would draw upon "a feeling of justice toward those who still suffer within our country whether they be white or whether they be black." Yes, he knew this was not the end of violence, lawlessness, disorder. "But the vast majority of white people and the vast majority of black people want to live together" in peace and harmony. "So I ask you tonight to return home to say a prayer for the family of Martin Luther King, that's true, but more importantly to say a prayer for our own country," a prayer for understanding and compassion for all its citizens.[24]

It was an incongruous sight: a powerful senator, scion of a wealthy family, quoting Greek verse to an audience learned mainly in the art of survival. Yet Kennedy's words broke through to his bereaved and embittered listeners. The crowd wept, then cheered for Kennedy. It cheered, too, at his hope of a peaceful, integrated nation, perhaps glimpsing in that moment the deeper understanding of which he spoke.

Few cities stayed as calm as Indianapolis. Stokely Carmichael heard the first reports in Washington and offered an early eulogy to King and all that he stood for. White society had made a mistake in killing King, Carmichael said, for he was "the one man of our race that this country's older generations, the militants and the revolutionaries and the masses of black people would still listen to."[25] Then Carmichael set out along spacious Pennsylvania Avenue, local blacks trailing, a gun belted to his body, to have a word with the white businessmen there.

The Reverend Walter Fauntroy of the SCLC tugged at Carmichael's arm trying to keep pace, pleading with him to avoid trouble. Carmichael continued to lunge ahead with long strides that carried along the much shorter minister. No, there would not be violence, Carmichael assured him as he advanced. He merely wished to request that merchants close their businesses that day in respect for King. Nearly all did so, moved by the tragedy, Carmichael's courteous demeanor, the presence of his revolver, and the large following that continued to gather behind him.[26]

Resentments of all kinds welled up in the residents as they followed Carmichael past each store. One youth recalled how he could never get eggs in a ghetto diner until noon, when leftovers were delivered from suburban restaurants. Another, who had studied for two years at Howard University until his money ran out, thought of ghetto buses that were so old they tilted heavily to one side, could scarcely reach a speed of twenty-five miles an hour, and stalled every time the driver stopped for a light or a passenger. Not so the buses in white neighborhoods: "When you go up on Connecticut Avenue you never see an old bus up there." The modern subways also were "for the crackers," with as many miles extending into white suburbs as served Washington itself. There was a simple reason for all this: the white authorities had "never in the past taken any interest in the community."[27]

As people in the crowd grew more restless, Carmichael tried to get them to disperse, if only to reorganize later more effectively. "Go home and get your guns," he said, whether to encourage violence or to deter police assault.[28] But King's murder had triggered anger that would not wait for expression. The first rocks crashed through store windows at ten in the evening. Over the next three days Americans could see their capital city from miles away by the light of seven hundred fires.

High school students and young unemployed men began the trashing of stores along Fourteenth Street, in the heart of the business district. Nonetheless, sociologists looking for distinctions between rioters and nonrioters would have had difficulty finding anyone for the second category, except the very young and the infirm. "I think almost everyone participated in the riots," a twenty-one-year-old native of Washington claimed, having been in the center of the rioting area. "I'm talking about women and children as well as adult males and also young adult males."[29]

Although rioters appeared to the public as wholly lacking in self-control, their sole common trait was that they had shaken free of outside control. There was, for example, the conduct of an articulate young man who rioted in his own, thoughtful way. While most of the looters in the Pep Boys appliance store came out with tires, lawn mowers, air conditioners, he recalled, "I stood in front of the store and tried to think of what I could use." He emerged with a big sponge, helpful for washing dishes. "I guess I might call myself a rational looter," he concluded. "I went into the store as though I was shopping." Did he then feel any guilt over his actions, which might account for his taking so little? None at all, the man evenly replied. He had advocated the burning of white-owned stores in the area. As for why he had been so moderate in looting, he surmised, "Perhaps because I'm a rather moderate person."[30]

Rioters selected their targets with greater care than outsiders realized. They consciously spared black-owned businesses and, for the most part, knew which stores merited protective treatment. A youth active in the looting and burning was indignant that white merchants would insult their intelligence by posting "soul brother" signs in their windows. "But the brothers know who owns the joint," he said. There were only a handful of black businesses, like Mama San's restaurant. Rioters burned shops all around it but left this black woman's establishment unharmed, and "she didn't have 'soul sister' up there. She wasn't even there!"[31]

Despite these precautions, not all blacks were as fortunate as Mama San. Black merchants sometimes lost their stores when fires spread, and black tenement dwellers above the stores on Fourteenth Street were left homeless. Riots simply were not conducive to precision vengeance. But regret mingled with a belief that in the long run people who lost their rat-infested, drafty dwellings, many of them lacking heat and hot water in the winter, would eventually find better homes. There was a sense, too, that such suffering was unavoidable. "Yeah, that happened, bro'," a rioter conceded, referring to losses in black property and lives. "But that's a part of war."[32]

The war cost nine lives in Washington. Nationally the toll was forty-six, of whom all but five were Negroes, in the most concentrated week of racial violence Americans had ever known. Though no city experienced the level of fury that struck Washington, over 130 lesser riots formed a bitter commemoration of King's murder. Some 2,600 fires exacted property damage of over $100 million, by conservative estimates. The disorders led to 20,000 police arrests and brought 130,000 troops and national guardsmen into domestic combat.

Throughout the rioting national Negro leaders pleaded for restraint, but with each appeal they drifted further from the mass of ghetto dwellers. Roy Wilkins appeared on national television, uncommonly distraught as he expostulated, "Looting . . . not sorrow, not anger . . . looting . . . Martin's memory is being desecrated. . . . "[33] Yes, a black youth told an interviewer weeks later, he remembered watching a television program in which "this cat from CORE," Roy Wilkins, "was rapping about this is no way to bring out a memorial" to King. When the interviewer identified Wilkins as head of the NAACP, not CORE, the youth shrugged that it was "all the same" because, "well, anyway, he's a Tom." He thought Wilkins should have blamed the whites, especially the assassin, because there might not have been a riot "if the honkey wasn't up there shooting like a goddamn maniac."[34]

Damage from the rioting included further erosion of support for black demands, though an unexpected legislative breakthrough obscured the full political toll. On April 11 Lyndon Johnson signed an open-housing act that prohibited discrimination in the sale or rental of about 80 percent of all housing. Coming at the very end of the weeklong rioting, this act widely appeared as a desperate response to the violence sparked by King's assassination. Yet as in the past congressmen acted with less regard for displays of ghetto defiance than for back-room maneuvering by civil rights leaders.

Since the open-housing measure was first proposed by liberal Democrats, in January 1968, virtually every lawmaker debating its merits agreed that the NAACP Washington chief, Clarence Mitchell, was the single dominant force in advancing the bill. One legislator decided the measure was worth a try because he "felt Mitchell deserved an effort by Congress to get this thing through." He added, "It demonstrates to the firebrands what moderate Negro leaders like Mitchell and Roy Wilkins can do."[35]

The civil rights bill of 1968 drew support not only from Democrats paying homage to Negro moderates but also from Republicans hoping to strengthen their party's record with black voters in an election year. Senate Minority Leader Everett Dirksen revived memories of his days as a leading man in earlier civil rights dramas by offering to support the bill in exchange for minor changes. Dirksen could not quite command the two-thirds majority needed to end Senate debate, but his switch pulled one powerful nonvoting party into the fray: Lyndon Johnson, who had doubted that any civil rights bill with an open-housing clause could survive, added decisive pressure that defeated a Southern filibuster on the fourth try. By a vote of 71 to 20 the Senate passed the amended civil rights bill on March 11, before stunned real estate lobbyists could organize against the measure.

The bill's prospects in the House of Representatives were still uncertain, but King's assassination changed its outlook much as Kennedy's death had done for an earlier civil rights measure. Delaying strategies by conservatives either dissolved or met defeat in roll-call votes. The Mississippi Democrat William M. Colmer, who chaired the House Rules Committee, said on the House floor that on Thursday evening, April 4, just before the assassination, "when I went home, in my humble judgment, as well as that of many others, we had the votes to send the bill to conference."[36] Overnight more than two dozen votes shifted, and the bill passed unamended on April 10. Lyndon Johnson signed the bill into law the next day. It was a landmark for the civil rights movement, though less a sign of resurgent reform than the coda to a passing era of legislative gains.

Like earlier civil rights laws the new measure focused narrowly on stopping acts of blatant discrimination, and whether it could do even this seemed doubtful. Although it covered more types of housing than the defeated civil rights bill of 1966, its enforcement provisions were far weaker and placed the burden of combating discrimination on individual litigants. In any case the web of social and economic restrictions on urban blacks was far more intricate and enveloping than were the intrigues of real estate agents. The legal scholar Alexander Bickel wrote while the bill was still under debate in the House, "The bill is a good thing, but it will not break up the ghettoes, and would not do so even if its enforcement provisions were stronger."[37]

The bill's most stringent punitive provisions were reserved for several antiriot amendments. Any person traveling interstate or using the mail, telegraph, telephone, radio, or television with intent to riot or incite to riot would be subject to a penalty of five years in jail and a fine of $10,000. Other clauses in this congressional homage to law and order focused on interstate conspiracies, as if to dismiss the notion of discontent in the ghettos. The bill's priorities were clear: modest federal involvement in black efforts to flee the ghetto, but overwhelming force to curb all restiveness within it.

These warning signals did not deter King's closest aide, Ralph Abernathy, from pursuing plans for a poor people's march on the capital. In his last days King himself had virtually stopped speaking about the march, becoming more concerned after Johnson's withdrawal not to embarrass the Democrats in an election year. But the Reverend Abernathy felt compelled to show through bold, even reckless, action that the movement after King remained a powerful force.

Abernathy had worked at King's side, and uncomplainingly in his shadow, since their joint efforts to launch the Montgomery boycott in 1955. Raised in rural Alabama, educated in a poor black college, Abernathy lacked King's polish but provided the common touch that sometimes eluded his erudite colleague. Frequently King would awe a Negro congregation with discourses on *agape* and other Christian or Gandhian terms, after which Abernathy would step in to say, "Now, let me tell you what that means for tomorrow morning," and explain the day's protest strategy.[38] Whenever King contemplated the likelihood of his own assassination, he emphasized his desire that Abernathy succeed him as head of the SCLC, though his equally fatalistic friend insisted this was pointless since they would surely be killed together. Now, in the spring of 1968, Abernathy had not only to establish his own style of leadership but also to direct the most ambitious black protest of the decade.

As conceived by King and his inner circle late in 1967, the Poor People's Campaign aimed to shift the focus of black activism to economic issues, develop a coalition of all poor groups, and pressure both government and private business in unprecedented ways. These included construction of glaring shantytowns in the capital to dramatize the plight of the poor, and repeated demonstrations courting arrest outside federal buildings. If this phase of nonviolent disruption could generate mass support, the campaign would then escalate to demands for corporate recruitment and training of poor people, backed by nationwide boycotts of reluctant companies. Here was a strategy for change far more militant than that of the earlier March on Washington in August 1963, a largely middle-class affair that had emphasized brotherhood and civil rights. Yet also unlike that earlier march, which occurred amid rising liberal enthusiasm, the Poor People's Campaign moved into a conservative headwind that swept over Congress and threatened even the mildest rallies with defiance.

Troubles descended on the campaign even as Abernathy and other SCLC ministers were invoking divine sanction for a righteous cause. On May 12, 1968, the first volunteers arrived before anyone quite knew what to do with them. Despite hurried attempts to house demonstrators, organizers discovered that their "Resurrection City" could not be built in a day. Construction crews managed to set up fifty tentlike, A-frame shanties of plywood and plastic for the first three hundred residents, who then shivered around open campfires and traded anxious rumors on the completion dates for electric power, water, and sewage facilities. Beginning May 23 heavy rains kept the marchers ankle deep in mud, depriving many of shelter, trash collection, and other spare amenities. The journalist Milton Viorst recorded that "preoccupation with physical survival diverted all attention from political questions, and kept the encampment shrouded in gloom. Almost no one attended the nightly revival meetings, which had been a standard feature of civil rights campaigns since Montgomery."[39]

Crippled by the elements, the Poor People's Campaign adjusted even less astutely to the inclement political climate. With Northerners on Capitol Hill averting their gaze from the shanties, and Southerners huffing about Communist-inspired rebellion, the ministers in the SCLC fumbled their once sure touch with the media and their own recruits. Slum dwellers parading as marshals harassed reporters and workers, yet the SCLC's leadership feared to dismiss these rough symbols of the ghetto poor. Instead the Reverend James Bevel insisted to annoyed journalists that an effective social movement must welcome the masses, not simply middle-class paragons of restraint. After ten days of explaining away the shoving, pummeling, and other "incidents," the SCLC's worried ministers at last ordered home two hundred street-gang members who, Bevel acknowledged, "went around and beat up on our white people."[40] But to many whites, and Negroes, too, this stand for nonviolence seemed a late, discouragingly faint echo of Dr. King's moral legacy.

From this rocky start the Poor People's Campaign moved on to repeated disappointment. Forty picketings of government buildings in the space of five weeks secured little attention and no aid to the poor. Abernathy briefly raised hopes for a massive culminating rally by enlisting the aid of Bayard Rustin, who had privately opposed the whole campaign as too prone to degenerate into violence. Rustin first tried to revive the campaign's image among white liberals by translating the ministers' militant rhetoric into limited and specific demands for jobs programs and welfare reform. But Abernathy publicly derided these initiatives as inadequate, and Rustin resigned. The Solidarity Day rally on June 19 still drew fifty thousand demonstrators, but it was small-scale in numbers and impact compared with the historic march in 1963 that inspired it. In this event, as in the campaign generally, Abernathy remained unclear about legislative priorities and unable to budge federal officials toward economic reform. Instead he settled for a bitter war of words with "a racist Congress"[41] and pointed vaguely to escalating protests.

Just who would provide the nonviolent muscle for these new measures remained in grave doubt. Few ghetto dwellers ever entered Resurrection City, whose total population never exceeded twenty-five hundred and usually hovered around five hundred. Cultural differences between Mexican-Americans, Indians, and blacks in the shanties outweighed any feelings of unity over economic goals. The Hispanic and Indian contingents especially resented the Negro ministers' tendency, ingrained over many earlier campaigns, to equate coalition with their own commands. Although the SCLC tried to reassure its prospective allies, ethnic tensions continued to jut out from a facade of class solidarity, at times to the point of public insult.

The New Mexican rebel Reies Lopez Tijerina, a latter-day caudillo whose armed posse patrolled a small southwestern principality, stood out among the SCLC's tentative partners. Tijerina clearly had little faith in nonviolence as an instrument of social change, nor was he much impressed by the SCLC's economic aims. His single-minded concern was to recover lands that he claimed the American government had illegally seized from his ancestors more than a century earlier. To placate the Hispanic leader, Abernathy adopted his demands, marched with him, and at a news conference hugged him as a visual proof of their unshakable alliance. Yet a single missed signal between the two groups could send tempers flaring, as in a highly personal shouting match between Tijerina and Hosea Williams over who had authority to approve marches.[42] In the aftermath of the misnamed Solidarity Day, Tijerina quietly sent his followers back to their desert dominion rather than swell the population of Resurrection City.

Even a détente among their leaders provided no assurance that the restive Negro, Indian, and Hispanic protesters would not turn against each other and all authority. The various ethnic contingents at one joint rally proved that proximity was a poor substitute for unity, as bored marchers smashed windows and tossed each other into public fountains. The final weeks of the campaign revealed little angelic feeling in Resurrection City. Incidents of robbery, assault, and rape were so common that Abernathy, Williams, Bevel, and other key organizers despaired of finding any way to enforce discipline. In contrast to the 1963 March on Washington, whose dignity drew presidential praise, the

1968 campaign confirmed the image of protesters as a rabble to be ignored or routed.

The debacle lingered on into the last week of June. Early on, Abernathy had pledged that demonstrators would besiege the capital indefinitely, but by the time Washington police had reluctantly arrested the 170 remaining denizens of Resurrection City, those who designed the campaign seemed more relieved than aggrieved. Hosea Williams, never sanguine about the campaign, confided his joy that the government got them out of "that mudhole" so that they could go back to pertinent organizing "instead of wasting half our energy trying to keep kids from throwing rocks." Andrew Young, who spoke for the SCLC during Abernathy's brief stay in jail, conceded at a press conference, "In one sense, whoever ran us out maybe did us a great favor."[43]

Although in his first leadership test Ralph Abernathy did not distinguish himself by tactical acumen, it is doubtful whether anyone, including King, could have guided the Poor People's Campaign to success. Part of Abernathy's difficulty stemmed from the fact that Washington was just emerging from its ordeal by arson the preceding month, leaving officials in no mood to reward or even humor new signs of militancy. But the minister's central problem was his goal, one that went far beyond the objectives of the earlier civil rights movement and of current political acceptability. His demands for an expanded federal commitment to end poverty came when the white middle class was already rebelling against the Great Society's much more limited initiatives. Had the marchers come in a spirit of conciliation during a stretch of sun-filled days, with King to speak and Rustin to anticipate every logistical trap, they would still have contended with a society in the throes of conservative reaction. Abernathy may well have been right in claiming afterward that had King lived, Washington would not have seen a poor people's march.

The presidential primary campaigns, overlapping and overshadowing the protests in the capital, revealed the public's abiding concern—law and order. On the left wing of the Democratic party Robert Kennedy gave a mild recital on the theme, reminding audiences that as a former attorney general he knew how important it was that people respect the law. Traveling in the right lane of the Republican race, Ronald Reagan spoke of expelling college demonstrators and punishing universities that encouraged disruptive student behavior. Reagan's stiff warnings to dissidents showed once more how intent many Americans were to curb disorder quite apart from any racial overtones. Yet those overtones were ever present. It was therefore logical that the leading purveyor of law and order was the third-party presidential candidate, George Corley Wallace of Alabama.

Once dismissed by political pundits as a relic of more primitive times, Wallace proved that his demagoguery was not limited to a single cause or era. In 1968 he spoke of freedom from big government and the right to choose one's neighbors and the school one's children attended. Law and order? Yes, Wallace believed in that with a vengeance, quite literally. Any protester who lay down in front of his automobile would not rise again, Wallace threatened. Wallace did not invoke explicitly racist slogans. He had no need. His obstruction of the Alabama schoolhouse was still a part of the country's collective memory. Wherever racial tensions rose, North or South, cries of "Wallace for President" became a favorite taunt among disgruntled whites.

Negro hopes of redirecting the national mood back toward goals of racial equality, or at least conciliation, rested on Robert Kennedy's belated but formidable drive for the presidency. Kennedy's surpassing popularity among blacks related only loosely to his left-of-center reliability on reform causes and his emphasis on racial issues. His opponents for the Democratic nomination, Senator Eugene McCarthy of Minnesota and (after Johnson's withdrawal) Vice-President Hubert H. Humphrey, were nearly as bedecked as Kennedy in liberal position papers, distinguishable mainly to aides versed in their fine print. But alone among major-party aspirants Kennedy drew equally loud cheers from veterans of ghetto riots, striking Mexican-American grape pickers, American Indians rebelling against the squalor of their reservations, and blue-collar white workers bitter about government "coddling" of nonwhites. Observers knowingly detected the old Kennedy magic at work, though on closer view the young, slight, somewhat rumpled "Bobby" lacked the same imposing presence and easy self-assurance of his martyred brother. Rather his charisma flowed from a haunted empathy with the alienated and from a stubborn faith, offered in high-pitched Boston Irish tones but at heart recalling the late Reverend King's soothing cadences, that somehow the country "can do better." To many Americans, rocked by the turbulence of the late 1960s, this mingling of vulnerability with heartening echoes of New Frontier resolve made for an appeal well suited to difficult times.

For black Americans, Kennedy's bid for the presidency meant even more, if possible, than his brother's candidacy eight years before. Since resigning as attorney general in 1964 and winning election as New York's junior senator, Bobby Kennedy continued to brood over the boundaries of possible change in American society. His reflections spilled over in many directions: siding with the demands of American Indians, whose vote-getting potential was negligible; breaking bread with the ailing migrant workers' union chief Cesar Chavez to end his long protest fast; organizing a black-run corporation in the Bedford-Stuyvesant ghetto of Brooklyn; evenly telling a friend that if the country's institutions could not meet the needs of the disadvantaged, "Then we will have to change the institutions."[44]

Acutely conscious of power politics, Bobby Kennedy enjoyed ties to old political bosses as well as New Left intellectuals. Whether he would ever fully vent his radical instincts, or survive them, drew conflicting speculations from political analysts—including the coterie of aides surrounding him. On June 5, 1968, when a lone gunman assassinated Robert Kennedy after a major primary victory in California, his potential leadership of a new coalition for change was still far from fully tested. What was evident to many, and painfully clear to black Americans, was that Kennedy's murder removed the last remaining figure able to calm the polarizing forces sweeping the country.

The major-party nominees did not try to rival George Wallace's imprecations against "pointy-headed bureaucrats" (big government) and "anarchists" (all dissenters), but both Democrats and Republicans reflected the country's conservative mood. Vice-President Hubert H. Humphrey, the Democratic party's clear choice for the presidency after Kennedy's assassination, had the greater distance to travel toward the new political center. Only two years earlier Humphrey had urged an expansion of social programs to end the causes of ghetto riots, and added that if he were forced to live like an animal in a tenement slum, he would have "enough spark left" in him "to lead a mighty good revolt."[45] Humphrey's updated liberal orations now included an admission that the Great Society should not become too great; smaller government could be better government.[46] Humphrey also fortified his credentials on law and order when, in August 1968, Chicago police flailed away at disruptive white youths, peaceful dissidents, journalists, and other suspected troublemakers outside the Democratic convention. It was the most dismaying televised spectacle since the Selma march, but Humphrey praised Mayor Daley's vigor in combating anarchic forces. The Democratic presidential nominee saved his reflections on the horror of this episode for a few trusted colleagues, as he moved upstream against his own long record of tolerance toward dissent.

For the Republicans, Richard Nixon once again sought the middle way, this time between Humphrey and Wallace. He resisted advice to go after Southern white votes by any means necessary, including racist appeals. That seemed to Nixon too ignoble and probably self-defeating, since he could not outdo Wallace and might simply lose Northern Republican support. Still, Nixon had come to believe after the 1960 election that nothing he did would win over Negro voters. He therefore aimed in 1968 for détente with the white South and distance from black protesters.

Nixon's nomination of Spiro Agnew as his running mate and political hatchet man suggested his standards for a centrist campaign. Agnew had been a liberal governor in Maryland until riots in his state gave his rhetoric a strident cast, ignoring inner-city grievances and encouraging strong police measures. It proved to be the best-timed leap onto a bandwagon hurtling to the right since 1919, when Governor Calvin Coolidge of Massachusetts had shed his progressive labor record for an image of strikebreaker at the height of the Red Scare. While Agnew intoned "law and order" instead of "public safety," as Coolidge had done forty years before, the general result was similar: Republican leaders began thinking of him as providing sturdy ballast for a presidential ticket. The Nixon camp rejected the first choice of conservative Southern Republicans, Ronald Reagan, for fear of straining the party too far toward Goldwaterism. But the selection of Agnew pleased Senator Strom Thurmond of South Carolina, the Democrat turned Republican who had become Nixon's gateway to the South.

Once nominated, Agnew hammered at conservative themes with unrestrained vigor. His speeches featured ethnic epithets for Poles and Asians, swipes at Humphrey as soft on rioters and on communism, and almost nothing at all on Negro concerns. Whereas Nixon called for "a militant crusade against crime," insisting that "the right to be free from domestic violence has become the forgotten civil right,"[47] Agnew promised more. Addressing blue-collar workers in Norridge, a Chicago suburb not far from where King had been stoned in 1966, Agnew declared that a Republican victory would guarantee a curb on dissent. He explained that confusion over what constituted legitimate dissent had contributed to rising crime rates.[48] Agnew displayed less interest in the problems and opinions of inner-city blacks. When a reporter asked why he had spoken in only one ghetto during the campaign, Agnew retorted, "If you've seen one city slum you've seen them all."[49]

Nixon and Agnew, separately traveling high and low roads through the heartland of public opinion, reached the White House in November. Their victory was narrow enough to console civil rights leaders, nearly all of whom had endorsed Humphrey. With 43.4 percent of the vote against Humphrey's 42.7 percent, Nixon could scarcely claim a clear mandate for any new policy. He won, moreover, for many reasons unrelated to race or even his own candidacy: Humphrey's ties to Johnson, public discontent over the war, disaffection of young Democrats from a nominee representing the "Old Politics." Still, signs of racial reaction throughout the nation, and especially in the South, left black leaders in gloom. The reaction extended to relatively moderate states like Georgia, where George Wallace swept the presidential balloting. In greater Atlanta, whose residents saw themselves as models of racial progressivism, voters rejected two liberal congressional candidates in favor of extreme right-wing Republicans.

On the national level blacks found themselves sharply at odds with political currents for the first time since 1952. George Wallace, arch-opponent of the Great Society, drew a protest vote of 13.5 percent, the best showing by a third-party candidate in forty-four years. Nearly one in every seven voters had cast their ballot for a man whose one secure niche in history was as a defender of white supremacy in an age of black advancement. And while 85 percent of the Negro voters chose Humphrey, veteran of many campaigns for minority rights, 57 percent of the total electorate rejected this symbol of Great Society liberalism. For blacks, then, as for supporters of social reform generally, the most significant landmark of this election was the mandate voters had emphatically denied.

The Silenced Minority

Unlike his Democratic predecessors in the White House, Richard Nixon had always shied away from a strong public commitment to civil rights. Perhaps for that reason his vacillations on racial issues engendered a history of bitter criticism, encapsulated by Martin Luther King's private reference to Nixon as a "moral coward."[50] That he was now about to become President, still carrying his same uncertain moral compass, pointed to difficult days ahead for the remnants of the movement.

Nixon realized that he entered the White House to the groans of black spokesmen. Pained by their hostility, believing himself to be a friend of their cause, he made numerous overtures as President in hope of dispelling their cynicism. Yet in seeking recognition as a responsible leader on race issues, Nixon contended not only with festering suspicions but also with his own desire for the Wallace vote.

As President-elect, Nixon conferred with six Negro leaders, including Ralph Abernathy and the grand exalted ruler of the Improved and Benevolent Order of Elks, also known as the black Elks, but excluding militants. Nixon pledged to his guests that he would "do more for the underprivileged and more for the Negro than any President has ever done."[51] Shortly after the inauguration Roy Wilkins reluctantly accepted the President's invitation to a dinner gathering, at which Nixon encouraged candid criticism if he did "anything wrong." The NAACP chairman left predicting that the President fully intended to rectify the problem of Negro disaffection from him. Privately, though, Wilkins thought of an old folk saying: "He say so good—but he *do* so po'."[52]

Nixon in fact proved a domestic leader of vision, but without the resolve to follow any reform idea too far from his conservative political base. Convinced of the saving power of capitalism, he increased subsidies to the Office of Minority Business and pressed unions to adopt timetables for admitting minorities, beginning with Philadelphia's construction unions. He also advocated a guaranteed annual income for every American family, perhaps the boldest idea for welfare reform since the New Deal. Yet each one of these measures encountered strong opposition, and, one by one, Nixon abandoned them all. Concern to trim social spending kept aid to black entrepreneurs at minimal levels, while union pressures—including violent demonstrations against black workers—led Nixon to quietly close his Philadelphia experiment. An unexpected snare awaited his welfare reform measure: the usual conservative cries of extravagance were joined by liberal charges of tokenism for the poor. After the bill twice passed the House, only to die in the Senate, Nixon lost interest in reviving it. Instead he turned to familiar incantations on the need to get welfare cheats off the rolls.

The President gave more sustained attention to conservative themes, most of which placed him in conflict with civil rights groups. He approved an unfortunately worded memorandum from his urban affairs adviser Daniel Patrick Moynihan, stating that race relations could profit from "a period of benign neglect."[53] Endlessly explained, the phrase still suggested calculated indifference to Negro interests, and Nixon's specific policies tended to confirm this view. While black leaders urged more effective training and employment programs, Nixon relaxed pressure on federal agencies to employ members of minority groups and vigorously dismantled key Great Society agencies, including the Office of Economic Opportunity. Clifford Alexander, the black administrator of the OEO, charged that the President lacked commitment to increased corporate hiring of minorities. Alexander resigned within months of his appointment.[54]

Nixon's calls for "law and order" also became noticeably fainter when civil rights statutes were at issue. Lax enforcement negated the impact of open-housing legislation. Attorney General John Mitchell further opposed extension of the Voting Rights Act of 1965, on the grounds that there was no longer any special problem with discrimination in the South. NAACP lobbyists worked overtime to counteract Mitchell's attacks on the bill's vital "pre-clearance" clause, which required districts guilty of past discrimination to seek federal approval before amending their electoral procedures. Civil rights groups saved their sharpest howls of outrage, however, for the administration's repeated forays against the liberal Warren Court.

"The courts don't understand the folks," President Richard Nixon told his speech writer William Safire as he mulled a response to recent desegregation rulings. "Forced busing is wrong, and I don't care if it does sound like demagoguery—I want to say so loud and clear." Nixon emended his thoughts—he would not stoop to give "a Wallace-type speech." Governors, like Ronald Reagan in California, "can emphasize the negatives—all the failures of integration. Seventy-five per cent of the people, black and white, will agree—I know this country. But it's not right—maybe it's okay for a candidate, not for a President," who would have to carry out the law. Yet was this neither a time to rehash old civil rights laws nor "the place for a long defense of Negro rights." Americans were weary of changes in race relations, Nixon expounded. "Forget the polls," he said; "people don't tell the truth to pollsters in this. I think the majority of people are against integration. The majority are scared to death of the black militants, and of the white militants as well." And if Nixon would not act the demagogue, still he added, "We've got the support of the majority, white and black, on this, and I want them to know the President is strongly on their side."[55]

The President was reflecting on the major test of his civil rights commitment—the school desegregation issue that had run through every presidency since the *Brown* decision. In 1968 the Supreme Court changed the rules somewhat by requiring schools to prepare desegregation plans that promised "realistically to work *now.*" It suggested busing as one possible means to achieve racially mixed school systems.[56] In that same year the Department of Health, Education, and Welfare toughened its guidelines for compliance with the courts by calling for "terminal desegregation" on penalty of forfeiting federal funds. But if the law was clear-cut, the political cost of carrying it out appeared even more compelling to the President.

Southern Republicans called on Nixon to stand up to the polarizing partisans of the NAACP. They expected him to suspend the hated HEW guidelines until he could place enough strict constructionists on Southern courts and the Supreme Court to keep *Brown* forever vague. A more refined ultimatum arrived in the form of a letter from the Democratic senator John Stennis of

Mississippi, who was the indispensable floor leader for Nixon's top legislative issue, an antiballistic missile system. Stennis regretted that the unrest likely to arise from imminent school desegregation might require him to spend some time back home, away from his tasks on Capitol Hill. Faced with Stennis's quietly disarming threat, Nixon instructed Justice Department officials to stonewall the Court's desegregation ruling.

Although experts in the HEW's Office of Education had drafted complete plans for Mississippi districts, Justice Department lawyers told federal judges that they needed more time to prepare. On August 19, 1969, HEW Secretary Robert Finch overrode his own experts and alerted the federal judge John Brown that to desegregate on such short notice "must surely . . . produce chaos, confusion and a catastrophic educational setback to the 135,700 children, black and white alike, who must look to the 222 schools of these Mississippi districts for their only available educational opportunities."[57] Judge Brown chose to avoid catastrophe by postponing the issue until December, when HEW could present to the court a new set of terminal desegregation guidelines.

In the interim Nixon pirouetted left and right as Southern congressmen, civil rights leaders, and conflicting administration aides buffeted him with urgent advice and unavoidable courses of action. The President considered granting a sixty-day stay of any cutoff of school funds, to appease Thurmond and his allies, but under counterpressure from Finch he offered a compromise plan. The delinquent districts would lose their federal funds but could recover the full amount if they came up with acceptable desegregation plans within sixty days.

At a press conference on September 26, 1969, Nixon seized the middle ground on the school controversy and pronounced it the moral high ground: "It seems to me that there are two extreme groups. There are those who want instant integration and those who want segregation forever. I believe that we need to have a middle course between those two extremes." The speech writer William Safire characterized Nixon's approach to desegregation as "make-it-happen, but don't make it seem like Appomattox."[58]

Civil rights leaders thought Nixon's position more closely recalled images of Tara. The President's attempt to suspend enforcement of HEW's guidelines led the NAACP Legal Defense and Education Fund to sue the Justice Department. Even before a unanimous Supreme Court ruled for the plaintiff in October 1969, Roy Wilkins reached an informal verdict at an NAACP convention. Nixon was guilty of "breaking the law," he ruled. Wilkins departed from his normally unflappable demeanor to add, "It's almost enough to make you vomit. This is not a matter of too little, too late. Rather it's a matter of nothing at all."[59]

Lower-level officials provided the administration's only consistent civil rights initiatives. Nixon's retreat on school desegregation sparked virtual civil war in the Justice Department's Civil Rights Division. Some lawyers refused to defend the government's plan to defer enforcement of the HEW guidelines.

Others went further, either resigning in protest or secretly passing data to attorneys for the NAACP Legal Defense and Education Fund. John Mitchell attacked his own staff for disloyalty, while the head of the Civil Rights Division had to lecture his lawyers on their proper responsibility.

One zealous federal appointee succeeded in pulling the administration into a reluctant, silent partnership with the courts. On July 10, 1970, Commissioner of Revenue Randolph Thrower, a liberal Republican from Atlanta, revoked the tax exemption for contributions to lily-white schools. Strom Thurmond gave his most charitable interpretation of this outrage: "I can only conclude that a group of liberal advisers around the President are misleading him and that their advice will bring disruption to the nation."[60] Nixon assured Thurmond and other Southern Republicans of his solidarity. Yet Attorney General Mitchell sustained this adverse tax ruling. The offending commissioner also retained his post despite Southern demands that he be fired. Such minor slaps at segregationist schemes, however, were notable mainly for their rarity. For the President had made a "Southern strategy" the basis of his ambitions for 1972.

In looking South, Nixon followed a course largely set by political necessity. Elected a minority President, he had to expand his base of support. As liberals had proved when they dismissed his Family Assistance Plan as an inadequate gesture, the President could not hope to charm substantial numbers of Northern Democrats. Wallace voters were more pliable. They saw little future in the party of Hubert Humphrey, the party that had appeared to sweep them aside in order to raise up Negroes. By reaching out to these people, Nixon bid to strengthen his presidency by engineering an enduring political realignment.

A Southern strategy did not necessarily mean a desertion of civil rights aims. Rather it held the potential to free the civil rights movement of its anti-Southern image. For years liberals tended to portray the Mason-Dixon line as a moral border, inevitably to the detriment of white Southerners. Nixon had an opportunity to ease the psychological battering administered by Northern journalists and legislators. The "bully pulpit" of the presidency had passed to him, from which moral height he could praise the South's difficult passage toward racial equality as an example to inspire the nation. Such a course could appeal to sectional pride, while still keeping the aim of racial justice in the forefront of national concern. This was not, however, the Southern strategy Nixon chose when he pondered how to woo the constituency of George Wallace.

Nixon serenaded the South in a discordant key peculiarly his own. A man of deep insecurities and long-held grudges, he understood the undertones of white resentment, fear, and suspicion better than the region's harmonies. His polarizing style found ample play in a period when racial animosities remained dangerously exposed.

Vacancies on the Supreme Court gave Nixon a chance to show how doggedly he would pursue his Southern strategy. It also brought out the extent

to which his courtship of the South involved a defense of segregationist sentiment. To fill the seat of the departing justice Abe Fortas late in 1969, he chose
South Carolina's federal judge Clement Haynsworth. In an earlier time Haynsworth might have glided to a rapid confirmation, but Democrats were looking
to repay a Republican investigation that had led Fortas to resign amid financial
scandal. NAACP and AFL-CIO lobbyists prolonged Haynsworth's hearing
with reports of racist and anti-union conduct. Haynsworth objected that some
cases cited in his record went back to 1958, "when none of us was thinking or
writing as we are today."[61] The Senate probed further and uncovered financial
conflicts of interest in several of Haynsworth's rulings. With seventeen Republicans deserting their party leader, the Senate rejected Haynsworth 55 to 45.
Attorney General Mitchell snapped, "If we'd put up one of the twelve Apostles
it would have been the same."[62] President Nixon promptly nominated another
Southern justice, G. Harrold Carswell, still more conservative, antilabor, and
blatantly segregationist.

The NAACP and other critics of Carswell's nomination went through
Carswell's record, and this proved a devastating tactic. His legal abilities were
limited, as was evident in the frequent reversal of his decisions in higher courts.
Seven of eighteen judges in Carswell's jurisdiction refused to sign a telegram to
Nixon endorsing the nomination. Carswell's tolerance for blacks was still more
limited. In 1948, during a losing campaign for the Georgia legislature, he had
stated his belief in the doctrine of white supremacy. Later, as a federal judge in
the Fifth Judicial Circuit, Carswell implemented this belief by adopting a hostile attitude toward Negro plaintiffs and attorneys in civil rights cases. As a
private citizen he worked tirelessly to exclude blacks from his local social club.

Under this scrutiny, support of Carswell's nomination changed from a
responsibility to an embarrassment for Senate Republicans and Southern
Democrats. Senator Ernest Hollings, Jr., of South Carolina, who led the fight
for Haynsworth's confirmation, believed that Carswell "was not qualified to
carry Judge Haynsworth's law books,"[63] but voted for him anyway. Roman
Hruska of Nebraska admitted that Carswell did not approach the caliber of his
predecessors but insisted, "We can't have all Brandeises, Frankfurters, and
Cardozos." Hruska moved well beyond his lackluster defense of Carswell to
become a tribune of the lackluster. "There are a lot of mediocre judges and
people and lawyers," he noted, "and they are entitled to a little representation,
aren't they?"[64] Such rank egalitarianism won few votes from wavering senators.

Confronted with evidence of Carswell's racism, as well as incompetence,
Nixon pressed on. In an angry letter to the Senate he asserted his right as
President to have justices of his own choosing. By a vote of 51 to 45, the Senate
disagreed. In a press statement on April 9, 1970, Nixon found a common cause
in the rejection of his two nominees: "They had the misfortune of being born in
the South." He went on, as if spying the ghost of William Tecumseh Sherman
marching through the Senate chambers: "I understand the bitter feeling of
millions of Americans who live in the South about the act of regional discrimi-

nation that took place in the Senate yesterday. They have my assurance that the day will come when men like Judges Carswell and Haynsworth can and will sit on the high Court."[65]

No one could say how much Nixon's defiant oration was a matter of interest-group politics and how much fused Nixon's own bitter persona with the resentments of a whole region. It was, in any case, a more persuasive statement of empathy than any he had made on the plight of minorities or the poor. To many white Southerners—and blacks—Nixon had earned his stars and bars as an honorary son of the Lost Cause. "You know," one White House aide exclaimed to another, "the President really *believes* in that Southern strategy—more than he believes in anything else."[66]

With public opinion shifting away from minority interests and the President hunting for votes in Wallace country, black activists floundered without clear direction. Voter registration increased, along with the number of elected black officials—370 in 1968—but the movement to advance Negro rights abruptly ebbed. The Birmingham protests, the March on Washington, the Selma marches, and even the Poor People's Campaign seemed events of a remote era. At the NAACP Clarence Mitchell no longer pressed for sweeping reform legislation but instead labored mainly to save existing laws and stave off racist appointments. Ghetto risings in large cities declined while black communities recovered from past rioting. Black radicals meanwhile continued their helpless drift toward the margins of influence.

James Forman's lone demand in July 1969 that whites pay "reparations" to blacks for centuries of racism probably achieved more respectful attention than any other black militant thrust in the Nixon years. Forman's ability to catch a tide of white sympathy had less to do with his grasp of history than with his histrionics, as he stalked into New York's liberal Riverside Church, commandeered the pulpit, and tapped the congregants' deep reservoirs of racial guilt. The former SNCC leader insisted that the damage wrought by white America was incalculable, but he was willing to settle for three billion dollars, cash. He promised to use the funds to finance a black-led socialist revolution as the only way to achieve justice in America. His fund-raising efforts netted a three-year pledge of $450,000 by the Riverside Church for social programs, leading the NAACP's Roy Wilkins to confess his mistaken course in asking for justice instead of demanding revolution and black domination.[67] Wilkins had a deeper reason than personal jealousy to lament Forman's singularly effective stroke. In the conservative Nixon era white liberals were often inclined to pay black militants purely in guilt or its financial equivalent, while shrinking from substantial activity for political reform.

The Nixon years also witnessed a proliferation of Black Power conferences, yet these, too, generally offered symbolic affirmations of revolutionary unity in place of more substantive programs for advancement. Labor Day weekend in 1970 featured three such conventions, each racked by problems. CORE's six hundred delegates met at Mobile, Alabama, to renounce integration, while Director Roy Innis predicted "all-out war" with the NAACP.[68] But his bombast only thinly concealed CORE's dwindling membership and its expedient zigzags toward a policy. In 1968 Innis had backed Richard Nixon in hopes of winning federal patronage for black enterprise, then shifted to savage criticism of the administration after it shunned his overtures.

While Innis was holding forth on black nationalism, two separate black conferences struggled toward this same goal. The Congress of African People could forge only modest agreements from twenty-five hundred participants ranging from the strident Black Muslim separatist Louis Farrakhan to the Urban League's Great Society liberal Whitney Young, Jr. The Black Panther party meanwhile sponsored a more ambitious convention in California, joining some five thousand feminist, gay rights, and other activists to draw up a new American constitution.[69] By then, however, the Panther party was a dying organization, its small membership ridden with factional intrigues. The former "prime minister" Stokely Carmichael quit the party in July 1969 after giving a bitter valedictory on its "dogmatic," "dishonest," and "vicious" character.[70] The Panthers also suffered, like other black militant groups, from a collision with the Nixon administration's intense if selective commitment to law and order.

Nixon was largely color-blind in his hostility toward dissenters. Violent student extremists, unrestrained journalists, antiwar demonstrators, self-absorbed hippies, mocking yippies, and occasional, unwary Democrats were monitored and harassed. Still, ghetto-based groups that spoke of revolution against a background of gutted buildings made especially enticing targets. The best-known militant band, the Black Panther Party for Self-Defense, was the most severely treated, as an object lesson to dissidents of all ideological hues. Spiro Agnew called the Panthers a "completely irresponsible, anarchistic group of criminals."[71] J. Edgar Hoover termed them the single biggest threat to the nation's internal security and encouraged raids on their offices. The Justice Department cooperated by setting up a special task force to destroy the party. Cecil Poole, the only black U.S. attorney, resigned in disgust at these developments in January 1970, charging, "Whatever they say they're doing [at the Justice Department], they're out to get the Panthers."[72]

The example of federal policy encouraged eager local police to combat the Black Panthers by any means available. In Illinois the party chairman was sentenced to four years in prison after conviction for stealing $71 worth of ice cream bars. This did not satisfy Chicago police; late in 1969 they shot two party members dead, one of them (the chairman) while he slept.[73]

As outlets for political protest were clamped shut, cultural assertion became the most vigorous form of black militancy. Black students in high schools challenged white middle-class values by demanding acceptance of black cheerleaders, "soul food" in cafeterias, a day honoring Malcolm X, and courses in black studies. Their actions at times sharply divided students, teachers, and administrators, while adding to the causes of fistfights and school riots. Some observers still discerned progress of sorts, though covered by bitterness and bruises; blacks were now confident enough of survival in white schools to question the terms on which they would fit into the student body.

Calls for black studies shifted the center of black activism back to the college campus. Proponents drew inspiration from the freedom schools created in Mississippi earlier in the decade. The joy of discovery among black children affected activists returning north, where school systems paid little attention to blemishes on American history such as slavery or segregation. By the late 1960s dozens of universities looked favorably on demands for black studies as one way to ease growing campus unrest. This reasoning left much to be desired educationally; politically, it seldom produced the desired opiate effect. Instead the new academic programs helped forge enclaves of black militancy in mostly white schools.

Liberal university presidents tried in vain to keep pace with black demands. James Perkins of Cornell, who had vigorously recruited blacks since his arrival in 1963, acceded to demands for a separate black coed dormitory and a separate black student center. Then, in the spring of 1969, militants demanded a separate degree-granting college. To underscore their resolve some ran across tabletops in the dining hall. Later a group of militants, fearing attack by a white mob, barricaded themselves in a campus building, eventually to emerge carrying guns. Perkins resigned soon afterward.[74]

In contrast to the vast optimism of the first sit-ins, a tone of grim desperation now prevailed among black campus groups. It was evident even in institutions comparatively receptive to black demands, such as Brandeis University. This school featured vigorous minority recruitment and programs tailored to the interests of minority students. Yet in April 1970 black students disrupted classes for one day to protest against racism in all aspects of university life. The leaflets they distributed to students and teachers concluded, "We are beyond survival."[75] This defiant declaration, while not beyond melodrama, conveyed something of the bleak mood gripping black leaders, in places ranging from NAACP offices to college campuses and the poorest ghetto streets. Like the youths at Brandeis, they saw Americans, on up to the man in the White House, once more deciding that no Negro problem existed that could not be cured by a strong dose of law and order.

For many black Americans, Richard Nixon came to personify the country's flight from responsibility on race issues. Unlike civil rights leaders who believed that their moral protests would save society, Nixon envisioned a society already saved, in which agitators had no constructive role. Those uncomplaining middle Americans who helped elect him were themselves the nation's elect, the contented core of Nixon's untroubled community. Blacks as well as whites might enter this coalition; but the society, after years of turmoil, would remain at rest.

The dimensions of Nixon's ignorance of black America were reproduced in miniature by a Republican National Committee campaign pamphlet entitled "The Black Silent Majority." Adorned by a cover picture of Nixon in a rare conference with black federal officials, the pamphlet courted black voters for the 1970 election by portraying them as conservative supporters of the President. The former CORE leader James Farmer, who had accepted a post in HEW, saw a copy of this campaign tract and laughed out loud at the image of black Americans clinging contentedly to the social status quo.[76] As assistant secretary for education, Farmer had by then endured nearly two years of frustration in government—the administration's expedient course in school desegregation, its indifferent enforcement of civil rights codes, the desperate and dubious fight to save Carswell's nomination, Nixon's recrimination after Carswell's defeat. At last, in December 1970, Farmer had had enough. He left office bearing the President's good wishes and his comment "I just hope people will believe that I *do* care."[77] But Farmer, like other veterans of black protest campaigns, found his hopes for minority rights rapidly disappearing in the miasma of Nixon's Southern strategy.

Epilogue: The Shifting Politics of Race

LAGGING progress toward equality led blacks in the 1970s to propose new, bolder answers to the riddle of "all deliberate speed." Instead of seeking merely to punish overt acts of discrimination, some civil rights spokesmen urged the government to guarantee fair representation of blacks in schools, jobs, and other areas of society. This strategy, pursued mainly through a sympathetic judiciary, broadened the concept of equal opportunity and the frontiers of federal regulation. Yet the idea of race-conscious and at times preferential treatment of blacks, even to remedy past injustice, strained the civil rights coalition and brought further backlash in an age of prolonged liberal eclipse.

Education and the Courts

School grounds had served as battle sites for civil rights issues since 1957 when Governor Faubus of Arkansas vainly matched his guardsmen against President Eisenhower's airborne troops. In the early 1960s Charlayne Hunter, Hamilton Holmes, and James Meredith extended the roll call of black students whose bid for a better education touched off legal and political crises. During the 1970s schools once more turned into flash points of racial conflict, as the NAACP Legal Defense and Education Fund sued for federal action to end the long mockery of *Brown*.

When Earl Warren resigned as chief justice in 1969, integrated education was still a rarity in the South. Most communities had kept the courts at bay with devices for token compliance, such as permission for families to select their children's public school. In practice few black parents cared to brave threats and bureaucratic gauntlets for the privilege of sending their children in twos and threes to hostile white classes. More often these "freedom of choice" plans became a convenience for white parents to spirit their children out of interracial schools. In 1970, however, a federal judge in North Carolina undercut these delays by ordering crosstown busing of black and white pupils to each other's schools. His plan, lauded by all nine Supreme Court justices the following year in *Swann v. Charlotte-Mecklenburg,* opened a new era of civil rights activism—and massive white resistance.

School buses had been a basic, accepted feature of American education before they became vehicles of integration. By 1970 they transported some nineteen million children, or 42 percent of all public school pupils. Communities welcomed busing as a way to afford improved education, especially for rural children, in consolidated school systems. Race was seldom at issue in busing plans, except to maintain all-white private academies and segregated public facilities. Once school transportation and civil rights were paired, however, public approval of busing plummeted and neighborhoods began tensing against a federally imposed black presence.

NO FORCED BUSING bumper stickers became standard equipment on white-owned cars in Charlotte. Eighty thousand signatures reinforced the point on antibusing petitions to Congress. Ministers preaching Sunday sermons included busing among the vices to be devoutly resisted. Antibusing placards ringed the post office, the federal courthouse, and the liberal *Charlotte Observer,* which thereafter curbed its editorial enthusiasm for busing. The voice of popular reaction was amplified by extremists, who firebombed the office of the black attorney Julius Chambers, a prime actor in the Charlotte case. Whites also held an uninvited lawn party outside the home of the federal judge James McMillan, author of the busing plan; he could view his image being hanged in effigy.[1]

Although racial concerns fueled these campaigns, many protesters saw themselves as embattled patriots staving off a foreign intruder. Defense of the neighborhood, a racial as well as a geographic ideal, became the focus of white activism. One volunteer for the antibusing cause summed up his record for freedom: "I served in Korea, I served in Vietnam, and I'll serve in Charlotte if I need to."[2]

Charlotte managed to avoid full-scale busing war. After several troubled years community leaders calmed the county's would-be vigilantes by emphasizing the primacy of good, peaceful schools. The small proportion of blacks in Mecklenburg County (29 percent) eased the adjustment to integrated education; and perhaps the years of black activism helped impart an undercurrent of inevitability to the Court decision. That moderating outlook was less evident elsewhere as court busing orders began to include liberal Northern communities—and the ghettos nearby.

The federal judge Arthur Garrity required seventy pages to detail Boston's "systematic program of segregation affecting all of the city's students, teachers and school facilities," and its funding policies that left black schools "the most crowded, the oldest, the least well maintained, and the most poorly staffed." He accompanied this indictment, in June 1974, with an equally sweeping remedy: mandatory busing of seventeen thousand pupils throughout the city in order to break down unacceptable "racial concentrations" in public schools.[3] Garrity's decree was juridically sound but socially impolitic; white

Bostonians were soon banding together for extralegal appeals that turned public education into a violent ordeal.

Opening day of classes at South Boston High, a formerly all-white school, was notable in 1974 for the absence of students, thanks to a white boycott better than 90 percent effective. Black students who had been bused in from the Roxbury ghetto were pelted with stones on leaving the school, then sprayed with shattered glass when rocks crashed through the bus windows. Unlike Little Rock, Arkansas, in 1957, Boston had a black student presence substantial enough to give racial violence a double edge. The stabbing of a white student in mid-October during a racial melee brought 450 national guardsmen to Hyde Park High School but no peace for the students. After nearly two more months of daily incidents a white mob trapped 135 black students in South Boston High for four hours in retaliation for another stabbing. Local school officials could do little more than give the warring parties a breathing space: they ordered an early Christmas vacation, which lasted a full month, then welcomed back the 400 students, including 31 blacks, with a 500-man police guard.[4]

White teenagers who assaulted their black classmates sometimes had records as juvenile delinquents; more often, though, they were expressing values learned in the home and the wider community. Although Boston was known as a beacon of liberalism—home of Harvard and the Kennedys, of nineteenth-century abolitionists and 1960s freedom riders—it also included close-knit communities, short on wealth but long on ethnic and local pride. Residents of South Boston and Charlestown saw busing as a plan by affluent liberals, whose children attended private or suburban schools, to foist experiments in race relations on poorer neighborhoods. Their reaction was simple: they refused to be working-class conscripts in a rich man's war on segregation.

Resentment of outside mandarins, rather than racism, wove through white declarations of war on court-ordered busing. The "Southie" resident Clarence McDonough shared the common view of Judge Garrity, who lived in suburban Wellesley, as an ethnic turncoat disrupting communities without cause. McDonough found a bitter joke in busing his "kid half way around Boston so that a bunch of politicians can end up their careers with a clear conscience." Jimmy Kelley was among those ready to fight for his neighborhood. Apart from the Irish lilt his message could well have come from Little Rock, New Orleans, or Birmingham two decades earlier: "You heard of the Hundred Years War? This will be the eternal war. It will be passed down from father to son."[5]

While white students fought the war in the schools, their parents gathered in the streets at antibusing rallies sponsored by ROAR (Restore Our Alienated Rights) and POWDERKEG. Boston politicians noted the names of these groups and the numbers behind them and either denounced busing or avoided comment. On October 4, 1974, an antibusing march of five thousand through the streets of south Boston drew state legislators, members of the school committee, and all but one member of the Boston City Council. The all-white school committee meanwhile opposed Garrity's court order with all its means short of open lawbreaking. "I will not go any further than doing what Judge Garrity directly orders me to do," the chairman said. "And I will not end up as a salesman for a plan which I do not believe in."[6]

The absence of clear lines between white extremists and public officials contributed to a climate that endangered black adults as well as students. Ted Landsmark, a Yale-educated black lawyer hurrying across the Boston City Hall plaza for a talk with the mayor, found that his briefcase and three-piece suit were a poor shield against white rage. A crowd had already gathered on the plaza, waving antibusing placards and bicentennial banners, when Landsmark came within view. From an upstairs window in City Hall, Mayor Kevin White watched helplessly as four white youths darted from the crowd and pummeled the black stranger. One assailant struck a glancing blow on Landsmark's face with an American flag, using the pole as a spear.[7]

Boston's racial upheaval shook all but the most dogmatic liberals from their faith that attempts to impose integration would inevitably benefit society. Black families, too, expressed conflicting emotions over busing plans, which did not even guarantee "racial balance" in return for the harassment that their children endured. In the first four years after Judge Garrity began hearings on school segregation, in September 1972, nearly twenty thousand white students fled Boston's public school system for parochial schools, private academies, or other cities. By the end of 1976, blacks, Hispanics, and other "minorities" were a majority of Boston's school population, and soon afterward blacks alone formed a majority. The thrust of events had effectively resegregated Boston's schools, which became, in the words of the journalist J. Anthony Lukas, largely "the preserve of the black and the poor."[8]

In 1974, the same year that racial conflicts flared over Judge Garrity's decree, the Supreme Court considered a school busing plan of vastly greater scope. The federal judge Stephen Roth had joined fifty-three white suburban school systems with the schools of Detroit, a predominantly black city still smoldering with memories of the worst urban riot in twentieth-century America. Roth's busing edict, affecting three hundred thousand black and white pupils from kindergarten level, was challenged by Governor William Milliken of Michigan on behalf of suburban whites who claimed autonomy from Detroit and innocence of its racial problems. The legal conflict, which took two years to reach the Supreme Court, posed a task critical to civil rights reform: fixing the bounds of Earl Warren's dictum that "in the field of public education the doctrine of separate but equal has no place."

Roth had arrived at his bold verdict along a bedrock path of legal precedents. The Supreme Court had already required communities to desegregate schools at once, approved crosstown busing as one way to accomplish this, and afforded judicial latitude in tailoring remedies to the circumstances of each case. Roth further recognized that only a busing plan encompassing both Detroit and its suburbs could overcome the effects of racially segregated housing. Yet the judge was treading on a thin political base, for he invoked the logic of judicial activism at a time when the busing cause was becoming a lightning rod for resentment of all federal power and black demands.

An angry political uproar muffled Roth's legal arguments. George Wallace denounced judicial meddling in local affairs and coasted to victory in the 1972 Michigan Democratic primary over Hubert Humphrey and the still more liberal George McGovern. Congressmen, reminiscent of Southern state legislators after *Brown,* felt a surge of local chauvinism at the mention of court-ordered busing. They debated bills "to cut off the gasoline for school buses, to permit resegregation of southern schools, and to tell the Supreme Court how to handle its school cases."[9] By 1974 the Court was listening attentively.

Four Nixon appointees sat on the Court that heard the appeal of Judge Roth's order, in *Milliken v. Bradley.* [10] All four, headed by Chief Justice Warren Burger, emphasized the overriding importance of limiting federal authority in local matters. Their votes anchored the five-to-four majority that overturned the metropolitan-wide busing decree on the grounds that the suburbs had not caused Detroit's segregation and therefore need not help solve the problem. In reaching that decision, the Court ignored evidence of pervasive housing discrimination that kept the suburbs nearly all-white. The Court disregarded, too, the report of the President's Commission on Civil Disorders, issued in 1968, which stated that "white society is deeply implicated in the ghetto." The Court in *Milliken v. Bradley* effectively absolved white suburban America from responsibility.

Dissent from the majority opinion ranged from caustic (William Douglas) to bitter (Thurgood Marshall). Justice Douglas asserted that local control had been invoked as a cover for segregation. "If this were a sewage problem or a water problem, or an energy problem" rather than a race problem, the wisdom of a metropolitan remedy would not be disputed. Michigan's school districts, Douglas noted, were mere creations of the state and extensively supervised by it.[11] Justice Marshall, the aging hero of *Brown,* saw the Court's retreat from federal intervention as a sign of diminishing interest in civil rights: "Today's holding, I fear, is more a reflection of a perceived public mood that we have gone far enough in enforcing the Constitution's guarantee of equal justice than it is the product of neutral principles of law."[12]

Neutral principles of law were not, in any case, sufficient tools for most civil rights reformers by the 1970s. Their advocacy of busing accompanied a broad shift in the movement for equality, from a focus on individual rights to one on group remedies. In business, industry, the professions, and academe, civil rights leaders sought recognition of special black needs as a first, "affirmative" step to overcome the effects of discrimination.

White liberals were indispensable midwives to this new, color-conscious approach to reform. John F. Kennedy first mentioned "affirmative action" with regard to race in a 1961 directive that required firms with federal contracts to recruit blacks. Four years later Lyndon Johnson issued guidelines for affirmative action that led to numerical goals for corporate employment of blacks. Neither presidential order envisioned a policy of racial preference, but rather an effort to ensure blacks a chance to win positions on merit. Yet these measures soon evolved, amid rising black militancy over poverty, into programs to compensate dark-skinned workers for a history of white racism.

Lyndon Johnson appeared to endorse a policy of racial reparations as early as June 1965, in a speech brimming with confidence in the healing power of government. "We seek . . . not just equality as a right and a theory," Johnson told the mostly black graduates of Howard University, "but equality as a fact and equality as a result."[13] In May 1968 the Labor Department set "goals and timetables" that cranked up the pressure on corporations to find, hire, and promote minorities to match their proportion of the general population. The directive stopped short of requiring "quotas," or rigid patterns of racial selection. But it cleared the way for a reinterpretation of federal law to make "benign" racial preference a legitimate public policy.

Not even the presidency of Richard Nixon or his appointment of "strict constructionist" judges halted affirmative action, which had become symbolic of civil rights activity. The Burger Court, though shifting awkwardly for a balance between compensatory justice and employer judgment, still penalized firms that appeared laggard in employing minorities at all levels. In 1973 AT&T acceded to federal pressure by signing a landmark consent decree to grant $15 million in back pay and assure rapid promotions to minority and female employees. By the mid-seventies racial classification and outreach toward minorities had become standard employment practice even for executives who had once looked only to flowcharts and profit margins for shaping corporate concerns.

Like school busing, affirmative action achieved legal standing more easily than it won hearts and minds. Such programs meant a centralization of bureaucracy beyond any previous federal effort to monitor race relations. During the sixties federal leaders had imposed national standards of justice on one region; now, with less public approval, the government was imposing new, more complex ground rules on every region. Moreover the tacit thrust of affirmative action, toward equality of condition, struck some critics as subversive of capitalistic values. Finally, many whites and some blacks regarded the substance of this new regulatory zeal as "reverse racism"—unwarranted, unfair, and unconstitutional. In 1978 Allan Bakke, a rejected medical school applicant turned litigant, tested these propositions before the Supreme Court, in a case that brought two conceptions of racial justice squarely into conflict.

The man who became identified with white challenges to affirmative action was thirty-three years old when he first applied to medical school, submitting a record of outstanding academic achievement, success as an aerospace engineer, and service as a Marines captain in Vietnam. Yet Allan Bakke was turned down by a dozen schools, including one—the University of California at Davis—that featured a biracial admissions program. Sixteen of the one hundred places in the entering class were automatically reserved for blacks,

Hispanics, and members of other minorities, most of whom had grades and test scores far below Bakke's. "I realize that the rationale for these quotas is that they attempt to atone for past racial discrimination," the frustrated applicant wrote to an officer at Davis; "but insisting on a new racial bias in favor of minorities is not a just situation."[14] As he pressed the point through four years of litigation, white outpourings of sympathy let Bakke know that he was not alone.

Beginning in California trial court Bakke asserted that racial quotas violated the Fourteenth Amendment guarantee to equal protection of the laws, and Title VI of the 1964 Civil Rights Act, which barred discrimination in federally assisted institutions. The wording of these measures appeared to support Bakke, but their intent could also be construed as favoring programs to aid black progress. As the case moved through two appeals to the Supreme Court, these technical points became enmeshed in broad policy conflicts over the limits of government, notions of economic justice, and how best to atone for a racist past, at what cost, and to whom. Before the Supreme Court could begin its deliberations on the case, late in 1977, activists of every persuasion were transforming *Bakke* into a lobbyists' Armageddon.

A record fifty-eight parties filed amicus curiae briefs on the *Bakke* case, climaxing a trend toward "public litigation" that assumed justice would lean toward the strongest political battalions. Liberals marshaled the more numerous forces on behalf of affirmative action, including the NAACP Legal Defense and Education Fund, Americans for Democratic Action, Protestant, educational, civil liberties, and labor groups, and the American Bar Association. Whether or not such a roster could impress the Supreme Court, it had its effect on the executive branch. President Jimmy Carter's Justice Department, initially siding with Bakke, reversed itself to assert the merits of race-conscious programs, including the use of quotas. After years of open conflict civil rights leaders and the federal government seemed once again to be operating in tandem.

Several glaring absences marred the reunion of liberal forces that had buttressed earlier civil rights campaigns. Jewish community organizations, unexpectedly allied with other white ethnic, police, and conservative groups, offered the most articulate briefs opposing preferential treatment. Their stand reflected the peculiar cost of affirmative action for Jews, who were disproportionately employed in the civil service, academic, and municipal jobs most vulnerable to black pressure. The emotional quality of Jewish reaction went deeper, however, to traumatic group memories of persecution in Europe and, until the 1940s, exclusion from American universities and varied industries. "A racial quota cannot be benign," Philip Kurland insisted for the Anti-Defamation League, "it must always be malignant because it defies the constitutional pronouncement of equal protection of the law; malignant because it reduces individuals to a single attribute, *skin color,* and this is the very antithesis of equal opportunity."[15]

Kurland's categorical moral lines typified the clash of litigants and lobbyists in the *Bakke* case. Opponents of affirmative action posed the choice between individual and racial judgments, while most civil rights advocates equated support for Bakke with hostility toward minority aspirations. In fact, though, *Bakke* involved a tangle of imperfect options, far more complicated than the bellicose briefs that were polarizing national opinion.

Partisans of affirmative action defied steep logical pitfalls in claiming the moral high ground for an approach contrary to the plain meaning of earlier civil rights demands. In place of color-blind treatment, blacks—joined by Hispanic, women, and Asian-American leaders—pressed for rewards based on group demographics. This entailed practical difficulties as well as moral dilemmas, for it risked formalizing a racial spoils system, with ethnic ratios for each field and locality determined by increasingly fractious lobbying. Whatever the long-term results, "preferential treatment" seemed to many critics a troubling stretch from Dr. King's plea that individuals be judged not by their color but by their character.

Affirmative action presented one more burden too heavy even for some blacks, such as the economist Thomas Sowell. Out of step with the civil rights establishment but claiming to reflect black sentiment, Sowell charged that affirmative action was scarcely a means of mass uplift. Instead it secured positions mainly for educated blacks who were likely to succeed anyway in an economy favoring skilled workers. The result was to stigmatize blacks, however inadvertently and unjustifiably, as the recipients of white charity.[16]

To Sowell it was no surprise that a Gallup poll in 1977 showed not only that whites overwhelmingly opposed preferential treatment for minorities but that a majority of blacks did so as well.[17] It is less clear that blacks defined such treatment as expansively as whites. Still, the evidence suggests that many who favored racial equality thought affirmative action a poorly designed tool for surgery on the body politic.

Opponents of affirmative action had the virtue of apparent consistency: they argued that preferential treatment could never be justified at the expense of individual merit. Yet this simplicity betrayed a selective memory of American history. It overlooked, first, that group preference was already ingrained in public policy, ranging from veterans' benefits to farm payments for crops not planted, tax credits to businessmen, and welfare programs for native Americans. Not until blacks sought compensation for the effects of white racism did the country undergo paroxysms of principle over assistance based on special group need or entitlement.

Scruples that affirmative action punished innocent individuals, while aiding the less deserving, tended to slight the impact of American race relations. For centuries racism had set limits on black achievement, conferring a competitive edge on those who, like Allan Bakke, belonged to the white majority. Admittedly Bakke had shown rare talent and drive (an admissions officer thought him as grimly determined as "a character out of a Bergman film"); but inferences that he rose without prejudice to black rights rested on shaky evidence. Bakke had grown up in segregated Coral Gables, Florida, attended the racially exclusive public schools, and benefited from all the options, counseling, and encouragement available to promising whites.[18] To look at Bakke's résumé alone, therefore, was to say much about his achievement but little about the society that, from the outset, had scrutinized and approved his "group characteristics."

Claims that affirmative action set a dangerous precedent for higher education by tampering with a rigorous merit system ignored the bias that already riddled the admissions process. Bakke's rejections, for example, resulted mainly from considerations of age, not race; medical schools accepted few applicants over thirty regardless of talent because most such students were expected to have shorter careers. The quality of merit was further strained by class and caste distinctions so routine that they escaped Bakke's notice and went unchallenged in court. The dean of the medical school at Davis intervened over the years in hundreds of cases ("on the side of fairness," he testified), admitting applicants who sometimes fell below minimum standards but compensated in family lineage. Beneficiaries of the dean's push for fairness— up to five individuals each year—included candidates related to a retired Davis chancellor, a former president of the county medical society, and the chairmen of the state legislature's finance committees that set the medical school budget.[19]

The defense of "merit" encouraged charges that affirmative action programs recruited unqualified persons; but here, too, the evidence suggested otherwise. The Davis special admissions program filled only fifteen of the sixteen allotted minority spaces in 1974 rather than accept a candidate it considered below school standards. Assertions that Bakke was more qualified than minority students at Davis rested chiefly on his standardized test scores for general, mathematical, scientific, and verbal knowledge. Yet such tests had scant predictive value for student performance after the first two years of medical school, and no value for gauging subsequent clinical work as a physician. Medical admissions committees at least tacitly agreed, for each year they turned down hundreds of students with high test scores and grades, while accepting hundreds more—mostly whites—with lower marks.[20] Such vagaries of the admissions process were accepted as routine judgments of overall student suitability—until minority admissions programs generated a clamor for "protection of standards."

Even apart from white racism and pervasive bias in admissions procedures, the claims for a system of "merit selection" free of racial factors left much to be desired. The term "merit" was appealing but also nebulous and arbitrary. It stretched credibility to assume that grades and test scores, ranked and rewarded with undeviating rigor, could provide a reliable index of human potential. Such competition, moreover, tended to substitute for policies aimed at developing the nation's social resources. Strict limits on the accreditation and funding of medical schools required those in operation to reject thousands of qualified applicants, while the country remained near the bottom among industrial nations in health care. This Darwinian battle for limited educational facilities coincided with the interests of a largely white, male elite, but it made a doubtful contribution to the wider society.

In all, supporters of "affirmative action" and "merit selection" were contesting a gray moral expanse that made the *Bakke* case as difficult as it was divisive. How were judges to weigh Allan Bakke's individual rights and record against the wrongs done to more than twenty million black citizens? And if blacks were entitled to compensation, how far could the Court sanction racial policies in a society that had so recently acknowledged the evils of all discrimination? Whatever the verdict, *Bakke* guaranteed only discord for the civil rights coalition.

Unlike *Brown,* which posed a clear moral choice that the Court decided with one voice, *Bakke* rent the Supreme Court as it had the nation. Four justices ruled to admit Bakke and strike down preferential treatment as contrary to the Civil rights Act of 1964. Four justices upheld affirmative action and the denial of admission to Bakke, as consistent with efforts to overcome the effects of white racism. It fell to the ninth justice, Lewis Powell, a Southern conservative chosen by Nixon in 1971, to shape a consensus from this unpromising material. His ruling—both for Bakke and for affirmative action—sought a middle ground amid a standoff of legal and moral absolutes.

Like other Nixon appointees, Powell had arrived on the high court to the laments of black leaders. John Conyers of the Congressional Black Caucus warned that Powell's segregationist leanings, close ties to corporate giants, membership in the largest all-white law firm in Richmond, Virginia, and defense of the status quo made poor references for a prospective Supreme Court justice. Yet Powell also brought to the bench a hard-earned sensitivity to racial issues: as chairman of the Richmond school board after *Brown,* he had defused a campaign of white resistance that threatened to disrupt public education. Social peace and stability were Powell's guiding principles, and in 1978 this courtly Virginia gentleman understood that to preserve race-conscious programs from white assault was the better part of conservative valor.

Powell wove carefully among his eight colleagues by offering a qualified endorsement of affirmative action. He disallowed the separate admissions program at Davis, which insulated minorities "from comparison with all other candidates."[21] He rejected, too, the idea of affirmative action to remedy general social ills. Instead he rested his approval on more unifying grounds: the right of universities to seek diversity, consistent with the First Amendment guarantee of free speech and its implied promise of a broad traffic in ideas. To what degree then could race shape admissions policy? And what would prevent such policy from acting as a disguised quota? Powell refused, in the interest of consensus, to refine the issue.

In the end Powell wrought a judicial majority so fragile that his middle way became the "judgment of the Court" although five other justices wrote separate concurrences or dissents and none would sign his opinion. Yet his approach placated most universities (which retained broad discretion in admissions policies), Bakke (who was admitted by Court order to study at Davis), and civil rights groups (affirmative action in some form could continue). In this three-way overture the Court's collective judgment, though an ill-fitting patchwork of legal opinions, formed a diplomatic master stroke.

Bakke encouraged other white challenges to affirmative action. Dozens of corporations cut back on their programs, and new litigants took Bakke's part in assailing preferential treatment as contrary to the Fourteenth Amendment and the Civil Rights Act of 1964. Yet the NAACP Legal Defense and Education Fund and other groups staved off most of these assaults. In 1979 the Court rejected the suit of the white union worker Brian Weber and noted that the Kaiser Aluminum Company could favor blacks in training and promotion.[22] The following year the Court upheld a congressional act that set aside 10 percent of all federal contracts on public works projects for minority businesses.[23] Both cases were notable for approving remedial programs even when discrimination by an individual company had been neither proven nor conceded. These issues still produced sharp dissents, but by 1980 the Burger Court had reinforced the shelter that *Bakke* had built for affirmative action.

Presidential Leadership from Ford to Reagan

Judicial burdens in race relations grew during the 1970s partly because issues of busing and affirmative action were considered too sensitive for congressional or executive resolution. Opinion polls showed that most Americans approved racial equality in principle but favored no specific program that would burden the white middle class. Both Democrats and Republicans therefore focused on consolidating past reforms, an approach that displayed concern for black rights yet did not disturb the social order.

The brief presidency of Gerald Ford, following Nixon's scandal-ridden exit in August 1974, tilted racial politics modestly to the right. During his twenty-nine-month administration Congress was resolutely quiescent toward black interests; it defeated bills to weaken civil rights laws and ban school busing, but it also buried measures to aid the ghettos. Ford himself, though known for diatribes against liberals, tried to restore national harmony after Watergate. The new President met early with civil rights leaders, named the black attorney William T. Coleman secretary of transportation, and, apart from a few antibusing statements, was content to maintain the status quo on racial issues. This stalemate carried over into the administration of Ford's Democratic successor, Jimmy Carter, who had tied his career to the South's emancipation from racist tradition.

Carter personified the New South with rare versatility. A folksy, broad-grinned peanut farmer, he also happened to be an Annapolis graduate, wealthy entrepreneur, prominent realtor, and systems engineer. Raised in segregated Plains, Georgia, Carter early absorbed the tolerant values of his mother, "Miss Lillian," the town's lone white opponent of racial bigotry during the forties and fifties. This moral sense did not wholly crowd out Carter's political pragmatism. In 1970 he campaigned for the governorship by identifying with the segregationist incumbent, Lester Maddox. But once ensconced in the governor's mansion, Carter changed the political symbolism of the state by hanging a portrait of Martin Luther King in his office. While Maddox sputtered, the new governor delivered an inaugural epitaph for the politics of prejudice: "I say to you quite frankly that the time for racial discrimination is over. . . . No poor, rural, weak, or black person should ever have to bear the additional burden of being deprived of the opportunity of an education, a job, or simple justice."[24]

Six years later a record 64 percent of all registered black voters turned out to boost Jimmy Carter's presidential campaign and complete the return of the South—a reconstructed South—to national respectability. An overwhelming black vote for Carter (94 percent) helped him win key Northern industrial states and every Southern state except Virginia. The close contest ultimately rested on returns from Mississippi, where newly enfranchised blacks tipped the state toward Carter despite a clear white majority for the incumbent Gerald Ford. For the civil rights leader Andrew Young, a close aide to Carter, the vote added up to a second emancipation: "When I heard that Mississippi had gone our way, I knew that the hands that picked cotton finally picked the president."[25]

Carter quickly began repaying debts to his core constituency. He named blacks to a record number of federal jobs, including Secretary of Housing and Urban Development Patricia Harris, the first black woman Cabinet officer. His fellow Georgian Andrew Young became ambassador to the United Nations, from which forum the maverick moralist denounced Western colonialism, American racism, and South African apartheid. Civil rights leaders hailed Carter as potentially another Lyndon Johnson in his loyalties and activist vision; but the consensus for reform that had brightened Johnson's first years in office eluded Carter throughout his presidency.

Few of Carter's initiatives for black progress survived intact. His support helped launch a jobs program for youths but at levels too low to curb black teenage unemployment, which reached 40 percent in 1980. Ambitious public works measures, of particular value to the inner cities, died quietly in Congress and went largely unmourned by the public. Carter was more effective in conveying personal support for minority opportunities. But in 1979 his main liaison with the civil rights movement, Andrew Young, resigned under pressure after reports that he had met with Palestinian guerrillas in violation of U.S. policy. The episode compounded black disenchantment with Carter, who now appeared suspect even in the area of political symbolism.

Carter's personal weaknesses made an inviting target for critics of his stalled agenda for reform. There were his poor relations with Congress, the media, and other Washington power centers; the embarrassing antics of his brother, Billy, who delighted in swilling beer, representing foreign governments, and generally distressing his famous sibling; and the President's public manner, which combined extremes of informality and piety. Yet Carter's salient problem was one of timing rather than of talent. His election in 1976 had temporarily halted the defection of white ethnics, union workers, and Southerners from the New Deal Democratic coalition. But the country was still listing to the right, and Carter—a self-declared political outsider ascending in the wake of Watergate—could not stem the conservative tide.

Foremost among the barriers to reform—and especially damaging to black hopes—was an economic downturn in the 1970s. Since World War II, liberals basking in a quarter century of rapid growth had claimed that greater aid to the poor would not unsettle the rest of society. But a tripling of inflation (which peaked at 12.4 percent in 1980), shrinking productivity gains (under 1 percent yearly since 1973), and a deficit approaching one trillion dollars imposed an unaccustomed sense of limits. With most Americans set against tax increases, Congress shunned new jobs programs and income transfers to the poor, two-thirds of whom were white. Black calls for "freedom budgets" to end poverty and "Marshall plans" to end slums—bold ideas even in the sixties— were foredoomed.

The new fiscal prudence mingled with resentments, concentrated among Southern whites and affluent Catholics, that blacks had already received too much federal support—that such aid was symptomatic of growing national ills. These beliefs helped energize a network of diverse conservative foundations, several thousand political action committees (PACs), and direct-mail campaigns against busing, affirmative action, and other egalitarian experiments. Another group neglected during the sixties, religious fundamentalists, clamored for school prayer and for curbs on abortion, issues that displaced black rights as the focus of morality in politics.

Within the liberal coalition a profusion of groups made it more difficult for any single one to enact a reform agenda. Consumer and environmental movements pushed federal regulation in new directions, often at odds with black interests in business growth and full employment. A human rights explosion encompassed feminists, homosexuals, the elderly, and the handicapped, all galvanized by the success of black nonviolent campaigns. The term "civil rights," once synonymous with black demands, now ranged from native American land claims in Maine to Hispanic concerns with bilingual education and immigration. For black groups this emulation came at the cost of increased competition for funds and a diffusion of civil rights aims. Most important, perhaps, the cause of black rights lost the unique moral stature so crucial to earlier triumphs.

While new demands were stretching the liberal alliance, old members were drawing back, often because of racial conflicts. Unions balked when affirmative action eroded the seniority system that sheltered whites from layoffs and exposed black recruits to the brunt of recessions. Jewish groups, already incensed over quotas, bristled at growing black criticism of Israel as an outpost of Western imperialism and a friend to racist South Africa. In the sixties such comments had been confined to the black nationalist fringes, but in 1979 Jesse Jackson and the SCLC's president, Joseph Lowery, embraced Arab leaders accused of terrorist acts against Israel. Charges and countercharges between black and Jewish groups drained resources that in the past had strengthened campaigns against discrimination.

A measure of the liberal disarray that President Carter inherited was the emergence of a "neoconservative" faction among intellectuals who had infused the Kennedy and Johnson era with a vision of social change. By the late 1970s such eminent apostates as Daniel Patrick Moynihan and the editor of *Commentary,* Norman Podhoretz, were assailing reform values that had shaped the movement for racial equality. The neoconservatives took a dour view of minority demands, which they saw as undervaluing social peace, overrating the expertise of reformers, outstripping society's resources, and encouraging undue expectations of government. Their influential writings, weighty with disillusion, touched popular misgivings that the Great Society had gone awry and, worse, was still spinning out of control.

Racial equality and other commitments of Great Society vintage fell into jeopardy in 1980, with the election of Ronald Reagan as President. Known for the good-humored charm he had shown as a Hollywood star through the 1950s, Reagan effectively humanized the right wing of the Republican party. Compared with Barry Goldwater, to whom he paid televised homage in 1964, Reagan conveyed an innocence even when opposing bills to protect black rights. He did not act out of prejudice, Reagan insisted, but to guard against government dictation. By 1980 the nation's conservative drift enabled Reagan to shed his extremist image without notably altering his views on politics or race. His outlook fused wide public resentment toward federal regulation with a tendency toward national amnesia about the racist roots of black inequality.

"Government cannot solve our problems. . . . [It] cannot eliminate poverty or provide a bountiful economy or reduce inflation or save our cities or cure illiteracy or provide energy."[26] Jimmy Carter had voiced this unfamiliar Democratic tenet midway through his presidency, in response to public frustration over his leadership. Three years later Ronald Reagan, unfettered by a need for liberal support, pressed the point further in his inaugural address. "Government is not the solution to our problem," he said. "Government is the problem."[27] Reagan aimed to reverse the accretion of federal programs since the early New Deal, including those for the protection of black rights.

As in the past Reagan disavowed any racist sentiment, but his call to undo a half century of liberal policies challenged black leaders along the spectrum of race-related issues. Unsympathetic to income transfers or subsidized employment, Reagan stated that poor blacks, like poor whites, would rise in an economy unfettered by burdensome taxes or welfare payments that discouraged work. He regarded race-conscious programs as perversions of color-blind justice, and his view of earlier civil rights laws was only marginally brighter. Reagan believed that blacks had already won basic equality, which reduced the need for civil rights laws that stigmatized the white South and denied free choice to all Americans. This philosophy contradicted the thrust of civil rights activism since the rise of W. E. B. Du Bois in the early twentieth century. But despite objections by black and liberal leaders, the sixty-nine-year-old President moved with vigor to implement his agenda for a free society.

Reagan's tax and spending cuts had a mixed impact on the economy, but the primary victims of this counterrevolution in fiscal policy were clearly the inner-city poor. Although entitlement payments to low-income groups, including welfare, food stamps, and child nutrition, absorbed less than a fifth of all funds for income maintenance, they suffered nearly 60 percent of the 1981 budget cuts. In two years Congress slashed $18 billion from such programs as Aid to Families with Dependent Children, Medicaid, Supplemental Security Income for the aged and disabled poor, free school meals, subsidies for fuel bills, low-income housing, job and compensatory education, legal services, food supplements for pregnant mothers, infants, and children under five, and social services for the poor.[28]

Although Reagan's Council of Economic Advisers acknowledged that income redistribution was no longer a federal goal, the President himself insisted that the poor were better off without artificial supports. But by 1983 the cumulative impact of Reagan's policies involved a $25 billion transfer in disposable income from the less well-off to the richest fifth of Americans, and a rise in the number of poor people from 29.3 million in 1980 to 35.3 million. This dismal category now included one in seven Americans, the highest proportion since the War on Poverty began in 1965. George Gilder, a leading defender of "Reaganomics," explained the policy in terms congenial to nineteenth-century conservatives: "In order to succeed, the poor need most of all the spur of their poverty." In fact, as the historian Arthur Schlesinger, Jr., observed, this trickle-down theory of prosperity assumed that "the poor needed the spur of poverty and the rich the spur of wealth."[29]

No overt racism fueled Reaganomics, which benefited some affluent blacks and devastated millions of whites living at or below the poverty line. But in a society where race and class intertwined, blacks as a group lost their tenuous footing in the climb toward economic parity. Elimination of one million people from the food stamp program, and reduction of aid for the remaining twenty million, disproportionately hurt blacks, who formed a third of the recipients.[30] Ghetto dwellers were also least able to afford the cutbacks in both employment-training programs and unemployment benefits. By 1984 black poverty stood at nearly 34 percent, three times the rate for whites and a grim counterpoint to Reagan's claim to have saved blacks from the "tragic" consequences of the Great Society.[31]

Reagan's attack on big government included cutbacks in federal enforcement of civil rights laws. The Justice Department filed suit against busing and affirmative action programs as unsound paths to the goal of racial equality. More discreetly the administration scrutinized and rejected virtually all other paths as well. Jimmy Carter had proposed regulations to implement the neglected open-housing law of 1968; Reagan withdrew the guidelines. His first attorney general, William French Smith, sought to dilute the Voting Rights

Act by requiring proof of intent to discriminate beyond clear circumstantial evidence of black exclusion. Congress extended the act in 1982 with a clause pointedly upholding its enforcement standards (the Senate by a vote of 85 to 8 and the House unanimously), upon which Reagan signed the bill as a sign of "our unbending commitment to voting rights."[32]

Although Congress protected civil rights laws from the administration, Reagan effectively pared the agencies responsible for enforcement. From 1981 to 1985 the number of lawyers in the Justice Department's Civil Rights Division shrank from 210 to 57. Reagan attempted to disband altogether the U.S. Commission on Civil Rights, which since 1957 had annoyed every President since Dwight Eisenhower with outspoken reporting on executive leadership. Failing to terminate the commission outright, he ousted Father Theodore Hesburgh as chairman and appointed in his place a black conservative, Clarence Pendleton, who opposed affirmative action, school busing, and his own organization's existence. Looking to the day when Congress would terminate the commission, Pendleton exclaimed in 1985, "How many agencies do we need to do this civil rights business?"[33]

Indifference to the survival of civil rights agencies typified Reagan's appointment policy. To head the Equal Employment Opportunity Commission, a sub-Cabinet office with a staff of over three thousand and a budget of $140 million, Reagan nominated William Bell, a black businessman whose job placement firm lacked a telephone listing and had not helped any clients for at least eleven months. Bell's written answers to congressional inquiries at his confirmation hearing were evasive, uninformed, and riddled with misspelled words. Bell did admit, though, that he had never managed more than four employees and that he lacked a background in civil rights law. Black, Hispanic, and allied groups lobbied to block the appointment, fearing, in the words of an Urban League spokeswoman, "We can't afford this last citadel of equal opportunity to be run by an incompetent." A White House aide defended Reagan's nomination, which was later withdrawn: "We offered it to ten or twelve other blacks, and nobody wanted to take it."[34]

On school segregation Justice Department officials echoed Reagan's pre-*Brown* perspective. In addition to contesting court-ordered busing, they supported a Washington state law that required Seattle to end a busing plan that it had voluntarily implemented and asked to retain. Assistant Attorney General for Civil Rights William Bradford Reynolds believed the real problem was not segregation but federal meddling to achieve interracial schools. "We aren't going to compel children who don't want to have an integrated education to have one," he said.[35]

Other high officials also adopted the President's minimalist approach to school desegregation. Secretary of Education Terrel Bell approved the administration's decision in 1982 to overlook violations of civil rights law by colleges where federal aid involved only student loans. Bell explained to a sympathetic senator that a higher law overrode his apparent constitutional duties: "The courts may soon be after us for not enforcing civil rights laws and regulations. It seems that we have some laws that we shouldn't have, and my obligation to enforce them is against my own philosophy."[36]

The administration's philosophy on racial issues came into the open on January 8, 1982, when Reagan restored the federal tax exemptions for segregated private schools that Richard Nixon had ended in 1970. The Justice Department immediately conveyed its support to two openly racist academies: Bob Jones University, in Greenville, South Carolina, which expelled students for interracial dating, and the Goldsboro Christian Schools, in Goldsboro, North Carolina, which barred blacks on the grounds that God separated the races. The ruling also benefited more than one hundred other segregated schools, which would no longer pay unemployment, Social Security, and federal income taxes, while their benefactors could deduct contributions on their own income taxes. In effect Reagan's policy awarded these segregated schools a matching grant from the Treasury.[37]

This dubious legal reversal, which ignored the 1964 civil rights law that outlawed federal aid to segregated schools, led more than 100 of the 176 lawyers in the Civil Rights Division to protest in writing to Assistant Attorney General Bradford Reynolds. A Justice Department spokesman informed them on behalf of the administration that they were "welcome to leave."[38] Reagan maintained the tax breaks until the Supreme Court, in an eight-to-one decision, strongly condemned the impropriety of subsidizing school segregation. (William Rehnquist, the lone dissenter, became Reagan's choice for the post of chief justice of the Supreme Court when Warren Burger resigned, in 1986.)

Reagan was usually more circumspect in opposing civil rights laws, and his reversal of past commitments encountered mainly indifference outside the black community. Whenever his chilly relations with black leaders broke into open charges of racism, Reagan offered conciliatory words, echoing a campaign pledge that he was "heart and soul in favor of the things that have been done" for desegregation.[39] These pronouncements did not placate civil rights leaders who monitored the gap between Reagan's assurances and his actions. But the President's national popularity remained untarnished by his policies on race, despite the suspicions of many blacks that Reagan was more inclined to assume the existence of equal opportunity than to achieve it.

Ronald Reagan's assaults on desegregation stirred fears of a national resurgence of racism such as occurred in the late nineteenth century. Just as the sweeping civil rights reforms of the 1960s became known as the "Second Reconstruction," so the subsequent erosion of black rights seemed to some observers a second conservative "redemption," marked by the abandonment of concern for racial justice. For blacks, American history appeared to be repeating a pattern of false promise and harsh reaction.

Parallels abounded between the two eras of conservative ascendancy. In the 1870s Southern whites spearheaded a political drive against the mingled currents of black advancement, tax increases for social services, and growing federal authority over local and private affairs. Consolidation of power by the newly "redeemed" Southern governments led to tax cuts for wealthy landowners and budget reductions that gutted social services, including the fledgling public school systems and programs to care for orphans, the sick, and the insane. The new governments also reinforced a national trend toward subsidizing and protecting business at any cost to public resources and workers' rights. Officials frequently approved, and profited from, the leasing of mostly black convicts for hard labor at negligible pay. Northern reformers, shying from a protracted struggle for racial justice and caught up in the spirit of economic growth, withdrew behind speeches that individual initiative rather than government protection provided the only sound hope for minorities and the poor.[40]

The Reagan administration retraced that abdication of federal concern to achieve racial equality. Just as the Supreme Court in the late nineteenth century had renounced objections to segregation, so Reagan's declaration "Government is the problem," instead of unchecked racism or poverty, summed up the current tendency to roll back decades of black progress. Together the two eras suggest that the cycles of reform and reaction in American history pose a special threat to the struggle for black rights, requiring a more powerful running start up an incline that never quite leads to a secure plateau.

The Receding Civil Rights Vision

It is now clear that the more expansive hopes for civil rights progress were markedly inflated. Residential segregation, seen in the persistence of inner-city black ghettos and lily-white suburbs, has easily survived federal fiats against housing discrimination. De facto segregation of churches, social centers, and private schools also remains routine, suggesting that in important respects the society's newfound emphasis on interracial harmony has been more rhetorical than real. Wealth, too, is largely segregated along racial lines; the median family income of blacks is barely half that of whites, and blacks are three times as likely to be poor. As for black political power, it is still embryonic with regard to national office holding and access to the circles that make foreign and domestic policy. In all, the roots of racial inequality have proved too deeply embedded in centuries of American history to be washed away by a decade's liberal reform.

Race relations have changed at a glacial pace in much of the rural South, where only the hardiest civil rights activists could weather the repressive social climate. Southern whites understandably regard black militancy as an urban malady, for only in the cities have blacks developed an independent business and professional class able to lead sustained protests. In many outlying towns, where whites monopolize credit and own the farms and textile mills that provide crucial jobs, the etiquette of racial deference persists.

Unwritten rules of segregation in small Southern communities still have the force of law. Harassment and occasional beatings discourage blacks from approaching the polls on election day, whatever the language of federal statutes. Blacks also know to avoid restaurants where they will draw stares instead of service, hotels that will always be "fully booked," and golf courses where management sand traps will foil their bids for access. Even white physicians who treat persons of both races commonly route their patients into separate waiting rooms with pre-1960 firmness. Here progress in race relations often comes in rudimentary concessions to black dignity, as in the recent removal of a chain-link fence dividing black and white plots in a Georgia county cemetery. Until that headline-making decision, black funeral processions had entered the cemetery through a back gate.[41]

Challenges to old racial mores can bring spiraling retaliation. In Ludowici, Georgia, where students picked separate white and black homecoming queens until 1984, an argument in the high school lunchroom over interracial dating degenerated into an interracial brawl. Discipline was swift and selective: several students were expelled, all of them black. After local black leaders protested, hooded Klansmen visited the town, and within hours the home of a civil rights activist was burned to the ground. Fire marshals blamed faulty wiring, but Joseph Lowery of the Southern Christian Leadership Conference thought it absurd to deny the real problem: faulty white racial attitudes. The former SNCC worker Charles Sherrod observed, "Those people who shot at us, and blew up churches and all that 20 years ago, they haven't gone anywhere. The attitudes are still there. Their behavior has changed because we have got a little power. They won't do anything they can't get away with."[42]

Few officials anywhere in the South still defy civil rights laws openly, for events in the 1960s showed the futility of shrill racist posturing. Softer sabotage, however, still limits the impact of federal guarantees. After passage of the Voting Rights Act in 1965, whites generally acquiesced in the registration of blacks but devised ways to undermine the new electorate. Testimony in 1982 before the Senate Judiciary Committee revealed that nearly half the counties of Alabama, Georgia, Louisiana, and South Carolina had disregarded the act's "preclearance" requirement by changing electoral laws—often for transparent racial reasons—without first obtaining federal approval. Cities with large black populations imported white voters by annexing adjacent suburbs, and cities with a few predominantly black areas discarded district elections for at-large voting. Legislators have also excluded black voters from communities through redistricting schemes of rare cartographic cunning. The understaffed Justice Department has trailed such infractions at a discouraging distance. An amendment to the North Carolina constitution, designed to gerrymander away the influence of new black voters, escaped challenge from federal attorneys until 1981, fourteen years after it was illegally implemented.[43]

Outside the South racism treads more softly but still sequesters most blacks in ghettos. Blacks formed 6 percent of the suburban population in 1980 (up from 5 percent in 1970), and even this figure was inflated by spillover into older, industrial suburbs that white flight turned into segregated enclaves. Federal studies show pervasive discrimination by white realtors and residents, resulting in hundreds of census tracts in New York, Cleveland, and other metropolitan areas that contain no nonwhites. Nor is housing bias entirely covert. Obscene phone calls, curses, threats, firebombings, and rocks and bricks crashing through windows are among the dozens of incidents that each year impart a rough frontier quality to black settlement in white neighborhoods. Such experiences confirm that the open-housing legislation of the 1960s has meant little beside the resolve of whites to maintain property values and "ethnic purity" in their communities.

Racial violence and harassment, a central target of civil rights protest, still occurs daily in every region of the country. The Justice Department conservatively recorded a rise in racist attacks from 99 in 1980 to 276 in 1986; the count by individual cities is more extensive. New York City's police department charted an increase in bias-related clashes from four a week to ten a week in early 1987. Chicago reported 240 episodes of racially motivated violence and harassment in 1986, an increase for the third consecutive year. The spark is often no more than the presence of a black person in a store, on the street, in a new home. For dejected white students at the University of Massachusetts at Amherst, the defeat of the Boston Red Sox in the 1986 World Series was enough reason to beat a black New York Mets fan unconscious and injure several others. Several months earlier, at Howard Beach, New York, three black "outsiders" fled an attack by eleven whites; one of the blacks, twenty-three-year-old Michael Griffith, was killed when he ran onto a parkway of speeding cars in his attempt to escape a beating. Kevin Nesmith, a black student at the Citadel Military School, in Charleston, South Carolina, resigned after whites in Klan robes burst into his room at two in the morning shouting racial slurs and hazing him. Something akin to a freedom ride befell black students returning from Newton North High School to their homes in Boston when whites smashed the bus windows with stones and a tire iron. These and other recent episodes do not approach the systematic, officially sanctioned terror against blacks that once scarred American history. They nonetheless point to the continued difficulty blacks face in securing basic civil rights.[44]

Police each year kill dozens of blacks, including children. Defenders of police conduct stress the extreme danger facing officers in some ghetto neighborhoods, their need to use deadly force on occasion to survive, and their able protection of blacks, notably during civil rights marches that have drawn white hecklers. Still, cases abound of unprovoked, cold-blooded police shootings of ghetto residents that almost invariably go unpunished.

The criminal justice system is less blatantly harsh toward blacks than in the past, but patterns of punishment still appear skewed by racial prejudice. Blacks average longer prison terms than whites for the same offense and are the primary victims of capital punishment.[45] Criminals of any race, moreover, are treated more severely for victimizing whites. In 1987 a case that challenged the death penalty as being tainted, in practice, by racial bias showed that in Georgia, even after accounting for 230 other factors, killers of white persons were four times more likely to be executed than killers of blacks. Despite corroborating evidence of prejudice in meting out capital punishment, the Supreme Court narrowly upheld the death penalty. The majority opinion asserted, in language shades removed from *Plessy v. Ferguson,* that the treatment of black and white prisoners was admittedly different but not discriminatory.[46]

Failure to include blacks fully in the nation's prosperity is the most glaring limitation of the movement for racial justice. In the South two-thirds of all black workers, compared with one-third of all whites, hold low-income jobs. The national economy today relegates more than half of all black workers to menial jobs, perpetuates a black underclass of deepening antisocial bent, and confines even educated blacks to the margins of wealth and opportunity. These problems can be traced to various causes—racial differences in family structure, education, and job experience among them—but they are also rooted in both past and persistent discrimination.

Title VII of the 1964 Civil Rights Act did not end bias in employment but drove it behind closed office doors. Managers commonly assigned blacks to dead-end jobs, minimized their executive role, scrutinized them more harshly than comparably trained whites, and excluded them from the after-hours fraternizing that can advance careers. In 1982 only one in thirty black men (compared with one in ten whites) filled management or administrative jobs, reflecting a ten-year increase so minute that it was probably a matter of statistical error. No black headed a corporation in *Fortune* magazine's top 1,000, and few had risen above the level of vice-president in any major firm. Tokenism thus became more intricate in the era of affirmative action, permitting a greater minority presence in the office but seldom in the conference suites where deals, promotions, and salaries are decided.[47]

An aura of the closed medieval guild still surrounds craft unions, which have countered civil rights laws with subtler means of racial exclusion. One AFL-CIO union, representing New York City's electrical contractors, avoided punishment for racist practices by devising an "outreach training program" for minorities in 1971. Over a decade later state investigators charged that the program required black and Hispanic trainees to work eleven years before they could reach class A journeyman status, compared with five years for white apprentices. Nonwhite trainees were also taught a curriculum separate from that of whites, with obsolete textbooks and without the fifth year of classroom instruction needed to pass the union exam and obtain work at journeymen's wages. Many other AFL-CIO locals have also been exposed for turning affirmative action programs into a permanent racial obstacle course for minorities.[48]

Despite a minutely detailed skein of evidence that shows racism permeating the economy, Americans frequently cite two apparent exceptions—the entertainment industry and professional sports—as proof that merit, not color, determines success. It is true that the presence of black athletes, and in some sports their predominance, is now taken for granted. So, too, is the celebrity of black television and film stars such as Bill Cosby, Richard Pryor, and Eddie Murphy. Even in these fields, however, blacks have strained against a color line placed well before the limits of their talent and drive.

While blacks have fared better in films and on television than before the civil rights movement, they still receive few parts not written specifically for a black. Leading roles are confined mainly to escapist "situation comedies" that affirm their right to be caricatured as sharply as whites. The versatile Broadway performer Ben Vereen complained that casting directors too often envisioned him in the role of janitor.[49] A Hollywood agent confirmed that Vereen's experience was the norm for black actors: "They're looking for druggies, athletes or men struggling out of the ghetto." Regarding black actresses, the agent said, "If you're beautiful, you can play a prostitute; if you're fat, you can play a mother; and if you're ugly, you can play a maid."[50] Bill Cosby, among the few blacks to transcend such stereotyping, has refused to appear as an Oscar-night presenter "because this industry just does not represent [black] America."[51]

As in all of American life since the civil rights movement, Hollywood executives express their prejudices (or reflect those of their audience) mainly in sub rosa messages. One NBC memorandum on how to promote a show with an ethnically mixed cast warned against highlighting its most seasoned performer, Debbie Allen, because of racial considerations: "On *Fame:* Spot you sent has to be more generic and less black. . . . [Show] VARIOUS TEACHERS. CAN USE LYDIA BUT ALSO NEED WHITE TEACHERS."[52] Similar indiscretions confirm that the advance of tolerance since the heyday of "Amos 'n' Andy" can still be measured in degrees.

Athletics, too, has seen blacks advancing in powerful strides but still unable to leap the highest racial hurdles. Fans now glory in black triumphs—the speed of Edwin Moses, the airborne agility of basketball's Michael Jordan, the destructive power of the boxer Mike Tyson. But there are limits. Racist loyalties are easily stirred, as boxing promoters have shown by building up white contenders of often limited skill, for the box office appeal of a "great white hope" battling a black champion. And while black physical skills are no longer disparaged, as in the days when athletic leagues were segregated, blacks have yet to receive recognition for mental and leadership qualities in any American sport.

Forty years after Jackie Robinson entered the major leagues, jobs as managers and administrators are nearly beyond the reach of blacks. The Los Angeles Dodgers vice-president Al Campanis explained on television in April 1987 that this was due not to racism but to the fact that blacks lacked the "necessities" for these executive positions. The seventy-year-old Campanis, unaccustomed to the media spotlight, was immediately fired for his expression of views doubtless known to his colleagues over many decades.[53] Yet the policy of tokenism in baseball's upper echelons continued.

Racial stereotyping pervades other sports as well. "Thinking" and leadership positions in football, such as those of quarterback and coach, are generally reserved for whites no matter how many blacks stand out elsewhere in the lineup. And in basketball, where blacks hold nearly every record except that for frequency of promotion to administrative roles, it is common to see five black players huddled around a white coach.

More ominous for blacks than the racism in sports and entertainment is the public view that these fields provide broad avenues of mobility for blacks with initiative. In fact they permit no more than a trickle of talented individuals to escape poverty, which would be true even if all professional athletes and entertainers were black. The visibility and lucrative contracts of several hundred media heroes belie the misery of millions in the black underclass, whose lot has generally worsened since the height of civil rights protest.

Flaming buildings in Watts brought the ghettos into national view in 1965. Twenty years later a study of Watts commissioned by the city and county of Los Angeles revealed isolated improvements amid systemic decay. Watts in 1985 featured a new hospital, a civic center, better bus service, and a shopping center named for Dr. King that featured the first full-service supermarket built since the riot. But unemployment, a major cause of the riot, had risen from under 12 percent at the time of the 1960 census to nearly 20 percent in 1980. The estimated actual jobless rate in Watts, including those no longer seeking work and those who never entered the labor force, was 30 percent for adults and 50 percent for teenagers.[54]

"There ain't no middle class right now—either you're up or you're down," said Duane Randolph, one of many Watts residents hurt by the loss of low-skilled factory jobs to automation and to suburban settings. Randolph formerly worked as a warehouse laborer and as a janitor for day-care centers but had held no job since the late seventies. "I've been on hold for a long time now," he said. "I'll be 29 next month, and my good thing ain't come around right now."[55] More fortunate was a resident who traveled up to two hours from Watts to his job, and back again, as a housekeeping porter at a hospital north of downtown Los Angeles. The slim rewards of such ambition could at best send mixed signals to other young black males seeking meaningful employment.

Government services since the riot have fallen further behind the need for better jobs and education. In 1985 not one comprehensive job-training or placement program operated in Watts. Existing programs were poorly coordinated and were further hurt when state officials closed the local office overseeing fair employment and housing. Public schools have also lost ground since the sixties. Overcrowding has forced year-round sessions, and the refusal of veteran teachers to accept assignment to Watts has led to staffing hundreds of classrooms with a series of temporary teachers. According to the government report, educational problems "remain critical and may be growing worse."[56]

As in 1965, Watts today encapsulates the outlook of urban black America. There are nearly ten million poor blacks—more than in 1960—and their numbers are growing faster than are those of the middle class. In 1960 three-quarters of all black men were employed, but barely half held jobs in 1980. Even this count was optimistic, for the Census Bureau was unable to find an additional 15 to 20 percent of all black men twenty to forty years old, who were presumed to have neither employment nor permanent residences. A realistic estimate, then, was that more than half of all black adult males did not have jobs, a figure twice the national unemployment level during the Great Depression.[57]

The unraveling of family ties has accompanied and aggravated this descent into the underclass. The proportion of single-parent, female-headed households grew from one-fifth of all black families in 1960 to nearly one-half in 1986, accounting for about 75 percent of all black children raised in poverty.[58] This is not a black problem alone; since 1970, births to single women have become more prevalent throughout American society, more than doubling among whites, to 14.5 percent in 1985. But among blacks the incidence of such births reached 60 percent.[59] It is a disastrous trend in a society where female-headed families, regardless of race, are four times as likely to be poor as all other families. In 1986 the median income for households headed by women was $13,647, compared with $32,805 for two-parent families of all races.[60]

Diminishing choices for young black men in particular have sharpened their survival skills, which take them outside the regular economy and, in many cases, the law. Young blacks in prison—over 56,000 males twenty to twenty-four years old in 1984—exceed by more than 25 percent the number of young blacks living in college dormitories.[61]

Violence in ghetto neighborhoods has grown with the burgeoning drug economy that produces immense wealth for major suppliers, affords "negative idols" for the young, and generates wars that recognize no bystanders as innocent. Adult prison gangs in Watts now deploy youth gangs as street troops to sell cocaine and murder rivals. Teens are increasingly armed and deadly to anyone caught in gang shootouts. Forty thousand gang members patrolled Los Angeles County in 1985, an increase of twelve thousand from 1980, and a number rising by 10 percent each year.[62]

For black males in the inner city, prison rather than college or career speeds the coming of age. The Harlem-born novelist Claude Brown observed that young blacks view the prospect of imprisonment with "nothing more than the mild apprehension or anxiety that attends, for instance, a bar mitzvah, joining the Marines or any other manhood initiation ritual in any normal society. One goes into the Marines as a young boy and comes out a 'real man.' It is the same with going into the 'joint,' as prison is called."[63]

At New Jersey's Trenton State Prison, Brown spoke with a black inmate, not quite old enough to shave, who was serving fifteen years—a "dime and nickel" sentence—for armed robbery. Brown painted for the youth a future of certain tragedy if he continued to pursue his criminal ways. Each time he went on the prowl for a victim or an establishment, there was a 60 percent likelihood of his being killed, permanently maimed, or ending up doing a long "bit" in jail. Even if he successfully carried off nine or ten robberies for $1,000 or more, in a few days to a week at most he'd be back where he started. The boy responded,

I see where you comin' from, Mr. Brown, but you got things kind of turned around the wrong way. You see, all the things that you say could happen to me is dead on the money, and that is why I can't lose. Look at it from my point of view for a minute. Let's say I go and get wiped [killed]. Then I ain't got no more needs, right? All my problems are solved. I don't need no more money, no more nothing, right? O.K., supposin' I get popped, shot in the spine and paralyzed for the rest of my life—that could happen playin' football, you know. Then I won't need a whole lot of money because I won't be able to go no place and do nothin', right? So, I'll be on welfare, and the welfare check is all the money I'll need, right? Now if I get busted and end up in the joint pullin' a dime and a nickel, like I am, then I don't have to worry about no bucks, no clothes. I get free rent and three squares a day. So you see, Mr. Brown, I really can't lose.

This logic, at once murderous and suicidal, left Brown relieved that the youth was serving a fifteen-year sentence: "It would be twice as comforting to know that this young cynic was doing a 30-year bit."[64] Still, as Brown realized, the problem reached beyond the fate of one prisoner, to racial legacies that neither time nor civil rights laws alone could redeem.

A Record of Change

Like other reform movements the crusade for racial justice inevitably fell short of the utopian goals that sustained it. Still, if America's civil rights movement is judged by the distance it traveled rather than by barriers yet to be crossed, a record of substantial achievement unfolds. In communities throughout the South, "whites only" signs that had stood for generations suddenly came down from hotels, rest rooms, theaters, and other facilities. Blacks and whites seldom mingle socially at home, but they are apt to lunch together at fast-food shops that once drew blacks only for sit-ins. Integration extends equally to Southern workers, whether at diner counters or in the high-rise office buildings that now afford every Southern city a skyline.

School desegregation also quickened its pace and by the mid-1970s had become fact as well as law in over 80 percent of all Southern public schools. Swelling private school enrollments have tarnished but not substantially reversed this achievement. A privileged 5 to 10 percent of all Southern white children may find shelter from the *Brown* verdict at private academies; but the words "massive resistance" have virtually disappeared from the region's political vocabulary.

Hate groups once flourished without strong federal restraint, but the civil rights movement has curbed the Ku Klux Klan and other extremist threats. Beginning in 1964 the FBI infiltrated the Klan so thoroughly that by 1965 perhaps one in five members was an informant. During the 1980s, amid a rise in racial assaults, synagogue bombings, and armed robberies to bankroll fringe groups, the federal government mounted the largest campaign against organized subversion since World War II. In 1987, members of the Florida Realm of the United Klans of America were convicted of illegal paramilitary training exercises, and leaders of the Identity Movement, which preaches a theology of hatred toward Jews and blacks, were indicted for conspiring to overthrow the government. Federal action has encouraged private lawsuits, including one that bankrupted the United Klans of America. After a black teenager in Mobile, Alabama, was murdered by Klansmen and left hanging from a tree in 1981, the boy's family won a $7 million judgment. To pay damages the Klan had to cede its two-story national headquarters, near Tuscaloosa, Alabama, to the black litigants. Reeling from legal and financial adversity, Klan membership declined from 10,000 in 1981 to less than 5,500 in 1987, the lowest since the early seventies.[65]

Protection of voting rights represents the movement's most unalloyed success, more than doubling black voter registration, to 64 percent, in the seven states covered by the 1965 act. Winning the vote literally changed the complexion of government service in the South. When Congress passed the Voting Rights Act, barely 100 blacks held elective office in the country; by 1989 there were more than 7,200, including 24 congressmen and some 300 mayors. Over 4,800 of these officials served in the South, and nearly every Black Belt county in Alabama had a black sheriff. Mississippi experienced the most radical change, registering 74 percent of its voting-age blacks and leading the nation in the number of elected black officials (646).[66]

Black influence in electoral politics acquired a compelling symbol during the 1980s with the emergence of the Reverend Jesse Jackson of Chicago as a presidential contender. As a young aide to Dr. King from 1966 to 1968, Jackson had stood out for his eloquence, élan, and ambition. In the 1970s Jackson won national acclaim for spurring ghetto youths to excel in school, but his denunciations of American society as racist, capitalist, and imperialist kept him on the fringes of public life. Over the next decade, however, as blacks increasingly protested President Reagan's neglect of minorities and the poor, Jackson began to temper his revolutionary message in hopes of forging a revitalized reform coalition.

Jackson campaigned in the 1984 Democratic presidential primaries, drawing large crowds and intense media coverage with his mixture of evangelical fervor, nimble wit, and self-conscious identification with minority hopes. He spoke of a "Rainbow Coalition" that would transcend racial lines, though his campaign chiefly focused on mobilizing black voter registration and turnout with the aid of Negro churches. This strategy enabled Jackson to win nomination contests in South Carolina, Louisiana, and Washington, D.C., and to finish third in delegates at the Democratic National Convention. Partly offsetting this achievement was Jackson's failure to draw even 5 percent of the white voters, whether because of his race, radical image, or suspect character. (Jews in particular recoiled at Jackson's ties with the Black Muslim Louis Farrakhan, who had branded Judaism a "gutter religion.")[67] Despite these weaknesses Jackson's campaign legitimized Black Power to the American people in a way that Stokely Carmichael and others in the 1960s had vainly tried to do from outside the political mainstream.

In 1988 Jackson hewed closer to the political center and reached well beyond his core supporters, in a second bid for the Democratic presidential nomination. The now seasoned candidate trimmed his radical rhetoric, conciliated many who had thought him opportunistic and divisive, and emphasized broadly appealing liberal themes of economic opportunity for all citizens. Jackson's approach, which this time afforded him second place among seven competitors, reflected and fostered a new openness toward blacks in the Democratic party and in the nation. An especially prominent landmark of political change was Jackson's Michigan primary victory, with 54 percent of the vote, just twenty years after that state's Democratic contest had gone to the Alabama segregationist George Wallace. The candidate's progress, as in 1984, remained in key respects exceedingly personal, for it did not appreciably change his party's stand on key issues nor dispel racism as a factor in national politics. Still, more than any black leader since Martin Luther King, Jr., Jackson had inspired Americans with the faith—crucial to every reform movement—that the decisive stage of America's democratic odyssey lay just ahead.

Despite unsettling parallels with the aftermath of Reconstruction, the modern civil rights movement should prove better able to resist the undoing of black gains. A salient difference is the greater reluctance in recent times to risk convulsing society by spurning the ideal of equality. Blacks during Reconstruction had exerted relatively minor influence over the white leadership that instituted—and then abandoned—measures for racial justice. By contrast blacks a century later shook whole cities with mass demonstrations, demanded and secured sweeping changes in federal law, and reshaped the political agenda of two strong-minded chief executives. These protests brought a new respect for Afro-Americans, breaking forever the comfortable myth that blacks were content with a biracial society and proving that they had the rare courage needed to challenge it.

New currents in world affairs have reinforced the consensus to guarantee black civil rights. During the late nineteenth century Americans were largely indifferent to the nonwhite world except for the growing possibilities of colonizing or otherwise controlling it. The European nations that most influenced this country were themselves indulging in imperialism based on racial as well as national interests. Global pressures today are vastly different. Competition for the support of nonwhite nations and the near-universal ostracism of South Africa, which asserts a racist ideology, require American society to pay at least nominal homage to racial equality.

Pluralism is also more firmly rooted in American values than ever before. The black revolution stimulated others, including women, homosexuals, Hispanics, native Americans, and Asians, who frequently modeled their actions on the values and tactics popularized by Martin Luther King, Jr. Each emerging movement, while pursuing a discrete agenda, has bolstered the principle that government must guarantee equal rights and opportunities to all citizens.

Racism lost more than legal standing with the triumph of civil rights campaigns; it lost social standing. Even the Daughters of the American Revolution, an organization known for its racially exclusive character, apologized in 1982 for having spurned the singer Marian Anderson over four decades earlier. The DAR's president general, a native of Beulah, Mississippi, invited Anderson to perform at the organization's ninety-first convention in Constitution Hall. The eighty-year-old singer was by then too frail to attend, but the black soprano Leontyne Price, who treated the DAR to a concert ending with "The Battle Hymn of the Republic," assured her interracial audience that Anderson was "here in spirit."[68]

The deepening interest in racial harmony has encouraged recognition of the black experience as central to American history. The 1977 television drama "Roots," which engaged audiences in the trauma of racial slavery and the struggle for freedom, became the most widely viewed special series in the history of the medium. Six years later Congress created a holiday to honor Martin Luther King, Jr., and by extension the civil rights movement he symbolized. Such a tribute had eluded Thomas Jefferson, Andrew Jackson, both Roosevelts, and other giants of American history. President Reagan, who had originally opposed enacting a holiday for King as an unwise "ethnic" precedent, signed the popular bill into law while standing alongside King's widow, Coretta.

In the South, as in the rest of the nation, few whites seriously contemplate returning to the state of race relations before 1960. This outlook differs strikingly from Southern intransigence after Reconstruction and reflects the disparate ways in which the two eras of racial change occurred. Reconstruction came as a sudden, violently imposed upheaval in Southern race relations that virtually nothing in the region's history had prepared it to accept. The civil rights movement instead advanced nonviolently, secured small gains over decades, and fostered progress from within the region. The campaigns that ended legalized segregation in the sixties marked the culmination of this gradual change. Many white Southerners had by then reconciled themselves to reforms that seemed inevitable and even, perhaps, beneficial.

Freed from the albatross of defending Jim Crow at the expense of national respect and regional peace, Southerners could focus on tasks of economic and social modernization. Mississippi's leading journal, the *Jackson Clarion-Ledger,* offered a glimpse into this revolution in priorities. After the March on Washington in 1963, a front-page story reported that the capital was "clean again with Negro trash removed." Twenty years later the paper won a Pulitzer Prize in public service for exposing the need for fuller desegregation and better funding of public schools.[69]

Southern memories of black protests have mellowed to the point where both races treat them as parts of their history to be proud of. Montgomery motorists now drive down the Martin Luther King, Jr. Expressway, and the Dexter Baptist Church, where King was pastor, has become a national landmark. The prison cell King occupied in Birmingham is set aside as a library for inmates, his "Letter from a Birmingham Jail" framed on the wall. In Georgia's capitol a portrait of King hangs near a bust of Alexander Stephens, the Confederate vice-president. One elderly black tour guide, assigned to interpret these landmarks of the past, ignored the bust of Stephens, and beamed, "Here is Nobel Prize winner Martin Luther King, Jr. He was born and bred right here in Atlanta on Auburn Avenue."[70]

Political calculation has sealed this acceptance of racial change. Over a quiet bourbon and branch water in his Senate office, Mississippi's arch-segregationist James Eastland confided, "When [blacks] get the vote, I won't be talking this way anymore."[71] Later Eastland was among the many officials who jettisoned their tested appeals to prejudice, learned to pronounce "Negro" in place of more casual epithets, and prefaced the names of newly valued black constituents with the once forbidden appellation "Mister."

Even the past master of race baiting, Alabama's George Wallace, was struck color-blind on the road to Montgomery in his 1982 gubernatorial campaign. Wallace, who like most politicians believed above all in winning elections today, tomorrow, and forever, spent much of his hard-fought contest kissing black babies and humbly supplicating their parents' support, assuring them of his reborn attitudes on race matters. (He won the campaign with the aid of a forgiving black electorate and welcomed several blacks to positions in his cabinet.) Whatever Wallace's deepest sentiments, his actions were a striking testament to the legacy of the civil rights protests that he once vowed to crush but that instead have left an indelible imprint on the nation's moral landscape.

The full impact of civil rights campaigns has yet to be felt. The movement could not wholly sweep away old Jim Crow hierarchies, but rather superimposed new patterns of behavior on a still race-conscious society. Cities like Selma, Alabama, where black activists battled white supremacists in the 1960s, today reflect two eras of race relations at once, giving no final sign of which will prevail.

Segregated neighborhoods persist in Selma, along with segregated social patterns. The Selma Country Club has no black members and until 1983 would not allow a black dance band inside. Elks Club members attend separate white and black chapters. Nearly a thousand white students attend two private academies founded with the express purpose of excluding blacks. Racial lines run through the city's economy: the overall jobless rate in Selma in 1985 was 16 percent but nearly twice as high for blacks as for whites. And in politics, residents tend to make racial choices for public office. The black community leader Frederick Reese won 40 percent of the mayoral vote in 1984 but only a handful of white supporters; Joseph Smitherman received 10 to 15 percent of the black vote but stayed in office with nearly 100 percent of the white vote.

Yet race relations in Selma have noticeably changed since the city's landmark civil rights demonstrations in 1965. The onetime "moderate segregationist" Smitherman began to tend an image as a facilitator of black mobility. In 1984 Smitherman observed proudly that 40 percent of the police force was black, including the assistant chief, several lieutenants, captains, and key department heads. The city's personnel board had three blacks and two whites, the eight-person library board was evenly composed of blacks and whites, and the school board had five blacks to four whites. Asphalt pavement, which had often stopped short of black neighborhoods, now stretched for miles throughout the town, covering over dirt roads and, with them, an era of flagrant neglect of black residents.

Perhaps most important to Selma's blacks and many whites, the movement reduced ignorance, fear, and hate. The black lawyer and civil rights activist J. L. Chestnut remarked in 1985, on the twentieth anniversary of his city's civil rights marches, that new attitudes were taking root: "My children don't think of white children as devils, and I don't think white children see my kids as watermelon-eating, tap-dancing idiots. If there is hope, it is in the fact that children in Selma today don't have to carry the baggage that Joe Smitherman and J. L. Chestnut carry. And that means they will never be scared the way we used to be scared." Teenagers at Selma's integrated public high school knew about the events of "Bloody Sunday" but viewed them as a mystery from another time. "Kids today, they're used to the way things are," explained Karyn Reddick, a black student. "Try as you can, you can't believe that white people once treated black people that way. It seems like something that happened long, long ago."[72]

ABBREVIATIONS

AC   *Atlanta Constitution*

CD   *Chicago Defender*

CORE Papers   CORE Archives, 1941–67, on microfilm, 49 reels, from King Center

CORE Papers Addendum   CORE Archives, 1944–68, further materials emphasizing CORE's growing militancy in response to the Black Power movement, on microfilm, 25 reels, from State Historical Society of Wisconsin, Madison, Wisconsin

CRDP   Civil Rights Documentation Project, Oral History Collection, at Howard University, Washington, D.C.

Johnson Library   Lyndon B. Johnson Library, Austin, Texas

Kennedy Library   John F. Kennedy Library, Boston, Massachusetts

King Center   Martin Luther King, Jr., Center for Nonviolent Change, Atlanta, Georgia

NAACP Papers   Records of the NAACP at the Library of Congress, Washington, D.C.

NUL Papers   Records of the National Urban League at the Library of Congress, Washington, D.C.

NYT   *New York Times*

PC   *Pittsburgh Courier*

SNCC Papers   Student Nonviolent Coordinating Committee Archives, 1959–72, on microfilm, 72 reels, from King Center

Wilkins Papers   Roy Wilkins Papers at the Library of Congress, Washington, D.C.

Notes

1. Origins of the Movement

1. Howell Raines, ed., *My Soul Is Rested: Movement Days in the Deep South Remembered* (New York: Penguin Books, 1983), p. 75.
2. Miles Wolff, *Lunch at the Five and Ten: The Greensboro Sit-ins: A Contemporary History* (New York: Stein and Day, 1970), pp. 25–26.
3. Raines, *My Soul Is Rested,* p. 76.
4. Wolff, *Lunch at the Five and Ten,* p. 16.
5. Raines, *My Soul Is Rested,* pp. 77–78; Pat Watters, *Down to Now: Reflections on the Southern Civil Rights Movement* (New York: Pantheon Books, 1971), p. 74.
6. Raines, *My Soul Is Rested,* p. 77.
7. Ibid., p. 78.
8. Ibid., p. 77.
9. Wolff, *Lunch at the Five and Ten,* p. 41.
10. Cleveland Sellers with Robert Terrell, *The River of No Return: The Autobiography of a Black Militant and the Life and Death of SNCC* (New York: William Morrow, 1973), p. 18.
11. Thomas F. Gossett, *Race: The History of an Idea in America* (Dallas: Southern Methodist University Press, 1963), p. 272.
12. John Hope Franklin, "History of Racial Segregation in the United States," *Annals of the Academy of Political and Social Science* 304 (March 1956): 1–9; on the persistent exclusion of blacks from Southern libraries, see *NYT,* Mar. 16, 1962, p. 19, which details the first attempt by blacks to break racial barriers at a public library in Montgomery, Alabama, since the institution was founded in 1898.
13. Watters, *Down to Now,* p. 34.
14. Herbert Garfinkel, *When Negroes March: The March on Washington Movement in the Organizational Politics for FEPC* (New York: Atheneum, 1969), p. 17.
15. Ibid., p. 21.
16. John M. Blum, *V Was for Victory: Politics and American Culture during World War II* (New York: Harcourt Brace Jovanovich, 1977), p. 190.
17. Lenora E. Berson, *The Negroes and the Jews* (New York: Random House, 1971), p. 96.
18. Gunnar Myrdal, with the assistance of Richard Sterner and Arnold Rose, *An American Dilemma: The Negro Problem and Modern Democracy* (New York: Harper and Bros., 1944), 2:1021.
19. Peter Lyon, *Eisenhower: Portrait of the Hero* (Boston: Little, Brown, 1974), p. 563.
20. *CD,* Feb. 20, 1960, p. 1.
21. James Farmer, *Lay Bare the Heart: An Autobiography of the Civil Rights Movement* (New York: Arbor House, 1985), p. 80.
22. Martin Luther King, Jr., *Stride toward Freedom: The Montgomery Story* (New York: Harper, 1958), p. 37.
23. Jo Ann Gibson Robinson, *The Montgomery Bus Boycott and the Women Who Started It,* ed. David J. Garrow (Knoxville: University of Tennessee Press, 1987), p. 46.
24. Raines, *My Soul Is Rested,* p. 45.
25. Ibid., pp. 48–49.
26. Henry David Thoreau, *Walden and Civil Disobedience,* ed. Owen Thomas (New York: W. W. Norton, 1966), p. 233.
27. Walter Rauschenbusch, *Christianity and the Social Crisis* (New York: Harper and Row, 1964; originally published in 1907), p. 418.
28. King, *Stride toward Freedom,* pp. 96–97.
29. Stephen B. Oates, *Let the Trumpet Sound: The Life of Martin Luther King, Jr.* (New York: Harper and Row, 1982), p. 8.
30. Ibid.
31. Ibid., p. 15; William Miller, *Martin Luther King, Jr.: His Life, Martyrdom and Meaning for the World* (New York: Weybright and Talley, 1968), pp. 7–10.
32. Interview with Richmond Smiley by Judy Barton, Jan. 27, 1972, p. 10, King Center, Oral History Collection.
33. King, *Stride toward Freedom,* pp. 136–37.
34. Ibid., p. 78.
35. Ibid., p. 160.
36. Ibid., p. 162.

37. Roy Wilkins with Tom Mathews, *Standing Fast: The Autobiography of Roy Wilkins* (New York: Viking Press, 1982), pp. 221, 246.

38. Aldon D. Morris, *The Origins of the Civil Rights Movement: Black Communities Organizing for Change* (New York: Free Press, 1984), pp. 188, 198.

2. The Sit-ins

1. Cleveland Sellers with Robert Terrell, *The River of No Return: The Autobiography of a Black Militant and the Life and Death of SNCC* (New York: William Morrow, 1973), p. 18.
2. Ruby Doris Smith and Robert Moses are quoted in Howard Zinn, *SNCC: The New Abolitionists,* 2d ed. (Boston: Beacon Press, 1965), p. 17.
3. Pat Watters, *Down to Now: Reflections on the Southern Civil Rights Movement* (New York: Pantheon Books, 1971), p. 82.
4. Robert J. Norvell, *Reaping the Whirlwind: The Civil Rights Movement in Tuskegee* (New York: Alfred A. Knopf, 1985), p. 171f., treats the quickening of student activism at Tuskegee in February 1960.
5. Miles Wolff, *Lunch at the Five and Ten: The Greensboro Sit-ins: A Contemporary History* (New York: Stein and Day, 1970), p. 64.
6. Letter by Martin Smolin (undated), reprinted in *Sit-ins: The Students Report* (New York: Congress of Racial Equality, 1960).
7. Clayborne Carson, *In Struggle: SNCC and the Black Awakening of the 1960s* (Cambridge: Harvard University Press, 1981), p. 21; Raines, *My Soul Is Rested,* p. 73.
8. Ibid.
9. Ibid., p. 22, provides background on Lawson's early years.
10. Martin Oppenheimer, "The Genesis of the Southern Negro Student Movement (Sit-in Movement): A Study in Contemporary Negro Protest" (Ph.D. thesis, University of Pennsylvania, 1963), pp. 189–91.
11. Bond's poem was later published in Langston Hughes and Arna Bontemps, eds., *The Poetry of the Negro, 1746–1970,* rev. ed. (Garden City, N.Y.: Anchor Press/Doubleday, 1970), p. 434.
12. Howell Raines, ed., *My Soul is Rested: Movement Days in the Deep South Remembered* (New York: Penguin Books, 1983), p. 84.
13. Ibid., p. 85; *AC,* Mar. 9, 1960, pp. 13, 60.
14. Raines, *My Soul Is Rested,* p. 86.
15. Ibid., pp. 86–87.
16. Ibid., p. 87.
17. *NYT,* Mar. 16, 1960, p. 27.
18. Ibid., Mar. 30, 1960, p. 25.
19. *AC,* Mar. 11, 1960, p. 2.
20. Ibid., Mar. 21, 1960, p. 2.
21. CORE Papers, reel 17, frame 01044.
22. Ibid., frame 01056.
23. Ibid., frame 01048.
24. Ibid., frame 01038.
25. Richard Haley, "Humdrum in Huntsville," 1962, ibid., frame 01059.
26. Zinn, *SNCC,* pp. 20, 25.
27. Ibid., p. 21.
28. CORE Papers, Addendum, reel 3, frame 0543.
29. Ibid., frame 0542.
30. Arnold Taylor, *Travail and Triumph: Black Life and Culture in the South since the Civil War* (Westport, Conn.: Greenwood Press, 1976), p. 241.
31. Zinn, *SNCC,* pp. 19–20.
32. CORE Papers, reel 31, frame 00048.
33. Raines, *My Soul Is Rested,* p. 87.
34. August Meier and Elliott Rudwick, *CORE: A Study in the Civil Rights Movement, 1942–1968* (New York: Oxford University Press, 1973), p. 118.
35. Jerome Smith, field report, May 25, 1962, CORE Papers, reel 17, frame 00414.
36. James Kilpatrick in the *Richmond News Leader,* Feb. 22, 1960, cited in Raines, *My Soul Is Rested,* p. 99.
37. Watters, *Down to Now,* p. 85.
38. Zinn, *SNCC,* p. 39.
39. Ibid., p. 14.
40. Raines, *My Soul is Rested,* p. 99; Zinn, *SNCC,* p. 19.
41. On the sources of dependency by Southern Negro leadership on white elites, see Louis Lomax, *The Negro Revolt* (New York: New American Library, 1963), esp. pp. 167–68. On the characteristics and attitudes of Southern Negro leadership, see Everett Carll Ladd, Jr., *Negro Political Leadership in the South* (Ithaca: Cornell University Press, 1966).
42. Lomax, *The Negro Revolt,* p. 209; see also *NYT,* Apr. 11, 1960, p. 25, on the expulsion of student demonstrators from Southern University.
43. *AC,* Mar. 11, 1960, p. 2.
44. *AC,* Mar. 3, 1960, p. 1.
45. Zinn, *SNCC,* p. 31.
46. Sellers, *The River of No Return,* p. 26.
47. Carson, *In Struggle,* p. 20. Capitalization has been standardized for purposes of clarity.
48. SNCC Papers, reel 1, frame 0001.
49. Ibid., frame 0007, 0009.
50. Carson, *In Struggle,* p. 24.
51. James M. Lawson, Jr., "From a Lunch-Counter Stool," reprinted in Francis L. Broderick and August Meier, ed., *Negro Protest Thought in the Twentieth Century* (Indianapolis: Bobbs-Merrill, 1965), pp. 274–81; quoted lines are on pp. 279–80. See also Sellers, *The River of No Return,* pp. 35–36, on reactions to Lawson's address.
52. Carson, *In Struggle,* p. 13.
53. Sellers, *The River of No Return,* pp. 36, 45.

54. See John M. Orbell, "Protest Participation among Southern Negro College Students," *American Political Science Review* 61 (June 1967): 446–56. Orbell gathered his data in 1962, when middle-class blacks still clearly predominated in protest campaigns. Later studies did not always reveal such pronounced middle-class characteristics among black protesters, which reflected a general rise in lower-class activism. See, for example, Anthony M. Orum and Amy W. Orum, "The Class and Status Bases of Negro Student Protest," *Social Science Quarterly* 49 (Dec. 1968): 521–33, based on data gathered in 1964.

55. Sellers, *The River of No Return,* pp. 40–41.

56. Ibid., p. 40; Meier and Rudwick, *CORE,* p. 113.

57. Zinn, *SNCC,* p. 21. The Reverend C. T. Vivian observed that "Fisk, for all its talk of being liberal, was far more restrictive of its students' participation" than some other schools, despite the "beautiful statements" of its president. See interview with C. T. Vivian, by Vincent J. Browne, Feb. 20, 1968, p. 18, CRDP.

58. John Neary, *Julian Bond: Black Rebel* (New York: William Morrow, 1971), p. 56.

59. Raines, *My Soul Is Rested,* pp. 87–88.

60. John Morsell, memorandum for staff discussion, May 2, 1960, in NAACP Papers, group IV, series A, container 3. This confidential memorandum and the ones by James Farmer and Robert L. Carter, cited below, were misfiled in an unrelated, and happily unrestricted, folder treating miscellaneous correspondence.

61. Robert L. Carter to John Morsell, May 5, 1960, p. 1, ibid.

62. James Farmer to John Morsell, May 6, 1960, p. 2, ibid.

63. Oppenheimer, "Genesis of the Southern Negro Student Movement," pp. 102.

64. Zinn, *SNCC,* p. 23.

65. See, for example, Oppenheimer, "Genesis of the Southern Negro Student Movement," pp. 245–54, treating the protest campaigns in Montgomery, Alabama.

66. William Brophy, "Active Acceptance—Active Containment: The Dallas Story," in *Southern Businessmen and Desegregation,* ed. Elizabeth Jacoway and David R. Colburn (Baton Rouge: Louisiana State University Press, 1982), pp. 146–50.

67. Raines, *My Soul Is Rested,* p. 92.

68. Ibid.

69. Ibid., p. 93.

70. *CD,* May 7, 1960, p. 1.

71. Sellers, *The River of No Return,* p. 44.

72. Ibid., pp. 42–43. An exception was Jane Stembridge, the first white member of SNCC's executive committee, who resigned in protest against the exclusion of Bayard Rustin.

73. Carson, *In Struggle,* p. 28.

74. *NYT,* Mar. 17, 1960, p. 16.

75. Elmo Richardson, *The Presidency of Dwight D. Eisenhower* (Lawrence: Regents Press of Kansas, 1979), p. 109.

76. "Billy Graham Says: 'Jim Crow Must Go,' " *CD,* Apr. 23, 1960, pp. 1–2.

77. Ibid.

78. Ibid., Dec. 24–30, 1960, p. 3.

3. Mass Protest in the Kennedy Years

1. Carl Brauer, *John F. Kennedy and the Second Reconstruction* (New York: Columbia University Press, 1977), p. 33.

2. Ibid.

3. "LBJ 'Bares Soul' over Civil Rights," *PC,* July 23, 1960, p. 6.

4. Arthur M. Schlesinger, Jr., *A Thousand Days: John F. Kennedy in the White House* (New York: Ballantine Books, 1965), pp. 59–60.

5. *AC,* Sept. 2, 1960, p. 1.

6. Roy Wilkins with Tom Mathews, *Standing Fast: The Autobiography of Roy Wilkins* (New York: Viking Press, 1982), p. 277.

7. King's arrest and its impact on the presidential election are recounted by Harris Wofford, *Of Kennedys and Kings: Making Sense of the Sixties* (New York: Farrar, Straus, and Giroux, 1980), pp. 11–28; Theodore H. White, *The Making of the President, 1960* (New York: Atheneum, 1961), pp. 345, 350–52; and Richard M. Nixon, *Six Crises* (New York: Doubleday, 1962), pp. 362–63, 403.

8. Interview with William Hartsfield by Charles T. Morrissey, Jan. 6, 1966, pp. 3–6, Kennedy Library, Oral History Project.

9. Wofford, *Of Kennedys and Kings,* pp. 21–22.

10. Ibid., p. 28; White, *The Making of the President, 1960,* p. 352.

11. Stephen B. Oates, *Let the Trumpet Sound: The Life of Martin Luther King, Jr.* (New York: Harper and Row, 1982), p. 159.

12. Wofford, *Of Kennedys and Kings,* p. 141.

13. Brauer, *John F. Kennedy and the Second Reconstruction,* p. 84.

14. Ibid., p. 71.

15. See E. Frederic Morrow, *Forty Years a Guinea Pig: A Black Man's View From the Top* (New York: Pilgrim Press, 1980), pp. 140–42.

16. Victor S. Navasky, *Kennedy Justice* (New York: Atheneum, 1971), p. 96.

17. Wofford, *Of Kennedys and Kings,* pp. 134–35.

18. Ibid., p. 135.

19. Ibid.

20. Ibid., p. 151.

21. Text quotation is in *CD,* July 2, 1960, p. 2; additional information on the boycott is found in *CD,* May 7, 1960, p. 12; July 2, 1960, pp. 1,10; July 16, 1960, p. 10; Oct. 8, 1960, p. 10; Jan. 7–13, 1961, p. 22.

22. Wofford, *Of Kennedys and Kings,* p. 136.
23. Ibid., pp. 136, 138.
24. Brauer, *John F. Kennedy and the Second Reconstruction,* pp. 120–23.
25. Wofford, *Of Kennedys and Kings,* p. 127–28; see *CD,* Jan. 28–Feb. 3, 1961, p. 3, on complaints by African officials.
26. August Meier and Elliot Rudwick, *CORE: A Study in the Civil Rights Movement, 1942–1968* (New York: Oxford University Press, 1973), p. 131.
27. Wofford, *Of Kennedys and Kings,* p. 151.
28. Medgar W. Evers to Gordon Carey, May 4, 1961, CORE Papers, reel 25, frame 00300.
29. Wilkins, *Standing Fast,* p. 283.
30. James Farmer, *Lay Bare the Heart: An Autobiography of the Civil Rights Movement* (New York: Arbor House, 1985), p. 195.
31. Meier and Rudwick, *CORE,* p. 136.
32. Howell Raines, ed., *My Soul Is Rested: Movement Days in the Deep South Remembered* (New York: Penguin Books, 1983), p. 111.
33. Farmer, *Lay Bare the Heart,* p. 201.
34. Genevieve Hughes, field report, May 15, 1961, CORE Papers, reel 25, frame 00014.
35. Ibid.; Albert Bigelow, report, May 25, 1962, ibid., reel 17, frame 00424.
36. See Raines, *My Soul Is Rested,* p. 114, and Peter Joseph, ed., *Good Times: An Oral History of America in the Nineteen Sixties* (New York: Charterhouse, 1973), p. 115.
37. Genevieve Hughes, field report, May 15, 1961, CORE Papers, reel 25, frame 00014.
38. Ibid., frame 00015.
39. Wofford, *Of Kennedys and Kings,* p. 152.
40. Brauer, *John F. Kennedy and the Second Reconstruction,* p. 99.
41. Wofford, *Of Kennedys and Kings,* p. 152.
42. Ibid, pp. 152–53.
43. Pat Watters, *Down to Now: Reflections on the Southern Civil Rights Movement* (New York: Pantheon Books, 1971), p. 103.
44. Ibid., p. 104.
45. Dick Cluster, ed., *They Should Have Served That Cup of Coffee: Seven Radicals Remember the Sixties* (Boston: South End Press, 1978), p. 5; Wofford, *Of Kennedys and Kings,* pp. 153–54.
46. Watters, *Down to Now,* p. 105.
47. Wofford, *Of Kennedys and Kings,* p. 154.
48. Juan Williams, with the "Eyes on the Prize" production team, *Eyes on the Prize: America's Civil Rights Years, 1954–1965* (New York: Viking Penguin, 1987), p. 155.
49. Interview with Burke Marshall by Anthony Lewis, June 14, 1964, p. 85, Kennedy Library, Oral History Project.
50. Farmer, *Lay Bare the Heart,* p. 205.
51. Navasky, *Kennedy Justice,* p. 24.
52. Farmer, *Lay Bare the Heart,* p. 206.
53. Wofford, *Of Kennedys and Kings,* p. 156.
54. Ibid.
55. Raines, *My Soul Is Rested,* p. 123.
56. Ibid., pp. 123–24.
57. *CD,* May 27–June 2, 1961, p. 1.
58. Meier and Rudwick, *CORE,* p. 141.
59. Ibid. pp. 141–42; Howard Zinn, *SNCC: The New Abolitionists,* 2d ed. (Boston: Beacon Press, 1965), p. 57; *The Progressive,* Nov. 1961.
60. Raines, *My Soul Is Rested,* p. 129. James Farmer estimated the total cost of all civil rights cases since the Greensboro sit-ins (there were no exact figures) in excess of $2,000,000. See James Farmer to Marvin Rich, CORE Papers, reel 17, frame 00415.
61. Brauer, *John F. Kennedy and the Second Reconstruction,* p. 108.
62. Ibid, p. 109.
63. Wofford, *Of Kennedys and Kings,* p. 160.
64. Cluster, *They Should Have Served That Cup of Coffee,* p. 16.
65. Wilkins, *Standing Fast,* p. 286; see also Louis Lomax, *The Negro Revolt* (New York: New American Library, 1963), p. 108f., on tensions between black student activists and the established civil rights groups in Albany, as well as between local and national black leaders. Marion Page, executive secretary of the Albany movement, explains how internal divisions led to its final collapse, in Watters, *Down to Now,* pp. 147ff.
66. David L. Lewis, *King: A Biography,* 2d ed. (Urbana: University of Illinois Press, 1978), pp. 152–53.
67. Ibid., pp. 163–64.
68. Oates, *Let the Trumpet Sound,* p. 191.
69. Lewis, *King,* p. 151; see also *Newsweek,* Aug. 13, 1962, p. 18, which notes Pritchett's study of Gandhi in order to outmaneuver the civil rights leadership.
70. Lewis, *King,* p. 159; David J. Garrow, *Bearing the Cross: Martin Luther King, Jr., and the Southern Christian Leadership Conference* (New York: William Morrow, 1986), pp. 203–4, reveals the secret arrangement among local leaders to end King's imprisonment.
71. Brauer, *John F. Kennedy and the Second Reconstruction,* p. 171.
72. Ibid., p. 172.
73. Watters, *Down to Now,* p. 220.
74. Oates, *Let the Trumpet Sound,* p. 199.
75. Lewis, *King,* p. 169.
76. Navasky, *Kennedy Justice,* p. 190.
77. Schlesinger, *A Thousand Days,* p. 947; Brauer, *John F. Kennedy and the Second Reconstruction,* pp. 192–93.
78. Schlesinger, *A Thousand Days,* p. 943.
79. Brauer, *John F. Kennedy and the Second Reconstruction,* p. 204.
80. Schlesinger, *A Thousand Days,* p. 966.
81. Lewis, *King,* p. 173.
82. Martin Luther King, Jr., *Why We Can't Wait* (New York: Mentor Books, 1964), p. 143.
83. Oates, *Let the Trumpet Sound,* pp. 219–20.
84. "Letter from Birmingham Jail" is reprinted in King, *Why We Can't Wait,* pp. 76–95.
85. Oates, *Let the Trumpet Sound,* p. 232.
86. King, *Why We Can't Wait,* p. 96.
87. Oates, *Let the Trumpet Sound,* p. 233.

88. King, *Why We Can't Wait,* p. 98; Raines, *My Soul Is Rested,* p. 171.
89. *NYT,* May 7, 1963, p. 33.
90. *NYT,* May 8, 1963, p. 28.
91. Lewis, *King,* p. 198, details the economic pressures that the Kennedy administration applied to Birmingham merchants.
92. King, *Why We Can't Wait,* p. 104.
93. Oates, *Let the Trumpet Sound,* p. 235.
94. Watters, *Down to Now,* p. 242.
95. According to the Southern Regional Council there were 14,733 arrests related to civil rights protests in eleven Southern states between April and November 1, 1963; 10,420 of these arrests occurred between April 3 and June 24. See *New South* 18 (Oct.–Nov. 1963): 20.
96. Schlesinger, *A Thousand Days,* p. 963.
97. Ibid.
98. Ibid.; see also the interview with Robert Kennedy conducted by John Bartlow Martin, Apr. 30, 1964, pp. 425–26, Kennedy Library, Oral History Collection, for Kennedy's account of the meeting.
99. Brauer, *John F. Kennedy and the Second Reconstruction,* p. 245.
100. Telephone conversation between Johnson and Theodore Sorensen, June 3, 1963, Johnson Library, Pre-Presidential files.
101. Brauer, *John F. Kennedy and the Second Reconstruction,* p. 247.
102. Ibid., p. 253.
103. Kennedy's speech of June 11, 1963, is reprinted in *Public Papers of the Presidents of the United States: John F. Kennedy, 1963* (Washington, D.C., U.S. Government Printing Office, 1964), pp. 468–71.
104. Brauer, *John F. Kennedy and the Second Reconstruction,* pp. 259–60.
105. King, *Why We Can't Wait,* p. 144.
106. Wilkins, *Standing Fast,* p. 290.
107. Herbert Garfinkel, *When Negroes March: The March on Washington Movement in the Organizational Politics of the FEPC* (New York: Atheneum, 1969), pp. 68–69.
108. Milton Viorst, *Fire in the Streets: America in the 1960's* (New York: Simon and Schuster, 1979), p. 206.
109. Ibid., pp. 199–231, is the main source of information for passages treating Bayard Rustin; it is supplemented by Meier and Rudwick, *CORE,* pp. 9–38, and two interviews with Rustin by the author.
110. Viorst, *Fire in the Streets,* p. 217.
111. Wilkins, *Standing Fast,* pp. 291–92.
112. Viorst, *Fire in the Streets,* p. 226.
113. Ibid., p. 223.
114. Nancy J. Weiss, "Whitney M. Young, Jr.: Committing the Power Structure to the Cause of Civil Rights," in *Black Leaders of the Twentieth Century,* ed. John Hope Franklin and August Meier (Urbana: University of Illinois Press, 1982), p. 342.
115. Schlesinger, *A Thousand Days,* pp. 969–71.
116. Arthur M. Schlesinger, Jr., *Robert Kennedy and His Times* (Boston: Houghton Mifflin, 1978), pp. 357–58. Taylor Branch, *Parting the Waters: America in the King Years, 1954–63* (New York: Simon and Schuster, 1988), pp. 566–69, details Hoover's use of personal as well as political pressure to extract approval from the Kennedys for FBI surveillance of King.
117. Schlesinger, *Robert Kennedy,* pp. 358–59.
118. An advance text of Lewis's speech is in NUL Papers, part 2, series 5, container 12.
119. Wilkins, *Standing Fast,* p. 293.
120. Clayborne Carson, *In Struggle: SNCC and the Black Awakening of the 1960's* (Cambridge: Harvard University Press, 1981), p. 93.
121. Peter Goldman, *The Death and Life of Malcolm X,* 2d ed. (Urbana: University of Illinois Press, 1979), p. 107.
122. A larger estimate of 400,000 is persuasively argued by Seymour Posner, public relations director for the March on Washington, in a letter of Aug. 29, 1983, "Uncounted in the 1963 March on Washington," in *NYT,* Sept. 5, 1983, p. 18.
123. Wilkins, *Standing Fast,* p. 292.
124. *Boston Globe,* Aug. 27, 1983, p. 1.
125. Oates, *Let the Trumpet Sound,* pp. 261–62.
126. James Baldwin, *No Name in the Street* (New York: Dial Press, 1972), p. 140.
127. *Public Papers of the Presidents of the United States: John F. Kennedy, 1963,* p. 572.
128. Ibid., p. 645.
129. Goldman, *The Death and Life of Malcolm X,* p. 107.
130. Schlesinger, *A Thousand Days,* p. 968.
131. Brauer, *John F. Kennedy and the Second Reconstruction,* p. 299.
132. Ibid., p. 297.
133. Ibid., p. 300.
134. Ibid., p. 301.
135. *Public Papers of the Presidents of the United States: John F. Kennedy, 1963,* p. 849.

4. The Great Society

1. Coretta Scott King, *My Life with Martin Luther King, Jr.* (New York: Holt, Rinehart and Winston, 1969), pp. 243–45.
2. Lyndon Baines Johnson, *The Vantage Point: Perspectives of the Presidency, 1963–1969* (New York: Holt, Rinehart and Winston, 1971), p. 155.
3. Ibid.
4. Ibid., p. 157.
5. Speech of Nov. 27, 1963, reprinted in *Public Papers of the Presidents of the United States: Lyndon B. Johnson, 1963–64* (Washington, D.C., U.S. Government Printing Office, 1965), bk I, pp. 8–9.

6. Johnson, *The Vantage Point,* p. 157.
7. Doris Kearns, *Lyndon Johnson and the American Dream* (New York: Harper and Row, 1976), p. 191.
8. Ibid., p. 192; Roy Wilkins with Tom Mathews, *Standing Fast: The Autobiography of Roy Wilkins* (New York: Viking Press, 1982), p. 296.
9. Kearns, *Lyndon Johnson and the American Dream,* p. 192.
10. Wilkins, *Standing Fast,* p. 296.
11. Ibid.
12. Johnson, *The Vantage Point,* p. 37.
13. Wilkins, *Standing Fast,* pp. 299–300.
14. Ibid., pp. 233–34.
15. Eric F. Goldman, *The Tragedy of Lyndon Johnson* (New York: Alfred A. Knopf, 1969), p. 69.
16. Charles Whalen and Barbara Whalen, *The Longest Debate: A Legislative History of the 1964 Civil Rights Act* (Cabin John, Md.: Seven Locks Press, 1985), pp. 116–17.
17. *NYT,* Feb. 9, 1964, p. 52.
18. Whalen, *The Longest Debate,* p. 117.
19. Wilkins, *Standing Fast,* pp. 300–301.
20. Whalen, *The Longest Debate,* p. 165.
21. Ibid., p. 201.
22. Speech by Senator Dirksen, on June 10, 1964, reprinted in the *Congressional Record,* vol. 110, pt. 10, 88th Cong., 2d sess., (Washington, D.C.: U.S. Government Printing Office, 1964), p. 13319.
23. *NYT,* July 10, 1964, pp. 1, 10.
24. Whalen, *The Longest Debate,* p. 205.
25. Wilkins, *Standing Fast,* p. 302.
26. Whalen, *The Longest Debate,* p. 205.
27. *NYT,* May 20, 1964, p. 1.
28. Medgar Evers as told to Francis H. Mitchell, "Why I Live in Mississippi," *Ebony,* Nov. 1958, p. 70.
29. Ibid., p. 69.
30. Juan Williams, with the "Eyes on the Prize" production team, *Eyes on the Prize: America's Civil Rights Years, 1954–1965* (New York: Viking Press, 1987), p. 52.
31. Wilkins, *Standing Fast,* p. 222.
32. Len Holt, *The Summer That Didn't End* (London: William Heinemann, 1965), p. 104.
33. *Ebony,* Nov. 1958, p. 67.
34. Medgar Evers, Annual Report to the NAACP, Nov. 14, 1957, Wilkins Papers, box 27, "Mississippi" folder.
35. On Lewis Allen, see Seth Cagin and Philip Dray, *We Are Not Afraid: The Story of Goodman, Schwerner, and Chaney and the Civil Rights Campaign for Mississippi* (New York: Macmillan, 1988), pp. 227–28.
36. See David J. Garrow, *Protest at Selma: Martin Luther King, Jr., and the Voting Rights Act of 1965* (New Haven: Yale University Press, 1978), p. 20; and Victor S. Navasky, *Kennedy Justice* (New York: Atheneum, 1971), pp. 117–19.
37. Howard Zinn, *SNCC: The New Abolitionists,* 2d ed. (Boston: Beacon Press, 1965), pp. 188–89.

38. Howell Raines, ed., *My Soul Is Rested: Movement Days in the Deep South Remembered* (New York: Penguin Books, 1983), p. 274.
39. Mary A. Rothschild, *A Case of Black and White: Northern Volunteers and the Southern Freedom Summers, 1964–1965* (Westport, Conn.: Greenwood Press, 1982), pp. 31–47, analyzes the backgrounds and motivations of volunteers for the freedom summer project.
40. James Atwater, "If We Can Crack Mississippi," *Saturday Evening Post,* July 25–Aug. 1, 1964, pp. 16–17.
41. Ibid., p. 17.
42. *NYT,* July 3, 1964, p. 8.
43. Young is quoted in Pat Watters, *Down to Now: Reflections on the Southern Civil Rights Movement* (New York: Pantheon Books, 1971), p. 137.
44. See Holt, *The Summer That Didn't End,* p. 46.
45. Ibid., p. 282.
46. Cleveland Sellers with Robert Terrell, *The River of No Return: The Autobiography of a Black Militant and the Life and Death of SNCC* (New York: William Morrow, 1973), pp. 79–80.
47. Holt, *The Summer That Didn't End,* p. 49.
48. Ibid., p. 50.
49. Lenora E. Berson, *The Negroes and the Jews* (New York: Random House, 1971), p. 121.
50. "Mississippi — 'Everybody's Scared,'" *Newsweek,* July 6, 1964, p. 15.
51. Holt, *The Summer That Didn't End,* p. 21.
52. Sellers, *The River of No Return,* p. 84.
53. Elizabeth Sutherland, ed., *Letters from Mississippi* (New York: McGraw-Hill, 1965), p. 27.
54. Raines, *My Soul Is Rested,* p. 289.
55. Sutherland, *Letters from Mississippi,* p. 68.
56. Zinn, *SNCC,* pp. 181–82.
57. Sutherland, *Letters from Mississippi,* p. 77.
58. Rothschild, *A Case of Black and White,* pp. 102, 106.
59. Paul Jacobs and Saul Landau, *The New Radicals: A Report with Documents* (New York: Random House, 1966), pp. 131–35.
60. Alice Walker, *Meridian* (New York: Pocket Books/Washington Square Press, 1977), pp. 130, 166.
61. Sara Evans, *Personal Politics: The Roots of Women's Liberation in the Civil Rights Movement and the New Left* (New York: Vintage Books, 1979), p. 87.
62. Rothschild, *A Case of Black and White,* pp. 138–39, 152 n. 29.
63. *NYT,* May 13, 1967, p. 21.
64. Rothschild, *A Case of Black and White,* p. 59.
65. *NYT,* Aug. 9, 1964, p. 62.
66. Sellers, *The River of No Return,* p. 107.
67. Ibid., p. 94.
68. Rothschild, *A Case of Black and White,* p. 73.
69. Watters, *Down to Now,* p. 285.

70. August Meier and Elliott Rudwick, *CORE: A Study in the Civil Rights Movement, 1942–1968* (New York: Oxford University Press, 1973), p. 324.
71. Kearns, *Lyndon Johnson and the American Dream*, p. 192; *NYT*, July 30, 1964, p. 1.
72. Interview with James Farmer by Paige Mulhollan, July 20, 1971, tape 2, p. 3, Johnson Library, Oral History Project.
73. Stokely Carmichael and Charles V. Hamilton, *Black Power: The Politics of Liberation in America* (New York: Vintage Books, 1967), p. 93; Len Holt, *The Summer That Didn't End*, p. 163.
74. Interview with Fannie Lou Hamer, Nov. 1966, in Anne Cooke Romaine, "The Mississippi Freedom Democratic Party through August, 1964" (M.A. thesis, University of Virginia, 1969), pp. 213–14.
75. Ibid., p. 214.
76. Interview with Joseph Rauh, June 1967, ibid., pp. 306–7.
77. Cagin and Dray, *We Are Not Afraid*, pp. 413–14.
78. Interview with Fannie Lou Hamer, in Romaine, "The Mississippi Freedom Democratic Party through August, 1964," pp. 214–15; interview with Edwin King, Aug. 1966, ibid., p. 271.
79. Clayborne Carson, *In Struggle: SNCC and the Black Awakening of the 1960's* (Cambridge: Harvard University Press, 1981), p. 125.
80. Holt, *The Summer That Didn't End*, p. 169.
81. Governor Johnson ultimately sanctioned a walkout by Mississippi regular Democrats from the national convention and refused to endorse President Johnson's candidacy. See *NYT*, Aug. 26, 1964, p. 28, and Aug. 27, 1964, p. 23.
82. Interview with Edwin King, who claimed Hubert Humphrey as his source, in Romaine, "The Mississippi Freedom Democratic Party through August, 1964," p. 269.
83. Interview with Joseph Rauh, June 1967, ibid., pp. 336–37.
84. Holt, *The Summer That Didn't End*, p. 171.
85. David J. Garrow, *Bearing the Cross: Martin Luther King, Jr., and the Southern Christian Leadership Conference* (New York: William Morrow, 1986), p. 348; Rauh discusses his convention role, in Romaine, "The Mississippi Freedom Democratic Party through 1964," pp. 301–53, and with Paige Mulhollan, Aug. 8, 1969, pp. 12–23, Johnson Library, Oral History Project.
86. James Forman, *The Making of Black Revolutionaries* (Washington, D.C.: Open Hand, 1985), p. 391.
87. Holt, *The Summer That Didn't End*, p. 171.
88. Forman, *The Making of Black Revolutionaries*, p. 392.
89. Ibid., p. 392; Arthur I. Waskow, "Notes on the Democratic National Convention, Atlantic City," August 1964, p. 30, in Anne Romaine Oral History Collection, box 1, folder 16, King Center.
90. Interview with Edwin King, in Romaine, "The Mississippi Freedom Democratic Party through August, 1964," p. 279.
91. Forman, *The Making of Black Revolutionaries*, p. 393.
92. Rothschild, *A Case of Black and White*, p. 70.
93. Forman, *The Making of Black Revolutionaries*, p. 393.
94. Ibid., p. 395.
95. An editorial in the *Washington Post*, Mar. 2, 1965, p. A16, "May It Please the Courts," reflected the mainstream liberal view that Leventhal's role in handling the Freedom party challenge was "statesmanly as well as politic."
96. Johnson, *The Vantage Point*, p. 101.
97. Stephen B. Oates, *Let the Trumpet Sound: The Life of Martin Luther King, Jr.* (New York: Harper and Row, 1982), p. 311.
98. Goldman, *The Tragedy of Lyndon Johnson*, pp. 234, 244; Theodore H. White, *The Making of the President, 1964* (New York: Atheneum, 1965), p. 382; Johnson, *The Vantage Point*, p. 110.
99. White, *The Making of the President, 1964*, pp. 400–401.
100. Ibid., p. 403.
101. Carson, *In Struggle*, p. 127.
102. Camichael and Hamilton, *Black Power*, p. 96.
103. Lawrence Guyot and Mike Thelwell, "The Politics of Necessity and Survival in Mississippi," *Freedomways* 6, no. 2 (Spring 1966): 132.
104. Holt, *The Summer That Didn't End*, p. 176.

5. The Voting Rights Campaign

1. Eric F. Goldman, *The Tragedy of Lyndon Johnson* (New York: Alfred A. Knopf, 1969), p. 318.
2. David J. Garrow, *Protest at Selma: Martin Luther King, Jr., and the Voting Rights Act of 1965* (New Haven: Yale University Press, 1978), pp. 27–28.
3. Ibid., p. 23.
4. Interview with Bernard Lafayette, conducted by the author, July 25, 1984.
5. Ibid.
6. Howard Zinn, *SNCC: The New Abolitionists*, 2d ed. (Boston: Beacon Press, 1965), p. 149.

7. Stephen B. Oates, *Let the Trumpet Sound: The Life of Martin Luther King, Jr.* (New York: Harper and Row, 1982), p. 336.

8. Zinn, *SNCC*, pp. 158–62.

9. Ibid., pp. 163–64.

10. Oates, *Let the Trumpet Sound*, p. 328; see also Charles Fager, *Selma 1965: The March That Changed the South* (New York: Scribner's, 1974), p. 9.

11. Cleveland Sellers with Robert Terrell, *The River of No Return: The Autobiography of a Black Militant and the Life and Death of SNCC* (New York: William Morrow, 1973), p. 119.

12. Howell Raines, ed., *My Soul Is Rested: Movement Days in the Deep South Remembered* (New York: Penguin Books, 1983), p. 197.

13. Oates, *Let the Trumpet Sound*, p. 335.

14. Ibid., p. 335.

15. Raines, *My Soul is Rested*, p. 198.

16. Ibid., p. 199.

17. Garrow, *Protest at Selma*, p. 43.

18. Fager, *Selma*, p. 35.

19. Oates, *Let the Trumpet Sound*, pp. 336–37.

20. "Selma—Notes on Strategy and Statements, Feb. 1965," King Papers 22:6, King Center.

21. Oates, *Let the Trumpet Sound*, p. 342.

22. *Time*, Feb. 12, 1965, p. 16.

23. Coretta King, *My Life with Martin Luther King, Jr.* (New York: Holt, Rinehart and Winston, 1969), p. 256.

24. Garrow, *Protest at Selma*, p. 57.

25. Ibid., p. 56; *NYT*, Feb. 13, 1965, p. 17.

26. Fager, *Selma*, p. 67.

27. Goldman, *The Tragedy of Lyndon Johnson*, p. 311; Fager, *Selma*, pp. 68–69; *NYT*, Feb. 13, 1965, p. 17.

28. Sheyann Webb and Rachel West Nelson, as told to Frank Sikora, *Selma, Lord, Selma* (New York: William Morrow, 1980), p. 69.

29. *NYT*, Feb. 13, 1965, p. 1.

30. Fager, *Selma*, p. 70; *NYT*, Feb. 17, 1965, p. 35.

31. Oates, *Let the Trumpet Sound*, p. 346.

32. Fager, *Selma*, pp. 89–90.

33. Oates, *Let the Trumpet Sound*, p. 347.

34. Fager, *Selma*, p. 93.

35. *NYT*, Mar. 8, 1965, p. 20.

36. Fager, *Selma*, p. 95.

37. George B. Leonard, "Midnight Plane to Alabama," *Nation*, May 10, 1965, p. 502.

38. Garrow, *Protest at Selma*, pp. 177–78.

39. See ibid., pp. 133–78, esp. p. 157. A nationwide Gallup poll in late March 1965 showed 76 percent of all Americans in favor of federal action to guarantee voting rights, compared with only 16 percent opposed. Among Southern whites, a plurality of 49 percent approved such action, with 37 percent opposed.

40. Fager, *Selma*, p. 101.

41. *NYT*, Mar. 8, 1965, pp. 1, 20.

42. Sellers, *The River of No Return*, pp. 123–24.

43. Ibid., p. 124.

44. Harris Wofford, *Of Kennedys and Kings: Making Sense of the Sixties* (New York: Farrar, Straus, and Giroux, 1980), p. 182.

45. Ibid., p. 183.

46. Fager, *Selma*, p. 105.

47. Wofford, *Of Kennedys and Kings*, pp. 184–85.

48. David L. Lewis, *King: A Biography*, 2d. ed. (Urbana: University of Illinois Press, 1978), p. 285.

49. Speech of March 15, printed in *Public Papers of the Presidents of the United States: Lyndon B. Johnson, 1965* (Washington, D.C.: U.S. Government Printing Office, 1966), pp. 281–87. Quotations are from pp. 281, 284.

50. Wofford, *Of Kennedys and Kings*, p. 188.

51. Oates, *Let the Trumpet Sound*, p. 350.

52. Ibid., pp. 355–56.

53. Lewis, *King*, p. 287.

54. Lyndon Baines Johnson, *The Vantage Point: Perspectives of the Presidency, 1963–1969* (New York: Holt, Rinehart and Winston, 1971), p. 163; Goldman, *The Tragedy of Lyndon Johnson*, pp. 314–15.

55. Johnson, *The Vantage Point*, p. 163.

56. Oates, *Let the Trumpet Sound*, pp. 356–57.

57. Ibid., p. 356.

58. Wofford, *Of Kennedys and Kings*, p. 188.

59. Oates, *Let the Trumpet Sound*, pp. 358–59.

60. Ibid., pp. 359–60.

61. Wofford, *Of Kennedys and Kings*, p. 192.

62. *NYT*, Mar. 23, 1965, p. 28.

63. *Newsweek*, Apr. 5, 1965, p. 25; Wofford, *Of Kennedys and Kings*, pp. 191–92.

64. *King: From Montgomery to Memphis*, unabridged film, in King Center.

65. Kathy Lange, the marcher, is quoted in "Marching through Alabama," *Peace News*, Apr. 16, 1965, pp. 3, 11, reprinted in CORE Papers, reel 17, frame 01008.

66. Wofford, *Of Kennedys and Kings*, pp. 196–97.

67. Ibid., p. 199.

68. The text is transcribed from the film *King: From Montgomery to Memphis.*

69. Fager, *Selma*, p. 164. Three members of the Ku Klux Klan were convicted of murdering Viola Liuzzo, and sentenced to a ten-year prison term, the maximum under a federal law of 1870 designed to protect against racially motivated violence. See *NYT*, Dec. 4, 1965, p. 1.

70. Goldman, *The Tragedy of Lyndon Johnson*, p. 327.

71. Doris Kearns, *Lyndon Johnson and the American Dream* (New York: Harper and Row, 1976), p. 226.

72. Goldman, *The Tragedy of Lyndon Johnson*, p. 328.

73. Wilkins, *Standing Fast*, p. 311.

74. Goldman, *The Tragedy of Lyndon Johnson*, pp. 328–29.

75. Ibid., p. 330.

76. Ibid., p. 331.

77. Interview with James Farmer by Paige Mulhollan, July 20, 1971, tape 2, p. 5, Johnson Library, Oral History Project.

78. *Public Papers of the Presidents of the United States: Lyndon B. Johnson, 1965,* bk. 2, p. 840.

79. Garrow, *Protest at Selma,* pp. 159–60.

80. Goldman, *The Tragedy of Lyndon Johnson,* p. 334.

6. The Ghettos Erupt

1. *NYT,* Jan. 6, 1964, p. C67.

2. John Hope Franklin, *From Slavery to Freedom: A History of Negro Americans,* 5th ed. (New York: Alfred A. Knopf, 1980), p. 478.

3. Charles C. Alexander, *Holding the Line: The Eisenhower Era, 1952–1961* (Bloomington: Indiana University Press, 1975), p. 116.

4. U.S. Bureau of the Census, *U.S. Census of Population: 1960, General Social and Economic Characteristics, United States Summary,* Final Report PC(1)-1C (Washington, D.C.: U.S. Government Printing Office, 1962), table 88; U.S. Bureau of the Census, *Historical Statistics of the United States: Colonial Times to 1970,* pt. 1 (Washington, D.C.: U.S. Government Printing Office, 1975), G 1-15, pp. 290, and G 189-204, p. 305; U.S. Bureau of the Census, Current Population Reports, series P-23, no. 42, *The Social and Economic Status of the Black Population in the United States, 1971* (Washington, D.C.: U.S. Government Printing Office, 1972), p. 53.

5. On New York State's decision to end this discriminatory practice, see *NYT,* Apr. 3, 1962, p. 27.

6. "Racism in Organized Labor: A Report of Five Years of the AFL-CIO, 1955–1960," NAACP Report, 1961, reprinted in CORE Papers, Addendum, reel 2, p. 7 of report, frame 0272.

7. Ibid., pp. 4–5, frame 0271.

8. Ibid., p. 2, frame 0270.

9. Mary Frances Berry and John W. Blassingame, *Long Memory: The Black Experience in America* (New York: Oxford University Press, 1982), p. 212.

10. U.S. Bureau of the Census, *Statistical Abstract of the United States: 1972* (Washington, D.C.: U.S. Government Printing Office, 1972), p. 329.

11. William Julius Wilson, *The Declining Significance of Race: Blacks and Changing American Institutions,* 2d ed. (Chicago: University of Chicago Press, 1980) p. 93, citing a study of the nation's twelve largest metropolitan areas from 1947 to 1970.

12. *Report of the National Advisory Commission on Civil Disorders* (New York: Bantam Books, 1968), p. 263.

13. Ibid., p. 267.

14. Ibid., p. 261, states that 23.7 percent of all nonwhite families in 1966 were headed by women, compared with 8.9 percent of all white families.

15. Ibid.

16. *NYT,* Jan. 11, 1964, p. 1.

17. Morris Renek, "Unpolished Nigger," *New Republic,* Sept. 9, 1967, p. 7.

18. Bayard Rustin, *Down the Line: The Collected Writings of Bayard Rustin* (Chicago: Quadrangle Books, 1971), p. 190.

19. James Farmer, "New York's Finest," reprinted in CORE Papers, Addendum, reel 1, frame 0107.

20. James Baldwin, *Nobody Knows My Name: More Notes of a Native Son* (New York: Dial Press, 1961), pp. 65–66.

21. Robert Conot, *Rivers of Blood, Years of Darkness* (New York: William Morrow, 1968), p. 14.

22. Ibid., p. 15–16.

23. William Manchester, *The Glory and the Dream: A Narrative History of America, 1932–1972* (New York: Bantam Books, 1975), p. 1063.

24. Ibid., p. 1062; Milton Viorst, *Fire in the Streets: America in the 1960's* (New York: Simon and Schuster, 1979), pp. 310, 318–19; *New South* 20 (Nov. 1965): 3–4.

25. Jim F. Heath, *Decade of Disillusionment: The Kennedy-Johnson Years* (Bloomington: Indiana University Press, 1975), pp. 250–51.

26. Roy Wilkins with Tom Mathews, *Standing Fast: The Autobiography of Roy Wilkins* (New York: Viking Press, 1982), p. 313.

27. Bayard Rustin, *Down the Line,* p. 146.

28. Ibid.

29. David L. Lewis, *King: A Biography,* 2d ed. (Urbana: University of Illinois Press, 1978), p. 306; see also Rustin, *Down the Line,* p. 142.

30. U.S. Bureau of the Census, *Historical Statistics of the United States: Colonial Times to 1970,* pt. 1 (Washington, D.C.: U.S. Government Printing Office, 1975), G 1-15, p. 289.

31. Economic justice was a recurrent though secondary theme in King's speeches and writings during the early 1960s. See, for example, *Why We Can't Wait* (New York: Mentor Books, 1964), esp. pp. 138–39.

32. Whitney M. Young, Jr., "The Social Revolution: Challenge to the Nation" (Address at the 1963 National Conference of the Urban League), reprinted in *Negro Protest Thought in the Twentieth Century,* ed. Francis L. Broderick and August Meier (Indianapolis: Bobbs-Merrill, 1965), pp. 287–96; see esp. p. 294.

33. Carl Brauer, "Kennedy, Johnson, and the War on Poverty, *Journal of American History* 69 (June 1982): 105.

34. Ibid., pp. 113–16.

35. Ibid., p. 114.
36. Eric F. Goldman, *The Tragedy of Lyndon Johnson* (New York: Alfred A. Knopf, 1969), pp. 186–87.
37. On the contrasts between Powell and Landrum, see ibid., pp. 184–85.
38. Daniel P. Moynihan, *Maximum Feasible Misunderstanding: Community Action in the War on Poverty* (New York: Macmillan, 1969), pp. 91–92; Goldman, *The Tragedy of Lyndon Johnson*, pp. 187–88.
39. James T. Patterson, *America's Struggle against Poverty, 1900–1980* (Cambridge: Harvard University Press, 1981), p. 141.
40. Stephen B. Oates, *Let the Trumpet Sound: The Life of Martin Luther King, Jr.* (New York: Harper and Row, 1982), p. 310.
41. *NYT,* Aug. 21, 1965, p. 10.
42. Ibid., Nov. 17, 1965, p. 1.
43. On community action programs, see Moynihan, *Maximum Feasible Misunderstanding;* Patterson, *America's Struggle against Poverty*, pp. 138–41, 145–52; George Brager and Francis Purcell, eds., *Community Action against Poverty: Notes from the Mobilization Experience* (New Haven: College and University Press, 1967); Ralph M. Kramer, *Participation of the Poor: Comparative Case Studies in the War against Poverty* (Englewood Cliffs, N.J.: Prentice-Hall, 1969), pp. 237–38, 266–73; and Kenneth J. and Annette C. Pollinger, *Community Action and the Poor: Influence vs. Social Control in a New York City Community* (New York: Praeger, 1972).
44. John E. Schwarz, *America's Hidden Success: A Reassessment of Public Policy from Kennedy to Reagan,* rev. ed. (New York: W. W. Norton, 1988), offers a strongly positive evaluation of the War on Poverty.
45. Patterson, *America's Struggle against Poverty,* pp. 148–52; the quotation is on p. 152.
46. Passages on Young's background and achievements draw on information in Nancy J. Weiss, "Whitney M. Young, Jr.: Committing the Power Structure to the Cause of Civil Rights," in *Black Leaders of the Twentieth Century,* ed. John Hope Franklin and August Meier (Urbana: University of Illinois Press, 1982), pp. 331–58.
47. Ibid., p. 340.
48. Ibid., pp. 334–35.
49. Ibid., p. 335.
50. August Meier and Elliott Rudwick, *CORE: A Study in the Civil Rights Movement, 1942–1968* (New York: Oxford University Press, 1973), p. 182.
51. Ibid., pp. 237–39.
52. Ibid., p. 249.
53. Ibid., p. 183.
54. Interview with Cecil B. Moore by John H. Britton, Sept. 26, 1967, CRDP. p. 35.
55. Meier and Rudwick, *CORE,* p. 249.
56. Peter Goldman, *The Death and Life of Malcolm X,* 2d ed. (Urbana: University of Illinois Press, 1979), p. 51.
57. On the Nation of Islam, see C. Eric Lincoln, *The Black Muslims in America,* rev. ed. (Boston: Beacon Press, 1973); and E. U. Essien-Udom, *Black Nationalism: A Search for an Identity in America* (Chicago: University of Chicago Press, 1962).
58. Goldman, *The Death and Life of Malcolm X,* p. 36.
59. Malcolm X as told to Alex Haley, *The Autobiography of Malcolm X* (New York: Ballantine Books, 1973; originally published 1965), pp. 6–7.
60. Ibid., p. 14.
61. Ibid., pp. 21–22.
62. Ibid., pp. 29, 36–37; the quotations are on p. 37.
63. Ibid., p. 251.
64. Ibid., p. 266.
65. Essien-Udom, *Black Nationalism,* p. 71.
66. Malcolm X, *Autobiography,* p. 246.
67. Malcolm X, *Malcolm X Speaks,* ed. George Breitman (New York: Grove Press, 1965), p. 9.
68. Malcolm X, *Autobiography,* pp. 280–81.
69. Goldman, *The Death and Life of Malcolm X,* p. 17.
70. Ibid., p. 8. The quotation is Peter Goldman's paraphrase of Young's comment.
71. Wilkins, *Standing Fast,* p. 317.
72. Malcolm X, *Autobiography,* p. 284.
73. Ibid. (epilogue by Alex Haley), p. 394.
74. Goldman, *The Death and Life of Malcolm X,* p. 14.
75. Ibid., p. 105.
76. James Farmer, *Lay Bare the Heart: An Autobiography of the Civil Rights Movement* (New York: Arbor House, 1985), pp. 225–27.
77. Malcolm X, *Malcolm X Speaks,* p. 171.
78. Malcolm X, *Autobiography* (epilogue by Alex Haley), p. 429.
79. Malcolm X, *Malcolm X Speaks,* p. 69.
80. Goldman, *The Death and Life of Malcolm X,* p. 150.
81. Ibid., p. 148.
82. Ibid., p. 189. The quotation is Peter Goldman's phrasing of Malcolm's message.
83. See, for example, the transcript of Malcolm's speech on June 28, 1964, at the founding rally of the Organization for Afro-American Unity, reprinted in Malcolm X, *By Any Means Necessary,* ed. George Breitman (New York: Pathfinder Press, 1970), esp. p. 37.
84. Malcolm X, *Autobiography* (epilogue by Alex Haley), p. 371.
85. Ibid., p. 400.
86. Malcolm X, *Malcolm X Speaks,* p. 213.
87. Ibid., p. 197.
88. Goldman, *The Death and Life of Malcolm X,* p. 143.

89. Malcolm X, *Autobiography* (epilogue by Alex Haley), p. 420.
90. Ibid., p. 429.
91. Goldman, *The Death and Life of Malcolm X,* pp.279–374, examines the evidence relating to Malcolm's murder.
92. Oates, *Let the Trumpet Sound,* p. 380.
93. Lewis, *King,* p. 313, citing Arnold Schuchter, *White Power, Black Freedom* (Boston: Beacon Press, 1968), p. 64; see also Harold M. Baron, "Black Powerlessness in Chicago," *Transaction* 6 (Nov. 1968); 27–33.
94. Oates, *Let the Trumpet Sound,* p. 369.
95. Coretta Scott King, *My Life with Martin Luther King, Jr.* (New York: Holt, Rinehart and Winston, 1969), p. 276.
96. Oates, *Let the Trumpet Sound,* p. 389; on the Lawndale "hearing" see also *NYT,* Jan. 28, 1966, p. 13.
97. Oates, *Let the Trumpet Sound,* p. 391; Thomas Morgan, "Requiem or Revival," *Look,* June 14, 1966, p. 75.
98. Coretta King, *My Life with Martin Luther King, Jr.,* pp. 280–81.
99. Oates, *Let the Trumpet Sound,* pp.392–93.
100. Lewis, *King,* p. 317.
101. Ibid., p. 318; Oates, *Let the Trumpet Sound,* p. 394.
102. Martin Luther King, Jr., *Where Do We Go from Here: Chaos or Community?* (Boston: Beacon Press, 1968), p. 45.
103. Ibid., p. 114.
104. Lewis, *King,* p. 332.
105. Oates, *Let the Trumpet Sound,* pp. 409–10; *NYT,* July 16, 1966, pp. 1, 8.
106. Oates, *Let the Trumpet Sound,* p. 412; *NYT,* Aug. 6, 1966, pp. I, 52.
107. Oates, *Let the Trumpet Sound,* pp. 412–13; see also *NYT,* Aug. 6, 1966, pp. 1, 52.
108. *NYT,* Aug. 24, 1966, p. 34.
109. Paul Good, "Bossism, Racism and Dr. King," *Nation,* Sept. 19, 1966, p. 239.
110. *NYT,* Aug. 27, 1966, p. 1.
111. Lewis, *King,* p. 346.
112. Good, "Bossism, Racism and Dr. King," p. 238.
113. Ibid., p. 242.
114. Oates, *Let the Trumpet Sound,* p. 418.

7. Reformers at the Crossroads

1. See Carleton Mabee to James Farmer, Sept. 19, 1962, and Farmer to Mabee, Oct. 8, 1962, in CORE Papers, reel 5, frames 00140-41.
2. *NYT,* Jan. 19, 1964, p. 43.
3. See, for example, the testimony of Lawrence Guyot in Howell Raines, ed., *My Soul Is Rested: Movement Days in the Deep South Remembered* (New York: Penguin Books, 1983), p. 290.
4. Howard Zinn, *SNCC: The New Abolitionists,* 2d ed. (Boston: Beacon Press, 1965), p. 92.
5. Raines, *My Soul Is Rested,* pp. 107–8.
6. Ibid., p. 107.
7. Alvin Poussaint, "A Negro Psychiatrist Explains the Negro Psyche," *NYT Magazine,* Aug. 20, 1967, pp. 75–76.
8. Raines, *My Soul Is Rested,* p. 265.
9. Ibid., p. 266.
10. Stephen B. Oates, *Let the Trumpet Sound: The Life of Martin Luther King, Jr.* (New York: Harper and Row, 1982), pp. 375–76.
11. Ibid.
12. Ibid., p. 376.
13. See David Halberstam, "The Second Coming of Martin Luther King," *Harper's,* Aug. 1967, p. 40.
14. Oates, *Let the Trumpet Sound,* p. 376.
15. Clayborne Carson, *In Struggle: SNCC and the Black Awakening of the 1960's* (Cambridge: Harvard University Press, 1981), p. 187.
16. Ibid..
17. Carson, *In Struggle,* p. 188; James Forman examines Younge's life and the impact of his murder on SNCC youths, in *Sammy Younge, Jr.* (New York: Grove Press, 1968).
18. Carson, *In Struggle,* p. 189.
19. John Neary, *Julian Bond: Black Rebel* (New York: William Morrow, 1971), pp. 92–129, and Herbert Shapiro, "Julian Bond: Georgia's 'Uppity' Legislator," *Nation,* Feb. 7, 1966, pp. 145–47, detail the circumstances of Bond's exclusion from the Georgia state legislature.
20. David L. Lewis, *King: A Biography,* 2d ed. (Urbana: University of Illinois Press, 1978), p. 311.
21. Ibid., p. 312.
22. *NYT,* June 3, 1966, p. 21.
23. On Nabritt's leadership of the committee and its handling of the antiwar resolution, see ibid.
24. Carson, *In Struggle,* p. 128.
25. Cleveland Sellers with Robert Terrell, *The River of No Return: The Autobiography of a Black Militant and the Life and Death of SNCC* (New York: William Morrow, 1973), p. 151.
26. Carson, *In Struggle,* p. 164.
27. Stokely Carmichael and Charles V. Hamilton, *Black Power* (New York: Vintage Books, 1967), p. 104.
28. Andrew Kopkind, "The Lair of the Black Panther," *New Republic,* Aug. 13, 1966, p. 12; Carmichael elaborated on his views of major party politics in *PC,* June 4, 1966, pp. 1, 4.
29. Carson, *In Struggle,* p. 166.

30. Ibid., p. 203.
31. *NYT,* June 7, 1966, p. 1. The assailant pleaded guilty and received a five-year prison term with three years suspended; see *NYT,* Nov. 22, 1966, p. 1.
32. Ibid., June 8, 1966, p. 26.
33. Martin Luther King, Jr., *Where Do We Go from Here: Chaos or Community?* (Boston: Beacon Press, 1968), p. 25.
34. Ibid., pp. 25–26.
35. *NYT,* June 8, 1966, p. 26.
36. Roy Wilkins with Tom Mathews, *Standing Fast: The Autobiography of Roy Wilkins* (New York: Viking Press, 1982), p. 315.
37. *NYT,* June 8, 1966, p. 26.
38. Wilkins, *Standing Fast,* pp. 315–16; Carmichael's version of this meeting is recorded in Milton Viorst, *Fire in the Streets: America in the 1960's* (New York: Simon and Schuster, 1979), p. 372.
39. *NYT,* June 9, 1966, p. 1.
40. Ibid., June 11, 1966, pp. 1, 19.
41. Sellers, *The River of No Return,* pp. 166–67; see also *NYT,* June 17, 1966, pp. 1, 33.
42. Paul Good, "The Meredith March," *New South* 21 (Summer 1966): 9.
43. Gene Roberts, "The Story of Snick: From 'Freedom High' to 'Black Power,' " *NYT Magazine,* Sept. 25, 1966, p. 27.
44. King, *Where Do We Go from Here,* p. 30.
45. Ibid., pp. 30–31.
46. Ibid., p. 31.
47. Ibid.
48. Renata Adler, *Toward a Radical Middle: Fourteen Pieces of Reporting and Criticism* (New York: Random House, 1969), p. 158.
49. *NYT,* June 23, 1966, p. 23.
50. Oates, *Let the Trumpet Sound,* p. 403.
51. Paul Good, "Odyssey of a Man—and a Movement," *NYT Magazine,* June 25, 1967, p. 44.
52. *NYT,* June 25, 1966, p. 15.
53. Oates, *Let the Trumpet Sound,* p. 404.
54. *NYT,* June 25, 1966, p. 15; Oates, *Let the Trumpet Sound,* p. 404.
55. *NYT,* June 27, 1966, p. 29.
56. Ibid., June 28, 1966, p. 22.
57. Carson, *In Struggle,* p. 211.
58. *NYT* June 27, 1966, p. 29.
59. Ibid.
60. Paul Good, "Odyssey of a Man—and a Movement," *NYT,* June 25, 1967, p. 44.
61. *NYT,* July 11, 1966, p. 19; CORE Papers, Addendum, reel 5, frame 0159.
62. Frantz Fanon, *The Wretched of the Earth,* tr. Constance Farrington (New York: Grove Press, 1968), p. 94.

63. Speech by Roy Wilkins, July 5, 1966, in NAACP Papers, group IV, series A, container 3.
64. Wilkins, *Standing Fast,* p. 316.
65. Bayard Rustin, "Black Power and Coalition Politics," *Commentary,* Sept. 1966, pp. 35–36.
66. Peter Joseph, ed., *Good Times: An Oral History of America in the Nineteen Sixties* (New York: Charterhouse, 1973), p. 98.
67. Ibid.
68. Carson, *In Struggle,* p. 220.
69. William Manchester, *The Glory and the Dream: A Narrative History of America, 1932–1972* (New York: Bantam Books, 1975), p. 1065.
70. "Violence in the City," *New Republic,* July 30, 1966, p. 5.
71. Social conditions in Hough are detailed ibid.; Roldo S. Bartimole and Murray Gruber, "Cleveland: Recipe for Violence," *Nation,* June 26, 1967, pp. 814–17; and Ruth Fischer, "Why Hough Got Tough: The Real Agitators," *New Republic,* Sept. 10, 1966, pp. 9–10. Langston Hughes is quoted ibid., p. 10.
72. Bartimole and Gruber, "Cleveland: Recipe for Violence," *Nation,* June 26, 1967, p. 816.
73. *The Report of the National Advisory Committee on Civil Disorders* (New York: Bantam Books, 1968), p. 39.
74. "Fair Housing in Trouble," *New Republic,* July 2, 1966, p. 9.
75. "Backlash Jitters," *New Republic,* Oct. 22, 1966, pp. 5–6.
76. Ibid., p. 6.
77. Ibid.
78. *NYT,* Sept. 30, 1966, p. 39; *Time,* Oct. 7, 1966, p. 30; *Newsweek,* Oct. 17, 1966, p. 29.
79. *NYT,* Aug. 12, 1964, p. 1; Robert G. Sherrill, "Strange Decorum of Lester Maddox," *Nation,* May 1, 1967, p. 553.
80. Jim F. Heath, *Decade of Disillusionment: The Kennedy-Johnson Years* (Bloomington: Indiana University Press, 1975), p. 226.
81. Analyses of the election results as they affected racial politics include Paul Good, "Blue Notes from Dixie," *Nation,* Nov. 28, 1966, pp. 570–75; Milton Viorst, "The Two Faces of the GOP," *Nation,* Dec. 12, 1966, pp. 630–32; "GOP '66: Back on the Map," *Newsweek,* Nov. 21, 1966, pp. 31–34; and "A Party for All," *Time,* Nov. 18, 1966, pp. 23–32.
82. Senators Mansfield and Dirksen are quoted in *Time,* Nov. 18, 1966, p. 26.

8. The Radical Movement

1. Preamble to the constitution of the Universal Negro Improvement Association, reprinted in Marcus Garvey, *Philosophy and Opinions of Marcus Garvey,* ed. Amy Jacques-Garvey, 2 vols. (New York: Atheneum, 1986), 1:102.

2. Jules Tygiel, *Baseball's Great Experiment* (New York: Oxford University Press, 1983), p. 343.
3. *PC,* June 4, 1966, p. 13.
4. James Baldwin, *Notes of a Native Son* (Boston: Beacon Press, 1955), p. 2.
5. James Baldwin, *The Fire Next Time* (New York: Dell, 1962), p. 127.
6. Ibid.
7. Ibid., p. 84.
8. Ibid., p. 115.
9. Ibid., p. 141.
10. Ray Charles and Aretha Franklin, in *CD,* Nov. 30–Dec. 6, 1968, p. 15.
11. Alex Poinsett, "The Controversial Jim Brown," *Ebony,* Dec. 1964, p. 66.
12. Arthur R. Ashe, Jr., *A Hard Road to Glory: A History of the African-American Athlete since 1946* (New York: Warner Books, 1988), p. 97.
13. Stokely Carmichael, *Stokely Speaks* (New York: Random House, 1965). p. 160.
14. "Ka 'Ba," in Imamu Amiri Baraka, *Black Magic: Collected Poetry, 1961–1967* (Indianapolis: Bobbs-Merrill, 1969), p. 146.
15. "Note on Commercial Theatre," in Langston Hughes, *Selected Poems* (New York: Vintage Books, 1974), p. 190.
16. Abraham Chapman, ed., *Black Voices* (New York: New American Library, 1968), p. 352.
17. *NYT,* Dec. 26, 1984, p. A15.
18. Harold Cruse, *The Crisis of the Negro Intellectual* (New York: Quill, 1967), p. 475.
19. Ibid., p. 9.
20. Ibid., p. 395.
21. Ibid., p. 395.
22. Ibid., pp. 7–8.
23. Ibid., p. 8.
24. Ibid., p. 317.
25. Ibid., p. 111.
26. Ibid., p. 195.
27. Ibid., pp. 343–44.
28. LeRoi Jones, *Home: Social Essays* (New York: William Morrow, 1966), pp. 250–51.
29. Eldridge Cleaver, *Soul on Ice* (New York: McGraw-Hill, 1968), p. 14.
30. Ibid., p. 106.
31. Ibid., p. 27.
32. Ibid., p. 99.
33. Ibid., p. 103.
34. Julian Mayfield, "The New Mainstream," *Nation,* May 13, 1968, p. 638; Richard Gilman, "White Standards and Negro Writing," *New Republic,* Mar. 9, 1968, p. 26.
35. Nikki Giovanni, *Black Feeling—Black Talk—Black Judgement* (New York: Quill, 1979), pp. 46–47.
36. James H. Cone, *Black Theology and Black Power* (New York: Seabury Press, 1969), p. 1.
37. Ibid., p. 135.
38. Ibid., p. 53.
39. Ibid., p. 143.
40. Albert B. Cleage, Jr., *The Black Messiah* (New York: Sheed and Ward, 1968), p. 3.
41. Ibid., p. 44.
42. Ibid., p. 4.
43. Ibid., p. 46.
44. Joseph R. Washington, Jr., *Black Religion: The Negro and Christianity in the United States* (Boston: Beacon Press, 1964); Joseph R. Washington, *The Politics of God: The Future of the Black Churches* (Boston: Beacon Press, 1967).
45. Malcolm X, *By Any Means Necessary,* ed. George Breitman (New York: Pathfinder Press, 1970), p. 37.
46. Peter Goldman, *The Death and Life of Malcolm X,* 2d ed. (Urbana: University of Illinois Press, 1979). p. 221.
47. Malcolm X, *Malcolm X Speaks,* ed. George Breitman (New York: Grove Press, 1965), p. 198.
48. Cleveland Sellers with Robert Terrell, *The River of No Return: The Autobiography of a Black Militant and the Life and Death of the SNCC* (New York: William Morrow, 1973), p. 153.
49. Ibid., pp. 153–54.
50. Ibid., p. 154.
51. Ibid
52. Alphonso Pinkney, "Contemporary Black Nationalism," in *Black Life and Culture in the United States,* ed. Rhoda L. Goldstein (New York: Thomas Y. Crowell, 1971), pp. 246–47.
53. Edward Witten, "The New Left: Rhetoric of Ambivalence," *Nation,* Dec. 16, 1968, pp. 646–48.
54. Malcolm X, *Malcolm X Speaks,* p. 42.
55. Martin Mayer, "The Full and Sometimes Very Surprising Story of Ocean Hill, the Teachers' Union and the Teacher Strikes of 1968," *NYT Magazine,* Feb. 2, 1969, p. 20. Ferguson's conviction is reported in *NYT,* Oct. 4, 1968, p. 20. Mayer's article is the primary source of information for passages treating the conflict in Ocean Hill, and is supplemented by William O'Neill, *Coming Apart: An Informal History of America in the 1960's* (Chicago: Quadrangle, 1971), pp. 183–87, and *NYT.*
56. Mayer, ". . . Ocean Hill,", p. 71.
57. Ibid., p. 70.
58. Ibid.; see also *NYT,* Dec. 1, 1968, p. 153.
59. Robert G. Weisbord and Arthur Stein, *Bittersweet Encounter: The Afro-American and the American Jew* (Westport, Conn.: Negro Universities Press, 1970), pp. 139–42; Brown is quoted on p. 139.
60. Sellers, *The River of No Return,* p. 202; interview with Julian Bond, p. 51, CRDP.
61. Sellers, *The River of No Return,* p. 203.
62. Ibid.
63. Ibid., pp. 194–97; Bob Zellner is quoted on p. 197.
64. August Meier and Elliot Rudwick, *CORE: A Study in the Civil Rights Movement 1942–1968* (New York: Oxford University Press, 1973), pp. 293–94.
65. *NYT,* July 6, 1967, p. 1.
66. Lee Rainwater and William L. Yancey,

The Moynihan Report and the Politics of Controversy (Cambridge: MIT Press, 1967), pp. 409–11.

67. *PC*, Jan. 1, 1966, p. 2.
68. Program of Oct. 30, 1966, tape no. 200, James Forman Collection, King Center.
69. Martin Luther King, Jr., *Where Do We Go from Here: Chaos or Community?* (Boston: Beacon Press, 1968), p. 186.
70. Ibid., p. 162.
71. Ibid., p. 164.
72. Ibid., p. 166.
73. *NYT*, Apr. 2, 1967, p. 76.
74. Ibid., Oct. 2, 1966, p. 1.
75. King, *Where Do We Go from Here*, p. 7.
76. *NYT*, Sept. 18, 1966, p. 72.
77. Preamble to "A Black Anti-Draft Program," Aug. 1966, in SNCC Papers, reel 21, frame 0790.
78. Stephen B. Oates, *Let the Trumpet Sound: The Life of Martin Luther King, Jr.* (New York: Harper and Row, 1982) p. 431.
79. Ibid., p. 434; King's speech is reprinted in *A Testament of Hope: The Essential Writings of Martin Luther King, Jr.,* ed. James M. Washington (San Francisco: Harper and Row, 1987), pp. 231–44.
80. *NYT* Nov. 19, 1964, p. 1.
81. Criticisms of King by the FBI and by Congressman Waggonner are quoted in Oates, *Let the Trumpet Sound*, p. 437.
82. "Dr. King's Disservice to his Cause," *Life*, Apr. 21, 1967, p. 4.
83. Kenneth Crawford, "The Non-Debate," *Newsweek*, Apr. 17, 1967, p. 46.
84. *NYT*, Apr. 7, 1967, p. 36.
85. Rowan and Bunche are quoted in Oates, *Let the Trumpet Sound*, pp. 437–38.
86. David Halberstam, "The Second Coming of Martin Luther King," *Harper's*, Aug. 1967, p. 49.
87. Stanley Goff and Robert Sanders with Clark Smith, *Brothers: Black Soldiers in the Nam* (New York: Berkley Books, 1985), p. 151.
88. Ibid., p. 149–50.
89. Wallace Terry, *Bloods: An Oral History of the Vietnam War by Black Veterans* (New York: Random House, 1984), pp. 115, 121–22.
90. Oates, *Let the Trumpet Sound*, p. 434.
91. Sellers, *The River of No Return*, p. 191.
92. *NYT*, Sept. 1, 1967, p. 18.
93. Carmichael's letter, in July 1969, is quoted in Abraham Chapman, ed., *New Black Voices* (New York: New American Library, 1972), p. 39.
94. Eldridge Cleaver, "An Open Letter to Stokely Carmichael," ibid., p. 40.
95. Passages on the Chicago conference are drawn chiefly from Richard Blumenthal, "New Politics at Chicago," *Nation*, Sept. 25, 1967, pp. 273–76, supplemented by Walter Goodman, "When Black Power Runs the New Left," *NYT Magazine*, Sept. 24, 1967, pp. 28ff. The quotation is in Blumenthal, p. 274.
96. Milton Viorst, *Fire in the Streets: America in the 1960's* (New York: Simon and Schuster, 1979), p. 412.
97. Blumenthal, "New Politics at Chicago," p. 274.
98. Ibid..
99. Ibid., p. 275.
100. Ibid., p. 276.
101. *NYT*, Sept. 3, 1967, p. 1.
102. David J. Garrow, *The FBI and Martin Luther King, Jr.* (New York: Penguin Books, 1983), pp. 182–83.
103. James Farmer, *Lay Bare the Heart: An Autobiography of the Civil Rights Movement* (New York: Arbor House, 1985), p. 215.
104. Ibid., p. 216.
105. Manning Marable, *Race, Reform and Rebellion: The Second Reconstruction in Black America, 1945–1982* (Jackson: University Press of Mississippi, 1984), p. 120.
106. Cruse, *The Crisis of the Negro Intellectual*, p. 456.
107. Ibid., p. 475.
108. Carson, *In Struggle*, p. 253.
109. Ibid., pp. 255–56.
110. Howard Zinn, "The Old Left and the New: Emancipation from Dogma," *Nation*, Apr. 4, 1966, p. 387.
111. Sellers, *The River of No Return*, p. 251.

9. Law and Order

1. *NYT*, July 5, 1967, p. 18.
2. Clayborne Carson, *In Struggle: SNCC and the Black Awakening of the 1960's* (Cambridge: Harvard University Press, 1981), pp. 259–60.
3. *NYT*, July 14, 1967, p. 34.
4. Ibid., July 1, 1967, p. 10.
5. *Report of the National Advisory Commission on Civil Disorders* (New York: Bantam Books, 1968), p. 67.
6. Ibid., pp. 67–69.
7. Ibid., p. 68.
8. Ibid., p. 97.
9. Ibid., p. 92.
10. "Blow Up in the Cities," *New Republic*, Aug. 5, 1967, p. 6.
11. *Newsweek*, Aug. 7, 1967, p. 19.
12. *NYT*, July 26, 1967, p. 19.
13. Robert M. Fogelson, *Violence as Protest: A Study of Riots and Ghettos* (New York: Anchor Books, 1971), pp. 26–27.
14. *Newsweek*, Aug. 7, 1967, p. 28.
15. "Blow up the Cities," *New Republic*, Aug. 5, 1967, p. 6; *NYT*, July 26, 1967, p. 19.

16. David S. Broder, *The Party's Over: The Failure of Politics in America* (New York: Harper and Row, 1971), p. 48.
17. Interview with Edith Green by Robert Wright, Feb. 21, 1968, p. 7, CRDP.
18. Jerome H. Skolnick, *The Politics of Protest* (New York: Simon and Schuster, 1969), p. 230.
19. Ibid., p. 231.
20. Martin Luther King, Jr., *Where Do We Go from Here: Chaos or Community?* (Boston: Beacon Press, 1968) p. 63.
21. Martin Luther King, Jr., *The Trumpet of Conscience* (New York: Harper and Row, 1968), pp. 14–15.
22. Interview with Mr. "B" by James M. Mosby, Apr. 24, 1968, p. 16, CRDP.
23. Martin Luther King, Jr., "I See the Promised Land", in *A Testament of Hope: The Essential Writings of Martin Luther King, Jr.,* ed. James Melvin Washington (San Francisco: Harper and Row, 1986), p. 286.
24. Robert Kennedy's speech is transcribed here from a tape provided by the John F. Kennedy Library, in Boston, Mass. The sequence of the last two sentences has been inverted.
25. Carson, *In Struggle,* p. 288.
26. Theodore H. White, *The Making of the President, 1968* (New York: Atheneum, 1969), p. 208.
27. Interview with Mr. "B," p. 41, CRDP.
28. White, *The Making of the President, 1968,* p. 208.
29. Interview with Mr. "A" by James Mosby, Apr. 26, 1968, p. 11, CRDP.
30. Ibid., pp. 4, 9.
31. Interview with Mr. "C" by James Mosby, May 16, 1968, pp. 7–8, CRDP.
32. Ibid., p. 9.
33. White, *The Making of the President, 1968,* p. 209.
34. Interview with Mr. "C," pp. 32–33, CRDP.
35. "Open Housing Law Credited to Mitchell's Lobbying," *Congressional Quarterly,* Apr. 26, 1968, p. 931.
36. Ibid., p. 934.
37. "The Belated Civil Rights Legislation of 1968," *New Republic,* Mar. 30, 1968, p. 12.
38. Howell Raines, ed., *My Soul Is Rested: Movement Days in the Deep South Remembered* (New York: Penguin Books, 1983), p. 54.
39. Milton Viorst, *Fire in the Streets: America in the 1960's* (New York: Simon and Schuster, 1979), p. 438.
40. Charles E. Fager, *Uncertain Resurrection: The Poor People's Washington Campaign* (Grand Rapids, Mich.: William B. Eerdmans, 1969), p. 52.
41. Ibid., p. 88.
42. Ibid., p. 58.
43. Ibid., p. 118.
44. David Halberstam, *The Unfinished Odyssey of Robert Kennedy* (New York: Random House, 1968), p. 129.
45. *NYT,* July 19, 1966, p. 19.
46. *NYT,* Aug. 1, 1968, p. 18.
47. Ibid., p. 1.
48. Ibid., Sept. 16, 1968, p. 38.
49. White, *The Making of the President, 1968,* p. 371.
50. Interview with Martin Luther King, Jr., by Berl I. Bernhard, Mar. 9, 1964, p. 12 of transcript, Kennedy Library, Oral History Project.
51. Rowland Evans, Jr., and Robert D. Novak, *Nixon in the White House: The Frustration of Power* (New York: Vintage Books, 1971), p. 134.
52. Roy Wilkins with Tom Mathews, *Standing Fast: The Autobiography of Roy Wilkins* (New York: Viking Press, 1982), pp. 332–33.
53. *Time,* March 9, 1970, p. 9.
54. Evans and Novak, *Nixon in the White House,* p. 150.
55. William Safire, *Before the Fall: An Inside View of the Pre-Watergate White House* (New York: Ballantine, 1977), pp. 304, 620–23, quoting Nixon in 1970 and 1972.
56. The Supreme Court ruled in *Green v. County Board of New Kent Co.* (Virginia), 391 U.S. 430 (1968).
57. Evans and Novak, *Nixon in the White House,* p. 154.
58. Safire, *Before the Fall,* p. 297.
59. Evans and Novak, *Nixon in the White House,* p. 149.
60. Ibid., p. 174.
61. Ibid., p. 161.
62. Ibid., p. 162.
63. Ibid., p. 164.
64. *NYT,* Mar. 17, 1970, p. 21.
65. Evans and Novak, *Nixon in the White House,* p. 171.
66. Ibid., p. 163. A defense of Nixon's Southern strategy is offered by Harry S. Dent, *The Prodigal South Returns to Power* (New York: John Wiley, 1978), pp. 175–84.
67. William L. O'Neill, *Coming Apart: An Informal History of America in the 1960's* (Chicago: Quadrangle Books, 1971), p. 189; *NYT,* Mar. 2, 1970, p. 41.
68. *NYT,* Sept. 7, 1970, p. 1.
69. Ibid., p. 13.
70. Ibid., July 4, 1969, p. 1.
71. O'Neill, *Coming Apart,* p. 187.
72. *CD,* Jan. 17–23, 1970, p. 3.
73. *NYT,* Dec. 5, 1969, pp. 1, 34.
74. William H. Friedland and Harry Edwards, "Confrontation at Cornell," in *The Transformation of Activism,* ed. August Meier (New York: Aldine, 1970), pp. 69–89.
75. Leaflet from Brandeis University, undated.
76. Evans and Novak, *Nixon in the White House,* p. 135n.
77. Ibid., p. 134.

Epilogue: The Shifting Politics of Race

1. *Black Enterprise,* July 1987, p. 66.
2. J. Harvey Wilkinson III, *From Brown to Bakke: the Supreme Court and School Integration, 1954–1978* (New York: Oxford University Press, 1979), p. 138.
3. Ibid., p. 206.
4. Ibid., p. 208.
5. Ibid., pp. 211–12.
6. Ibid., p. 209.
7. J. Anthony Lukas, *Common Ground: A Turbulent Decade in the Lives of Three American Families* (New York: Alfred A. Knopf, 1985), pp. 324–26.
8. Ibid., pp. 649–50; the quotation is on p. 650.
9. Wilkinson, *From Brown to Bakke,* p. 219, quoting Gary Orfield.
10. Milliken v. Bradley, 418 U.S. 717 (1974).
11. Ibid., p. 758.
12. Ibid., p. 814.
13. Lyndon Baines Johnson, *The Vantage Point: Perspectives of the Presidency, 1963–1969* (New York: Holt, Rinehart and Winston, 1971), p. 166.
14. Robert Lindsey, "White/Caucasian—and Rejected," *NYT Magazine,* Apr. 3, 1977, p. 44.
15. Joel Dreyfuss and Charles Lawrence III, *The Bakke Case: The Politics of Inequality* (New York: Harcourt Brace Jovanovich, 1979), p. 98.
16. Thomas Sowell, "A Black Conservative Dissents," *NYT Magazine,* Aug. 8, 1976, p. 43; Sowell, *Black Education, Myths, and Tragedies* (New York: McKay, 1972), p. 292; see also his more recent critiques of affirmative action, for example, "Poor Aim in War on Bias," *NYT,* Aug. 11, 1981, p. A17, and *Civil Rights: Rhetoric or Reality?* (New York: Quill, 1984), pp. 37–60.
17. Sowell, *Civil Rights,* p. 40.
18. Dreyfuss and Lawrence, *The Bakke Case,* p. 15.
19. Ibid., p. 42.
20. Ibid., p. 113.
21. Wilkinson, *From Brown to Bakke,* p. 302.
22. United Steelworkers of America v. Weber, 99 Supreme Court, 2855 (1979).
23. Fullilove v. Klutznick, 100 Supreme Court 2758 (1980).
24. Jack Bass and Walter DeVries, *The Transformation of Southern Politics: Social Change and Political Consequence since 1945* (New York: Basic Books, 1976), p. 144.
25. Steven F. Lawson, *In Pursuit of Power: Southern Blacks and Electoral Politics, 1965–1982* (New York: Columbia University Press, 1985), p. 256.
26. State of the Union Message, Jan. 19, 1978, in *Public Papers of the Presidents: Jimmy Carter, 1978,* bk. 1 (Washington, D.C.: U.S. Government Printing Office, 1979), p. 91.
27. Inaugural address, Jan. 20, 1981, *Public Papers of the Presidents: Ronald Reagan, 1981* (Washington, D.C.: U.S. Government Printing Office, 1982), p. 1.
28. John M. Blum et al., *The National Experience,* 6th ed. (New York: Harcourt Brace Jovanovich, 1984), p. 883; Ronnie Dugger, *On Reagan: The Man and His Presidency* (New York: McGraw-Hill, 1983), pp. 287–88.
29. Blum et al., *The National Experience,* p. 883; *NYT,* Aug. 25, 1982, pp. A1, A24.
30. Dugger, *On Reagan,* pp. 287–88. 303.
31. *NYT,* Sept. 16, 1982, p. A1.
32. Michael Goldstein, "How Ronald Reagan, Henry Hyde, and William French Smith Became Voting Rights Heroes," *UCLA Center for Afro-American Studies Report* 7 (May 1983): 1, 10–12; the quotation is on p. 1.
33. *NYT,* July 26, 1985, p. A9.
34. *Newsweek,* Nov. 16, 1981, p. 37.
35. Dugger, *On Reagan,* p. 205.
36. Ibid., p. 215.
37. Ibid., p. 212.
38. Ibid., p. 214.
39. Ibid., p. 195.
40. See Eric Foner, "Redemption II," *NYT,* Nov. 7, 1981, p. 23.
41. *NYT,* Apr. 6, 1985, p. 7.
42. E. R. Shipp, "Across the Rural South, Segregation as Usual," *NYT,* Apr. 27, 1985, p. 41.
43. Goldstein, "How Ronald Reagan, Henry Hyde, and William French Smith Became Voting Rights Heroes," p. 10.
44. "Racism on the Rise," *Time,* Feb. 2, 1987, pp. 18–21; Walter Leavy, "What's Behind the Resurgence of Racism in America?" *Ebony,* Apr. 1987, pp. 132–39; Alphonso Pinkney, *The Myth of Black Progress* (Cambridge: Cambridge University Press, 1984), pp. 58–80 passim.
45. Pinkney, *The Myth of Black Progress,* p. 79.
46. *NYT,* Jan. 5, 1984, p. A18; Apr. 24, 1987, p. A30; Apr. 28, 1987, p. A31.
47. Based on figures in *Time,* Dec. 6, 1982, p. 53, and *Newsweek,* May 23, 1983, p. 60.
48. Herbert Hill, "Labor's Enemy: Labor," *NYT,* Sept. 5, 1982, p. E17.
49. "Capturing the Black Experience," *TV Guide,* Nov. 29, 1986, pp. 10–14; the quotation is on p. 14.
50. Arthur Lubow, "Blacks in Hollywood," *People,* May 17, 1982, p. 33.
51. Ibid., p. 32.
52. *TV Guide,* Oct. 16, 1982, pp. 39–41.
53. *NYT,* Apr. 9, 1987, p. B14.
54. *NYT,* Aug. 12, 1985, p. A11.
55. Ibid.
56. Ibid.
57. "Income Gap between Races as Wide as in 1960," *NYT,* July 18, 1983, p. A1.
58. U.S. Bureau of the Census, Current Population Reports, series P-20, no. 419, *House-*

hold and Family Characteristics: March 1986 (Washington, D.C.: U.S. Government Printing Office, 1987), p. 9, table F; U.S. Bureau of the Census, Current Population Reports, series P-60, no. 160, *Poverty in the United States: 1986* (Washington, D.C.: U.S. Government Printing Office, 1988), table 7, pp. 27, 29.

59. U.S. Bureau of the Census, *Statistical Abstract of the United States: 1988* (Washington, D.C.: U.S. Government Printing Office, 1987), table 86, p. 62.

60. Ibid., table 714, p. 434; U.S. Bureau of the Census, *Current Population Reports,* series P-60, no. 159, *Money Income of Households, Families, and Persons in the United States: 1986* (Washington, D.C.: U.S. Government Printing Office, 1988), table A, p. 3.

61. Manning Marable, *Black American Politics: From the Washington Marches to Jesse Jackson* (London: Verso, 1985), p. 103, quoting Marian Wright Edelman.

62. *NYT,* Aug. 12, 1985, p. A11.

63. Claude Brown, "Manchild in Harlem," *NYT Magazine,* Sept. 16, 1984, p. 44.

64. Ibid.

65. *NYT,* June 11, 1987, p. A22.

66. Figures were provided by the Joint Center for Political Studies, Washington, D.C.

67. *NYT,* June 28, 1984, p. A22.

68. *Newsweek,* May 3, 1982, p. 23.

69. *Time,* May 2, 1983, p. 78.

70. *Newsweek,* Aug. 29, 1983, p. 17.

71. Lloyd Cutler, "Using Morals, Not Money on Pretoria," *NYT,* Aug. 3, 1986, p. E23.

72. *NYT,* Mar. 1, 1985, pp. A1, 12.

Further Reading

OVERVIEWS of the civil rights movement include Harvard Sitkoff, *The Struggle for Black Equality, 1954–1980* (New York: Hill and Wang, 1981); Manning Marable's socialist critique, *Race, Reform and Rebellion: The Second Reconstruction in Black America from 1945 to 1982* (Jackson: University Press of Mississippi, 1984); sociological studies by Doug McAdam, *Political Process and the Development of Black Insurgency, 1930–1970* (Chicago: University of Chicago Press, 1982), Rhoda Lois Blumberg, *Civil Rights: The 1960s Freedom Struggle* (Boston: Twayne, 1984), and Jack M. Bloom, *Class, Race, and the Civil Rights Movement* (Bloomington: Indiana University Press, 1987); Juan Williams with the "Eyes on the Prize" production team, *Eyes on the Prize: America's Civil Rights Years, 1954–1965* (New York: Viking Press, 1987), and Henry Hampton and Steve Fayer with Sarah Flynn, *Voices of Freedom: An Oral History of the Civil Rights Movement from the 1950s through the 1980s* (New York: Bantam Books, 1990), both companion volumes to the two PBS television documentary series, "Eyes on the Prize"; and Pat Watters, *Down to Now: Reflections on the Southern Civil Rights Movement* (New York: Pantheon Books, 1971), a white journalist's sympathetic account of changing race relations in his native South.

The Greensboro sit-in that sparked a decade's civil rights protest is examined by Miles Wolff, *Lunch at the Five and Ten: The Greensboro Sit-ins: A Contemporary History* (New York: Stein and Day, 1970); William H. Chafe, *Civilities and Civil Rights: Greensboro, North Carolina, and the Black Struggle for Freedom* (New York: Oxford University Press, 1980), observes the limits of reform through the 1970s. Milton Viorst, *Fire in the Streets: America in the 1960's* (New York: Simon and Schuster, 1979), incisively depicts the March on Washington and other episodes of black activism. Len Holt, *The Summer That Didn't End* (London: William Heinemann, 1965), describes the racial awakening among Mississippi's black population during the first freedom summer project in 1964; Mary Aickin Rothschild, *A Case of Black and White: Northern Volunteers and the Southern Freedom Summers, 1964–1965* (Westport, Conn.: Greenwood Press, 1982), and Doug McAdam, *Freedom Summer* (New York: Oxford University Press, 1988), explore the motivations and experiences of young white civil rights workers in Mississippi; Seth Cagin and Philip Dray, *We Are Not Afraid: The Story of Goodman, Schwerner, and Chaney and the Civil Rights Campaign for Mississippi* (New York: Macmillan, 1988), recounts the murders of three volunteers in the first freedom summer project. David J. Garrow, *Protest at Selma: Martin Luther King, Jr., and the Voting Rights Act of 1965* (New Haven: Yale University Press, 1978), details the way civil rights leaders precipitated white racist violence to stir public support and federal intervention. The journalist Charles E. Fager recounts two critical protests in *Selma, 1965: The March That Changed the South* (Boston: Beacon Press, 1985; reprint of 1974 ed.), and *Uncertain Resurrection: The Poor People's Washington Campaign* (Grand Rapids, Mich.: William B. Eerdmans, 1969).

An excellent introduction to the politics of civil rights at the national level is Richard Kluger, *Simple Justice* (New York: Vintage Books, 1977), which treats the Supreme Court's landmark desegregation ruling in *Brown v. Board of Education.* Carl M. Brauer, *John F. Kennedy and the Second Reconstruction* (New York: Columbia University Press, 1977), is a superb study of presidential leadership in a time of rising black protest. Harris Wofford, *Of Kennedys and Kings: Making Sense of the Sixties* (New York: Farrar, Straus, and Giroux, 1980), discusses nonviolent direct action from a distinctive vantage point as both an advocate of Gandhian protest and an aide to President Kennedy. The civil rights record of Attorney General Robert Kennedy is analyzed by Victor S. Navasky, *Kennedy Justice* (New York: Atheneum, 1971). Two partisan but still compelling histories of the Kennedys, including appraisals of their civil rights leadership, are *A Thousand Days: John F. Kennedy in the White House* (Boston: Houghton Mifflin, 1965) and *Robert Kennedy and His Times* (Boston: Houghton Mifflin, 1978), both by Arthur M. Schlesinger, Jr. Eric F. Goldman, *The Tragedy of Lyndon Johnson* (New York: Alfred A. Knopf, 1969), contains spirited accounts of President Johnson's legislative initiatives against discrimination. The workings of the Congress are charted by Charles Whalen and Barbara Whalen, *The Longest Debate: A Legislative History of the 1964 Civil Rights Act* (Cabin John, Md.: Seven Locks Press, 1985).

Ghetto life and race riots receive probing treatment in *The Report of the National Advisory Commission on Civil Unrest* (New York: Bantam Books, 1968), also known as the Kerner Commission Report; in Robert Conot's study of Watts, *Rivers of Blood, Years of Darkness* (New York: William Morrow, 1968); in Bayard Rustin, *Down the Line: The Collected Writings of Bayard Rustin* (Chicago: Quadrangle Books, 1971); and in Robert M. Fogelson, *Violence as Protest* (Garden City, N.Y.: Doubleday, 1971).

Organizational histories are proliferating as scholars confront the diversity of protest campaigns throughout the South. A good background survey is Aldon D. Morris, *The Origins of the Civil Rights Movement* (New York: Free Press, 1984), which focuses on black clerical, civic, and civil rights groups in the years before 1960. Howard Zinn, *SNCC: The New Abolitionists,* 2d ed. (Boston: Beacon Press, 1965), is a vivid and provocative account by a scholar-activist. Clayborne Carson offers a comprehensive study of SNCC, *In Struggle: SNCC and the Black Awakening of the 1960's* (Cambridge: Harvard University Press, 1981). August Meier and Elliott Rudwick, *CORE: A Study in the Civil Rights Movement, 1942–1986* (New York: Oxford University Press, 1973), exhaustively charts the history of that organization through the late sixties.

Adam Fairclough, *To Redeem the Soul of America: The Southern Christian Leadership Conference and Martin Luther King, Jr.* (Athens: University of Georgia Press, 1978), illuminates the strengths and limitations of the SCLC as a force for social change.

Memoirs, biographies, and oral histories are among the richest sources on the civil rights movement. Howell Raines, ed., *My Soul Is Rested: Movement Days in the Deep South Remembered* (New York: Penguin Books, 1983), is a splendid compilation of interviews with participants in diverse campaigns. Martin Luther King, Jr., is the subject of a probing study by David L. Lewis, *King: A Biography,* 2d ed. (Urbana: University of Illinois Press, 1978); an absorbing, if reverent, portrait by Stephen B. Oates, *Let the Trumpet Sound: The Life of Martin Luther King, Jr.* (New York: Harper and Row, 1982); a monumental work by David J. Garrow, *Bearing the Cross* (New York: William Morrow, 1986); and a superbly written volume by Taylor Branch, *Parting the Waters: America in the King Years, 1954–1963* (New York: Simon and Schuster, 1988). David Garrow delves into FBI Director J. Edgar Hoover's campaign to destroy the minister, in *The FBI and Martin Luther King, Jr.* (New York: Penguin Books, 1983). King himself left various personal and political testaments, including a history of the Montgomery bus boycott of 1955–56, *Stride toward Freedom: The Montgomery Story* (New York: Harper and Row, 1958); a prescription for civil rights progress, *Why We Can't Wait* (New York: New American Library, 1964); and a call for comprehensive social change, *Where Do We Go from Here: Chaos or Community?* (Boston: Beacon Press, 1968). James Farmer, *Lay Bare the Heart: An Autobiography of the Civil Rights Movement* (New York: Arbor House, 1985), provides a wealth of engaging vignettes on his days in CORE. Roy Wilkins with Tom Mathews, *Standing Fast: The Autobiography of Roy Wilkins* (New York: Viking Press, 1982), relates the activities of the NAACP from the perspective of its dominant figure.

The growing militancy of black protest forms a central theme in the writings of many activists. Cleveland Sellers with Robert Terrell, *The River of No Return: The Autobiography of a Black Militant and the Life and Death of SNCC* (New York: William Morrow, 1973), poignantly traces the experiences that radicalized a young Southern black. SNCC's key organizer, James Forman, argues the inadequacy of liberal reform, in *The Making of Black Revolutionaries* (Washington, D.C.: Open Hand, 1985). Stokely Carmichael and Charles V. Hamilton expound on the changing politics of racial protest in *Black Power* (New York: Vintage Books, 1967); Eldridge Cleaver's *Soul on Ice* (New York: McGraw Hill, 1968), offers a series of personal meditations on the same theme. The most seminal and searing critic of white society is the subject of a brilliant biography by Peter Goldman, *The Death and Life of Malcolm X,* 2d ed. (Urbana: University of Illinois Press, 1979). *The Autobiography of Malcolm X,* as told to Alex Haley (New York: Ballantine Books, 1965), remains among the most formidable tracts in the record of black American protest.

Index